MARK TWAIN'S
HAWAII

MARK TWAIN'S HAWAII

A Humorous Romp through History

MARK TWAIN

with additional material by
JOHN RICHARD STEPHENS

TWODOT®

GUILFORD, CONNECTICUT
HELENA, MONTANA

To Elaine Molina Stephens

A · TWODOT® · BOOK

An imprint of Globe Pequot,
the trade division of The Rowman & Littlefield Publishing Group, Inc.
4501 Forbes Blvd., Ste. 200
Lanham, MD 20706
www.rowman.com

Distributed by NATIONAL BOOK NETWORK
Copyright © 2022 by John Richard Stephens
Palm tree art © Oleksandr Melnyk/iStock/Getty Images Plus

British Library Cataloguing in Publication Information available

Library of Congress Cataloging-in-Publication Data
Names: Stephens, John Richard, editor.
Title: Mark Twain's Hawaii : a humorous romp through history / Mark Twain
  with additional material by John Richard Stephens.
Description: Guilford, Connecticut : TwoDot, [2022] | Includes
  bibliographical references. | Summary: "Combines Twain's own writings on
  Hawaii with personal reminiscences by others who met him at that time,
  and traces Twain's journey through the region just as he experienced it
  in 1866"— Provided by publisher.
Identifiers: LCCN 2021043681 (print) | LCCN 2021043682 (ebook) | ISBN
  9781493053124 (hardback) | ISBN 9781493053131 (epub)
Subjects: LCSH: Twain, Mark, 1835-1910—Travel—Hawaii. |
  Hawaii—Description and travel. | Authors, American—19th
  century—Biography.
Classification: LCC PS1332 .M364 2022 (print) | LCC PS1332 (ebook) | DDC
  818/.409—dc23/eng/20211122
LC record available at https://lccn.loc.gov/2021043681
LC ebook record available at https://lccn.loc.gov/2021043682

∞™ The paper used in this publication meets the minimum requirements of American
National Standard for Information Sciences—Permanence of Paper for Printed Library
Materials, ANSI/NISO Z39.48-1992.

ACKNOWLEDGMENTS

John Richard Stephens would like to thank Elaine Molina Stephens; Martha and Jim Goodwin; Scott Stephens; Marty Goeller and Dorian Rivas; Terity, Natasha, and Debbie Burbach; Brandon, Alisha, and Kathy Hill; Jeff and Carol Whiteaker; Christopher and Doug Whiteaker; Jeffrey Seibert; Sean Stephens Morrison; Gabriel, Aurelia, Elijah, Sereya, Nina, and Justin Weinberger; Jayla, Anthony, and Bobby Gamboa; Baba and Mimi Marlene Spencer; Anne and Jerry Buzzard; Krystyne Göhnert; Norene Hilden; Doug and Shirley Strong; Barbara Main; Joanne and Monte Goeller; Irma and Joe Rodriguez; Danny and Mary Schutt; Les Benedict; Jeanne Sisson; Michael and Roz McKevitt; Dr. Rick Roth; and my agent, Charlotte Cecil Raymond.

LIST OF CARGO

INTRODUCTION
Mark Twain and I

IN RESEARCHING THIS BOOK, I GATHERED virtually everything Mark Twain wrote about Hawai'i. Some of it comes from obscure newspaper and magazine articles. Other bits come from his personal letters and notes. Still others come from speeches he made. I've searched far and wide and have found many lost and forgotten selections. But there is way too much material to include in this book, so I've had to winnow it down to the more interesting and relevant parts. Twain intended to write a book on Hawai'i himself but eventually gave up on the idea. I'm very grateful I was able to act as his editor in compiling this.

Normally, each article, letter, and so on would be presented in the order it was published, but this would put things out of order from how he experienced them. His articles on the Big Island's volcanoes were written and published after he had returned to California, while his visit to Maui preceded the Big Island, but that portion wasn't published until seven years later. Even rearranging the articles to match his trip doesn't quite work since portions would still be out of order. One article explains what happened before and after his trip.

As this book is not concerned with the publishing history or even in the articles themselves, I've decided to break the selections up and rearrange the pieces in the order he experienced them as well as combining the best of different versions of particular accounts while also inserting current information on the sites he visited. This will better enable us to follow his journey through the Islands and his rise to international celebrity status.

I have written about Twain and included his writings in more than half of my twenty-three books, so it's probably fitting that this book is about him. And while my writing is not quite as popular as his, I can't hold that against him. He *is* one of my favorite authors after all.

Aside from being one of America's greatest and most popular authors, I believe Mark Twain is the most American of all our authors. England has Shakespeare, Russia has Pushkin, and the United States has Twain.

Mark Twain—the nom de plume of Samuel Clemens—is best known as the author of *The Adventures of Tom Sawyer*, *The Adventures of Huckleberry Finn*, *The Prince and the Pauper*, *A Connecticut Yankee in King Arthur's Court*, and "The Celebrated Jumping Frog of Calaveras County." William

Faulkner labeled him "the father of American literature." He was also one of the first stand-up comics, as you will see later in the book.

He was a top-notch humorist, and that is what initially made him famous. As the *Encyclopedia Americana* noted, "Twain liberated humor, raising it to high art. . . . Instead of subduing his humor to seriousness, Twain invaded the citadels of seriousness and freed the humor held captive there." He also shocked people with what was at the time considered his crudeness and brashness. In that respect, he was much like many comedians today.

Twain came to prominence during a period when America was still strongly divided into North and South, but oddly he was a blend of the two, with a heavy dose of the West thrown in. Twain is the one author who is pure American.

Throughout his life, beginning at an early age, he worked in the publishing industry as a printer's devil (errand boy), typesetter, printer, letter

An average American loves his family. If he has any love left over for some other person, he generally selects Mark Twain.
—THOMAS EDISON, A SPEECH AT THE ENGINEERS' CLUB, DECEMBER 9, 1907

To my mind Mark Twain was beyond question the largest man of his time, both in the direct outcome of his work and more important still, if possible, in his indirect influence as a protesting force in an age of iron Philistinism.
—RUDYARD KIPLING, NOVEMBER 30, 1935, COMMEMORATING THE CENTENNIAL YEAR OF MARK TWAIN'S BIRTH

All modern American literature comes from one book by Mark Twain called *Huckleberry Finn*. American writing comes from that. There is nothing before. There has been nothing as good since.
—ERNEST HEMINGWAY, GREEN HILLS OF AFRICA, 1935

Mark Twain and I are in very much the same position. We have to put things in such a way as to make people who would otherwise hang us, believe that we are joking.
—GEORGE BERNARD SHAW, A CONVERSATION WITH HIS BIOGRAPHER ARCHIBALD HENDERSON, PRE-1911

contributor, reporter, correspondent, freelancer, travel writer, editor, magazine writer, book author, columnist, part owner of a newspaper, and investor in a typesetting machine. He tried his hand at other jobs, such as a clerk, prospector, and miner. Unsuccessful, he returned to the publishing industry, assuming his famous pen name (although I am partial to his first pen name—Thomas Jefferson Snodgrass—while another of his half dozen or so pseudonyms, W. Epaminondas Adrastus Blab, probably would never have caught on). He gave several versions of how he got the name, but its meaning came from his days as a riverboat pilot, when approaching a dangerous sandbar, someone would test the depth of the water and call it out to the pilot. A call of "mark twain" meant two fathoms, or twelve feet (3.7 meters), which was safe for the riverboat to pass over.

It was his jumping-frog story that jump-started Twain's career as a humorist, even though his form of humor almost landed him in several duels. But it was his visit to Hawai'i that quickly led him to become an international celebrity. His writing and speeches helped reunite the deeply divided country, but they also turned him into an informal ambassador to the world. Even today, he remains tremendously popular.

TWAIN
BEFORE TWAIN

BEFORE WE SCOOT OFF WITH TWAIN TO HAWAI'I, we need a quick recap of Twain's life up to that point.

Twain's or, rather, Samuel Clemens's father died when Sam was eleven years old. His father had done well as a lawyer and a judge, but suddenly things became tough for the Clemens family, so Sam left school on completing the fifth grade and began a three-year apprenticeship at the *Hannibal Courier* as a printer's devil and a typographer. That paper was owned by his brother Orion, and the position was unpaid—like an intern. He then figured he could strike it rich by importing coca leaves from the Amazon and set out east from Missouri, spending time in New York City, Philadelphia, Cincinnati, and St. Louis working for printers but this time for pay.

Setting off once again for the Amazon, he reached New Orleans, only to discover there were no ships going to the Amazon from there, so he became a steamboat pilot on the Mississippi River. He loved this job, but when the Civil War broke out, traffic on the river ceased, and he was suddenly unemployed.

He and his friends talked themselves into forming an informal volunteer guerilla unit. There were eleven (or fifteen) of them, and they elected Twain as second lieutenant. A colonel then administered to them the oath of allegiance to the Missouri State Guard, making them "swear to uphold the flag and Constitution of the United States,"[1] which left them wondering which side they were actually on. But they were to assist the Confederates in protecting their state. According

Twain at around 18 years old holding a typesetting tool, on which he set his name.

to Twain, he then set about achieving his "self-appointed great task of annihilating the Federal armies and breaking up the Union."[2]

They didn't have uniforms, and they brought their own weapons. One of their number said Twain rode a mule, was armed with a squirrel rifle, and carried a carpet bag and an umbrella. But his heart wasn't in it, especially after tramping around in the wilderness for a couple of weeks. By then, he later said, "the desire to kill people to whom I had not been introduced had passed away."[3] So either the company disbanded or he resigned.

When his brother Orion, who had campaigned for Lincoln, received a political appointment as secretary of the Nevada Territory, Twain decided to join him. Twain had saved money as a pilot and paid for their stagecoach trip. It cost him $300—or about $7,500 in today's dollars—and took twenty days to travel from St. Louis to Carson City, Nevada Territory. Once there, he worked for Orion as a clerk and then as a silver miner before taking up newspaper reporting.

It was as a reporter that he began getting himself in hot water.

Wild Reporters of the Wild West

For the most part, newspaper reporting was very different from what it is today. Most newspapers were small, being run by fewer than a dozen people. They were usually of one political bent or another, or they catered to a particular audience; for example, the *San Francisco Daily Morning Call*'s readers were primarily Irish. This made it easier for reporters to get articles approved by the editor that would never be published today.

Opinions were often mixed in with news reporting. Reporters would blend fiction with fact to spice up their stories. On slow news days, they sometimes just made up stories. In addition, rival newspapers were constantly sniping at each other, sometimes breaking out into verbal wars. Some were mock battles played out between friends. Others were very serious, and the attacks could become very personal and libelous. There was also a tradition in the West of raising tall tales to the level of art—the more exaggerated and outrageous, the better.

Twain loved all of that and was able to get away with it at Nevada's leading newspaper, the *Territorial Enterprise*.

Mark Twain ca. 1865. Pen names were common among journalists at this time. Regarding his, he said, "It is an old river term, a leads-man's call, signifying two fathoms—twelve feet. It has a richness about it. It was always a pleasant sound for a pilot to hear on a dark night. It meant safe water."[4]

The Petrified Man

One of his hoaxes that got him into trouble made it around the world. It is called a hoax, but I'm not sure he intended it to be. He carefully included clues that his story of the petrified man was a joke.

As he later wrote, "In the fall of 1862, in Nevada and California, the people got to running wild about extraordinary petrifications and other natural marvels. One could scarcely pick up a paper without finding in it one or two glorified discoveries of this kind. The mania was becoming a little ridiculous. I was a brand-new local editor in Virginia City [of the *Territorial Enterprise*], and I felt called upon to destroy this growing evil [. . .]."[5]

He did so by writing of the discovery of a petrified man, subtly describing him as being in "a sitting posture, and leaning against a huge mass of croppings; the attitude was pensive, the right thumb resting against the side of the nose; the left thumb partially supported the chin, the fore-finger pressing the inner corner of the left eye and drawing it partly open; the right eye was closed, and the fingers of the right hand spread apart."

Twain added that the petrified man was cemented to the spot, and while some people wanted to give him a proper burial, "Judge S. refused to allow the charitable citizens to blast him from his position."[6] Judge Sewall was a new coroner whom Twain disliked and wanted to make fun of.

THE PETRIFIED MAN.

This 1875 illustration of the petrified man was made from Twain's memory of the original story and is a bit inaccurate, but it makes the satire even more obvious.

His readers took the story at face value, and it "swept the great globe and culminated in sublime and unimpeached legitimacy in the august London *Lancet*"[7], which is still one of the world's premier medical journals.

Another of his hoaxes got him into trouble a year later. This was a fictional report titled "A Bloody Massacre near Carson City," which was a satire of the sensationally violent reporting that was common there in 1863, particularly by the *Gold Hill Daily News*. He included various impossible details and inconsistencies. He also put it under the pen name he used for humorous pieces—Mark Twain—but most of his readers didn't notice. The news shot up and down the coast, and when it was discovered to be false, some termed it a hoax and called for his resignation.

He had to fight off the criticism for quite a while. About three weeks later, he wrote of "the revolting details of Another Bloody Massacre!," explaining how 1,000 men were slaughtered by a criminal named Samson using a jawbone of an ass, adding a postscript predicting that the editor of the *San Francisco Journal* would again label Twain a hoaxer before discovering that the story was from the Bible and the jawbone was from one of the editor's ancestors.

Five years after he wrote the bloody massacre story, he reminisced, "To find a petrified man, or break a stranger's leg, or cave an imaginary mine, or discover some dead Indians in a Gold Hill tunnel, or massacre a family at Dutch Nick's, were feats and calamities that we never hesitated about devising when the public needed matters of thrilling interest for breakfast. The seemingly tranquil *Enterprise* office was a ghastly factory of slaughter, mutilation and general destruction in those days."[8]

Off to San Francisco

In spite of the controversies—or perhaps because of them—Twain's humor attracted an audience, building his popularity on the West Coast. When an article he wrote as a joke was published by mistake, he ended up infuriating women who ran a local charity fund-raiser, and then he nearly had to fight a duel. Deciding it was time to move on, he and Steve Gillis—one of his friends at the *Territorial Enterprise*—quit their jobs and headed to San Francisco.

Once there, he began working for the *San Francisco Daily Morning Call*. Now he had to stick closer to the facts, and much of his work was just traditional local reporting without a byline. The reporting was bland and required long hours. It soon became routine and boring to him. He later described it as "soulless drudgery."[9] Still, he continued sending correspondence to the *Daily Territorial Enterprise*, where he had more freedom.

Of course he rebelled at the *Call*'s editorial restrictions. After Rudyard Kipling heard stories about Twain from this time, he wrote, "In San Francisco the men of the *Call* told me many legends of Mark's apprenticeship in their paper five-and-twenty years ago; how he was a reporter delightfully incapable of reporting according to the needs of the day. He preferred, so they said, to coil himself into a heap and meditate until the last minute. Then he would produce copy bearing no sort of relationship to his legitimate work—a copy that made the editor swear horribly and the readers of the *Call* ask for more."[10]

Twain was something of a social reformer, speaking out against hypocrisy, corruption, cruelty, injustices, and discrimination against Blacks and the Chinese. At that time, speaking out for Blacks was tolerated since the Civil War was going on but not for the Chinese. One such incident contributed to his leaving the *Call*.

He later wrote in his autobiography, "One Sunday afternoon I saw some hoodlums chasing and stoning a Chinaman who was heavily laden with the weekly wash of his Christian customers, and I noticed that a policeman was observing this performance with an amused interest—nothing more. He did not interfere. I wrote up the incident with considerable warmth and holy indignation."[11]

His editor killed the story, not wanting to offend the prejudices of their readership. Twain lost interest in his work and began neglecting it. A month later, he was fired, or, as Twain put it, he retired at the solicitation of the publisher.

This was October 1864. While he continued to send letters to the *Territorial Enterprise*, he entered a period where he was often short of money.

A couple of months after leaving the *Call*, Twain and his friends Steve and Jim Gillis decided to try their hands at gold mining, so they headed off to Jackass Hill for three months, where the Gillises and Dick Stoker owned a cabin. They didn't strike it rich, but it was while mining that Twain heard a number of tall tales that he later wrote down—including the jumping-frog story that he would make famous.

Going Gonzo

It was during this period that Twain developed a style that Hunter S. Thompson would later call "gonzo journalism." Essentially, Twain would create a narrative spiced with humor, social commentary, and general outrageousness. It was iconoclastic, violated norms, and didn't shy away from hurling insults. It would be based on actual events, with fictional elements and himself right in the middle of it all. While it wouldn't be accurate, it would ring true. Some people felt it was more truthful than authentic news articles.

In his 1871 *Roughing It* lecture, he said, "A reporter has to lie a little, of course, or they would discharge him. That is the only drawback to the profession. [...] Reporting is fascinating, but then it is distressing to have to lie so. Lying is bad—lying is very bad. Every individual in this house knows that by experience. I think that for a man to tell a lie when he can't make anything by it, is wrong."[12]

In his autobiography, Twain wrote, "all through my life: whenever I have diverged from custom and principle and uttered a truth, the rule has been that the hearer hadn't strength of mind enough to believe it."[13]

While traditional journalism punishes writers who invent sources, characters, and quotations and otherwise incorporate fictional elements into their work, many journalists admire gonzo and secretly wish they had the freedom to write it. Hunter Thompson flirted with it in his classic novel *Fear and Loathing in Las Vegas*, but he really let loose in his articles for *Scanlan's Monthly* and *Rolling Stone*, even inventing a story of 1972 presidential candidate Edmund Muskie using the obscure hallucinogenic drug ibogaine that other journalists thought was true and repeated in their own reporting as being factual, much like Twain's hoaxes.

Thompson also took Twain's talent for creative insults to new levels, such as describing Richard Nixon as "a foul caricature of himself, a man with no soul, no inner convictions, with the integrity of a hyena and the style of a poison toad."[14] And, "If there were any such thing as true justice in this world, his rancid carcass would be somewhere down around Easter Island right now, in the belly of a hammerhead shark."[15]

Twain cultivated his talent for creative insults, describing a reporter for the *Virginia City Evening Bulletin* as an "oyster-brained idiot." Describing a Kingdom of Hawai'i government official Charles Harris, Twain wrote that "this stately figure, which looks so like a Washington monument in the distance, is nothing but a thirty-dollar windmill when you get close to him." Regarding the wife of poet and novelist Thomas Bailey Aldrich, he wrote, "I do not believe I could learn to like her except on a raft at sea with no other provisions in sight." Of his lawyer, he noted, "He is a great fat good-natured, kind-hearted, chicken-livered slave; with no more pride than a tramp, no more sand than a rabbit, no more moral sense than a wax figure, and no more sex than a tapeworm. He sincerely thinks that he is honest; he sincerely thinks that he is honorable. It is my daily prayer to God that he be permitted to live and die in those superstitions." After an editor tried to correct his language, he fumed, "This long-eared animal, this literary kangaroo, this bastard of the muse, this illiterate skull full of axle grease. . . ." When comparing another author to Jane Austen, he said, "I could read his prose on salary, but not Jane's. Jane is entirely impossible. It seems a great pity that they allowed her to die a natural death." And on another occasion, he mused, "Every time I read *Pride and Prejudice* I want to dig her up and beat her over the skull with her own shinbone."

Much American humor at that time featured colloquial speech, such as that of Josh Billings, Artemus Ward, and Petroleum V. Nasby. Twain tried that when he was young but cast it aside, preferring to use his own voice. And unlike anything else at the time, Twain's work was subversive, exposing society's evils and hypocrisies. His humor forced people to think after they laughed, much like the humor of Lenny Bruce, George Carlin, and Stephen Colbert. He sometimes went out of his way to shock people, feeling that if he could knock them off balance, they'd be more susceptible to his humor. He made fun of his enemies, his friends, and even himself. And while he was close friends with many missionaries, he made fun of them too. His satire was so advanced that it often went over the head of many of his readers and listeners.

Twain incorporated all of these elements in some of his correspondence from Hawai'i, mixed in with his more traditional business and travel articles.

Famous Frog

By October 1865, Twain was beginning to realize that his path forward was through humor. In a letter he wrote to his brother Orion and his brother's wife, he said, "I have had a 'call' to literature, of a low order—i.e. humorous. It is nothing to be proud of, but it is my strongest suit."[16]

This was the same month that he finished writing and submitted "Jim Smiley and His Jumping Frog." Appearing in New York's *Saturday Press*, it was a big hit and was reprinted in American and British newspapers and pirated in at least one book. A year and a half later, he featured a modified version of it in his own collection of Western stories, titled *The Celebrated Jumping Frog of Calaveras County, and Other Sketches* (1867). This would be his first book.

But when the story was first published, the *San Francisco Alta* proclaimed it "has set all New York in a roar, and he may be said to have made his mark. I have been asked fifty times about it and its author, and the papers are copying it near and far. It is voted the best thing of the day."[17]

Nowadays it seems a bit odd that the story made so much noise. It's just a tall tale about a stranger that comes into Angel's Camp—a gold mining town—and is challenged by an inveterate gambler to bet on a jumping-frog race, but the gambler loses after the stranger surreptitiously slips a handful of shotgun pellets down the throat of the gambler's frog, preventing him from jumping. But it's not so much the story as the way it was written that caught people's attention. The *New York Tribune*'s critic explained that "the style of the letter was so singularly fresh, original, and full of character as to attract prompt and universal attention."[18]

Here is an excerpt:

> Thish-yer Smiley had a mare—the boys called her the fifteen-minute nag, but that was only in fun, you know, because, of course, she was faster than that—and he used to win money on that horse, for all she was so slow and always had the asthma, or the distemper, or the consumption, or something of that kind. They used to give her two or three hundred yards' start, and then pass her under way; but always at the fag-end [last part] of the race she'd get excited and desperate-like, and come cavorting and straddling up, and scattering her legs around limber, sometimes in the air, and sometimes out to one side amongst the fences, and kicking up m-o-r-e dust, and raising m-o-r-e racket with her coughing and sneezing and blowing her nose—and always fetch up at the stand just about a neck ahead, as near as you could cipher it down.

Twain had a natural style that people liked. Instead of being rather formal and grammatically correct—even as much writing still is today—it was very conversational and reflects the way people *really* talk. He would even purposefully pause in the middle of a thought and jump to something else to make it seem spontaneous.

While he didn't think much of the story, in his autobiography he noted, "It certainly had a wide celebrity, [. . .] but I was aware that it was only the frog that was celebrated. It wasn't I. I was still an obscurity."[19]

But it was a start.

Trouble in California

By the end of 1865, Twain accepted an assignment as the San Francisco correspondent for the *Daily Territorial Enterprise*, submitting daily reports for $90 a month, or roughly $2,300 a month in today's dollars. He was also writing for the *San Francisco Dramatic Chronicle* for $40 a month and the *Napa County Reporter*, along with freelance contributions to the *Californian* and the *New York Weekly Review*.

But he was also involved in a war of words with journalist Albert Evans. Twain accused Evans—who used the pen names Fitz Smythe, Stiggers, and Amigo—of being a poor writer, of drinking too much, of being a liar, and of blindly glorifying the police, saying he "invariably and eternally slobbers them over with his slimy praise."[20] Evans, on the other hand, insinuated that Twain had venereal disease. Each of them wanted to kill the other.

He was also relentlessly criticizing the San Francisco police, accusing them of corruption and racism in his *Daily Territorial Enterprise* articles. He even attacked the police chief personally, saying, "I have not the remotest idea of meddling with his private affairs. Even if he kept a mistress, I would hardly parade it in the public prints; nor would I object to his performing any gymnastic miracle which might suggest itself to his mind as being calculated to afford her wholesome amusement. [. . .] But Chief Burke don't keep a mistress. On second thoughts, I only wish he did. I would call it malfeasance in office and publish it in a minute!"

The barrage of attacks prompted Chief Martin Burke to file a lawsuit against the newspaper, but it was thrown out because the newspaper was in another state and outside of the court's jurisdiction. But his officers were looking for any opportunity to grab Twain and throw him in the slammer. And they got their chance in mid-January 1866, jailing him overnight for public drunkenness, probably on an exaggerated charge, although he was drinking heavily during this period.

A few days later. he wrote a letter to his mother and sister, saying, "I wish I was back there piloting up and down the [Mississippi] river again." And he added that he received an invitation to sail on the maiden voyage of the steamship *Ajax* to Honolulu, "but I could not accept it, because there would be no one to write my correspondence while I was gone. But I am so sorry now. If the *Ajax* were back I would go quick and throw up the correspondence."[21]

Even two years earlier when he was still in Virginia City, he wanted to go to the "Sandwich Islands"—an old name for the Hawaiian Islands that was used throughout the nineteenth century. He wrote to his sister, referring to the editor and owner of the *Territorial Enterprise*, saying, "Joe Goodman is gone to the Sandwich Islands. [. . .] I wanted to go with Joe, but the news-editor was expecting every day to get sick (he has since accomplished it), and we could not all leave at once."[22]

In a February 19, 1866, squib, the *San Francisco Dramatic Chronicle* noted,

> **Important**
>
> Up to 12 o'clock on Saturday night, "Mark Twain" had not been cowhided. But at half-past 11, Fitz Smythe was "hunting him" around at his favorite bowling alley on Pine Street. At a quarter before 12, the ferocious and bloodthirsty proprietor of the Napoleonic moustache and the gorgeously caparisoned charger was "laying" for the unsuspecting and defenseless jokist at the Faust Cellar. We would earnestly advise "Mark" to leave town for a week or two. Sagebrush Joe would like to see him.[23]

They were referring to Joe Goodman in Nevada, essentially suggesting Twain leave the state for a bit—which he accomplished two and a half weeks later.

Becoming a Foreign Correspondent

The idea of going to Hawai'i must have become very attractive to Twain, for he decided that his *Daily Territorial Enterprise* correspondence was not that important after all, and so a friend of his, Charles Webb—the editor of the *Californian* and the *Sacramento Daily Union*'s San Francisco correspondent—approached the owners of the *Daily Union* with the idea of sending Twain to write a series of articles from the Islands.

Webb somehow sensed Twain was going to be a great success in spite of Twain's professed laziness. Just four months earlier, he wrote in his correspondence to the *Sacramento Daily Union*, "To my thinking, Shakespeare had no more idea that he was writing for posterity than Mark Twain has at the present time, and it sometimes amuses me to think how future Mark Twain scholars will puzzle over that gentleman's present hieroglyphics and occasionally eccentric expressions."[24]

There were no complimentary tickets for the *Ajax*'s second voyage, but Webb later said he bought Twain's ticket.

Sacramento is the capital of California, and at that time, the *Sacramento Daily Union* was the most important newspaper in the West. As the name "Mark Twain" was now fairly well known in California and Nevada and the jumping-frog story was well received in the East, the managers of the *Union* must have figured Twain's dispatches from the Kingdom of Hawai'i would garner attention. Hawai'i was still its own country then, led by a king.

Reminiscing in 1898, Twain wrote that he went to "the Islands to write letters for the weekly edition of the *Sacramento Union*, a rich and influential daily journal which hadn't any use for them, but could afford to spend twenty dollars a week for nothing. The proprietors were lovable and well-beloved men: long ago dead, no doubt, but in me there is at least one person who still holds them in grateful remembrance; for I dearly wanted to see the Islands, and they listened to me and gave me the opportunity when there was but slender likelihood that it could profit them in any way."[25]

Actually, there already was interest in the Islands by the business community. The gold rush was coming to an end, and the West was looking for new opportunities to expand its economy. Passenger ships regularly sailed there, but the introduction of the steamship *Ajax* promised to cut travel time from roughly twenty-eight days to eleven days. And Congress had just voted to fund a mail steamer to China by way of Hawai'i and Japan. Businessmen wanted to know more about the sugar industry, whaling, and trade. Most of the businesses there were already run by Americans. California was importing agricultural products from the Kingdom, and this had increased during the Civil War. Routine news from the Islands was regularly printed in newspapers all across the country, and churches closely followed the work of the missionaries. There was also considerable interest in Hawai'i as an exotic paradise, and since few people could afford to go there, they vicariously visited the Islands through reading travel books and articles.

Twain's dispatches from Hawai'i gave him the opportunity to use a wide range of styles. They contain straight business information with statistics, reliable news reporting, politics, social commentary, travel writing, and a wide variety of humor, including subtle irony, wit, ridicule, satire, and even slapstick. In his Nevada writings, he often made fun of tenderfoots. In Hawai'i, *he* was a tenderfoot, but that didn't stop him from continuing to spoof them and himself, along with "the myth of grandiose expectations" and their expectation that they've crossed over into "hostile territory" when in fact they hadn't.[26]

Twain emphasized the contrast between the sentimental views of the Islands and the realistic through the use of a fictional traveling companion named Mr. Brown. Brown is a crude, rather uncouth, ignorant character—at least in the beginning. He's the realist, in contrast to Twain's sentimentalism. When Twain starts drifting into sentimentality, Brown abruptly brings him back to reality. Brown sometimes acts as Twain's alter ego, and Twain also uses him as a foil. While Brown appears at various points throughout the *Union* letters, Twain deleted him—except for three brief mentions—when he prepared the correspondence for a book on his Hawai'i travels, which was unfortunate. Brown reappeared later on in more of his newspaper correspondence—such as those from New York and Washington—but the two characters gradually melded into one, and Twain eventually dropped Brown altogether.

Oddly, he deleted some of his best material from his Hawai'i manuscript, replacing it with some dull stuff only obliquely related to Hawai'i. Much of the added material were tall tales of the West that were told to him in a public room on Maui. On realizing he no longer had enough material for a book and needing to pad out the subscription edition of *Roughing It*—his book of Nevada and California writings—he ended up adding the revised Hawai'i material to the end of that book, although it and all of the illustrations were soon removed from most later editions.

Twain's humor in his Hawai'i articles transitions between the exaggerated tall tale humor of the West and the more refined humor of his second book, *The Innocents Abroad* (1869). In the *Union* letters, he was able to experiment with different forms of humor—some successful and some not. I'm going to spare you from his tedious and droll vomit jokes, although I will mention them in passing so you'll be thankful of what you're missing. Perhaps being out of the country gave him a sense that he was writing for a broader audience. After the jumping frog's success, he did have his eye on making a name for himself back East. While his *Union* letters were widely read in the western United States, large and small parts were reprinted in newspapers around the country for decades to come, although even his later humor was specifically designed to shock those with refined sensibilities.

In preparing to leave, Twain wrote this letter home to let them know of his sudden departure:

> San Francisco, March 5, 1866.
>
> My Dear Mother and Sister,
>
> I start to the Sandwich Islands day after tomorrow (I suppose Annie [his niece] is geographer enough by this time to find them on the map) in the steamer *Ajax*. We shall arrive there in about twelve days. My friends seem determined that I shall not lack acquaintances, for I only decided today to go, and they have already sent me letters of introduction to everybody down there worth knowing, the King included, I believe.
>
> I am to remain there a month and ransack the Islands, the great cataracts and the volcanoes completely, and write twenty or thirty letters to the *Sacramento Union*—for which they pay me as much money as I would get if I staid at home.
>
> If I come back here I expect to start straight across the continent by way of the Columbia River, the Pend d'Oreille Lakes, through Montana and down the Missouri river—only 200 miles of land travel from San Francisco to New Orleans.
>
> Goodbye for the present.
> Yours,
> Sam.[27]

He ended up staying four months in the Islands, not one, and he never made that trip to New Orleans.

As Hawai'i had very few hotels or rooming houses—mainly in Honolulu—Twain's friends loaded him down with letters of introduction to everyone they knew in Hawai'i so he would receive a warm welcome and have someplace to stay when he ventured out of the town.

Then on March 7, 1866, his friends at the *San Francisco Dramatic Chronicle* bid him bon voyage:

For the Islands

"Mark Twain," the funniest man now on top of the earth, so far as heard from, sails for the Sandwich Islands in the *Ajax* today. He will correspond with the *Sacramento Daily Union*, and everyone who knows "Mark's" quality will join with us in the wish that his letters may be frequent and long. We enjoin it upon the commander of the *Ajax* to take especial care of "Mark," for he is worth more than all the ship's cargo. In these dismal days who shall put an estimate upon the value of a man who can make you laugh as "Mark" can?

A few days later, Virginia City's *Montana Post* wrote, "*The Golden Era* says that the great California humorist, Mark Twain, is now on his way to the Sandwich Islands on the steamer *Ajax* and it would not be surprising if passengers and crew had humor breaking out all over them before arriving at Honolulu."[28]

JOURNEY TO
PARADISE

The *Ajax* docked at San Francisco's Greenwich Street wharf in 1866. Note the paddle wheel housing on the far side of the foremast.

[MARCH 7–18, 1866:]

Although Twain had been a riverboat pilot for four years, was very familiar with boats, and made many ocean voyages after this, this was his first time at sea—still, he handled it a lot better than many of the other passengers. The journey took eleven days, some of it in very rough weather.

"Making Sail"

Leaving all care and trouble and business behind in the city, now swinging gently around the hills and passing house by house and street by street out of view, we swept down through the Golden Gate and stretched away toward the shoreless horizon. It was a pleasant, breezy afternoon, and the strange new sense of entire and perfect emancipation from labor and responsibility coming strong upon me, I went up on the hurricane deck so that I could have room to enjoy it. I sat down on a bench, and for an hour I took a tranquil delight in that kind of labor which is such a luxury to the enlightened Christian—to-wit the labor of other people. [. . .]

[Soon after leaving port, they hit rough weather.]

The ship was rolling fearfully. At this point I got up and started over to ask the captain if it wouldn't be a good idea to belay a little for a change, but I fell down. I then resumed my former seat. For twenty minutes after this I took careful note of how the captain leaned his body hard to port when the ship lurched to starboard, and hard to larboard when she lurched to port, and then got up to practice a little. I only met with moderate success, though, and after a few extraordinary evolutions, fetched up against the mainmast. The concussion did not injure the mast perceptibly, but if it had been a brick house the case might have been very different. I proceeded below, rather discouraged.[1]

We had some thirty passengers; among them a cheerful soul by the name of Williams, and three sea-worn old whaleship captains going down to join their vessels. These latter played euchre in the smoking room day and night, drank astonishing quantities of raw whiskey without being in the least affected by it, and were the happiest people I think I ever saw.[2]

[The storm continued for four days, and all but about half a dozen passengers got horribly seasick. But even without seasickness, the storm was rough on Twain.]

You can take that four-days dose of your infamous "Pacific," Mr. Balboa, and digest it; and you may consider it well for your reputation in California that we had pretty fair weather the balance of the voyage. If we hadn't, I would have given you a blast in this letter that would have made your old dry bones rattle in your coffin—you shameless old foreign humbug![3]

—⋞

In his next *Union* letter, Twain did blast Balboa for about six column inches, calling him such things as an "infatuated old ass" and a "Balboa-constrictor," complaining in extended detail that for most of the year, the Pacific was not pacific.

In his book *Roughing It*, Twain also introduced a character nicknamed "Admiral," although this man had never been in the Navy. The old Admiral was actually inspired by whaling captain James Smith. The very long profile of the Admiral starts out sympathetic, with him being as "tender-hearted as a girl," but by the end he's a very disagreeable character—an ignorant blowhard. He begins as a strong Unionist but ends as a strong Confederate, without really understanding what the war was about.

Twain wrote that "his face was the lodestone that chained the eye. It was a sultry disk, glowing determinedly out through a weather beaten mask of mahogany, and studded with warts, seamed with scars, 'blazed' all over with unfailing fresh slips of the razor; and with cheery eyes, under shaggy brows, contemplating the world from over the back of a gnarled crag of a nose that loomed vast and lonely out of the undulating immensity that spread away from its foundations."

And when "the Admiral's fires began to wax hot, the atmosphere thickened, the coming earthquake rumbled, he began to thunder and lighten. Within three minutes his volcano was in full eruption and he was discharging flames and ashes of indignation, belching black volumes of foul history aloft, and vomiting red-hot torrents of profanity from his crater."[4]

When trapped in an argument, the Admiral began to make stuff up about a nonexistent war atrocity, but he was soundly put in his place by a quiet passenger named Williams, who seemed to agree with the Admiral, complimenting him while actually slapping him down with similar false evidence of another imagined war atrocity.

In the Middle of Nowhere

Twain spent a lot of time talking to people on the voyage gathering as much information as he could about the Islands. Unfortunately, he picked up a lot of false information, along with their prejudices, which he repeated in his initial letters to the *Union*. He corrected many of these later on as he got to know the Islands and its people better. The whaling captains provided him with a lot of information about whaling, and he talked with missionaries, along with their sons and daughters, some who had been born and raised in the Islands. The parents of Rev. Thomas Thurston and his sister Mary Hayden were on the first ship of missionaries to arrive. William Henry Dimond's father was part of the seventh company of missionaries.

The two *Ajax* voyages were not profitable, so it ceased service to the Islands until May 1870 when it began carrying mail to Australia and New Zealand, stopping off in Honolulu with passengers and freight. It regularly visited Honolulu until November 1872.

Eleven days at sea seems like a long time to us since we can fly from the mainland in five or six hours, but that was fastest at that time. Normally, it was much longer. For people sailing from the East Coast, it could take many months. Hawai'i is the most remote inhabited spot on Earth.

Because of the curvature of the Earth, the closest spots are Hilo on the eastern side of Big Island and San Francisco—a distance of 2,315 miles. Here are a few other distances, moving farther away:

Los Angeles, California	2,563
Tahiti	2,755
Anchorage, Alaska	2,787
Tokyo, Japan	3,860
Chicago, Illinois	4,254
New York City, New York	4,965
Sydney, Australia	5,080
Manila, Philippines	5,305
London, England	7,236
Delhi, India	7,408
Cape Town, South Africa	11,549

Note that these are the shortest distances by air. Many airline routes are longer, particularly if they have to refuel. For example, it's unlikely you'll be able to fly nonstop from Cape Town over Antarctica to Hawai'i as I've measured here.

The Hawaiian Islands also include the Northwestern Hawaiian Islands, which are 131 smaller islands, islets, shoals, and atolls that continue the Hawaiian archipelago up to the northwest, extending for 1,523 miles—about the distance from the Mississippi River to Los Angeles. None of these are inhabited, except for the Midway Atoll, where four to five dozen US Fish and Wildlife Service employees and contract workers live. All of these islands, except for three Midway Islands, are part of the state of Hawai'i.

I should also note, just in case you don't live or spend much time here, that Hawai'i is the name of the largest and southeasternmost island of the Hawaiian Islands. It is also the name for the eight largest islands as a group. Because of the confusion that can be caused by having the island and the group of islands using the same name, we commonly refer to the island of Hawai'i as the Big Island.

O'AHU

HONOLULU 1866

WHILE TWAIN DIDN'T GET SEASICK ON THE VOYAGE, four days before reaching Honolulu, he came down with the mumps and didn't recover until after his arrival.

[March 18, 1866:]

On a certain bright morning the Islands hove in sight, lying low on the lonely sea, and everybody climbed to the upper deck to look. After two thousand miles of watery solitude the vision was a welcome one.[1]

We came in sight of two of this group of islands, Oʻahu and Molokai[2] (pronounced O-WAW-hoo and Mollo-KI), on the morning of the 18th, and soon exchanged the dark blue waters of the deep sea for the brilliant light blue of "soundings." The fat, ugly birds (said to be a species of albatross) which had skimmed after us on tireless wings clear across the ocean, left us, and an occasional flying-fish went skimming over the water in their stead.

Oʻahu loomed high, rugged, treeless, barren, black and dreary, out of the sea, and in the distance Molokai lay like a homely sway-backed whale on the water.[3]

As we approached, the imposing promontory of Diamond Head rose up out of the ocean its rugged front softened by the hazy distance, and presently the details of the land began to make themselves manifest: first the line of beach; then the plumed coconut trees of the tropics; then cabins of the natives; then the white town of Honolulu, said to contain between twelve and fifteen thousand inhabitants spread over a dead level; with streets from twenty to thirty feet wide, solid and level as a floor, most of them straight as a line and few as crooked as a corkscrew.[4]

The Hawaiian Flag

As we rounded the promontory of Diamond Head (bringing into view a grove of coconut trees, first ocular proof that we were in the tropics), we ran up the stars and stripes at the main-spencer-gaff, and the Hawaiian flag at the fore. The latter is suggestive of the prominent political elements of the Islands. It is part French, part English, part American

In 1866, this was the flag of the Kingdom of Hawai'i. Now it's the state flag. This one has a small fishing shrine at its base above the palm frond where offerings are still made to Ku'ula, Kū, or Kanaloa, the primary fishing gods. Whether this is a cultural or a religious practice depends on the individual's intentions and beliefs.
AUTHOR'S PHOTO

and is Hawaiian in general. The union jack in the corner has the crosses of England, Ireland, and Scotland; the remainder of the flag (horizontal stripes) looks American, but has a blue French stripe in addition to our red and white ones.

The flag was gotten up by foreign legations in council with the Hawaiian government. The eight stripes refer to the eight islands which are inhabited; the other four are barren rocks incapable of supporting a population.

[In 1816 a British captain designed the Hawaiian Kingdom's flag for King Kamehameha. While no one is sure what it looked like, it's thought to have looked like the current flag. The British flag—with its three styles of crosses of the patron saints of England, Scotland, and Ireland—is in the top left corner to represent that the Kingdom was under Britain's protection, although Britain never officially recognized Hawai'i as a protectorate. The Kingdom's flag was retained when Hawaiʻi became a U.S. territory in 1898, and again when Hawaiʻi became the Union's fiftieth state in 1959.]

Reflections

As we came in sight we fired a gun, and a good part of Honolulu turned out to welcome the steamer. It was Sunday morning, and about church time, and we steamed through the narrow channel to the music of six different church bells, which sent their mellow tones far and wide, over hills and valleys, which were peopled by naked, savage, thundering barbarians only fifty years ago!

Six Christian churches within five miles of the ruins of a pagan temple, where human sacrifices were daily offered up to hideous idols in the last century! We were within pistol shot of one of a group of islands whose ferocious inhabitants closed in upon the doomed and helpless Captain Cook and murdered him, eighty-seven years ago; and lo! their descendants were at church! Behold what the missionaries have wrought!

Not All That Savage

Okay, the Hawaiians didn't murder a "doomed and helpless" Captain Cook. While that was the popular idea of what happened, Twain soon discovered it was wrong, and later on he gives an accurate account of what really took place.

Also, the Hawaiians were not nearly as savage as people thought. Their culture is very interesting and complex. In some ways, it's better than Western culture, particularly when it comes to generosity and caring for one another.

Lawyer and sailor Richard Henry Dana wrote in his famous sea voyage exposé, *Two Years before the Mast* (1840), regarding Hawaiians,

> I would have trusted my life and all I had in the hands of any one of these people; and certainly, had I wished for a favor or act of sacrifice, I would have gone to them all, in turn, before I should have applied to one of my own countrymen on the coast, and should have expected to see it done, before my own countrymen had got half through counting the cost.

Their customs, and manner of treating one another, show a simple, primitive generosity which is truly delightful, and which is often a reproach to our own people. Whatever one has, they all have. Money, food, clothes, they share with one another, even to the last piece of tobacco to put in their pipes. I once heard old Mr. Bingham [a Hawaiian named after the missionary] say, with the highest indignation, to a Yankee trader who was trying to persuade him to keep his money to himself, "No! we no all 'e same a' you! Suppose one got money, all got money. You, suppose one got money lock him up in chest. No good!"

"Kānaka all 'e same a' one!"

This principle they carry so far that none of them will eat anything in sight of others without offering it all round. I have seen one of them break a biscuit, which had been given him, into five parts, at a time when I knew he was on a very short allowance, as there was but little to eat on the beach.

[. . .] they were the most interesting, intelligent, and kind-hearted people that I ever fell in with. I felt a positive attachment for almost all of them; and many of them I have, to this day, a feeling for, which would lead me to go a great way for the pleasure of seeing them, and which will always make me feel a strong interest in the mere name of a Sandwich Islander.[5]

Sailor Ebenezer Townsend Jr. wrote in 1798, "These Islanders are neat in their persons, respect their legislators and their laws, are cheerful and obliging to each other. And they were extremely religious."[6]

A lot of the so-called savage elements of their society arose from misunderstandings and from a general lack of knowledge of what Cook and other explorers were witnessing. If someone finds themselves in unfamiliar and possibly dangerous surroundings, they tend to fill in the blanks with the worst possible explanation in order to play it safe. And on the other side, some of what Cook's men said and did made the Hawaiians wonder how Cook's men could be so savage.

Even in 1873, after receiving many concerned inquiries, travel writer Isabella Bird felt it necessary to insist, "The natives are not savages, most decidedly not. They are on the whole a quiet, courteous, orderly, harmless, Christian community."[7]

The missionaries fostered the idea that the ancient Hawaiians were savage because it made their work and achievements seem that much greater and helped them raise money, but I'm sure they would be just as horrified at our modern society.

Twain's articles occasionally stray into racist territory, usually by attributing negative or unsavory attributes or actions to persons of other nationalities—Europeans and Hawaiians. He also inadvertently absorbed some of the false impressions that, no doubt, were circulating at the time regarding the native Hawaiians. It is unfortunate that he passed these on to his readers.

Twain eventually realized this and poked fun at his audience's false beliefs by titling his lectures "Our Fellow Savages of the Sandwich Islands." Still, it's important to remember that Twain was one of the more liberal and most antiracist authors in his day, and he often caught flak for it. And, as Lawrence Downes put it, "readers should try to forgive Twain's culture-bound ethnic insensitivity and remember that his misanthropy is refreshingly all-inclusive."[8]

We'll discuss the human sacrifices shortly, but they weren't much different than the executions in America and Europe, except in Hawai'i they were much less gruesome and didn't involve torture. Remember that the witch trials and the Spanish Inquisition, which resulted in executions of many innocent people, were also based on warped religious ideas.

I'd also like to quickly point out that the term "Hawaiian" in Hawai'i refers only to those of native Hawaiian ancestry and their culture. Everyone else who lives here is a "Hawai'i resident," even if they were born here. The term "local" is a bit broader. A local can be anyone who has a deep emotional connection to the land and a strong appreciation of the many different cultures and people here. A lot of the people who live here are not really locals. The term "kama'āina" means "child of the land" or "one who was born here," but merchants have broadened this by offering kama'āina discounts to anyone with a Hawai'i ID.

At the top is King Kamehameha's compound at Honolulu in 1816, painted by a ship's artist. Fort Honolulu is in the back on the left. This is the only early picture I know of that shows Kamehameha's flag, which is upside down from the way we fly it now. The compound was along the shore between what is now Nuʻuanu Avenue and Fort Street. Below is downtown Honolulu today looking across Kahanamoku Lagoon.

(TOP) LOUIS CHORIS; (BOTTOM) AUTHOR'S PHOTO

Surrounded by Wonders

By the time we had worked our slow way up to the wharf, under the guidance of McIntyre, the pilot, a mixed crowd of 400 or 500 people had assembled— Chinamen, in the costume of their country; foreigners and the better class of natives, and "half whites" in carriages and dressed in Sacramento summer fashion; other native men on foot, some in the cast-off clothing of white folks, and a few wearing a battered hat, an old ragged vest, and nothing else— at least nothing but an unnecessarily slender rag passed between the legs; native women clad in a single garment—a bright colored robe or wrapper as voluminous as a balloon, with full sleeves.

This robe is "gathered" from shoulder to shoulder, before and behind, and then descends in ample folds to the feet—seldom a chemise or any other under garment—fits like a circus tent fits the tent pole, and no hoops. These robes were bright yellow, or bright crimson, or pure black occasionally, or gleaming white; but "solid colors" and "stunning" ones were the rule.

The view of Nuʻuanu Avenue from a ship in 1877 (or 1884).

This is what happens when missionaries become fashion designers. Finding the female form indecent, they covered the women in choir robes. The Hawaiians called these voluminous dresses holokūs, and the Americans called them Mother Hubbards. The version of this dress without the high neck yoke and buttons is called a muʻumuʻu, now commonly pronounced as moo-moo.
MENZIES DICKSON

They wore little hats such as the sex wear in your cities, and some of the younger women had very pretty faces and splendid black eyes and heavy masses of long black hair, occasionally put up in a "net." Some of these dark, gingerbread colored beauties were on foot—generally on bare-foot, I may add—and others were on horseback—astraddle; they never ride any other way, and they ought to know which way is best, for there are no more accomplished horsewomen in the world, it is said.

The balance of the crowd consisted chiefly of little half-naked native boys and girls. All were chattering in the catchy, chopped-up Kanaka language; but what they were chattering about will always remain a mystery to me.

"Kanaka" is the Hawaiian word for "Hawaiian." Literally it means "human being." I've read of a number of other cultures who refer to themselves as simply "the people" or something similar, like this.

Climatic

We arrived here today at noon, and while I spent an hour or so talking, the other passengers exhausted all the lodging accommodations of Honolulu. So I must remain on board the ship tonight. It is very warm in the stateroom, no air enters the ports. Therefore, have dressed in a way which seems best calculated to suit the exigencies of the case. A description of this dress is not necessary. I may observe, however, that I bought the chief article of it at "Ward's" [Ward's Shirt Store in San Francisco].

There are a good many mosquitoes around tonight and they are rather troublesome; but it is a source of unalloyed satisfaction to me to know that the two millions I sat down on a minute ago will never sing again.[9]

The upper photograph shows downtown Honolulu in the late 1860s. The lower picture—taken in 1865 from Quarantine Island (now part of Sand Island)—shows rain approaching the suburbs, where most of the foreigners lived. Part of this area is now Chinatown.
(BOTTOM IMAGE) CHARLES WEED

Top: A barber shop ca. 1877 at the north corner of King and Bethel streets near the wharves and about a block from the *Pacific Commercial Advertiser* newspaper office, one of the first places Twain went in Honolulu. Bottom: A barbershop on Fort Street ca. 1869, also near where Twain was on his first day in Honolulu.

Almost a King

I had not shaved since I left San Francisco—ten days. As soon as I got ashore I hunted for a striped pole, and shortly found one. I always had a yearning to be a king. This may never be, I suppose. But at any rate it will always be a satisfaction to me to know that if I am not a king, I am the next thing to it—I have been shaved by the King's barber.

Landsmen on "Sea Legs"

Walking about on shore was very uncomfortable at first; there was no spring to the solid ground, and I missed the heaving and rolling of the ship's deck. It was unpleasant to lean unconsciously to an anticipated lurch of the world and find that the world did not lurch, as it should have done. And there was something else missed—something gone—something wanting, I could not tell what—a dismal vacuum of some kind or other—a sense of emptiness.

But I found out what it was presently. It was the absence of the ceaseless dull hum of beating waves and whipping sails and fluttering of the propeller, and creaking of the ship—sounds I had become so accustomed to that I had ceased to notice them and had become unaware of their existence until the deep Sunday stillness on shore made me vaguely conscious that a familiar spirit of some kind or other was gone from me. Walking on the solid earth with legs used to the "giving" of the decks under his tread, made Brown sick, and he went off to bed and left me to wander alone about this odd-looking city of the tropics.[10]

Mark Twain's Headquarters

One of the first places Mark Twain went on arriving in Honolulu was the offices of Hawai'i's largest newspaper—the *Pacific Commercial Advertiser*. Its editor and publisher, Henry Whitney, reminiscing forty-three years later in 1899, wrote,

> It was in the early sixties, when a stranger entered its sanctum, and introduced himself as the correspondent of a California paper—the *Sacramento Daily Union* perhaps—and offered to assist in newspaper work, if agreeable. Having then one good assistant—Nat Ingalls—who was a very clever writer, no opening offered for him. Still, an occasional joke played on an unsuspecting victim, and racy items of news, made the stranger's visits very welcome, and showed that he had a fund of humor ready for any occasion.

> He was not only an inveterate joker, but also smoker, at least one box of cigars disappearing every week on an average. He made himself perfectly at home in my office, but would seldom leave without a parting joke.

> I became quite attached to the stranger, who proved to be Mark Twain—a *nom de plume* then hardly known beyond the borders or California, as he was just commencing his literary career.[11]

Left: The *Pacific Commercial Advertiser* office is the second building from the left. Called the Honolulu Hale, it was originally built for the Kingdom of Hawai'i's legislature. This photograph is from ca. 1885. When Twain was here, the bottom floor housed Henry Whitney's bookstore on one side of the room and Honolulu's post office on the other. Whitney was also Hawai'i's first postmaster. On the roof is a semaphore. Another semaphore on Telegraph Hill would use flags to signal here the arrival of ships containing the mail, news, or VIPs. Then church and factory bells would ring all over the city, and cannons were fired. Even ordinary ships prompted people to head to the wharves in excitement. Parties and celebrations often began at the docks. Right: Henry Whitney was the publisher of the *Pacific Commercial Advertiser* and a Hawaiian-language newspaper and also published books.

William Brash, who worked for Whitney, also remembered Twain's arrival. When Brash was interviewed for the statewide celebration of Mark Twain Day to commemorate what would have been Twain's eightieth birthday in 1915, he said,

> I remember that visit of Mark Twain with much pleasure. You know I was a printer on the *Advertiser* in my early days before entering the service of the Wilder Steamship Company, so it was natural that I should see a good deal of the young correspondent during his stay in Honolulu.

About the first thing Mark Twain did when he arrived here, on the seventeenth [actually it was the eighteenth] of March, 1866, was to drop into the *Advertiser* office, and everyone there soon knew him. With the editor (the late Henry M. Whitney) he got along famously—but did not land a job, for Nat Ingalls was assisting in getting out the paper then and there was not enough work to keep two reporters going.

Nevertheless Mark Twain virtually made the *Advertiser* his headquarters, and Mr. Whitney liked to have him around, as did the printers. It was not so many years before that, you know, that Clemens was working at the printing trade himself and naturally he drifted back and forth from the editorial room to the composing room a good deal.

Thus Mark Twain immediately felt at home in Honolulu. Among his acquaintances, beside Mr. Whitney, he soon numbered others of prominence in the community, notably the Rev. S. C. Damon, then the editor of *The Friend*, and Henry Macfarlane. He had plenty of fun with each of them and they with him, and they became fast friends.

Of course Mark Twain's first writings about life in Hawaii were full of exaggerations, but no one minded in the least. Everything he wrote was eagerly read and produced great merriment. That he, with all his fun-making, deeply loved Hawaii was evidenced in later years, and especially so in the prose poem now so widely used in the literature descriptive of the Islands.[12]

The prose poem is a quotation from one of Twain's after-dinner speeches. We'll take a closer look at it a little later.

Twain tried to get Whitney to give him a job, but we don't know whether it was so he could earn some extra money while he was in Hawai'i or whether it was because he wanted to stay there. Either way, Whitney probably felt Twain's style of humor wasn't right for his paper. Whitney did say that Twain occasionally contributed "quaint anecdotes" to the paper.[13] Unfortunately, we don't know what they were.

New Scenes and Strong Contrasts

The further I traveled through the town the better I liked it. Every step revealed a new contrast—disclosed something I was unaccustomed to. In place of the grand mud-colored brown fronts of San Francisco, I saw dwellings built of straw, adobes, and cream-colored pebble-and-shell-conglomerated coral, cut into oblong blocks and laid in cement; also a great number of neat white cottages, with green window-shutters; in place of front yards like billiard-tables with iron fences around them, I saw these homes surrounded by ample yards, about like Portsmouth Square [in Chinatown, San Francisco] (as to size), thickly clad with green grass, and shaded by tall trees, through whose dense foliage the sun could scarcely penetrate; in place of the customary geranium, calla lily, etc., languishing in dust and general debility on tin-roofed rear additions or in bedroom windows, I saw luxurious banks and thickets of flowers, fresh as a meadow after a rain, and glowing with the richest dyes; in place of the dingy horrors of San Francisco's pleasure grove, the "Willows," and the painful sharp-pointed shrubbery of that funny caricature of nature which they call "South Park," I saw huge-bodied, wide-spreading forest trees, with strange names and

Fort Street in the 1860s or early 1870s, showing its intersection with Hotel Street (where the white pole is on the left), looking toward Nuʻuanu Valley.
PHOTO BELIEVED TO BE BY HENRY L. CHASE

stranger appearance—trees that cast a shadow like a thunder-cloud, and were able to stand alone without being tied to green poles; in place of those vile, tiresome, stupid, everlasting gold-fish, wiggling around in glass globes, assuming countless shades and degrees of distortion through the magnifying and diminishing qualities of their transparent prison houses, I saw cats—Tom-cats, Mary Ann cats, long-tailed cats, bob-tailed cats, blind cats, one-eyed cats, wall-eyed cats, cross-eyed cats, gray cats, black cats, white cats, yellow cats, striped cats, spotted cats, tame cats, wild cats, singed cats, individual cats, groups of cats, platoons of cats, companies of cats, regiments of cats, armies of cats, multitudes of cats, millions of cats, and all of them sleek, fat, lazy and sound asleep.

I looked on a multitude of people, some white, in white coats, vests, pantaloons, even white cloth shoes, made snowy with chalk duly laid on every morning; but the majority of the people were almost as dark as negroes—women with comely features, fine black eyes, rounded forms, inclining to the voluptuous, clad in a single bright red or white garment that fell free and unconfined from shoulder to heel, long black hair falling loose, gypsy hats, encircled with wreaths of natural flowers of a brilliant carmine tint; plenty of dark men in various costumes, and some with nothing on but a battered stove-pipe hat tilted on the nose, and a very scant breech-clout [rag]; certain smoke-dried children were clothed in nothing but sunshine—a very neat fitting and picturesque apparel indeed.

In place of roughs and rowdies staring and blackguarding on the corners, I saw long-haired, saddle-colored Sandwich Island maidens sitting on the ground in the shade of corner houses, gazing indolently at whatever or whoever happened along; instead of wretched cobble-stone pavements, I walked on a firm foundation of coral, built up from the bottom of the sea by the absurd but persevering insect of that name, with a light layer of lava and cinders overlying the coral, belched up out of fathomless perdition long ago through the seared and blackened crater that stands dead and harmless in the distance now; instead of cramped and crowded streetcars, I met dusky native women sweeping by, free as the wind, on fleet horses and astride, with gaudy riding-sashes streaming like banners behind them; instead of the combined stenches of Sacramento Street, Chinadom and Brannan Street slaughter-houses, I breathed the balmy fragrance of jasmine, oleander, and the Pride of India; in place of the hurry and bustle and noisy confusion of San Francisco, I moved in the midst of a summer calm as tranquil as dawn in the Garden of Eden; in place of the Golden City's skirting sand hills and the placid bay, I saw on the one side a frame-work of tall, precipitous mountains close at hand, clad in refreshing green, and cleft by deep, cool, chasm-like valleys—and in front the grand sweep of the ocean; a brilliant, transparent green near the shore, bound and bordered by a long white line of foamy spray dashing against the reef, and further out the dead, blue water of the deep sea, flecked with "white caps," and in the far horizon a single, lonely sail—a mere accent-mark to emphasize a slumberous calm and a solitude that were without sound or limit. When the sun sunk down—the one intruder from other realms and persistent in suggestions of them—it was tranced luxury to sit in the perfumed air and forget that there was any world but these enchanted islands.[14]

—⟟—

Coming to Hawai'i is like going from black and white to color. It's like in the *Wizard of Oz* when the tornado abruptly relocates Dorothy's house and she opens her front door to see the wonderful Land of Oz. You are suddenly confronted with an endless summer filled with flowers in myriad hues, singing birds, majestic rainbows (which are often double rainbows), the most flavorful fruit you've ever tasted, languorous palm trees swaying lazily in the tropical breezes along soft, sandy beaches. Hawai'i is the land of hula dancers, luaus, volcanoes, tikis, and Mai Tais, but it's so much more than that, as Mark Twain quickly discovered.

Oddly, some people are immune to Hawai'i's charms. I just don't get it. It's as though they are color-blind. But for most people, this exotic paradise makes a lasting impression, so much so that if you're like me, you'll think about it every day you're not here—wishing you were back—as I did for years before I was finally able to move here. For the rest of his life, Mark Twain was haunted by Hawai'i and continually dreamt of returning here to live out his days in peaceful indolence. This was the start, when the scales fell from his eyes.

But while at heart Twain was a sentimentalist, he also had the practical streak of a realist.

Reality Bites!

It was such ecstasy to dream, and dream—till you got a bite.

A scorpion bite. Then the first duty was to get up out of the grass and kill the scorpion; and the next to bathe the bitten place with alcohol or brandy; and the next to resolve to keep out of the grass in the future. Then came an adjournment to the bed-chamber and the pastime of writing up the day's journal with one hand and the destruction of mosquitoes with the other—a whole community of them at a slap. Then, observing an enemy approaching—a hairy tarantula on stilts—why not set the spittoon on him? It is done, and the projecting ends of his paws give a luminous idea of the magnitude of his reach.[15]

At this moment, this man Brown, who has no better manners than to read over one's shoulder, observed:

"Yes, and hot. Oh, I reckon not (only 82 in the shade)! Go on, now, and put it all down, now that you've begun; just say, 'And more "santipedes," ' and cockroaches, and fleas, and lizards, and red ants, and scorpions, and spiders, and mosquitoes and missionaries'—oh, blame my cats if I'd live here two months, not if I was High-You-Muck-a-Muck and King of Wawhoo, and had a harem full of hyenas!" (Wahine—most generally pronounced Wyheeny [actually wah-HEE-nay]—seems to answer for wife, woman and female of questionable character, indifferently. I never can get this man Brown to understand that "hyena" is not the proper pronunciation. He says, "It ain't any odds; it describes some of 'em, anyway.")

I remarked, "But, Mr. Brown, these are trifles."

"Trifles be—blowed! You get nipped by one of them scorpions once, and see how you like it! There was Mrs. Jones, swabbing her face with a sponge; she felt something grab her cheek; she dropped the sponge and out popped a scorpion an inch and a half long! Well, she just got up and danced the Highland fling for two hours and a half—and yell!—why, you could have heard her from Lu-wow to Hoolahoola, with the wind fair! and for three days she soaked her cheek in brandy and salt, and it swelled up as big as your two fists.

"And you want to know what made me light out of bed so sudden last night? Only a 'santipede'—nothing, only a 'santipede,' with forty-two legs on a side, and every foot hot enough to burn a hole through a rawhide.

Don't you know one of them things grabbed Miss Boone's foot when she was riding one day? He was hid in the stirrup, and just clamped himself around her foot and sunk his fangs plum through her shoe; and she just throwed her whole soul into one war-whoop and then fainted. And she didn't get out of bed nor set that foot on the floor again for three weeks.

"And how did Captain Godfrey always get off so easy? Why, because he always carried a bottle full of scorpions and santipedes soaked in alcohol, and whenever he got bit he bathed the place with that devilish mixture or took a drink out of it, I don't recollect which. And how did he have to do once, when he hadn't his bottle along? He had to cut out the bite with his knife and fill up the hole with arnica, and then prop his mouth open with the boot-jack to keep from getting the lockjaw. [These were homeopathic treatments and would not be recommended today.]

"Oh, fill me up about this lovely country! You can go on writing that slop about balmy breezes and fragrant flowers, and all that sort of truck, but you're not going to leave out them santipedes and things for want of being reminded of it, you know."

I said mildly, "But, Mr. Brown, these are the mere ..."

"*Mere*—your grandmother! They ain't the mere anything! What's the use of you telling me they're the mere ... mere ... whatever it was you was going to call it? You look at them raw splotches all over my face—all over my arms—all over my body! Mosquito bites! Don't tell me about mere— mere things! You can't get around them mosquito bites.

"I took and brushed out my bar [mosquito net] good night before last, and tucked it in all around, and before morning I was eternally chawed up, anyhow. And the night before I fastened her up all right, and got in bed and smoked that old strong pipe until I got strangled and smothered and couldn't get out, and then they swarmed in there and jammed their bills through my shirt and sucked me as dry as a life-preserver before I got my breath again.

"And how did that dead-fall work? [A deadfall is a trap where a heavy weight falls and smashes the intended target, in this case, the mosquito.] I was two days making it, and sweated two buckets full of brine, and blame if the mosquito ever went under it, and sloshing around in my sleep I ketched my foot in it and got it flattened out so that it wouldn't go into a green turtle shell forty-four inches across the back.

"Jim Ayers grinding out seven double verses of poetry about Waw-*hoo*! and crying about leaving the blasted place in the two last verses; and you slobbering here about—there you are! Now—*now*, what do you say?

[Colonel James Ayers was the editor and one of the founders of the *San Francisco Morning Call*. He was on the *Ajax*'s first voyage, traveling to Honolulu to start the *Hawaiian Herald*.]

"That yellow spider could straddle over a saucer just like nothing—and if I hadn't been here to set that spittoon on him, he would have been between your sheets in a minute—he was traveling straight for your bed—he had his eye on it. Just pull at that web that he's been stringing after him—pretty near as hard to break as sewing silk; and look at his feet sticking out all round the spittoon. Oh, confound Waw-*hoo*!"

I am glad Brown has got disgusted at that murdered spider and gone. I don't like to be interrupted when I am writing—especially by Brown, who is one of those men who always looks at the unpleasant side of everything, and I seldom do.[16]

What a Pest

Well, there are a number of bothersome arachnids and insects here, all of which were imported from elsewhere, probably by accident. But as far as I know, there aren't any tarantulas in Hawai'i, unless they've been smuggled in as a pet. I think the yellow spider Twain referred to is the Hawaiian Garden Spider, but you're unlikely to find it indoors, and they don't look anything like a tarantula. They stick to gardens, where they make large webs.

This is the tropics, so there are a lot of bugs. On the other hand, I've been to places here where people leave their doors and windows wide open and don't seem to get any bugs inside. But if there's standing water nearby, chances are you'll have mosquitos.

The first mosquitoes arrived in 1826 at Lāhainā, Maui, in water barrels on the British whaling ship *Wellington*. At that time, the missionaries were trying to outlaw booze and nooky with the natives—things the whalers didn't want to do without. This led to a heated feud. One whaling crew marched with pistols, knives, and a black flag to the house of Rev. William Richards, where they threatened to kill him. A year later, the British whaling ship *John Palmer* fired its cannons at the missionaries' houses, but the five cannonballs missed their targets. It's said

Mark Twain was Here...in Honolulu

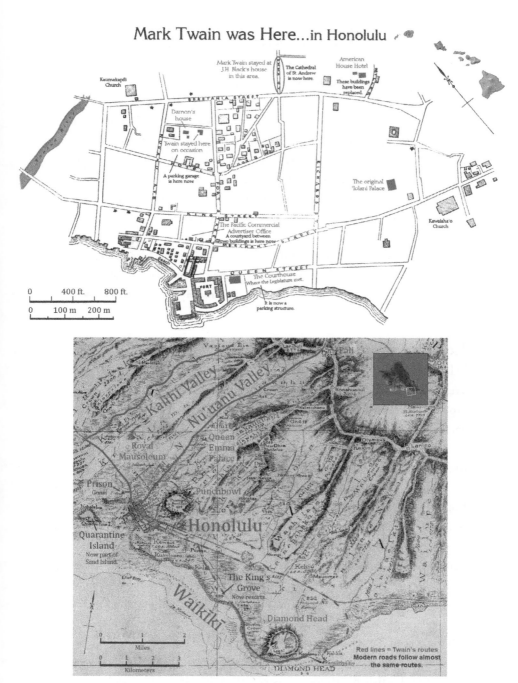

(TOP) AUTHOR'S GRAPHIC, USING A MODIFIED 1843 MAP, WITH AN INSERTED MODIFIED ISLANDS MAP BY FOREST STARR AND KIM STARR AT THE HAWAI'I STATE OFFICE OF PLANNING; (BOTTOM) AUTHOR'S GRAPHIC, USING AN 1881 HAWAIIAN GOVERNMENT SURVEY MAP, WITH AN O'AHU SATELLITE IMAGE FROM THE HAWAI'I STATE OFFICE OF PLANNING

that another way the whalers fought back was when the crew of the *Wellington* dumped a cask of wriggler-infested water into a pond behind the missionaries' houses. The mosquitoes quickly spread to the other islands.

Native tradition says that in the early 1800s, a native woman went out from Waimea in south Kaua'i to board a visiting ship. While on the ship, her lover rewarded her with a corked bottle and instructions not to open it until she was ashore. This she did. When she expectantly opened the bottle and looked inside, she didn't see anything. It was empty. Its occupants had already escaped. They were the first fleas in the Islands. While it was probably intended as a joke, albeit a rather sick one, it's doubtful the ignorant sailor ever knew of all the suffering his "joke" caused.

Scorpions are found primarily on the arid leeward side of the Islands, and they tend to stay outdoors. Centipedes are more of a problem, but they too stay mainly outside. They like moist places, like under trash cans, flowerpots, and piles of leaves. They usually eat insects but can eat mice and geckos.

Lodging at the American House

[March 19, 1866:]

We passengers are all at home now—taking meals at the American [House] Hotel, and sleeping in neat white cottages, buried in noble shade trees and enchanting tropical flowers and shrubbery.[17]

I did not expect to find as comfortable a hotel as the American, with its large, airy, well-furnished rooms, distinguished by perfect neatness and cleanliness, its cool, commodious verandas, its excellent table, its ample front yard, carpeted with grass and adorned with shrubbery, etcetera—and so I was agreeably disappointed.

One of our lady passengers from San Francisco, who brings high recommendations, has purchased a half interest in the hotel, and she shows such a determination to earn success that I heartily wish she may achieve it—and the more so because she is an American, and if common remark can be depended upon, the foreign element here will not allow an American to succeed if a good strong struggle can prevent it.

Several of us have taken rooms in a cottage in the center of the town, and are well satisfied with our quarters. There is a grassy yard as large as Platt's Hall [a large performance theater in San Francisco] on each of the three sides of the premises; a number of great tamarind and algeraba [algarroba, mesquite, or carob tree, known here as kiawe (pronounced KEY-ah-vay)] trees tower above us, and their dense, wide-spreading foliage casts a shade that palls our verandas with a sort of solemn twilight, even at noonday.

If I were not so fond of looking into the rich masses of green leaves that swathe the stately tamarind right before my door, I would idle less and write more, I think. The leaf of this tree is of the size and shape of that of our sickly, homely locust in the States; but the tamarind is as much more superb a tree than the locust as a beautiful white woman is more lovely than a Digger squaw who may chance to generally resemble her in shape and size. ["Digger" was a derogatory term popularly used in California at the time to refer to certain tribes of Native Americans who occasionally dug up roots for food.]

The algeraba (my spelling is guesswork) has a gnarled and twisted trunk, as thick as a barrel, far-reaching crooked branches and a delicate, feathery foliage which would be much better suited to a garden shrub than to so large a tree.

We have got some handsome mango trees about us also, with dark green leaves, as long as a goose quill and not more than twice as broad. The trunk of this tree is about six inches through, and is very straight and smooth. Five feet from the ground it divides into three branches of equal size, which bend out with a graceful curve and then assume an upright position. From these, numerous smaller branches spout. The main branches are not always three in number, I believe, but ours have this characteristic, at any rate.

We pay from five to seven dollars a week for furnished rooms, and ten dollars for board.

Further Particulars in This Connection

Mr. Laller, an American, and well-spoken of, keeps a restaurant [on Nuʻuanu Street] where meals can be had at all hours. So you see that folks of both regular and eccentric habits can be accommodated in Honolulu.[18]

—

This would have appealed to Twain since he was a night owl, often staying up until dawn.

This is the American House Hotel advertisement that Twain saw when he got off the *Ajax*. It was in the *Pacific Commercial Enterprise* for March 17, 1866.

The American House was a new hotel that had been open for only less than three weeks. It moved to a different location sometime in the following year or so. At that time, there were very few places to stay. The 1869 directory lists only six hotels, but four of them are described as being boardinghouses, although there were probably others. The American House was trying to be an upscale hotel, possibly Honolulu's first.

Twain stayed at various places while in Honolulu, but where he was and when is a bit sketchy. He did stay at J. H. Black's house on Queen Emma Place. Black was the printer at the *Pacific Commercial Advertiser*. Four years later, he became part owner of the newspaper. In addition, he was the Hawaiian government's printer for a while.

Twain also became good friends with Rev. Samuel Damon (not to be confused with the Father Damian, Damon was pastor of the Bethel Union Church, chaplain of the Honolulu branch of the American Seamen's Friend Society, and publisher of *The Friend* monthly newspaper), and he stayed in a cottage next to Rev. Damon's home on Chaplain Street—possibly a guest cottage. In his notebook, he jotted down, "Went with Mr. Damon to his cool, vine shaded home. No care-worn or eager, anxious faces in the land of happy contentment—God!

what a contrast with California and Washoe [County, Nevada]. Everybody walks at a moderate gait—though to speak strictly, they mostly ride."[19]

It's said he also stayed at Thomas Lacks's place on Queen Emma Street. If so, it was probably after his return from the Big Island since Thomas Lacks didn't seem to know Twain when Twain stopped at the Lacks plantation on the Big Island.

Twain continued,

—⊱

Washing is done chiefly by the natives; price, a dollar a dozen. If you are not watchful, though, your shirt won't stand more than one washing, because Kānaka artists work by a most destructive method. They use only cold water, sit down by a brook, soap the garment, lay it on one rock and "pound" it with another. This gives a shirt a handsome fringe around its borders, but it is ruinous on buttons. If your washerwoman knows you will not put up with this sort of thing, however, she will do her pounding with a bottle, or else rub your clothes clean with her hands. After the garments are washed the artist spreads them on the green grass, and the flaming sun and the winds soon bleach them as white as snow. They are then ironed on a coconut-leaf mat spread on the ground, and the job is finished. I cannot discover that anything of the nature of starch is used.

Board, lodging, clean clothes, furnished room, coal oil or whale oil lamp (dingy, greasy, villainous)—next you want water, fruit, tobacco and cigars, and possibly wines and liquors—and then you are "fixed," and ready to live in Honolulu.

The Essentials: Water, Fruit, Liquor, Cigars

WATER

The water is pure, sweet, cool, clear as crystal, and comes from a spring in the mountains, and is distributed all over the town through leaden pipes. You can find a hydrant spiriting away at the bases of three or four trees in a single yard, sometimes, so plenty and cheap is this excellent water. Only twenty-four dollars a year supplies a whole household with a limitless quantity of it.[20]

FRUIT

We have an abundance of fruit in Honolulu, of course. Oranges, pineapples, bananas, strawberries, lemons, limes, mangoes, guavas, melons, and a rare and curious luxury called the cherimoya, which is deliciousness itself.[21]

You must have fruit. You feel the want of it here. At any rate, I do, though I cared nothing whatever for it in San Francisco. You pay about twenty-five cents ("two reals," in the language of the country, borrowed from Mexico, where a good deal of their silver money comes from) a dozen for oranges; and so delicious are they that some people frequently eat a good many at luncheon. I seldom eat more than ten or fifteen at a sitting, however, because I despise to see anybody gormandize.

Even fifteen is a little surprising to me, though, for two or three oranges in succession were about as much as I could ever relish at home. Bananas are worth about a bit [12.5 cents] a dozen—enough for that rather over-rated fruit. Strawberries are plenty, and as cheap as the bananas. Those which are carefully cultivated here have a far finer flavor than the California article. They are in season a good part of the year.[22]

Then there is the tamarind. I thought tamarinds were made to eat, but that was probably not the idea. I had a curiosity to taste these things, and I knocked half-a-dozen off the tree and ate them the other day. It seemed to me that they were rather sour this year. They pursed up my lips, till they resembled the stem-end of a tomato, and I had to take my sustenance through a quill for twenty-four hours.

They sharpened my teeth up like a razor till I could have shaved with them, and gave them a "wire edge" that I was afraid would stay; but a citizen said "no, it will come off when the enamel does"—which was comforting, at any rate. [. . .]

I found, afterward, that only strangers eat tamarinds—but they only eat them once.[23]

Mangoes and guavas are plenty. I do not like them. The limes are excellent, but not very plentiful. Most of the apples brought to this market are imported from Oregon. Those I have eaten were as good as bad turnips, but not better. They claim to raise good apples and peaches on some of these islands. I have not seen any grapes, or pears or melons here. They may be out of season, but I keep thinking it is dead summertime now.[24]

Tamarinds are edible, but they're very sour when they're not ripe. Still, the unripe fruit is used as an ingredient in some savory dishes. When ripe, it's used in drinks, ice cream, candy, and jam, and you've probably had it in Worcestershire sauce.

The amount and types of fruit in Hawai'i are pretty amazing. There are at least 189 varieties of avocadoes and around fifty types of bananas. The ancient Hawaiians preferred the bananas that you cook over the ones we like to eat raw.

The fruits here taste different from the same fruits from elsewhere. If you've never had a mango from Hawai'i, don't imagine you know what good mangos taste like. I never cared for mangoes until I tried them from here. Now I can hardly wait for mango season. I'm not sure which of the more than sixty varieties of mangoes grows in the neighborhoods here—they're probably Haden mangoes—but they're *really* good.

You can sometimes find them in markets, although most of the store mangoes, bananas, and so on are imported from Central and South America and never taste as good, perhaps because they have to pick them before they're ripe. But then, some tests have shown that Hawai'i mangoes are about twice as sweet as those from elsewhere.

Other common popular fruits in Hawai'i include liliko'i (passion fruit), guava, starfruit, lychee, rambutans, dragon fruit, Surinam cherry, jackfruit, pomelo, and mangosteen. And then we have the more exotic fruits—poha berry, buddah's hand, peanut butter fruit, custard apple, longan, sapodilla, strawberry guava, snake fruit, cashew apple, kumquat, soursop, egg fruit, and ice cream bean—and we even have the either greatly loved or furiously dreaded durian.

As Twain said, even if you never had much fruit, when you're here, you must have fruit. And here, they even put it in your drinks.

WATER AGAIN

I must come back to water again, though I thought I had exhausted the subject.

As no ice is kept here, and as the notion that snow is brought to Honolulu from the prodigious mountains on the island of Hawai'i is a happy fiction of some imaginative writer, the water used for drinking is usually kept cool by putting it into "monkeys" and placing those animals in open windows, where the breezes of heaven may blow upon them. "Monkeys" are slender-necked, large bodied, gourd-shaped earthenware vessels, manufactured in Germany and are popularly supposed to keep water very cool and fresh, but I cannot endorse that supposition. If a wet blanket were wrapped around the monkey, I think the evaporation would cool the water within, but nobody seems to consider it worthwhile to go to that trouble, and I include myself among this number.[25]

CIGARS

The only cigars smoked here are those trifling, insipid, tasteless, flavorless things they call "Manilas"—ten for twenty-five cents; and it would take a thousand to be worth half the money. After you have smoked about thirty-five dollars' worth of them in a forenoon you feel nothing but a desperate yearning to go out somewhere and take a smoke.

They say high duties and a sparse population render it unprofitable to import good cigars, but I do not see why some enterprising citizen does not manufacture them from the native tobacco. A Kanaka gave me some Oʻahu tobacco yesterday, of fine texture, pretty good flavor, and so strong that one pipe full of it satisfied me for several hours.

(This man Brown has just come in and says he has bought a couple of tons of Manilas to smoke tonight.)[26]

—✦—

This was something very important to Twain. He loved cigars and smoked them all his life, except for a short period after he got married. Later in life, he said, "I am seventy-three and a half years old, and have been smoking seventy-three of them. But I never smoke to excess, that is, I smoke in moderation—only one cigar at a time."[27]

Writing in 1910, William Dean Howells, Twain's close friend and editor of *The Atlantic Monthly*, said, "Whenever he had been a few days with us, the whole house had to be aired, for he smoked all over it from breakfast to bedtime. He always went to bed with a cigar in his mouth, and sometimes, mindful of my fire insurance, I went up and took it away, still burning, after he had fallen asleep. I do not know how much a man may smoke and live, but apparently he smoked as much as a man could, for he smoked incessantly."[28]

Besides cigars, his other favorite activity was smoking his pipes. Twain described himself as a "perpetual smoker." Years later, his lecture tour manager, said, "He smokes constantly, and I fear too much also; still, he may stand it. Physicians say it will eventually kill him."[29]

Perhaps it did contribute to his death from a heart attack at the age of seventy-four.

O'AHU EXPLORATIONS
Going to Prison
[March 21, 1866:]

[O'ahu's prison was state of the art at that time and was modeled on one in Charleston, North Carolina. It was much more modern than Maui's crude coral-block prison in Lāhainā. The Honolulu Prison could hold one hundred and seventy inmates. Everyone who received a sentence of more than three months was sent there.]

Cantering across the bridge and down the firm, level, gleaming white coral turnpike [the Old Prison Road is now Ala Moana Boulevard and Nimitz Highway] that leads toward the south, or the east, or the west, or the north (the points of the compass being all the same to me, inasmuch as, for good reasons, I have not had an opportunity thus far of discovering whereabouts the sun rises in this country—I know where it sets, but I don't know how it gets there nor which direction it comes from), we presently arrived at a massive coral edifice which I took for a fortress at first, but found out directly that it was the government prison.

A soldier at the great gate admitted us without further authority than my countenance, and I suppose he thought he was paying me a handsome compliment when he did so; and so did I until I reflected that the place was a penitentiary.

However, as far as appearances went, it might have been the king's palace, so neat, and clean, and white, and so full of the fragrance of flowers was the establishment, and I was satisfied.

We passed through a commodious office, whose walls were ornamented with linked strands of polished hand cuffs and fetters, through a hall, and among the cells above and below. The cells for the men were eight or ten feet high, and roomy enough to accommodate the two prisoners and their hammocks, usually put in each, and have space left for several more. The floors were scrubbed clean, and were guiltless of spot or stain of any kind, and the painfully white walls were unmarred by a single mark or blemish. Through ample gratings, one could see the blue sky and get his hair blown off by the cool breeze. They call this a prison—the pleasantest quarters in Honolulu.

There are four wards, and one hundred and thirty-two prisoners can be housed in rare and roomy comfort within them.

There were a number of native women in the female department. Poor devils, they hung their heads under the prying eyes of our party as if they were really ashamed of being there.

In the condemned cell and squatting on the floor, all swathed in blankets, as if it were cold weather, was a brown-faced, gray-bearded old scallywag, who, in a frolicsome mood, had massacred three women and a batch of children—his own property, I believe—and reflects upon that exploit with

Inmates at the Oʻahu Prison share poi in the late 1800s.

genuine satisfaction to this hour, and will go to the gallows as tranquilly indifferent as a white man would go to dinner.

The prison-yard—that sad enclosure which, in the prisons of my native America, is a cheerless barren and yieldeth no vegetation save the gallows-tree, with its sorrowful human fruit—is a very garden! The beds, bordered by rows of inverted bottles (the usual style here), were filled with all manner of dainty flowers and shrubs: Chinese mulberry and orange trees stood here and there, well stocked with fruit; a beautiful little pine tree—rare, and imported from the far South Seas—occupied the center, with sprays of gracefully arching green spears springing outward like parasol tops, at marked and regular intervals, up its slender stem, and diminishing in diameter with mathematical strictness of graduation, till the sprouting plume at the top stood over a perfect pyramid.

Vines clambered everywhere and hid from view and clothed with beauty everything that might otherwise have been suggestive of chains and captivity.

There was nothing here to remind one of the prison save a brace of dovecotes, containing several pretty birds brought hither from "strange, strange lands beyond the sea." These, sometimes, may pine for liberty and their old free life among the clouds or in the shade of the orange groves, or abroad on the breezy ocean—but if they do, it is likely they take it out in pining, as a general thing. [...]

[Here Twain describes two prisoners who sound more like psychiatric patients than criminals.]

Upstairs in the prison are the handsome apartments used by the officers of the establishment;—also a museum of quaint and curious weapons of offense and defense, of all nations and all ages of the world.

The prison is to a great extent a self-supporting institution, through the labor of the convicts farmed out to load and unload ships and work on the highways, and I am not sure but that it supports itself and pays a surplus into the public treasury besides, but I have no note of this, and I seldom place implicit confidence in my memory in matters where figures and finance are concerned and have not been thought of for a fortnight.

This government prison is in the hands of W. C. Parke, Marshal of the Kingdom, and he has small need to be ashamed of his management of it.

Without wishing to betray too much knowledge of such matters, I should say that this is the model prison of the western half of the world, at any rate.[30]

In an 1875 guidebook, Twain's friend and publisher of the *Pacific Commercial Advertiser*, Henry Whitney wrote, "This state prison is one of the best kept institutions to be found in any country, and is well worth a visit from those interested in prison discipline."[31]

Twain's Stately Steed

[Still March 21, 1866:]
In my diary of our third day in Honolulu, I find this:

I am probably the most sensitive man in Hawai'i tonight—especially about sitting down in the presence of my betters. I have ridden fifteen or twenty miles [25 to 50 km] on horseback since 5 p.m., and to tell the honest truth, I have a delicacy about sitting down at all. I am one of the poorest horsemen in the world, and I never mount a horse without experiencing a sort of dread that I may be setting out on that last mysterious journey which all of us must take sooner or later, and I never come back in safety from a horseback trip without thinking of my latter end for two or three days afterward. This same old regular devotional sentiment began just as soon as I sat down here five minutes ago.

An excursion to Diamond Head and the King's Coconut Grove was planned today—time, 4:30 p.m.—the party to consist of half-a-dozen gentlemen and three ladies. They all started at the appointed hour except myself. I was at the government prison (with Captain [A. W.] Fish and another whaleship skipper, Captain [W. H.] Phillips, [Twain used their real names here but called them Captain Fitch and Captain Phelps when they were playing cards together on the *Ajax*]) and got so interested in its examination that I did not notice how quickly the time was passing. Somebody remarked that it was twenty minutes past five o'clock, and that woke me up.

It was a fortunate circumstance that Captain Phillips was along with his "turn-out," as he calls a top-buggy that Captain Cook brought here in 1778, and a horse that was here when Captain Cook came. Captain Phillips takes a just pride in his driving and in the speed of his horse, and

SAY WHAT?

Shortly, you will read that Twain named his horse Oahu, after the island. I have left out the " ' " ('okina) in the horse's name (and his other horse's name) to help distinguish his horse from the island. But the main thing I want to point out here is Twain's unusual pronunciation of the word. He says it's "O-waw-hee." Of course, he can pronounce his horse's name any way he wants. He gives the pronunciation of the island's name a bit more correctly elsewhere. O'ahu is actually pronounced "Oh AH-who," but most people just run the word together without the 'okina. The same applies to the islands of Hawai'i (huh-VAI ee or huh-WHY ee), Lāna'i (luh-nah ee), and Kaua'i (KAH-wah ee, never "cow-eye"). Leaving out the 'okina can give the word a different meaning. Lāna'i is the island, while lanai is a porch, verandah, or deck.

Actually, many Hawaiian words are commonly mispronounced today. Even Hawaiians use the Japanese pronunciation for Maui's north-shore town of Haiku (HI-koo) instead of the original Ha'ikū (ha EE-kooo). Whereas haiku is a type of Japanese poetry, the town is named after the kāhili flower because the kāhili trees were first planted there. And while I'm at it, I should also point out that the Hawaiians originally pronounce Maui as MOW-ee—not MAO-ee, as most people pronounce it today. In fact, the map made in the 1790s by Captain Cook's cartographer spells the name as "Mowee." I occasionally hear Hawaiian speakers pronounce it the old way, but it's rare.

Some of Twain's pronunciations are rather odd, such as Waikīkī (Wy-kee-ky), but it makes me wonder if he was just a greenhorn or whether they did pronounce the words that way back then.

to his passion for displaying them I owe it that we were only sixteen minutes coming from the prison to the American Hotel—a distance which has been estimated to be over half a mile.

But it took some fearful driving. The captain's whip came down fast, and the blows started so much dust out of the horse's hide that during the last half of the journey we rode through an impenetrable fog, and ran by a pocket compass in the hands of Captain Fish, a whaler captain of twenty-six years' experience, who sat there through the perilous voyage as self-possessed as if he had been on the euchre-deck of his own ship, and calmly said, "Port your helm—port," from time to time, and "Hold her a little free—steady—so," and "Luff—hard down to starboard!" and never once lost his presence of mind or betrayed the least anxiety by voice or manner.

When we came to anchor at last, and Captain Phillips looked at his watch and said, "Sixteen minutes—I told you it was in her! That's over three miles an hour!" I could see he felt entitled to a compliment, and so I said I had never seen lightning go like that horse.

And I never had.

The Steed Oahu

The landlord of the American [Hotel] said the party had been gone nearly an hour, but that he could give me my choice of several horses that could easily overtake them.

I said, never mind—I preferred a safe horse to a fast one—I would like to have an excessively gentle horse—a horse with no spirit whatever—a lame one, if he had such a thing.

Inside of five minutes I was mounted, and perfectly satisfied with my outfit. I had no time to label him "This is a horse," and so if the public took him for a sheep I cannot help it. I was satisfied, and that was the main thing. I could see that he had as many fine points as any man's horse, and so I hung my hat on one of them, behind the saddle, and swabbed the perspiration from my face and started.

I named him after this island, "Oahu" (O-waw-hee [sic]). The first gate he came to he started in; I had neither whip nor spur, and so I simply argued the case with him. He resisted argument, but ultimately yielded to insult and abuse. He backed out of that gate and steered for another one on

LOOKING FOR MISCHIEF.

Twain and Oahu from his book *Roughing It.*

the other side of the street. I triumphed by my former process. Within the next six hundred yards he crossed the street fourteen times and attempted thirteen gates, and in the meantime the tropical sun was beating down and threatening to cave the top of my head in, and I was literally dripping with perspiration and profanity. (I am only human and I was sorely aggravated. I shall behave better next time.)

He abandoned the gate business after that and went along peaceably enough, but absorbed in meditation. I noticed this latter circumstance, and it soon began to fill me with apprehension. I said to myself, this creature is planning some new outrage, some fresh deviltry or other—no horse ever thought over a subject so profoundly as this one is doing just for nothing. The more this thing preyed upon my mind the more uneasy I became, until the suspense became almost unbearable and I dismounted to see if there was anything wild in his eye—for I had heard that the eye of this noblest of our domestic animals is very expressive. I cannot describe what a load of anxiety was lifted from my mind when I found that he was only asleep.

I woke him up and started him into a faster walk, and then the villainy of his nature came out again. He tried to climb over a stone wall, five or six feet high. I saw that I must apply force to this horse, and that I might as well begin first as last. I plucked a stout switch from a tamarind tree, and the moment he saw it, he surrendered. He broke into a convulsive sort of a canter, which had three short steps in it and one long one, and reminded me alternately of the clattering shake of the great earthquake, and the sweeping plunging of the *Ajax* in a storm.[32]

—

In 1900, Henry Whitney, the editor of the *Pacific Commercial Advertiser*, recalled this story a little differently:

> His favorite pastime was riding horseback. We had no livery stables in those days, but every afternoon the natives would have horses saddled for hire. One day he took the first "plug" that came to the door, mounted him and started off for his accustomed ride to Waikīkī, scarcely looking to see what his animal was. Before reaching the seashore, the horse began to give out. The more he spurred the beast, the slower he went, till at last he came to a dead halt. Mark beating him as furiously as ever.
>
> A stranger came along and remonstrated with the rider; saying that his horse was asleep. He instantly dismounted and had to give up his ride for that day at least. The poor animal had probably had nothing to eat for a day or two.
>
> This ended Mark's ride, and as the tram cars were not then running, he had a long walk back to town. [. . .] After this adventure, Mark made sure of the quality of his steed before he mounted.[33]

Out of Prison, but in the Stocks

And now there can be no fitter occasion than the present to pronounce a left-handed blessing upon the man who invented the American saddle. There is no seat to speak of about it—one might as well sit in a shovel—and the stirrups are nothing but an ornamental nuisance.

If I were to write down here all the abuse I expended on those stirrups, it would make a large book, even without pictures. Sometimes I got one foot so far through, that the stirrup partook of the nature of an anklet; sometimes both feet were through and I was handcuffed by the legs; and sometimes my feet got clear out and left the stirrups wildly dangling about my shins. Even when I was in proper position and carefully balanced upon the balls of my feet, there was no comfort in it, on account of my nervous dread that they were going to slip one way or the other in a moment. But the subject is too exasperating to write about.[34]

Honolulu's Plague of Horses

Hawai'i's first horses were given to King Kamehameha I in 1803 and he was not sure what to make of them. He didn't see much use for them and thought they ate too much, but the Hawaiians soon took to them, loving to ride their horses as fast as they could go, especially on Saturdays when the women would get all dressed up and charge across the Honolulu plains at full gallop. They also kept horses as pets.

But the horses soon become a problem. In 1854 a committee of the Royal Hawaiian Agricultural Society submitted a report that said:

> In making up a report on horses the first thing we wish particularly to call attention to, is the lamentable increase of the miserable creatures to be seen every day in the streets of Honolulu and in all the horse breeding districts on the Islands. Horses are evidently fast becoming a curse and nuisance to the country and to most of their owners, especially to the lower classes of natives.
>
> About one-half of the horses on the island are never used for any purpose but multiplication—are never bitted or backed—are born, live and die without being of any advantage to anyone, or having served any purpose, useful or ornamental, but the impoverishment of the land, and the propagation of the nuisance.[35]

There were obviously missionaries on the committee, as they believed everything had to have a purpose, otherwise it was wasteful and ungodly.

Honolulu Prices for Horse Flesh

You can buy a pretty good horse for forty or fifty dollars, and a good enough horse for all practical purposes for two dollars and a half. I estimate Oahu to be worth somewhere in the neighborhood of thirty-five cents. A good deal better animal than he is was sold here day before yesterday for a dollar and six bits [seventy-five cents], and sold again today for two dollars and twenty-five cents; Brown bought a handsome and lively little pony yesterday for ten dollars; and about the best common horse on the island (and he is a really good one) sold yesterday, with good Mexican saddle and bridle, for seventy dollars—a horse which is well and widely known, and greatly respected for his speed, good disposition, and everlasting bottom.

You give your horse a little grain once a day; it comes from San Francisco, and is worth about two cents a pound; and you give him as much hay as he wants; it is cut and brought to the market by natives, and is not very good; it is baled into long, round bundles, about the size of a large man; one of them is stuck by the middle on each end of a six-foot pole, and the Kanaka shoulders the pole and walks about the streets between the upright bales in search of customers. These hay bales, thus carried, have a general resemblance to a colossal capital H.

These hay-bundles cost twenty-five cents apiece, and one will last a horse about a day. You can get a horse for a song, a week's hay for another song, and you can turn your animal loose among the luxuriant grass in your neighbor's broad front yard without a song at all—you do it at midnight, and stable the beast again before morning. You have been at no expense thus far, but when you come to buy a saddle and bridle they will cost you from $20 to $35. You can hire a horse, saddle, and bridle at from $7 to $10 a week, and the owner will take care of them at his own expense.

Well, Oahu worried along over a smooth, hard road, bordered on either side by cottages, at intervals, pulu swamps at intervals, fish ponds at intervals, but through a dead level country all the time, and no trees to hide the wide Pacific Ocean on the right or the rugged, towering rampart of solid rock, called Diamond Head or Diamond Point, straight ahead.[36]

Itchy Palms

In Twain's time, the Royal Coconut Grove—aka the King's Grove—was on Waikīkī Beach. This was once Kamehameha's compound after he conquered O'ahu in 1795 and was then the location of King Kamehameha V's beach house. Now on that spot stand the Sheraton Waikīkī, the Royal Hawaiian, and the Royal Hawaiian Shopping Center.

Top: Waikīkī kalo fields from McCully Street ca. 1910. Bottom: King Kamehameha V's cottage in King's Grove, also known as The Royal Grove. It was one of several buildings that made up the royal compound.
(TOP) RAY JEROME BAKER

[Still March 21, 1866:]

A mile and a half from town, I came to a grove of tall coconut trees, with clean, branchless stems reaching straight up sixty or seventy feet and topped with a spray of green foliage sheltering clusters of coconuts—not more picturesque than a forest of colossal ragged parasols, with bunches of magnified grapes under them, would be.

I once heard a gouty northern invalid say that a coconut tree might be poetical, possibly it was; but it looked like a feather-duster struck by lightning.

I think that describes it better than a picture—and yet, without any question, there is something fascinating about a coconut tree—and graceful, too.

About a dozen cottages, some frame and the others of native grass, nestled sleepily in the shade here and there. The grass cabins are of a grayish color, are shaped much like our own cottages, only with higher and steeper roofs usually, and are made of some kind of weed strongly bound together in bundles. The roofs are very thick and so are the walls; the latter have square holes in them for windows. At a little distance these cabins have a furry appearance, as if they might be made of bear skins. They are very cool and pleasant inside.

The King's flag was flying from the roof of one of the cottages, and His Majesty was probably within. He owns the whole concern thereabouts, and passes his time there frequently, on sultry days "laying off." The spot is called "The King's Grove."[37]

Waikīkī Village

[Still March 21, 1866:]

The little collection of cottages (of which I was speaking a while ago) under the coconut trees is a historical point. It is the village of Waikīkī (usually pronounced Wy-kee-ky), once the capital of the Kingdom and the abode of the great Kamehameha I.

In 1801, while he lay encamped at this place with seven thousand men, preparing to invade the island of Kaua'i (he had previously captured and subdued the seven [*sic*, six of the eight] other inhabited islands of the group, one after another) [he also didn't capture Ni'ihau], a pestilence broke out in O'ahu and raged with great virulence. It attacked the king's army and made great havoc in it. It is said that three hundred bodies were washed out to sea in one day.

[From 1803 to 1805, between 5,000 and 175,000 people died from a disease that is thought to have been yellow fever, Asiatic cholera, bubonic plague, dysentery, or typhoid fever. It killed people in less than twenty-four hours, and the bodies turned black. Whatever it was, King Kamehameha caught it but survived.]

There is an opening in the coral reef at this point, and anchorage inside for a small number of vessels, though one accustomed to the great bay of

San Francisco would never take this little belt of smooth water, with its border of foaming surf, to be a harbor, save for Whitehall boats or something of that kind. But harbors are scarce in these islands—open roadsteads are the rule here. The harbor of Waikīkī was discovered in 1786 (seven or eight years after Captain Cook's murder) by Captains Portlock and Dixon, in the ships *King George* and *Queen Charlotte*—the first English vessels that visited the Islands after that unhappy occurrence. This little bathing tub of smooth water possesses some further historical interest as being the spot where the distinguished navigator Vancouver, landed when he came here in 1792.

In a conversation with a gentleman today about the scarcity of harbors among the Islands (and in all the islands of the South Pacific), he said the natives of Tahiti have a theory that the reason why there are harbors wherever fresh water streams empty into the sea, and none elsewhere, is that the fresh water kills the coral insect, or so discommodes or disgusts it that it will not build its stony wall in its vicinity, and instanced what is claimed as fact, viz., that the break in the reef is always found where the fresh water passes over it, in support of this theory.[38]

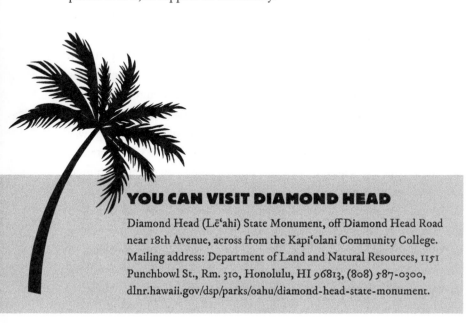

YOU CAN VISIT DIAMOND HEAD

Diamond Head (Lēʻahi) State Monument, off Diamond Head Road near 18th Avenue, across from the Kapiʻolani Community College. Mailing address: Department of Land and Natural Resources, 1151 Punchbowl St., Rm. 310, Honolulu, HI 96813, (808) 587-0300, dlnr.hawaii.gov/dsp/parks/oahu/diamond-head-state-monument.

The Equestrian Excursion Concluded

I wandered along the sea beach on my steed Oahu around the base of the extinct crater of Lēʻahi, or Diamond Head, and a quarter of a mile beyond the point I overtook the party of ladies and gentlemen and assumed my proper place—that is, in the rear—for the horse I ride always persists in remaining in the rear in spite of kicks, cuffs, and curses. I was satisfied as long as I could keep Oahu within hailing distance of the cavalcade—I knew I could accomplish nothing better even if Oahu were Norfolk himself.

We went on—on—on—a great deal too far, I thought, for people who were unaccustomed to riding on horseback, and who must expect to suffer on the morrow if they indulged too freely in this sort of exercise.

Finally we got to a point which we were expecting to go around in order to strike an easy road home; but we were too late; it was full tide and the sea had closed in on the shore.

Young Henry McFarlane said he knew a nice, comfortable route over the hill—a short cut—and the crowd dropped into his wake. We climbed a hill a hundred and fifty feet high, and about as straight up and down as the side of a house, and as full of rough lava blocks as it could stick—not as wide, perhaps, as the broad road that leads to destruction, but nearly as dangerous to travel, and apparently leading in the same general direction.

I felt for the ladies, but I had no time to speak any words of sympathy, by reason of my attention being so much occupied by Oahu. The place was so steep that at times he stood straight up on his tip-toes and clung by his forward toenails, with his back to the Pacific Ocean and his nose close to the moon—and thus situated we formed an equestrian picture which was as uncomfortable to me as it may have been picturesque to the spectators. You may think I was afraid, but I was not. I knew I could stay on him as long as his ears did not pull out.

It was a great relief to me to know that we were all safe and sound on the summit at last, because the sun was just disappearing in the waves, night was abroad in the land, candles and lamps were already twinkling in the distant town, and we gratefully reflected that Henry had saved us from having to go back around the rocky, sandy beach. But a new trouble arose while the party were admiring the rising moon and the cool, balmy night breeze, with its odor of countless flowers, for it was discovered that we had got into a place we could not get out of—we were apparently surrounded by precipices—our pilot's chart was at fault, and he could not extricate us, and so we had the prospect before us of either spending the night in the admired night-breeze, under the admired moon, or of clambering down the way we came, in the dark.[39]

However, a Kanaka came along presently and found a first-rate road for us down an almost imperceptible decline, and the party set out on a cheerful gallop again, and Oahu struck up his miraculous canter once more. By and by, we halted on the summit of a hill which commanded a far-reaching view. The moon rose and flooded mountain and valley and ocean a mellow radiance, and out of the shadows of the foliage the distant lights of Honolulu glinted like an encampment of fireflies. I was not sorry we had lately been in trouble, because the consciousness of being safe again raised our spirits and made us more capable of enjoying the beautiful scene than we would have been otherwise. I never breathed such a soft, delicious atmosphere before, nor one freighted with such fragrance. A barber shop is nothing to it.[40]

A Beach of Bones

[Still March 21, 1866:]

What Twain and his friends were doing was taking the beach trail past Diamond Head and out toward Koko Head, both of which are ancient volcanic tuff cones, but they made it only as far as Wai'alae Beach before turning back.

Nine years later, Twain's friend Henry Whitney would describe the route to Koko Head in his *The Hawaiian Guide Book for Travelers*, saying, "The ride to this southernmost point of O'ahu, ten miles from the hotel, must be performed on horseback. The road lies past the telegraph station, and through several little villages and coconut groves. This is an extinct crater [Koko Crater] and is flanked by a beautiful cove [Hanauma Bay], where tropical fishes are usually abundant. Returning, take the road along the beach and around Diamond Head, thus traversing the battleground of Wai'alae, where Kamehameha fought his first battle with the King of O'ahu—a sanguinary fight, in which thousands of warriors were slain, whose bodies were buried in the sand near the beach. Skulls have been frequently found here and hundreds carried off as relics. This battle was fought in 1790 or '91."[41]

Battleground Whose History Is Forgotten

[Still March 21, 1866:]

The halt was brief. Gayly laughing and talking, the party galloped on, and with set teeth and bouncing body I clung to the pommel and cantered after. Presently we came to a place where no grass grew—a wide expanse of deep sand. They said it was an old battleground. All around everywhere, not three feet apart, the bleached bones of men gleamed white in the moonlight.[42]

We picked up a lot of them for mementoes. I got quite a number of arm bones and leg bones—of great chiefs, maybe, who had fought savagely in that fearful battle in the old days, when blood flowed like wine where we now stood—and wore the choicest of them out on Oahu afterward, trying to make him go. All sorts of bones could be found except skulls; but a citizen said, irreverently, that there had been an unusual number of "skull hunters" there lately—a species of sportsmen I had never heard of before.

The conversation at this point took a unique and ghastly turn. A gentleman said:

"Give me some of your bones, Miss Blank; I'll carry them for you."

Another said:

"You haven't got bones enough, Mrs. Blank; here's a good shin-bone, if you want it."

Such observations as these fell from the lips of ladies with reference to their queer newly-acquired property:

"Mr. Brown, will you please hold some of my bones for me a minute?" And, "Mr. Smith, you have got some of my bones; and you have got one, too, Mr. Jones, and you have got my spine, Mr. Twain. Now don't any of you gentlemen get my bones all mixed up with yours so that you can't tell them apart."

These remarks look very irreverent on paper, but they did not sound so, being used merely in a business way and with no intention of making sport of the remains. I did not think it was just right to carry off any of these bones, but we did it, anyhow. We considered that it was at least as right as it is for the Hawaiian government and the city of Honolulu (which is the most excessively moral and religious town that can be found on the map of the world), to permit those remains to lie decade after decade, to bleach and rot in sun and wind and suffer desecration by careless strangers and by the beasts of the field, unprotected by even a worm-fence.

Call us hard names if you will, you statesmen and missionaries! but I say shame upon you, that after raising a nation from idolatry to Christianity, and from barbarism to civilization, you have not taught it the common respect for the dead. Your work is incomplete.[43]

Unfortunately, Twain didn't yet have the full picture of what was going on, so his castigation of the missionaries here is the complete opposite of reality. Twain and the others never would have considered collecting bones and skulls at the Gettysburg battle site. Neither would they have done it in their family cemetery. They wouldn't have known that there was a kapu, or restriction, that prevented Hawaiians from entering grave sites. Since the Hawaiians didn't enforce most kapus against foreigners, most foreigners were unaware of them. And they tended to ignore the kapus even when they were aware of them.

The Hawaiians have always had a tremendous amount of reverence for their ancestors—more so than Americans and Europeans since they considered all Hawaiians to be their extended family. They probably left the bones in situ out of respect, just as the Americans did at Gettysburg. Disturbing the dead is considered sacrilegious and is kapu. Today—and no doubt back then as well—they would be horrified at Twain's conduct, that is, unless the deceased was disliked, but this would not be the case of warriors who died in battle or the many sufferers who fell victim to deadly diseases.

As Twain later points out, the Hawaiians would make fishhooks out of bones, but he didn't understand the beliefs behind it. In these cases, it was only the bones of a hated or enemy chief. The idea was that the chiefs were close relatives of the gods; therefore, their bones were infused with mana, or spiritual power. They believed that the higher one's rank was in the social classes, the more mana they had. It was thought that mana in a chief's bones was so strong that it attracted fish and thus made excellent fishhooks. They also thought someone could use the bones or any other body part to summon the spirit of the deceased and command it to do his or her bidding. The bodies of enemies and kapu breakers could be treated with disrespect. But these were rare exceptions. In all other cases, the remains were handled with the deepest veneration.

Many ancient Hawaiian graveyards are in sandy areas. On islands where there's volcanic rock just about everywhere, where can you bury your deceased uncle? You could pile lava rocks on him, or you can bury him in sand. There are disadvantages to each. The lava rocks could crush his corpse, and the gaps in the rocks would allow critters in.

With sand, the wind and rain could carry the sand away, eventually exposing the remains. Also, you may have noticed that when you open a can of mixed nuts, the larger nuts are on top. If you shake the can, the larger ones rise to the surface as the smaller ones slip into the gaps below. Over many years, the same thing can happen to bones in sand. They eventually rise to the surface. But even today, iwi kapuna (ancestral bones) are found in inland sandy areas, usually during construction or when harvesting sand to make concrete.

Later in his newspaper articles, Twain tells of a Hawaiian man who refused to go anywhere near a grave site. While it's possible this was out of fear or superstition, which also played a part, I think it was more likely out of respect and honor. These feelings are not as strong in Western civilization, except for immediate relatives and those who die in the line of duty, such as soldiers, policemen, and firemen. Many people would think nothing of keeping an ancient tooth or skull they found. I have even seen tourists stand on Hawaiian graves to pose for photos. Most Hawaiians are deeply offended by such behavior.

So while Twain says the missionaries should have taught the Hawaiians to respect the dead, it was actually Twain and the others from Western cultures that needed to learn this respect. And this remains true today.

Now, much of Twain's humor was shocking for his time, and that's what he wanted. He went out of his way to make people feel uncomfortable, as it threw them off balance, so he loved joking about corpses and cannibalism. He had just come from the gold rush days of the West, where almost the entire population was male and in their twenties or thirties. There, a very rough sense of humor flourished. With his Hawai'i dispatches and lectures, Twain was transitioning from the crude humor of the West Coast to the refined humor of the East Coast that is found in his humorous Mediterranean travel book, *The Innocents Abroad*, but he never really gave up his cannibalism jokes. And later on, it became part of his social commentary, using it to point out to his readers that they weren't much different than the people they called savages.

Legendary

Nothing whatever is known about this place—its story is a secret that will never be revealed. The oldest natives make no pretense of being possessed of its history. They say these bones were here when they were children. They were here when their grandfathers were children—but how they came here, they can only conjecture.

Many people believe this spot to be an ancient battleground, and it is usual to call it so, and they believe that these skeletons have lain for ages just where their proprietors fell in the great fight. Other people believe that Kamehameha I fought his first battle here.

On this point, I have heard a story, which may have been taken from one of the numerous books which have been written, concerning these islands—I do not know where the narrator got it. He said that when Kamehameha (who was at first merely a subordinate chief on the island of Hawai'i), landed here, he brought a large army with him, and encamped at Waikīkī. The O'ahuans marched against him, and so confident were they of success that they readily acceded to a demand of their priests that they should draw a line where these bones now lie, and take an oath that, if forced to retreat at all, they would never retreat beyond this boundary. The priests told them that death and everlasting punishment would overtake any who violated the oath, and the march was resumed.

Kamehameha drove them back step by step; the priests fought in the front rank and exhorted them both by voice and inspiriting example to remember their oath—to die, if need be, but never cross the fatal line. The struggle was manfully maintained, but at last the chief priest fell, pierced to the heart with a spear, and the unlucky omen fell like a blight upon the brave souls at his back; with a triumphant shout the invaders pressed forward—the line was crossed—the offended gods deserted the despairing army, and accepting the doom their perjury had brought upon them, they broke and fled over the plain where Honolulu stands now—up the beautiful

Four portraits of King Kamehameha that were made during his lifetime. All but the bottom right picture were made by Louis Choris, artist in the brig *Rurik*, in 1816. Captain Otto von Kotzebue wrote that after finally convincing Kamehameha to have his portrait painted, "Choris succeeded in taking a very good likeness of him, though Kamehameha, in order to embarrass him, did not sit still a moment, and made all kinds of faces, in spite of my entreaties." Most of Kamehameha's later portraits were based on those by Choris. The bottom right portrait was made by Mikhail Tikhanov, the artist on board the *Kamchatka*, in 1818. The king had shaved the sides of his head in mourning for his sister.

(TOP AND BOTTOM LEFT IMAGES) LOUIS CHORIS: (BOTTOM RIGHT) MIKHAIL TIKHANOV

Nuʻuanu Valley—paused a moment, hemmed in by precipitous mountains on either hand and the frightful precipice of the Pari (pronounced Pally; intelligent natives claim that there is no "r" in the Kānaka alphabet [and now written as "Pali"]) in front, and then were driven over—a sheer plunge of six hundred feet![44]

The story is pretty enough, but Mr. Jarves's excellent history says the Oʻahuans were entrenched in Nuʻuanu Valley; that Kamehameha ousted them, routed them, pursued them up the valley and drove them over the precipice. He makes no mention of our boneyard at all in his book.

[Twain is referring to the book he used as his primary reference when writing about Hawaiʻi—James Jackson Jarves's *History of the Hawaiian or Sandwich Islands*, originally published in 1843, although Twain used the 1844 second edition. Jarves was also the editor of the Honolulu newspaper, *The Polynesian*. He was one of the few nonmissionary early historians of Hawaiian history and is considered to be the most accurate.]

There was a terrible pestilence here in 1804, which killed great numbers of the inhabitants, and the natives have legends of others that swept the Islands long before that [but after Cook's arrival]; and therefore many persons now believe that these bones belonged to victims of one of these epidemics who were hastily buried in a great pit. It is by far the most reasonable conjecture, because Jarves says that the weapons of the Islanders were so crude and inefficient that their battles were not often very bloody. If this was a battle it was astonishingly deadly, for in spite of the depredations of "skull hunters," we rode a considerable distance over ground so thickly strewn with human bones that the horses' feet crushed them, not occasionally, but at every step.[45]

[It was probably a cemetery for both warriors and people who died of other causes. While there was a group of warriors whose job it was to constantly train for battle, when a battle came, every able-bodied man was required to fight as well, and sometimes the women volunteered to join them—to fight as well as to treat the wounded. And the battles were very bloody. Tactics involved breaking bones, gouging eyes, noosing, spearing, and clubbing, and some weapons were lined with sharks' teeth for ripping open flesh.]

Sentiment

Impressed by the profound silence and repose that rested over the beautiful landscape, and being, as usual, in the rear, I gave voice to my thoughts.

I said, "What a picture is here slumbering in the solemn glory of the moon! How strong the rugged outlines of the dead volcano stand out against the clear sky! What a snowy fringe marks the bursting of the surf over the long, curved reef! How calmly the dim city sleeps yonder in the plain! How soft the shadows lie upon the stately mountains that border the dream haunted Mānoa Valley! What a grand pyramid of billowy clouds towers above the storied Pali! How the grim warriors of the past seem flocking in ghostly squadrons to their ancient battlefield again—how the wails of the dying well up from the. . . ."

At this point the horse called Oahu deliberately sat down in the sand. Sat down to listen, I suppose. Never mind what he heard. I stopped apostrophizing and convinced him that I was not a man to allow contempt of court on the part of a horse. I broke the backbone of a chief over his rump and set out to join the cavalcade again.[46]

Impressing the Ladies

[Still March 21, 1866:]

Very considerably fagged out we arrived in town at nine o'clock at night, myself in the lead—for when my horse finally came to understand that he was homeward bound and hadn't far to go, he threw his legs wildly out before and behind him, depressed his head and laid his ears back, and flew by the admiring company like a telegram. In five minutes he was far away ahead of everybody.

We stopped in front of a private residence—Brown and I did—to wait for the rest and see that none were lost. I soon saw that I had attracted the attention of a comely young girl and I felt duly flattered. Perhaps, thought I, she admires my horsemanship—and I made a savage jerk at the bridle and said, "Ho! will you!" to show how fierce and unmanageable the beast was—though, to say truly, he was leaning up against a hitching post peaceably enough at the time.

I stirred Oahu up and moved him about, and went up the street a short distance to look for the party, and "loped" gallantly back again, all the while making a pretense of being unconscious that I was an object of interest. I then addressed a few "peart" remarks to Brown, to give the young lady a chance to admire my style of conversation, and was gratified to see her step up and whisper to Brown and glance furtively at me at the same time. I could see that her gentle face bore an expression of the most kindly and earnest solicitude, and I was shocked and angered to hear Brown burst into a fit of brutal laughter

As soon as we started home, I asked with a fair show of indifference, what she had been saying.

Brown laughed again and said, "She thought from the slouchy way you rode and the way you drawled out your words, that you was drunk! She said, 'Why don't you take the poor creature home, Mr. Brown? It makes me nervous to see him galloping that horse and just hanging on that way, and he so drunk.'"

I laughed very loudly at the joke, but it was a sort of hollow, sepulchral laugh, after all. And then I took it out on Oahu.[47]

—⋖—

People often thought Twain was drunk. Ann Alexander, the daughter of Twain's missionary friend Rev. William Alexander, with whom he often visited during his stay on Maui, went riding with him on at least one occasion. She said that he wore a linen duster that was too big for him and that when it slid off one shoulder, he'd pull it up, and it would slip off the other. She thought he was a very poor rider, saying he leaned forward in the saddle swaying from side to side, all the while engaging in what she thought was foolish talk. She was sure he was either drunk or crazy.

When Lillain Woodman Aldrich's husband—the editor of *The Atlantic Monthly*—brought home an oddly dressed man one winter evening, not knowing who he was, she noted he was "clothed in a coat of sealskin, the fur worn outward [unusual for the time]; a sealskin cap well down over his ears; the cap half revealing and half concealing the mass of reddish hair underneath; the heavy mustache having the same red tint. The trousers came well below the coat, and were of a yellowish-brown color; stockings of the same tawny hue, which the low black shoe emphasized. May and December intermixed, producing strange confusion in one's preconceived ideas. Was it the dress for winter, or was it the dress for summer? Seemingly it all depended on the range of vision. If one looked up, winter; if one looked down, summer. But when the wearer spoke it was not difficult for the listener to believe that he was not entirely accountable for the strange gear. It was but too evident that he had looked upon the cup when it was red, for seemingly it had both cheered and inebriated, as the gentleman showed marked inability to stand perpendicular, but swayed from side to side, and had also difficulty with his speech; he did not stammer exactly, but after each word he placed a period."

She was convinced he was drunk, but her husband later explained that Mark Twain was always like that.[48]

Talk Like a Hawaiian
[March 22, 1866:]

On this day, Rev. Samuel Damon gave Twain a Hawaiian translation of *The Pilgrim's Progress*, probably before Twain began his excursion to the Pali, which began in the morning and may have lasted until well after dark, unless he made more than one excursion there, which is likely. He did pass through on his later trip around the island but probably wasn't there at night that time.

Paradise and the Pari (Joke)

Twain's headline for the next section refers to the Pali, but I have retained the old spelling here since updating it would remove Twain's pun. The Hawaiian alphabet only has thirteen letters—a, e, i, o, u, h, k, l, m, n, p, w, and ' (the 'okina). The 'okina indicates a break in the pronunciation called a glottal stop, which almost makes the word sound as if it's two words, such as we'd say "ah-oh." While there is no "r" in their alphabet, originally the Hawaiians pronounced "l"s or "r"s and "k"s or "t"s in words, depending on which island they were from or which side of the island. They were seemingly unable to notice the difference—both sounding the same to them—which caused considerable consternation among the missionaries who created the Hawaiian alphabet.[49] Since it is now pronounced "PAH-lee" and is spelled "pali" in Hawaiian, I have updated the spelling from this point forward.

Also, every word and syllable ends with a vowel. Syllables are only one or two letters long—if two letters, the first one is always a consonant—although nowadays people tend to run some syllables together, so kai or "kah-ee" has become "ky." Initially, every vowel made only one sound, but people don't follow that rule anymore. The kahakō (stress mark, or macron) over vowels indicates the sound is extended slightly, such as the difference when we say "be" and "bee." Okay! Now see how fast you can say humuhumunukunukuāpuaʻa, the name of Hawaiʻi's state fish.

The Pali from the windward side in 1836.
THEODORE AUGUSTE FISQUET

Pali means "cliff" in Hawaiian, and there are nā pali (the plural of pali) on all the Islands, but "the Pali" refers to one long, high cliff line to the northeast of Honolulu. And it particularly refers to one spot at the top of Nuʻuanu Valley where in 1895 Kamehameha—future first king of the Kingdom of Hawaiʻi—ended his most famous battle. He was later known as King Kamehameha I or Kamehameha the Great. Initially a lower-level chief on the Big Island, he rose to become that island's primary chief and then captured the island of Maui.

Setting out to conquer Oʻahu, most of his 10,000 to 16,000 men landed east of Diamond Head, with a few landing at Waikīkī. The battle began when they reached the foot of the Punchbowl and was fought with cannons, muskets, swords, knives, and their traditional weapons up Nuʻuanu Valley to the Pali, where estimates of 400 to more than 800 warriors were pushed over or jumped off the Pali, falling about 400 feet to their deaths (the drop is about 1,000 feet as you move farther out).

Riding into Fairyland

I have ridden up the handsome Nuʻuanu Valley; noted the mausoleum of the departed kings of Hawaiʻi by the wayside; admired the neat residences, surrounded by beautiful gardens that border the turnpike; stood, at last,

The Pali Overlook.
AUTHOR'S PHOTO

after six miles of travel, on the famous Pali—the "divide," we would call it—and looked down the precipice of six or eight hundred feet, over which old Kamehameha I drove the army of the King of Oʻahu three-quarters of a century ago; and gazed upward at the sharp peak close at my left, springing several hundred feet above my head like a colossal church spire—stood there and saw the sun go down and the little plain below and the sea that bordered it become shrouded in thick darkness; and then saw the full moon rise up and touch the tops of the billows, skip over the gloomy valley and paint the upper third of the high peak as white as silver; and heard the ladies say: "Oh, beautiful!—and such a strong contrast!" and heard the gentlemen remark: "By George! talk about scenery! how's that?"[50]

It was all very well, but the same place in daylight does not make so fine a picture as the Kalihi Valley (pronounced Kah-LEE-he). All citizens talk about the Pali; all strangers visit it the first thing; all scribblers write about it—but nobody talks or writes about or visits the Pali's charming neighbor, the Kalihi Valley. I think it was a fortunate accident that led me to stumble into this enchanted ground.

YOU CAN VISIT NUʻUANU VALLEY AND THE PALI

On his way up through Nuʻuanu Valley, Twain stopped at the Royal Mausoleum. And according to his notebook, he also stopped at King Kamehameha IV's summer palace—now known as the Queen Emma Summer Palace.

Maunaʻala—Royal Mausoleum State Monument, 2261 Nuuanu Ave., Honolulu, HI 96817, (808) 587-0300, dlnr.hawaii.gov/dsp/parks/oahu/royal-mausoleum-state-monument.

The Queen Emma Summer Palace, 2913 Pali Highway, Honolulu, HI 96817, (808) 595-3167, daughtersofhawaii.org/queen-emma-summer-palace.

The Pali is easy to get to. From H1 in Honolulu, you drive 5.6 miles up Highway 61 (Pali Highway) through Nuʻuanu Valley to the Nuʻuanu Pali State Wayside turnoff, which takes you into a good-sized parking lot. For more information and hours, go to dlnr.hawaii.gov/dsp/parks/oahu/nuuanu-pali-state-wayside.

Another Paradise

For a mile or two we followed a trail that branched off from the terminus of the turnpike that leads past the government prison, and bending close around the rocky point of a foothill we found ourselves fairly in the valley, and the panorama began to move. After a while the trail took the course of a brook that came down the center of the narrowing canyon, and followed it faithfully throughout its eccentric windings.

On either side the ground rose gradually for a short distance, and then came the mountain barriers—densely wooded precipices on the right and left, that towered hundreds of feet above us, and up which one might climb about as easily as he could climb up the side of a house.

It was a novel sort of scenery, those mountain walls. Face around and look straight across at one of them, and sometimes it presented a bold, square front, with small inclination out of the perpendicular; move on a little and look back, and it was full of sharp ridges, bright with sunlight, and with deep, shady clefts between and what had before seemed a smooth boulder, set in among the thick shrubbery on the face of the wall, was now a bare rampart of stone that projected far out from the mass of green foliage, and was as sharply defined against the sky as if it had been built of solid masonry by the hand of man.

Ahead the mountains looked portly—swollen, if you please—and were marked all over, up and down, diagonally and crosswise, by sharp ribs that reminded one of the fantastic ridges which the wind builds of the drifting snow on a plain. Sometimes these ridges were drawn all about the upper quarter of a mountain, checking it off in velvety green squares and diamonds and triangles, some beaming with sunlight and others softly shaded—the whole upper part of the mountain looking something like a vast green veil thrown over some object that had a good many edges and corners to it—then a sort of irregular "eaves" all around, and from this the main body of the mountain swept down, with a slight outward curve, to the valley below.

All over these highlands the forest trees grew so thickly that, even close at hand, they seemed like solid banks of foliage. These trees were principally of two kinds—the koa and the kukui—the one with a very light green leaf and the other with a dark green. Occasionally there were broad alternate belts of each extending diagonally from the mountain's bases to their summits, and here and there, in the midst of the dark green, were great patches of the bright light-colored leaves, so that, to look far down the valley, along the undulating front of the barrier of peaks, the effect was as if the sun were streaming down upon it through breaks and rifts in the clouds, lighting up belts at intervals all along, and leaving those intervening darkened by the shadows of the clouds; and yet there was not a shred of a cloud in the whole firmament!

It was very soft, and dreamy, and beautiful. And following down the two tall ridges that walled the valley in, we saw them terminate at last in two bold, black headlands that came together like a V, and across this gate ran a narrow zone of the most brilliant light green tint (the shoal water of the distant sea, between reef and shore), and beyond this the somber blue of the deeper water stretched away to the horizon.

The varied picture of the lights and shadows on the wooded mountains, the strong, dark outlines of the gate, and the bright green water and the belt of blue beyond, was one replete with charming contrasts and beautiful effects—a revelation of fairyland itself.

The mountain stream beside us, brawling over its rocky bed, leaped over a miniature precipice occasionally, and then reposed for a season in a limpid pool at her base, reflecting the dank and dripping vines and fans that clung to the wall and protruded in bunches and festoons through breaks in the sparkling cascade.

On the gentle rising ground about us were shady groves of forest trees— the kou, the koa, the breadfruit, the lauhala, the orange, lime, kukui, and many others; and, handsomest of all, the ʻōhiʻa, with its feathery tufts of splendid vermilion-tinted blossoms, a coloring so vivid as to be almost painful to the eye.

Large tracts were covered with large hau (how) bushes, whose sheltering foliage is so thick as to be almost impervious to rain. It is spotted all over with a rich yellow flower, shaped something like a tea cup and sometimes it is further embellished by innumerable white bell-shaped blossoms, that grow upon a running vine with a name unknown to me.

Here and there were wide crops of bushes completely overgrown and hidden beneath the glossy green leaves of another species of vine, and so dense was this covering that it would hardly be possible for a bird to fly through it.

Then there were open spaces well carpeted with grass, and sylvan avenues that wound hither and thither till they lost themselves among the trees. In one open spot a vine of the species I last mentioned had taken possession of two tall dead stumps and wound around and about them, and swung out from their tops and twined their meeting tendrils together into a faultless arch. Man, with all his art, could not have improved its symmetry.

Verily, with its rank luxuriance of vines and blossoms, its groves of forest trees, its shady nooks and grassy lawns, its crystal brook and its wild and beautiful mountain scenery, with that charming far-off glimpse of the sea, Kalihi is the Valley of Enchantment come again!

[Date unknown:]

Another journey that Twain took was to see O'ahu's west end. This time, he was accompanied by J. H. Black, the printer at the *Pacific Commercial Advertiser*. For a while, Twain stayed at J. H. Black's house on Queen Emma Place. The two took the long, hot, dusty road through 'Ewa, around to the west side of the island, and on up to Wai'anae. It's said that when Twain fell far behind, Black rode back to see what the trouble was and found that Twain's mule had fallen asleep. Twain was sitting backward in his saddle and was twisting the mule's tail, trying to get him to go.

Today, that area is a poorer area of the island and is referred to as the Wild West side. If you go there, be sure not to leave anything unattended or visible in your vehicle.

YOU CAN VISIT KALIHI VALLEY

Experiencing Kalihi Valley is a bit trickier than Nu'uanu Valley. Twain rode up through it on horseback. Now you pretty much have to rapidly pass through it on Highway 63 (Likelike Highway). There aren't any places along the highway where you can stop, but you can drive through the residential area on Kalihi Street.

PEOPLE WHO LIVE IN GRASS HOUSES

The Fearless Pāʻū Riders

[Either March 24 or 31, 1866:]

Mounted on my noble steed Hawaii (pronounced Hah-WY-ye—stress on second syllable), a beast that cost thirteen dollars and is able to go his mile in three—with a bit of margin to it—I departed last Saturday week for—for any place that might turn up.[51]

Passing through the market place we saw that feature of Honolulu under its most favorable auspices—that is, in the full glory of Saturday afternoon, which is a festive day with the natives. The native girls by twos and threes and parties of a dozen, and sometimes in whole platoons and companies, went cantering up and down the neighboring streets astride of fleet but homely horses, and with their gaudy riding habits streaming like banners behind them. Such a troop of free and easy riders, in their natural home, the saddle, makes a gay and graceful and exhilarating spectacle.

Pāʻū riders were initially known for riding very fast. This sketch from 1846 shows two women sailing past a startled man on the Honolulu plains in front of the Punchbowl.
A. PLUME

The riding habit I speak of is simply a long, broad scarf, like a tavern table cloth brilliantly colored, wrapped around the loins once, then apparently passed between the limbs and each end thrown backward over the same, and floating and flapping behind on both sides beyond the horse's tail like a couple of fancy flags; then, slipping the stirrup-irons between her toes, the girl throws her chest forward, sits up like a major general and goes sweeping by like the wind.

"Gay?" says Brown with a fine irony, "Oh, you can't mean it!"

The girls put on all the finery they can on Saturday afternoon—fine black silk robes; flowing red ones that nearly put your eyes out; others as white as snow; still others that discount the rainbow—and they wear their hair in nets, and trim their jaunty hats with fresh flowers, and encircle their dusky throats with homemade necklaces of the brilliant vermilion-tinted blossom of the 'ōhi'a; and they fill the markets and the adjacent streets with their bright presences, and smell like a rag factory on fire with their offensive coconut oil.[52]

The Poi Thickens

Moving among the stirring crowds, you come to the poi merchants, squatting in the shade on their hams, in true native fashion, and surrounded by purchasers. (The Sandwich Islanders always squat on their hams, and who knows but they may be the old original "ham sandwiches?" The thought is pregnant with interest.)

The poi looks like common flour paste, and is kept in large bowls formed of a species of gourd, and capable of holding from one to three or four gallons. Poi is the chief article of food among the natives, and is prepared from the kalo or taro plant (k and t are the same in the Kānaka alphabet, and so are l and r). [Like the words "pali" and "pari," the Hawaiians originally pronounced it both ways, but the letters t and r are not in the Hawaiian alphabet.] The kalo root looks like a thick, or, if you please, a corpulent sweet potato, in shape, but is of a light purple color when boiled. When boiled it answers as a passable substitute for bread. The buck Kānakas bake it underground, then mash it up well with a heavy lava pestle, mix water with it until it becomes a paste, set it aside and let it ferment, and then it is poi—and an unseductive mixture it is, almost tasteless before it ferments and too sour for a luxury afterward. But nothing is more nutritious.

When solely used, however, it produces acrid humors, a fact which sufficiently accounts for the humorous character of the Kānakas. I think there must be as much of a knack in handling poi as there is in eating with chopsticks. The forefinger is thrust into the mess and stirred quickly round several times and drawn as quickly out, thickly coated, just as if it were poulticed; the head is thrown back, the finger inserted in the mouth and the delicacy stripped off and swallowed—the eye closing gently, meanwhile, in a languid sort of ecstasy.

Many a different finger goes into the same bowl and many a different kind of dirt and shade and quality of flavor is added to the virtues of its contents. One tall gentleman, with nothing in the world on but a soiled and greasy shirt, thrust in his finger and tested the poi, shook his head, scratched it with the useful finger, made another test, prospected among his hair, caught something and ate it; tested the poi again, wiped the grimy perspiration from his brow with the universal hand, tested again, blew his nose . . .

"Let's move on, Brown," said I, and we moved.[53]

—≺

Of course, Twain is exaggerating, and eating with this method is not quite so unsanitary, as Twain's friend Charles Warren Stoddard explained:

How to eat paste without a spoon was the next question. The whole family volunteered to show us; drew up around the calabash in a hungry circle, and dipped in with a vengeance. Six right hands spread their first and second fingers like sign-boards pointing to a focus in the very center of that poi-paste; six fists dove simultaneously, and were buried in the luscious mass. There was a spasmodic working in the elbows, an effort to come to the top, and in a moment the hands were lifted aloft in triumph, and seemed to be tracing half a dozen capital O's in the transparent air, during which maneuver the mass of poi adhering to the fingers assumed fair proportions, resembling, to a remarkable degree, large, white swellings; whereupon they were immediately conveyed to the several mouths, instinctively getting into the right one, and, having discharged freight, reappeared as good as ever, if not better than before.

"Disgusting!" gasped Felix, as he returned to the water-side. I thought him unreasonable in his harsh judgment, assuring him that our own flour was fingered as often before it came, at last, to our lips in the form of bread.

"Moreover," I added, "this poi is glutinous: the moment a finger enters it, a thin coating adheres to the skin, and that finger may wander about the calabash all day without touching another particle of the substance. Therefore, six or sixteen fellows fingerings in one dish for dinner are in reality safer than we, who eat steaks that have been mesmerized under the hands of the butcher and the cook."[54]

Jack London realized the same thing, saying that "you stick your finger into a thick paste, and the finger is withdrawn coated with it. Ergo, your finger has touched nothing of what remains in the pot—or sack."[55]

Still, people tend to be squeamish.

Twain's description of eating poi was written shortly after his arrival in Hawai'i. In his notebook, he wrote, "poi not bad food."[56] Toward the end of his visit, he occasionally spent the night with Hawaiians in their grass houses when traveling around the Big Island, and his companion for part of the trip—Edward Howard—said a native gave them "some nasty paste he called 'poi' which Sam seemed to relish."[57]

Poi is usually made from the bulbous root of the kalo (or taro) plant. The Hawaiians had around 300 varieties of kalo, although only about eighty are known today. To make poi, the tuber part of the plant is steamed or baked underground, pealed or scraped, and then vigorously pounded on a board with a poi pounder stone while adding water until it turns into a dough, and then it's kneaded. It initially has little flavor, and its consistency is similar to pudding but slightly thicker and stickier. One Hawaiian I know calls it Hawaiian superglue because if you eat too much, it can stop you up.

Some eat it fresher when it's slightly sweet. Others would rather have it after it's fermented and is a bit sour. Personally, I like it both ways. If you haven't had it before, you might want to add either a little salt or sugar. It is an acquired taste, and you have to eat it a few times to really appreciate it, which is probably how Twain learned to relish it.

If you mix poi with sugar and coconut cream, it's called kūlolo and makes a good dessert. Other types of poi were made from sweet potatoes, cooked breadfruit, or bananas, which were mashed and mixed with water.

'Awa for Sale—Ditto Fish

Around a small shanty was collected a crowd of natives buying the 'awa root [pronounced "AH-vah", it is also known as kava]. It is said that but for the use of this root the destruction of the people in former times by venereal diseases would have been far greater than it was, and by others it is said that this is merely a fancy.

All agree that poi will rejuvenate a man who is used up and his vitality almost annihilated by hard drinking, and that in some kinds of diseases it will restore health after all medicines have failed; but all are not willing to allow to the 'awa the virtues claimed for it.

The natives manufacture an intoxicating drink from it, which is fearful in its effects when persistently indulged in. It covers the body with dry, white scales, inflames the eyes, and causes premature decrepitude.

Although the man before whose establishment we stopped has to pay a government license of eight hundred dollars a year for the exclusive right to sell 'awa root, it is said that he makes a small fortune every twelve-months, while saloon keepers—who pay a thousand dollars a year for the privilege of retailing whiskey, etc.—only make a bare living.

We found the fish market crowded; for the native is very fond of fish, and eats the article raw and alive! Let us change the subject.[58]

—⌇—

Raw fish is still very popular in the form of poke, sushi, and sashimi. Poke (pronounced POH-kay) is dice-sized cubes of raw tuna—a much higher grade than what comes in a can—and is so fresh that it doesn't have a fishy flavor—mixed with things like onion bits and seaweed, along with a sauce of different types depending on what style of poke it is. Supermarkets carry up to a dozen different styles, all freshly made, including Hawaiian style, spicy, shoyu, limu, and California style.

'Awa is still available today and can be found in health-food stores and other places. It has a sedative effect. It can help you sleep but can also make you feel drunk. Usually, it is used as a type of tea, but it's also available in other forms, such as candy bars.

Saturday Is Party Time

In old times here Saturday was a grand gala day indeed. All the native population of the town forsook their labors, and those of the surrounding country journeyed to the city. Then the white folks had to stay indoors, for every street was so packed with charging cavaliers and cavalieresses that it was next to impossible to thread one's way through the cavalcades without getting crippled.

In the afternoon the natives were wont to repair to the plain, outside the town, and indulge in their ancient sports and pastimes and bet away their week's earnings on horse races. One might see two or three thousand, some say five thousand, of these wild riders, skurrying over the plain in a mass in those days. And it must have been a fine sight.

At night they feasted and the girls danced the lascivious hula hula—a dance that is said to exhibit the very perfection of educated motion of limb and arm, hand, head, and body, and the exactest uniformity of movement and accuracy of "time."

It was performed by a circle of girls with no raiment on them to speak of, who went through an infinite variety of motions and figures without prompting, and yet so true was their "time," and in such perfect concert did they move that when they were placed in a straight line, hands, arms, bodies, limbs, and heads waved, swayed, gesticulated, bowed, stooped, whirled, squirmed, twisted, and undulated as if they were part and parcel of a single individual; and it was difficult to believe they were not moved in a body by some exquisite piece of mechanism.

Of late years, however, Saturday has lost most of its quondam gala features. This weekly stampede of the natives interfered too much with labor and the interests of the white folks, and by sticking in a law here, and preaching a sermon there, and by various other means, they gradually broke it up.

The demoralizing hula hula was forbidden to be performed, save at night, with closed doors, in the presence of few spectators, and only by permission duly procured from the authorities and the payment of ten dollars for the same. There are few girls now-a-days able to dance this ancient national dance in the highest perfection of the art.[59]

Wicked Hula

After King Kamehameha died in 1819, his twenty-two-year-old son Liholiho became King Kamehameha II. Kamehameha's favorite wife Ka'ahumanu became co-ruler with Liholiho, going from queen consort to kuhina nui (similar to a prime minister). The two cast off their old Hawaiian religion, and about four months later, the first missionaries arrived from Boston. The leader of the missionary group, Hiram Bingham, was quick to attack the Hawaiian's traditional dance, writing, "The whole arrangement and process of their old hulas were designed to promote lasciviousness, and of course the practice of them could not flourish in modest communities. They had been interwoven too with their superstitions, and made subservient to the honor of their gods, and then rulers, either living or departed or deified."[60]

This was a very distorted view of hula and one that would lead it to be suppressed for almost a century.

The Hawaiians didn't have a written language until the missionaries created one. Instead, they used chants to record and pass on their history, genealogy, myths, and legends. Chants were used to praise their chiefs, and it was one of their main sources of entertainment. Chants accompanied hula to make them more entertaining. Hula is at the heart of Hawaiian culture. Originally, it was considered a martial art—a form of training similar to tai chi—and only men were allowed to hula. It gradually evolved into an art form that requires years of training and countless hours of practice as a group. It also became a social activity that helps bind the community together.

The missionaries were unable to appreciate this. They were convinced hula was savage and Satanic. Most of the Westerners' perceptions of hula stemmed from misunderstandings, preconceived notions, and cultural biases.

These 1816 premissionary hula dancers were wearing their kapa or imported cloths. The women's short hair is bleached white along the front by a lime paste made from crushed coral, sometimes with a long violet curl combed back from the center of the forehead. The men's illustration shows three different poses, but in reality, their movements would have been synchronized like those of the women. The men are wearing boar-tusk bracelets and dog-teeth anklets. The anklets made a rattling sound as they danced, and they're holding feathered gourd rattles. One of the men is tattooed. Usually, it was only the wealthy and hula dancers who had tattoos. Their tattoos were of plant dyes that lasted from six months to a year. The men's movements are often different than the women's and are at times aggressive and threatening.

LOUIS CHORIS

Hula was not a part of the ancient religion. But religion was infused into every-thing they did, so they did make offerings before they danced. There were some sacred dances that featured the gods—usually Pele (pronounced PEH-lay), the goddess of volcanoes, lava, and one of the goddesses of hula—but they were danced for education, edification, and entertainment—not as part of their worship.[61]

The missionaries also had a problem with hula's skimpy attire, but then this was a time when Americans thought it was risqué for a woman to show her ankles, hence the tent-like dresses the missionaries made Hawaiian women wear.

While the Hawaiians still skinny-dipped in lakes, rivers, and the ocean, the hula was much less revealing. Women wore their traditional kapa (also tapa or bark cloth) pāʻū skirts or four layers of kapa cloth, creating a puffy covering around their hips. They would also wear skirts made from fresh ti leaves. Men wore either their usual malo or a puffy kapa covering similar to that of the women.

With pressure from the Christians, female hula dancers began wearing tops made from shortened holokū dresses (Mother Hubbards), with the puffy kapa cloth around their hips. Grass skirts were worn on a few other Polynesian islands but weren't used in Hawaiʻi until the 1870s. Some Hawaiians derisively call them shredded-wheat skirts, but these skirts had the advantage of being reusable—you didn't have to make fresh ones for each performance. As near as I can tell, coconut bras arrived here around the 1970s. While grass skirts and coconut bras are not traditionally Hawaiian, they've been adopted and are common now, just as West-ern-style music has replaced the chanting.

Nudity was just a part of everyday life for the Hawaiians in the early 1800s, so they probably didn't have a clue that Westerners saw female breasts as being erotic. If they did, they probably didn't understand why. After the explorers, most visitors to Hawaiʻi were sailors—either whalers or from merchant ships that sup-plied the whalers. The captains needed their men to work during the day, so they restricted hula show attendance to the night, and they insisted only women be allowed to dance. This probably made the dances seem more suggestive.

The early explorers and the missionaries saw half-naked people dancing around and assumed that hula was mainly about sex, but it wasn't. Of the twenty-eight types of hula, only one was primarily sexual. This was the hula maʻi, or genital hula. It was usually the final hula performed in a show and was meant to honor the chief.

For the Hawaiians, procreation was considered sacred, and sex was a pleasur-able part of everyday life. It was how the future generations were created. They felt no shame or that there was anything perverse about it, as the Western cultures tend to do. And talking about one's genitals was the same as talking about one's eyes, hands, or hairstyle. To them, sex was pleasurable for themselves and for others, and it was good for establishing friendships and expanding their families and good for the gods.

Whenever a child was born in a chiefly or a priestly family, a chant was composed honoring his or her genitals. This was more anticipative, predictive, and wishful than realistic, of course, since they were just a baby, but these would be chanted to honor them throughout their lives.

Still, it's no wonder the prudish missionaries were offended.

It's very unfortunate that something that had such deep meaning and cultural significance to one group of people would be viewed as salacious by another. The sailors totally missed what makes hula significant, and the missionaries were even further off mark. Today, many people still think only women dance the hula, which is sad considering the men are just as talented as the women.

In 1824, Queen Ka'ahumanu became a Christian, and in 1830, she issued an edict, banning—among other things—the hula, chants, music (except hymns), alcohol, 'awa (kava), cussing, and bathing in public by women. After her death two years later, this edict was largely ignored, but pressure by the Christians continued to push the hula into the background.

But it wasn't just sex that bothered the missionaries. They subscribed to the puritanical notion that hard work was a form of prayer. "Idle hands are the devil's workshop," so one must focus on work and devotion to God. Amassing wealth was considered by some to be God's reward for diligent labor.

The missionaries complained that the Hawaiians refused to work consistently throughout the day but had no problem dancing hula for hours on end in the hot sun. They and other Westerners created the myth that the Hawaiians—and all Polynesians—were lazy, while at the same time they were highly prized as sailors, cane cutters, and cowboys precisely because they were such hard workers. But part of the idea of laziness originated with misunderstandings of the Hawaiian culture. For centuries, the Hawaiians were able to get everything they needed to live with minimal work. Working to gain wealth made no sense to them.

Missionary Charles Stewart, in his 1828 book, wrote, "Notwithstanding the variety of apparently necessary employment falling both to men and women, few of either sex devote more than four or five hours of the twenty-four to work.

Though unavoidably more laborious than many other Polynesians, they partake of the indolence of character incident to the inhabitants of tropical climates, and sleep and lounge away more than half their time, while much of the remainder is given to amusement and pleasure. It is, however, difficult to determine how far the Sandwich Islanders partake of this indolence from the fact that there is no motive for industry presented to them, beyond the fear of starvation, and a dread of the displeasure of their chiefs."[62]

What the Hawaiians did and when they did it had been strictly regulated by their ancient religion. Certain days you could fish, and other days you couldn't. There were specific times for farming and others for making fishing nets. Also, they refrained from working in the heat of the day, confining their exertions to the cool early mornings and late afternoons.

And in the late fall and winter, there was the Makahiki festival (harvest and New Year's festival), where everyone—except the lowest class, similar to India's untouchables—took a vacation and celebrated for up to four months, being released from both work and most religious regulations.

But there was also another important factor.

Good and Bad Chiefs

The commoners supplied their chiefs with goods and food in exchange for protection from other chiefs and their warriors. In addition, the chiefs also interceded with the gods on the commoners' behalf, such as during times of drought. There was no point for commoners to try to amass wealth since whenever a chief saw something belonging to one of their commoners, he or she could take it. There was no incentive for them to work hard for gain, as in the end they wouldn't really gain anything. They lived simply, and if they were abused by their chief, they were free to move to land under the care of a more hospitable chief. If a chief lost his people, not only would it show his peers that he was a bad chief, he wouldn't have anyone to supply his needs. This gave the chiefs incentives to care for their people. If a chief was really horrible to his people, they could just kill him, and he'd be replaced with another, hopefully better, chief. This was permitted since it was directed against a particular chief and not against the system or the chiefs in general.

Chiefs were also trained to care for their people. David Malo, a native Hawaiian who grew up under King Kamehameha's reign, wrote ca. 1835–1836,

It was the policy of the government to place the chiefs who were destined to rule, while they were still young, with wise persons, that they might be instructed by skilled teachers in the principles of government, be taught the art of war, and be made to acquire personal skill and bravery.

The young man had first to be subject to another chief, that he might be disciplined and have experience of poverty, hunger, want and hardship, and by reflecting on these things learn to care for the people with gentleness and patience, with a feeling of sympathy for the common people [this should be a requirement of our leaders], and at the same time to pay due respect to the ceremonies of religion and the worship of the gods, to live temperately, not violating virgins ('a'ole lima koko kohe) [this was mistranslated—instead of "virgins," it should read "menstruating women"], conducting the government kindly to all.

This is the way for a king to prolong his reign and cause his dynasty to be perpetuated, so that his government shall not be overthrown. Kings that behave themselves and govern with honesty—their annals and genealogies will be preserved and treasured by the thoughtful and the good.[63]

The ancient Hawaiians believed everyone and everything were part of their family. They believed they were descended from Wākea, the sky father, and Papa, the earth mother. They felt the land was their ancestor—their great-great-etc. grandmother. It was all part of their collective family. The ali'i nui—or high chiefs—were considered direct descendants of the gods and were viewed as the elder siblings, while the commoners were thought of as the junior siblings. It was the duty of the elder siblings to protect the junior siblings from natural disasters and from the depredations of war, often by interceding with the gods. The chiefs also provided governmental organization and redistributed surpluses to help those in need. The junior siblings took care of the elder siblings by caring for the land, tending the crops, fishing, and producing products that everyone needed, such as kapa cloth and salt.

There weren't a lot of chiefs. In 1848, there were ten high chiefs, twenty-four lower chiefs, and 218 land stewards who managed the land for the chiefs—that was with a population of about 80,000. So supplying the needs of their chiefs wasn't usually a burden. And this system didn't cause the commoners to be selfish and to just work enough for their own needs. They had a very strong sense of community where generosity was highly valued. Their concept of 'ohana (family) refers primarily to their extended family but also to their community and more broadly to all Hawaiians or to people as a whole. In other words, they felt we're all in this together. When one person had something, he or she was honored to be able to share it with everyone else. Thus, for example, if one person didn't catch any fish—perhaps because he was sick or injured—others in the community would give him some. And later on when he had some, he would give to them. Seeing themselves as one big family is the source of their tremendous generosity. They saw no point in accumulating a surplus. They could feed their family by working a couple days a week, and if they needed more, they could get it whenever they needed it.

This was something the Westerners could have learned from, but it ran counter to Western civilization's idea of individuals putting their noses to the grindstone so they could pull themselves up by their own bootstraps in order to become rich and influential, amassing wealth like it's a competition—taking as much as you can so you can turn a profit from it.

Traditional Hawaiian life was also contrary to the idea of landownership since the community needed access to various types of land in order to supply their needs. Both owning land and the wage economy disrupted this by taking workers away from their extended families and communities. Those who continued to live outside the wage system were considered unproductive and indolent, but eventually, they had no choice and had to move into wage-paying jobs.

In addition, Westerners tend to take a dim view of communal living, falsely believing that it doesn't work and is doomed to failure. Thus, the growing dominance of Western culture in Hawai'i put an end to centuries of Hawaiian self-sufficiency.

Back to Dancing

As the missionaries began expanding into business ownership, particularly sugar plantations, they needed cheap labor, which gave further incentive to remove distractions from work. They wanted to ban hula as a "public evil" by saying it was preventing the people from engaging in legitimate labor. After years of trying, the missionary advisors finally got the government to pass a law against it in 1859. This basically restricted the dances to private events at certain locations in Honolulu—these are what Twain was talking about.

Lot was the king by the time Twain arrived in Hawai'i. He had been educated at the missionary school for ali'i (high chiefs and royalty), but he turned his back on this in favor of promoting Hawaiian culture. The laws restricting hula remained in effect, and there were still some dance halls in Honolulu when Twain was there that he could have easily visited, but there's nothing to indicate that he did. He took the missionaries' view of the dance.

The law banning hula was repealed in 1870, and in 1877, King Kalākaua—Hawai'i's seventh and last king, also known as the Merrie Monarch—revived hula in the 1880s, proclaiming, "Hula is the language of the heart and therefore the heartbeat of the Hawaiian people." The newspapers immediately began calling for another ban. Rev. Samuel Damon's *The Friend* described the king's cultural revival as fostering "destructive and poisonous practices," "vile," and "hideous deviltries." Even as late as 1898, one anonymous author wrote, "Civilization and Christianity have nearly succeeded in banishing all traces of barbarism from the Islands, although the hula-dances are still indulged in some sections—mostly for the diversion of tourists having depraved minds."[64]

But this didn't stop the king. For his Royal Jubilee in 1886, he staged three days of hula performances at the 'Iolani Palace. This has now become a tradition with the Merrie Monarch Festival held every year the week after Easter in Hilo on the Big Island. This important and popular event is televised live throughout the Islands. It is the Olympics of hula competitions.

The Influence of the Missionaries

The missionaries have clothed them, educated them, broken up the tyrannous authority of their chiefs, and given them freedom and the right to enjoy whatever their hands and brains produce, with equal laws for all and punishment for all alike who transgress them.

The contrast is so strong—the benefit conferred upon this people by the missionaries is so prominent, so palpable and so unquestionable, that the frankest compliment I can pay them, and the best, is simply to point to the condition of the Sandwich Islanders of Captain Cook's time, and their condition today. Their work speaks for itself.[65]

The missionaries have Christianized and educated all the natives. They all belong to the Church, and there is not one of them, above the age of eight years, but can read and write with facility in the native tongue. It is the most universally educated race of people outside of China. They have any quantity of books, printed in the Kānaka language, and all the natives are fond of reading.

They are inveterate church-goers—nothing can keep them away. All this ameliorating cultivation has at last built up in the native women a profound respect for chastity—in other people. Perhaps that is enough to say on that head. The national sin will die out when the race does, but perhaps not earlier.—But doubtless this purifying is not far off, when we reflect that contact with civilization and the whites has reduced the native population from *four hundred thousand* (Captain Cook's estimate,) to *fifty-five thousand* in something over eighty years![66]

—⋲—

Jack London echoed this forty years later: "Of the original Hawaiians, one thing is certain: They are doomed to extinction. [...] All of which is a pity, for the world can ill afford to lose so splendid and lovable a race."[67]

Fortunately they didn't die out, and the population hit a low of 37,656 in 1900 and then began recovering. No one knows how many people were here when Captain Cook arrived. Estimates of the size of the Hawaiian population vary from 130,000 to 1 million, although 400,000 to 800,000 appear to be most likely.

Twain gives the missionaries a bit more credit than they deserve. They did not break up the tyranny of the chiefs. The Hawaiians did that themselves before the missionaries arrived. The missionaries did create their written language and taught it to them, primarily so they'd be able to read the Bible, but the rapid spread of Christianity and reading throughout the Islands was because the royalty strongly encouraged it and later on required it. Education wasn't yet compulsory in the United States, so Twain is probably right that Hawai'i and China were the two most educated countries in the world at that time. Remember, Twain only had a fifth-grade education, and this wasn't unusual.

The missionaries also worked hard to save the Hawaiians from extinction while at the same time trying to restrict them from having sex. The Hawaiians had a difficult time understanding the missionaries' beliefs regarding sex since for centuries, the Hawaiians had felt that anything that was pleasurable must be good.

The leader of the first company of missionaries, Rev. Hiram Bingham, arrived on the Big Island in 1820. This group consisted of fourteen adults, five children, and three Hawaiian helpers.

Rev. Asa Thurston and his wife Lucy in 1859. Although they look like they were going to a funeral, this was taken on their wedding anniversary. Bingham and Thurston helped create the written Hawaiian language and worked on translating the Bible into that language.

Medical doctor Dr. Gerrit Judd and Laura were part of the third company that arrived in 1828. Judd became Hawai'i's unofficial prime minister, directing all aspects of the government in the 1840s and 1850s.

Teacher Daniel and Charlotte Dole, ca. 1853, arrived with the ninth company in 1841. Their son, Sanford Dole—a second cousin of James Dole—was a founder of the Hawaiian Pineapple Company, which eventually became the Dole Food Company. He also helped draft the Bayonet Constitution in 1887 that King Kalākaua was forced to sign, taking away most of his powers. Then in 1893, Sanford was involved in the the coup d'état that overthrew the Kingdom of Hawai'i and became the president of the Republic of Hawai'i and then the first governor of the Territory of Hawaii.

Minister and medical doctor Rev. Dr. Dwight Baldwin ca. 1854, next to a photograph of his wife Charlotte ca. 1860. They were part of the fourth company that arrived in 1831. One of their sons owned a Maui pineapple company, while another was the Baldwin in Alexander & Baldwin, which was one of the "Big Five" trading and agriculture corporations that dominated Hawai'i's economy in the early twentieth century and that some believe controlled Hawai'i's government for decades. The Big Five also controlled 90 percent of the sugar industry.

Teacher Amos Cooke and wife Juliette were also part of the eighth company. His daughter married the son of the Alexander in Alexander & Baldwin, and his son married the daughter of the Baldwin in Alexander & Baldwin. Another of his sons became president of C. Brewer & Co. and the Bank of Hawai'i. And his grandson married the granddaughter of Gerrit P. Judd.

Rev. William Alexander and Mary Ann came over with the fifth company in 1832. One of their sons was a cofounder of Castle & Cooke and of Alexander & Baldwin—two of the Big Five. Their daughter married the Baldwin in Alexander & Baldwin, while another daughter married James Dole the "Pineapple King," a founder of the Hawaiian Pineapple Company, which eventually became the Dole Food Company. He developed America's first nationwide consumer advertising campaign to sell his canned pineapples.

Bank teller Samuel Castle, shown in 1878, and his second wife, Mary Castle—who was his first wife's sister—is shown in 1889. They were with the eighth company, which arrived in 1837. Castle initially managed the mission's finances but went on to found Castle & Cooke, one of the Big Five corporations. He was on the Privy Council of King Kamehameha V and King Lunalilo.

Mark Twain's friend, Samuel Chenery Damon, and his wife, Julia, came with the tenth company in 1842. They are shown ca. 1860 with their four sons: (left to right) Francis, Samuel Mills, Edward, and William. Samuel Mills Damon married the daughter of missionary Dwight Baldwin. Her brother was the Baldwin in Alexander & Baldwin, one of the Big Five. Samuel Mills became minister of finance of the Kingdom of Hawai'i and the head of the bank that became First Hawaiian Bank. By the time he died in 1925, his estate was valued at more than $252 million. He was one of the biggest landowners in Hawai'i.

    The missionaries were not supposed to "go awhoring after filthy lucre," but many quit the mission in order to start their businesses. There's a popular saying in Hawai'i that the missionaries came to do good and did well.

Twain knew he had to praise the missionaries in his *Union* letters since they were considered to be God's heroes back home, and later on, he was caustically criticized when he joked about them, but in his notebook, he wrote, "S.[and-wich] Islanders never intended to work. Worse off now with all religion than ever before. Dying off fast. First white landed there was a curse to them."[68] And, "The missionary (I should say preacher), feature of insincerity and hypocrisy, marks the social atmosphere of the place."[69]

Although in one of his later *Union* letters, he did write,

> Now, therefore, when I say that the Sandwich Islands mission-aries are pious; hard-working; hard-praying; self-sacrificing; hospitable; devoted to the well-being of this people and the interests of Protestantism; bigoted; puritanical; slow; ignorant of all white human nature and natural ways of men, except the remnants of these things that are left in their own class or pro-fession; old fogy—fifty years behind the age; uncharitable toward the weaknesses of the flesh; considering all shortcomings, faults and failings in the light of crimes, and having no mercy and no forgiveness for such—when I say this about the missionaries, I do it with the explicit understanding that it is only my estimate of them—not that of a Higher Intelligence—not that of even other sinners like myself. It is only *my* estimate, and it may fall far short of being a just one.[70]

The missionaries learned the Hawaiian language and taught the Hawaiians in that. Very few were taught English—something the missionaries were criticized for at the time. And they were allowed to teach them only enough to read the Bible. This was well before the Republic outlawed the use of Hawaiian.

Nevertheless, it must strike a stranger with surprise to find all these demi-barbarians have been taught to read and write—exceedingly well too—indeed the clean, well-defined calligraphy of the Hilo nymphs will compare with that of the most fashionable style of the art in young ladies' seminaries at home—they pay a strict outward observance to the Sabbath, have a general knowledge of the Scriptures, and many of the youth, a tolerable share of education.
—US NAVY LIEUTENANT HENRY WISE, 1848[71]

Rev. Sereno Bishop, the son of missionaries, wrote in 1901 or 1902, "I have long regarded the most serious error of the missionary work as pursued in these islands as being the failure to begin by establishing, as fast as possible, training schools for the thorough civilizing and Christianizing of youth to become leaders of their people in all good things. [. . .] Many of the older missionaries were deeply impressed with the importance of that line of work." But the head of the Board of Missions refused. He added, "Had training schools for young boys and girls been conducted forty years earlier, I believe that Hawaiian civilization would have been greatly accelerated."[72] Several such schools were established, but they were eventually abandoned.

In addition, Hawai'i became, under the influence of the missionaries, what was probably the most Christian nation in the world at that time—even more so than the United States. The lives of the ancient Hawaiians were entirely suffused with religion, so after casting off their old religion, they followed their queen and other chiefs in accepting the new one. A single church service could easily have more than 1,000 worshipers, and they would sit there for hours taking it all in, sometimes several times a day. Their love and respect for their royalty ensured that nearly the entire nation converted to Christianity. Unfortunately, this worked to their disadvantage when the missionaries and their sons took their land away and overthrew their kingdom, as we shall see later on.

It also lasted only until the 1850s after the Catholics and Mormons arrived. In the 1860s, Kamehameha IV and Queen Emma switched to the Hawaiian version of the Church of England.

The Hawaiians arguably embraced Western civilization more wholeheartedly than any other people in the past few hundred years. With Captain Cook's arrival, they suddenly leapt from stone age to the modern era in the blink of eye. And while Twain admired how the missionaries brought civilization to the Hawaiians, he was also sorry about how certain aspects of their culture were lost.

It wasn't just hula that the missionaries tried to abolish. Because of Rev. Hiram Bingham's efforts, Captain Otto von Kotzebue noted that by 1825 in Honolulu, "The streets, formerly so full of life and animation, are now deserted; games of all kinds, even the most innocent, are sternly prohibited; singing is a punishable offence; and the consummate profligacy of attempting to dance would certainly find no mercy. On Sundays, no cooking is permitted, nor must even afire

Children just don't want to be like their parents. The Hawaiian culture rapidly changed in one generation. Hoʻolulu—sketched in 1819—was one of King Kamehameha's chief officers, while his daughter Mrs. Benjamin Pitman (Kinoʻoleoliliha)—painted here in 1849—was also a high chief. Hoʻolulu and his half brother were responsible for hiding King Kamehameha's bones, and his descendants are still the guardians of Maunaʻala, the Royal Mausoleum of Hawaiʻi in Honolulu.

be kindled: nothing, in short, must be done; the whole day is devoted to prayer, with how much real piety may be easily imagined."[73]

In 1840, Commodore Charles Wilkes added, "I was much struck with the absence of sports among the boys and children. On inquiry, I learned that it had, after mature deliberation and experience, been considered advisable by the missionaries to deprive them of all their heathenish enjoyments, rather than allow them to occupy their minds with anything that might recall old associations. The consequence is that the Hawaiian boys are staid and demure, having the quiet looks of old men. I cannot doubt that they possess the natural tendency of youth towards frolicsome relaxations; but the fear of offending keeps a constant restraint over them. It might be well, perhaps, to introduce some innocent amusements; and indeed I believe this has been attempted, for I occasionally saw them flying kites."[74]

ROYALTY AND ETIQUETTE

[MARCH 25, 1866:]

On Sunday, Twain went to church and then to a luau at J. L. Lewis's house in Waikīkī, where he met the admiral of the Hawaiian Navy and Lydia Kamaka'eha Pākī, who in 1891 became Queen Lili'uokalani, the last ruler of the Kingdom.

A Trip around the Island
[Sometime between March 25 and April 3, 1866:]

In late March, Twain took what was known as "the trip around the island" on horseback, although this eighty-mile journey left out large portions of O'ahu. He was accompanied much of the way by Henry Macfarlane. Twain didn't write about it, but his friend Henry Whitney did in *The Hawaiian Guide Book for Travelers* (1875), saying that it "may be accomplished comfortably in three or four days"

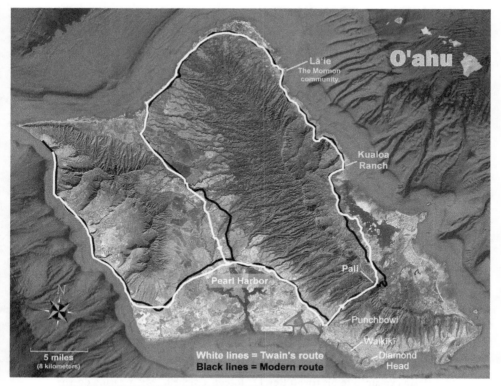

AUTHOR'S GRAPHIC WITH A SATELLITE IMAGE FROM THE HAWAI'I STATE OFFICE OF PLANNING

and that it began by taking the road over the Pali, where "having descended the mountain pass, a gallop of three miles takes the rider to the village of Kaneohe, where are located several sugar plantations. Thence a delightful ride of ten miles through cane fields, kalo and rice patches; also among hamlets, grazing fields, and on through the jungle of guava bushes to Judd's Ranch at Kualoa."

Medical doctor Garrit Judd was a missionary who became Kamehameha III's advisor and translator, then was successively the minister of foreign affairs, the minister of interior, the minister of finance; served in the House of Representatives; finally was the minister plenipotentiary to England, France, and the United States. At the time, people said he was the government of Hawai'i. But many people thought he had too much power and didn't like what he was doing, so he was ousted.

Twain's stack of letters of introduction enabled him to stay with some of Hawai'i's most prominent families. Elizabeth Wilder, Judd's daughter, said Twain stayed at the ranch for a week, but that's probably an exaggeration. At that time, the ranch was almost 3,000 acres. Another 1,000 was added later. It runs inland from and includes Mokoli'i, or Chinaman's Hat Island. A short-lived sugar plantation was in operation when Twain was there.

Laura Wilder, Judd's granddaughter, was about five years old at the time. She later said that Twain set her on his knee and asked how many Mother Goose rhymes she could recite. He also pulled on her ears, saying that would make them grow. She recalled her mother being a bit peeved because he wanted buckets of hot water taken into his bathroom every morning. And she added that she was shocked that he swore so much, so he put cotton in her ears.[75]

Among those who knew him, Twain was notorious for his swearing. He said, "When you're mad, count four; when you're very mad, swear! But most of us don't wait to count four! At least I don't!"[76] And, "If I cannot swear in heaven I shall not stay there."[77]

His housekeeper, Katy Leary, said that "of course his swearing never seemed really bad to me. It was sort of funny, and a part of him, somehow. Sort of amusing it was—and gay—not like real swearing, 'cause he swore like an angel."[78] His friend Hamlin Garland wrote, "Mark Twain swore with so much eloquence and with such an individual choice of words that we all excused it."

Twain explained to his friend Rev. Dr. Joseph Twichell, "My swearing doesn't mean any more to me, than your sermons do to you."[79]

Whitney continues with the tour around the island:

The scenery is of the most delightful character, bounded inland by magnificent palisades and seaward by the coral fringed ocean. From this point a barrier mountain, reaching far down toward the sea, shuts out the view of the road and leaves the traveler alone with the mountain and the sea. A good road entices him onward, new views of surpassing beauty open on the unwearied eye at every turn; now of a small hamlet in a well-watered valley, now of a stupendous cliff or of a deep bay surf bounded and coral paved.

A waterfall in the exquisite Valley of Hauʻula allure the traveler from the direct road; he wonders at the Mormon colony at Lāʻie, then spurs his horse on over the cattle trod plain of Kahuku. If a conchologist, he tarries on the beach at Waimea to gather the fluted univolvus, that shell-workers use, or, if a theologian, he diverges to the renowned heiau, or heathen temple, where human sacrifices once bleached on the altar.

Fifty miles from Honolulu, by the above route, is Waialua, formerly a populous village, but now noteworthy only for a girls' school and one or two sugar plantations and cattle ranches. From this point, a gradual ascent of eight miles leads the tourist to a pampas alive with cattle and horses. It is deeply scored by ravines and water courses, some

YOU CAN VISIT KUALOA RANCH

The ranch is now a popular tourist spot. Scenes in more than seventy movies have been filmed there, including *Pearl Harbor*, *Godzilla*, and the *Jurassic Park* films, along with TV shows like *Hawaii Five-O*, *Magnum P.I.*, and *Lost*. You can take their movie tours or enjoy many other activities. Kualoa Ranch, 49-560 Kamehameha Highway, Kāneʻohe, HI 96744, (808) 237-7321, kualoa.com.

requiring a detour of a mile or more to cross. As natural wonders they are worth the trip. Lofty mountains, hazy in the distance, bound these great plains, now treeless, but once densely shaded by a forest that was burnt in order to find its sandalwood.

Still ascending, but so gradually that the exhilarating gallop never flags, the summit brings in sight Diamond Head, Honolulu harbor and the panorama of the coast for thirty miles. Now descending we pass, after a few miles, the village of 'Ewa, the famous harbor of Pearl River, rice and sugar plantations, wonderful fish ponds on the distant left, then on again by the famous crater and its salt lake, and over the coral road, past the insane asylum, the reform school, and the prison, and again enter Honolulu and draw up at the hotel, after a ride that has no superior for comfort, ease and charming views, the Hawaiian Islands.[80]

The hotel mentioned was the Hawaiian Hotel, later renamed the Royal Hawaiian Hotel. The Hawaiian government went deeply in debt building it across the street from the 'Iolani Palace, hoping it would attract tourists. It could be considered Hawai'i's first luxury resort hotel and operated from 1872 to 1926. It was demolished a year before the current pink Royal Hawaiian Hotel was built in Waikīkī.

Honored as a Curiosity

Society is a queer medley in this notable missionary, whaling and governmental center. If you get into conversation with a stranger in Honolulu, and experience that natural desire to know what sort of ground you are treading on by finding out what manner of man your stranger is, strike out boldly and address him as "captain." Watch him narrowly, and if you see by his countenance that you are on the wrong tack, ask him where he preaches. It is a safe bet that he is either a missionary or captain of a whaler. I am now personally acquainted with seventy-two captains and ninety-six missionaries. The captains and ministers form one half of the population; the third fourth is composed of common Kānakas and mercantile foreigners and their families, and the final fourth is made up of high officers of the Hawaiian government. And there are just about cats enough for three apiece all around.

A solemn stranger met me in the suburbs yesterday, and said, "Good morning, your reverence. Preach in the stone church yonder, no doubt!"

"No, I don't. I'm not a preacher."

"Really, I beg your pardon, captain. I trust you had a good season. How much oil ..."

"Oil? What do you take me for? I'm not a whaler."

"Oh, I beg a thousand pardons, your Excellency. Major general in the household troops, no doubt? Minister of the Interior, likely? Secretary of War? First Gentleman of the Bedchamber? Commissioner of the Royal ..."

"Stuff, man. I'm no official. I'm not connected in any way with the government."

"Bless my life! Then who the mischief are you? What the mischief are you? and how the mischief did you get here? and where in thunder did you come from?"

"I'm only a private personage—an unassuming stranger—lately arrived from America."

"No! Not a missionary! not a whaler! not a member of his Majesty's government! not even Secretary of the Navy! Ah, Heaven! it is too blissful to be true—alas, I do but dream. And yet that noble, honest countenance—those oblique, ingenuous eyes—that massive head, incapable of ... of ... anything; your hand; give me your hand, bright waif. Excuse these tears. For sixteen weary years I have yearned for a moment like this, and ..."

Here his feelings were too much for him, and he swooned away. I pitied this poor creature from the bottom of my heart. I was deeply moved. I shed a few tears on him, and kissed him for his mother. I then took what small change he had, and "shoved."[81]

[Twain then proceeded to give a very long explanation of whaling slang.]

Proper Etiquette

Every section of our Western Hemisphere seems supplied with a system of technicalities, etiquette, and slang, peculiar to itself. The above chapter is intended to give you a somewhat exaggerated idea of the technicalities of conversation in Honolulu—bred from the great whaling interest which centers here, and naturally infused into the vocabulary of the place. Your favorite California similes were bred from the technicalities of surface mining—those of Washoe [County, Nevada, which includes Reno] come from the profound depths of the "main lead," and those of the Honoluluian were born of whalebone, blubber, and the traffic of the seas.

Perhaps no single individual would use more than two or three of the nautical and whaling phrases I have quoted, in any one conversation, but you might hear all of them in the course of a week, if you talked with a good many people.

And etiquette varies according to one's surroundings. In the mining camps of California, when a friend tenders you a "smile" or invites you to take a "blister," it is etiquette to say, "Here's hoping your dirt'll pan out gay." In Washoe, when you are requested to "put in a blast," or invited to take "your regular pison," etiquette admonishes you to touch glasses and say, "Here's hoping you'll strike it rich in the lower level." And in Honolulu, when your friend the whaler asks you to take a "fid" with him, it is simple etiquette to say, "Here's eighteen hundred barrels, old salt!" But "Drink hearty!" is universal. That is the orthodox reply, the world over.

In San Francisco sometimes, if you offend a man, he proposes to take his coat off, and inquires, "Are you on it?" If you are, you can take your coat off, too. In Virginia City [Nevada], in former times, the insulted party, if he were a true man, would lay his hand gently on his six-shooter and say, "Are you heeled?" But in Honolulu, if Smith offends Jones, Jones asks (with a rising inflection on the last word, which is excessively aggravating), "How much do you weigh?" Smith replies, "Sixteen hundred and forty pound—and you?"

"Two ton to a dot, at a quarter past eleven this forenoon—peel yourself; you're my blubber!"[82]

—⋖—

Twain went into a much more detailed explanation of the pros and cons of the whaling trade that would be of interest to only a whaling historian, so I've left those parts out.

Whaling vessels—primarily from Marblehead, Massachusetts—set out on three- to five-year voyages to the Pacific. Primarily, they hunted right whales—so called because they were considered the *right* whales to catch. Whale oil was used in oil lamps, for streetlights, for heating, in industry, and in soap. It was also used as a lubricant for everything from watches to guns. The baleen in the whale's mouth, which it used to filter the krill out of the water—its sole food—was called "whalebone" and was used to make skirt hoops, corsets, umbrellas, buggy whips, and fishing poles. They also caught sperm whales, as a wax in their heads was used to make smokeless, odorless candles. An extremely valuable substance found in their intestines is still used to make perfume. During the industry's peak year in 1850, they killed more than 8,000 whales.

The whalers stopped to get supplies in Hawai'i for about two weeks every October and March or April until they returned to the East Coast. Their primary ports of call were Honolulu, which had the best ship services, and Lāhainā, which had the best produce. The missionaries became upset because they felt the whalers encouraged drunkenness, prostitution, and lawlessness, while the whalers felt the missionaries were prissy spoilsports. This conflict occasionally descended into violence.

Whaling dominated Hawai'i from 1840 to 1860, with as many as 500 ships spending large amounts of money each year. Up through the 1820s, the chiefs controlled the land, which was farmed by their tenants. Whaling and Western culture shifted commerce to independent farmers. Then it shifted from the farmers to immigrant-owned trading companies, with most of the immigrants being Americans.

Then in 1859, petroleum was discovered in Pennsylvania, replacing whale oil for lamps and heating. The Civil War created a shortage of ships, while the Confederate warship CSS *Shenandoah* captured twenty-eight whalers, sinking twenty-four of them. Then in 1871, thirty whaling ships were caught in ice and lost in the Arctic. In addition, the whale population was in decline. And, as Twain had encouraged in his *Union* articles, San Francisco took over as the main resupply station in the Pacific.

Eventually, whaling was gone, but the whales are still here. Hawai'i has some pilot whales, false killer whales, melon-headed whales, and occasionally orcas that are here year-round, but it's the humpback whales that are the easiest to see.

Whale season runs from December to April when the humpbacks vacation here, using it as their breeding grounds. This is when whale watching becomes all the rage, and many residents become excited about their return.

The Best-Laid Plans of Mice and Twain

[April 3, 1866:]

In a letter to his mother and sister, Twain wrote, after dinner with the Kingdom's future and final king,

> I have been here two or three weeks, and like the beautiful tropical climate better and better. I have ridden on horseback all over this island (O'ahu) in the meantime, and have visited all the ancient battlefields and other places of interest. I have got a lot of human bones which I took from one of these battlefields—I guess I will bring you some of them.
>
> I went with the American Minister [James McBride] and took dinner this evening with the King's Grand Chamberlain [David Kalākaua, who later became king and ruled from 1874 to 1891], who is related to the royal family, and although darker than a mulatto, he has an excellent English education and in manners is an accomplished gentleman.
>
> The dinner was as ceremonious as any I ever attended in California—five regular courses, and five kinds of wine and one of brandy. He is to call for me in the morning with his carriage, and we will visit the King at the Palace—both are good Masons— the King is a Royal Arch Mason. After dinner tonight they called in the "singing girls" and we had some beautiful music, sung in the native tongue.
>
> The steamer I came here in [the *Ajax*] sails tomorrow, and as soon as she is gone I shall sail for the other islands of the group and visit the great volcano [on the Big Island]—the grand wonder of the world. Be gone two months.[83]

In his notebook, he wrote out his plans in more detail:

The original 'Iolani Palace was completed in about 1846. To the right is David Kalākaua in the 1860s.

Go to Hilo [on the east side of the Big Island], see Mr. Porter—use [H. D.] Dunn's name [a travel writer for the *San Francisco Bulletin* who came over on the *Ajax*'s first voyage] as being in Tahiti in '54—go to Kīlauea (Vol[cano]) [on the south side of the Big Island] by advice of Porter—Coming back get Capt. let me ashore at Lāhainā [on the west side of Maui]—there see Mr. [Rev. George] Mason [an Anglican priest in Lāhainā]—use Dunn's name—go to Wailuku [on the north side of Maui] and surrounding plantations and thence to [James] Makee's [Rose Ranch]—come back to Lāhainā and go to [the island of] Lāna'i and see Gibson's Mormonism—thence back to Lāhainā and thence to [the island of] Molokai by boat—thence back to Lāhainā—then to Honolulu—thence around O'ahu—thence to [the island of] Kaua'i—circuit and back to Honolulu— (Hoffslacker on Kaua'i)—On Hawai'i and Maui spend good deal time and make many inquiries.

He made it to Maui and the Big Island but not the other three and not in the order he intended. He probably went to Maui first because that's where an available ship was headed. Then he had to return to O'ahu before going to the Big Island. Traveling between the Islands was very difficult in those days, and going from one to another could take a week. Then you had to wait a week for a return trip. Hurrying to catch a weekly boat ended up causing Twain great pain later on.

Twain wouldn't leave the island for two more weeks. In the meantime, he had an invitation from David Kalākaua, the future king, to visit the ʻIolani Palace the following morning to meet the king. Unfortunately, the king wasn't there.

Inside the Royal Palace

[April 4, 1866:]

The King's palace stands not far from the melancholy Bungalow [a ruined, abandoned mansion], in the center of grounds extensive enough to accommodate a village. The place is surrounded by neat and substantial coral walks, but the gates pertaining to them are out of repair, and so was the soldier who admitted us—or at any rate his uniform was. He was an exception, however, for the native soldiers usually keep their uniforms in good order.

The palace is a large, roomy frame building, and was very well furnished once, though now some of the appurtenances have lost some of their elegance. But the King don't care, I suppose, as he spends nearly all his time at his modest country residence at Waikīkī.

King Kamehameha and one of his wives, Kaʻahumanu III (Kekāuluohi). Captain George Vancouver first met Kamehameha on Captain Cook's third voyage and after meeting him again in 1794 wrote that "I was agreeably surprised in finding that his riper years had softened that stern ferocity which his younger days had exhibited [...]"

(LEFT) JAMES GAY SAWKINS IN 1850 USING A PORTRAIT BY LOUIS CHORIS; (RIGHT) CHARLES B. KING IN THE 1840S USING A SKETCH BY ALFRED THOMAS AGATE

A large apartment in the center of the building serves as the royal council chamber; the walls are hung with life-size portraits of various European monarchs, sent hither as tokens of that cousinly regard which exists between all kings, at least on paper.

To the right is the reception room or hall of audience, and to the left are the library and a sort of ante room or private audience chamber.

In one of these are life-size portraits of old Kamehameha the Great and one or two queens and princes. The old war-horse had a dark brown, broad and beardless face, with native intelligence apparent in it, and something of a crafty expression about the eye; hair white with age and cropped short; in the picture he is clad in a white shirt, long red vest and with the famous feather war-cloak over all.

We were permitted to examine the original cloak. It is very ample in its dimensions, and is made entirely of the small, silky, bright yellow feathers of the man-of-war or tropic bird, closely woven into a strong, coarse netting of grass by a process which promises shortly to become a lost art, inasmuch as only one native, and he an old man, is left who understands it in its highest elegance.

These feathers are rare and costly, because each bird has but two of them—one under each wing—and the birds are not plenty. It required several generations to collect the materials and manufacture this cloak, and had the work been performed in the United States, under our fine army contract system, it would have cost the government more millions of dollars than I can estimate without a large arithmetic and a blackboard.

In old times, when a king put on his gorgeous feather war-cloak, it meant trouble; some other king and his subjects were going to catch it.

We were shown other war-cloaks, made of yellow feathers, striped and barred with broad bands of red ones—fine specimens of barbaric splendor.

The broken spear of a terrible chief who flourished seven hundred years ago, according to the tradition, was also brought out from among the sacred relics of a former age and displayed. It is said that this chieftain stood seven feet high without his boots (he was permanently without them), and was able to snake an enemy out of the ranks with this spear at a distance of forty to sixty and even a hundred feet; and the spear, of hard, heavy, native wood, was once thirty feet long.

The Palace's throne room and the royal bedroom, which were restored using some of the original pieces that had been auctioned off after the overthrow of the monarchy when the Palace was turned into government offices of the Republic of Hawai'i.
AUTHOR'S PHOTOS

The name of this pagan hero is sounded no more from the trumpet of fame, his bones lie none knows where, and the record of his gallant deeds is lost. But he was a "brick," we may all depend upon that. How the wood of the weapon has managed to survive seven centuries of decay, though, is a question calculated to worry the antiquaries.

But it is sunrise, now, and time for honest people to begin to "turn in."[84]

Early Birds Get Worms

[April 5, 1866:]

Twain wrote that comment about turning in at sunrise the following morning because he was a night owl and preferred writing at night, usually sleeping until 11 a.m. or later. Newspaper men often had to work late into the night. In his notebook he wrote, "Rise early, it is the early bird that catches the worm. Don't be fooled by this absurd saw: I once knew a man who tried it. He got up at sunrise and a horse bit him."[85] And toward the end of his visit, he also noted, "Well enough for old folks to rise early, because they have done so many mean things all their lives they can't sleep anyhow."[86]

This matched the island lifestyle. Twain's friend Charles Warren Stoddard wrote in the early 1880s, "As is usually the case with the happy-go-lucky Hawaiian, neither beast nor human appeared until nine o'clock in the day."[87]

Twain loved it. In his notebooks he wrote, "They live in the S.I.—no rush, no worry—merchant goes down to his store like a gentleman at nine—goes home at four and thinks no more of business till next day. Damn San F. style of wearing out life."[88]

[Around April 17, 1866:]

Twain left O'ahu for Maui sometime around April 17.

YOU CAN VISIT THE ROYAL PALACE

'Iolani Palace State Monument, 364 South King Street, Honolulu, HI 96813, (808) 522-0832, iolanipalace.org.

MAUI

A VACATION WITHIN A VACATION

[APRIL 25, 1866 (TWAIN LANDS ON MAUI):]

Since we're not sure which ship he took, we don't know where he landed. He may have left on April 14 aboard the *Mōʻi Keiki*, which landed at Kahului on the north side of the island, or on April 19 aboard the *Nettie Merrill* to Lāhainā on the west side or by some other ship, but most likely he took the *Mary Ellen* to Waiheʻe Landing, which is also on the north side.

Of the three islands he visited, Maui was Mark Twain's favorite, which isn't surprising, as even today it's the favorite for many people. The readers of *Condé Nast Traveler* magazine voted Maui the best island in the world for nineteen years in a row. Elaine and I live on Maui, so we understand that, but I'd like to point out that each of the Hawaiian Islands has its own personality and is wonderful in different ways. They all have their high points and are worth exploring. I find it very sad that he didn't make his planned trip to Kauaʻi. While we feel Maui is the best island to live on, Kauaʻi is the best one to visit, so we take most of our vacations there.

Twain spent five weeks on Maui researching the sugar industry and just enjoying the island. Unfortunately, he didn't write much about it except for a lot of statistics and business information that is now long out of date, so I haven't included that here.

Since Twain didn't write much about his stay, it's difficult to trace his steps. But some information can be gleaned from external sources. He appears to have

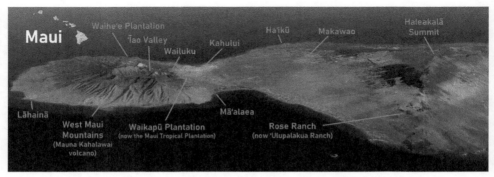

AUTHOR'S GRAPHIC, MODIFIED FROM GOOGLE, DATA LDEO-COLUMBIA, NSF, NOAA, DATA MBARI, DATA SIO, NOAA, US NAVY, NGA, GEBCO, DATA SOEST/UHM, DATA USGS, LANDSAT/COPERNICUS, MAXAR TECHNOLOGIES, TERRA METRICS, WITH AN INSERTED ISLANDS SATELLITE IMAGE FROM THE HAWAIʻI STATE OFFICE OF PLANNING

The Wailuku Sugar Mill in 1865—the year before Twain arrived—with the West Maui Mountains and the entrance to 'Iao Valley in the background. This was the most productive sugar mill in Hawai'i at that time. Twain stayed in the plantation's boardinghouse, which would be built on the far side of the vacant field between the mill and the long building in the foreground.

spent most of his time in Wailuku. At the Wailuku Sugar Plantation, he stayed for two weeks in the plantation's boardinghouse on the corner of Market Street and 'Olu Drive with the plantation bookkeeper—a man named Tallant—and his wife, who probably ran the boardinghouse. Twain later described Tallant as the oldest man on the island. It's also said that part of the time, he had a cottage all to himself. And according to Goodale Armstrong, Twain also stayed with him and his family while in Wailuku. Armstrong said he and Twain knew each other from their days in Virginia City.

When Twain's cousin Mildred Clemens visited Maui in 1916 and 1934, the old-timers told her that Twain usually wore a long linen duster that reminded them of the holokū dresses (Mother Hubbards) worn by Hawaiian women. They said he rode his horse all over Maui with the tails of his duster flapping in the wind, much like a female pā'ū rider. While his duster made the locals think of a man in drag, to us, he probably would have looked more of a Wild West movie gunfighter.

Hawaiian women riding horseback were called pāʻū riders because of their flowing pāʻū skirts. Unlike foreign women, they never rode sidesaddle, which many Americans at the time considered scandalous. This Honolulu pāʻū rider was Adele Kauilani Robinson in either 1910 or 1913.
RAY JEROME BAKER

Doctor Carl Andrews told her that Twain would appear in the garden outside of his cottage each morning wearing his duster. The local women began to suspect that it was the only garment he had on. To prove the point, one morning while watering next door, they turned the hose on him, pretending it was an accident. They apologized profusely, and Twain never suspected them, but they apparently proved their point.

In 1897, E. S. Goodhue interviewed Goodale Armstrong. Dr. Goodhue was a surgeon who lived on Kaua'i, but he was in Wailuku when he interviewed Armstrong, who was then a clerk of the Second Circuit Court on Maui.

"Yes, I knew Mark Twain, or Sam Clemens as we called him then," said Mr. Armstrong, as he clipped some leaves off a blood-red begonia. "I have never told the story for publication, because most of those interested were living.

"Sam lived in Wailuku for several weeks and boarded at our house. My wife was alive then, and my children were with me, but they are all gone," continued the old man, looking at his flowers, "and these are all I have left. Sam is an old man, too.

"It was in 1867 [1866], I think, and we lived down at the corner of the road by the old mill. There were no streets.

"I had met Mr. Clemens in Virginia City, where he lived. He was very careless in his dress, but I am told that his wife has changed all that. [Twain married in 1870.]

"Of course he had that peculiar Missouri drawl they talk about. He rode all over the country horseback, dressed in a linen duster which reached nearly down to his feet.

"This was enough to ruin the pride of any horse, and judging from what Sam has written about the horses he had, some of them were badly spoiled.

"It is reported here that he went about with only his duster on, wearing it as the natives do their holokūs, but I never saw him out with less than a pair of drawers.

"An old native, who died here lately, let Sam have a number of the horses he rode. He would ride down to the house, get his supper, then come out on the veranda, and, placing his feet alongside mine on the railing, smoke and talk for hours.

"One evening he seemed worried, and smoked harder than ever; then, with a dig of his foot, said, 'Damn him! he did me up, but a time may come when he'll be where I am, and I'll be writing easy checks.'

"He wasn't a bit mad when he said this, though there was fire in his eye, and he didn't say who the chap was that cut him up so.

"Sam liked to ride, and used to go a great deal with my wife's sister, who was then a young lady, and mighty fine looking if I do say so. I sometimes thought Sam was inclined to be soft, and I think that on one occasion he came near proposing. At any rate, my sister-in-law thought he did, but you can't always tell about the ways of a man with a maid. Being human and a man, Sam probably didn't know himself just how far he could trust himself with a pretty girl. For he hadn't a red cent—not even decent clothes.

"I wonder if he remembers the time one of the girls cut off about three inches from the bottom of his duster! [Note: That wouldn't have affected it much. More likely, she cut off three feet.]

"I'm sorry we didn't have a snapshot of him, but in those days photography wasn't out of the hands of experts.

"Mr. Clemens was writing for the *San Francisco Call*, the *Bulletin*, *Alta California*, and the *Sacramento Daily Union*. But he didn't get much pay, and was often hard up. Being generous himself, he wasn't bashful about asking for a loan. I've let him have many a half-dollar for cigars.

"He would write over at the other house, where he slept, until two or three o'clock in the morning, then sleep late next day. [. . .]

"Some say Sam sowed his 'wild oats' here. If so, I never saw any of his growing."[1]

The "other house" Armstrong refers to was probably his previous house—the one Twain stayed at—as Armstrong was living in a different one at the time of the interview. But it appears Dr. Goodhue may have been staying in this other house, as he wrote, "I am sitting in a roomy bungalow, under a mango tree, in a house that was probably old when the author of *Huckleberry Finn* sat writing in it. He slept here during several weeks, part of the night and a half of the next day, as was his wont, using this table as I am doing now." Unfortunately, Goodhue didn't mention where this house was located.

An ad for Bismark Sta-
bles that was in Henry
Whitney's *The Tourists'
Guide to the Hawaiian
Islands* (1895).

Twain said he didn't do much writing while on Maui, but he did take a lot of notes, especially regarding the sugar industry. His Maui notebook is now lost, which is regrettable, as it no doubt contained some interesting information.

When he wasn't collecting information and exploring the island, he spent his time loafing, smoking, and socializing. In those days before there were electronic devices to captivate people's attention, people would gather at someone's house in the evenings and entertain each other by telling stories, playing games, and singing together. Of course, Twain was a master at telling stories.

One place he enjoyed going was to the house of missionary Rev. William Alexander. The reverend's granddaughter Mary Alexander recalled, "He was often welcomed to supper at the Alexander home, and he and Mr. Alexander had jolly times together. He used to say that he thought too much of Mr. Alexander to put him into any of his books."[2]

Twain hung out with a wide variety of people. Another of those interviewed by Dr. Goodhue was Bill Goodness, who owned the Bismarck Stables, where Twain probably got his horses.

> Me, I knowed Sam Clemings. Higbee, his pardner, he come to Hawai'i with me. He tol' me Sam he was too pesky lazy to fetch the water to wash dishes when it come his turn in the mornin'. They "bached" it, you see, in a little cabin onto their claim [in California or Nevada]. But they never realized nothin'. Sam was too lazy to hussle.

Lāhainā's Front Street in 1912 looking south toward where the bottom photograph was taken. The lower picture shows Lāhainā's waterfront north of the harbor as seen from where Kamehameha's compound and the Brick Palace used to be.
(TOP) RAY JEROME BAKER; (BOTTOM) AUTHOR'S PHOTO

Me, I seen him lots of times—slim and sort of hump-back lookin', long nose like yourn, and downright far-seein' eye.

He'd walk around with his hands in his pockets, an' fer the life of me I couldn't tell him no lies. He'd wrote some fer the papers that beats mine.[3]

Lāhainā's Curious Character

Speaking of lies, it's not known when or how many times Twain visited Lāhainā, but he wrote a lengthy piece about Francis Oudinot, whom he met in public room there.[4] Oudinot was originally from Kentucky and was well known around Maui as a teller of tall tales and as an inveterate and compulsive liar. Calling him Markiss, Twain described him as an exceedingly annoying person and goes on at great length demonstrating it. Some of Oudinot's tall tales as retold by Twain became very popular, but these were about California—not Hawai'i. Twain said that when Oudinot died, because he left a suicide note, no one would believe he was dead because the note had to be a lie. On discovering he really was dead, they decided he must have gone insane since he wouldn't have told the truth if he were sane. This was the punch line to the Markiss story.

The environs of Lāhainā are like a garden. It would be difficult to find a soil more fertile, or a people who could turn it to greater advantage. [. . .] Every cabin has its enclosure, and every enclosure is well taken care of; it seems to suffice for the wants of the family. [. . .]

The space cultivated by the natives of Lāhainā is about three leagues in length, and one in its greatest breadth. Beyond this, all is dry and barren; everything recalls the image of desolation. Nevertheless, the soil and its resources are the same; whence therefore this apparently culpable neglect? It is a natural consequence of the mode of reasoning adopted by these people; they have all that is necessary at hand, what advantage would there be in seeking superfluities from afar? . . . Superfluities are thrown away on these people. Twenty acres of land will not produce them a better dinner than their square of kalo.

—JACQUES ARAGO, FRENCH WRITER, ARTIST, AND EXPLORER, 1819.[5] [THIS WAS BEFORE LĀHAINĀ BECAME A MAJOR WHALING PORT. THEN THEY HAD TO GROW FOOD TO SUPPLY ALL THE SHIPS.]

Unfortunately, Twain didn't write about Lāhainā, but he hinted that while in Lāhainā, he stayed with Maui's sheriff, who was also Lāhainā's postmaster, custom-house officer, and tax collector of the island of Lānaʻi. He also said that at one point, "we presently hired some natives and an outrigger canoe or two, and went out to overlook a grand surf-bathing [surfing] contest."[6] And in his tale about Oudinot, he makes it sound like he was there on four occasions, each a couple of weeks apart, but this may be an exaggeration for the story, although two of these could be stops the interisland schooner made on his way to and from the Big Island.

In his *The Hawaiian Guide Book for Travelers* (1875), Henry Whitney wrote this about Lāhainā:

> It is built in a grove of coconut, breadfruit, mango, tamarind, orange and other trees, which grow to the very ocean verge, whose rocky shore and sandy beach are ever fringed by the foam of the playful breakers that often rise into lofty rollers, the terror of any landing boat, but glorious playthings of the daring surf riders, many of whom live here and are frequently seen sporting in the breakers. For two miles along the coast the white dwellings seem to grow out of the trees, while the whole is bounded by an emerald border of rustling sugarcane. The background of the picture is grand in mountain majesty, rent into deep cliffs when the foot prints of Almighty power trod here in earthquake and volcanic eruption. The contrasts are violent, abrupt, prompt and worth coming afar to see. They are all distinctly seen from the sea, but when viewed from the summit above Lāhaināluna [the missionary school] in the afternoon, as the sunlight varies its brilliancy with the approach of delightful evening, the scene is far more beautiful. [. . .]
>
> In Hawaiian early history Lāhainā, was the city of the King, and the chief capital of Hawaiʻi [from 1820 to 1845]. Its harbor has been greatly renowned in the palmy days of the nearly extinct whale fishery. Its sheltered roadstead held at one time half a hundred ships with room for a thousand more. Its narrow streets held scores of shops and sailors' homes, and it was provided with a bethel, a consulate,

and a U.S. hospital. Now, Honolulu is the metropolis. The royal palace [Kamehameha's Brick Palace], 120 by 40 feet with its huge surrounding veranda has tumbled down; the old fort has been removed; the consulate, hospital and the land-shark sailor homes have all been abandoned, and Lāhainā is in decay. [. . .]

Lāhainā has no hotel or public place of entertainment; yet for a very reasonable stipend furnished dwellings can be obtained by the day or week for an individual, a family or a party; while meals can be obtained of Chinese cooks at fair rates by the day or week. [. . .]

There is not much to interest the traveler in this place.[7]

Today, travelers will find much of interest, and Lāhainā is now a very popular tourist spot.

YOU CAN VISIT THE LĀHAINĀ PRISON

If you regret not being able to see the long-gone Honolulu prison, you can hang out at the Lāhainā prison, which Twain may have visited (unofficially). In the 1830s, Lāhainā was the largest town in Hawai'i. The 1850s were the peak years of the whaling trade, and it was in the early part of this decade that the prison was built. Things were a bit more casual here than at most prisons. The inmates spent a lot of time sitting around the courtyard. Families could visit and bring food. And the prisoners could be hired out to employers for various jobs. When someone asked the warden what happened if they didn't return at night, he responded, "By golly, we lock 'em out!"

Hale Pa'ahao Lāhainā Prison, 187 Prison St., Lāhainā. Mailing address: Lāhainā Restoration Foundation, 120 Dickenson St., Lāhainā, HI 96761, (808) 661-3262, info@lahainarestoration.org, lahainarestoration.org/hale-paahao-prison.

Fields of Sugarcane

Since the main reason the *Sacramento Daily Union* sent Twain to Hawai'i was to report on the sugar industry, he spent considerable time researching it.

Hawai'i's first export was sandalwood, primarily to China. This was when Kamehameha was still alive. The kingdom ran out of sandalwood right about the time the Islands became the whaling center of Pacific. As whaling began to fail, sugar arose to take its place. Twain wrote in great detail about the sugar industry of the 1860s and packed his article full of statistics. Most of it is pretty mind-numbing, but here is one bit:

> The High Chief of Sugardom
>
> I have visited Haleakalā, Kīlauea, Wailuku Valley, the Petrified Cataracts, the Pathway of the Great Hog God [three of these are on the Big Island]—in a word, I have visited all the principal wonders of the island, and now I come to speak of one which, in its importance to America, surpasses them all. A land which produces 6,000, 8,000, 10,000, 12,000, yea, even 13,000 pounds of sugar to the acre on unmanured soil!
>
> There are precious few acres of unmanured ground in Louisiana—none at all, perhaps—which will yield 2,500 pounds of sugar; there is not an unmanured acre under cultivation in the Sandwich Islands which yields less. This country is the king of the sugar world, as far as astonishing productiveness is concerned.[8]

Initially, Twain favored the commercial exploitation of Hawai'i and strongly encouraged it—after all, the *Sacramento Daily Union* sent him there to write about the business prospects and to promote them—but this changed as he fell in love with the Islands and came to understand them better. He also came to understand the changes that were about to take place.

The rise of the sugar industry was something of a revolution that completely changed Hawai'i. While it brought considerable wealth to the Islands, primarily for a few elites, it was the biggest nail in the coffin of the Hawaiians' subsistence way of life and of their independence. It brought about the rise of the Big Five corporations, which essentially ruled Hawai'i for almost a century, and led to the overthrow of the Kingdom and it's being absorbed into the United States.

The Hawaiians had been cultivating sugarcane about 1,000 years before Captain Cook arrived. Cook noted fields of it near the Hawaiians' houses. In 1802, the Chinese began producing it on Lāna'i. The first plantation appeared at Kōloa, Kaua'i, in 1835. The redistribution of land in the Great Māhele of 1848 enabled individuals and corporations to amass great tracts of land for sugar cultivation, but it was during the Civil War that the sugar industry really began to take off. The war halted sugar cultivated in the South from being sold in the North, so Hawai'i became a major source for sugar.

When the war ended, American tariffs cut into the sugar profits. A free trade agreement with the United States in the 1870s helped save Hawai'i's economy, which was struggling as the whaling industry diminished, but it essentially removed Hawai'i from the world market, establishing the United States as its dominant trading partner. This was very controversial, as some Americans—especially those in the sugar industry, which was dominated by American missionaries and their sons—saw it as a step toward annexation, while this was strongly opposed by the Hawaiians as well as many Americans.

In order to renew the agreement, American businessmen—primarily sugar related—used the threat of assassination to force the king to sign away most of his authority with the Bayonet Constitution. They also forced him to give the United States control over Pearl Harbor. When the subsequent queen tried to restore that authority in the early 1880s, the businessmen, with the aid of the US military, overthrew the Kingdom. Because the coup was deemed illegal at the time, the United States initially refused to accept Hawai'i as part of the United States, but after a conservative administration entered the White House, they were able to make Hawai'i a territory. (A century later, the US government reconfirmed the coup was illegal and apologized.)

The sugar industry also changed the cultural makeup of the Islands. It was a very labor-intensive industry and required a lot of field hands. Initially, these were Hawaiians. As the industry was dominated by missionaries and their sons, they justified this by saying the work was good for building their characters. As a letter to King Kamehameha III signed by seven missionaries, including Samuel Castle and Amos Cooke—the founders of one of the Big Five corporations—put it, "As it is true that indolence begets vice, so it is true that industry promotes virtue. All successful efforts taken to produce industry by proper means tend to promote virtue and must be beneficial to that people on whom they are bestowed."[9]

But things didn't turn out that way. For instance, Henry Baldwin was the son of a missionary and cofounder of one of the Big Five corporations. A chemist who worked for him said he couldn't understand how the actions of the "deeply religious" Baldwin, "like those of many zealots, contradicted the religion in which he professed to believe. An example of this was his unrelenting attitude toward the indentured labor force." His workers' contracts contained a clause "which in effect kept the workers indefinitely in slavery. Just how his religion countenanced this attitude I couldn't understand."[10]

Initially, the missionaries wanted the Hawaiians to become small, independent commercial farmers, but this never happened, largely because much of their land was snatched up by sugar plantations and ranchers. The new economic system and changes in labor conditions put an end to subsistence farming and forced many Hawaiians from their land. The decimation of the Hawaiian population by disease also took a severe toll and contributed to the end of their traditional lifestyle. Some were encouraged to grow sugarcane, but they soon found themselves in debt, forcing them to surrender their land.

For many Hawaiians, the primary job open to them was field labor. This was very difficult backbreaking work that was tough to sustain for long periods of time. In return, they received poverty-level wages. As the Hawaiian population decreased and the plantations grew, the sugar corporations looked overseas for cheap labor. They first brought in Chinese on contracts that required them to work at three dollars a month for five years. When they finished working off their contract, they set up businesses of their own. To keep up with the demand for labor and changing conditions, they kept switching countries, bringing in hundreds of thousands of workers—Chinese (1852–1897), Portuguese (1878–1913), Japanese (1897–1907), Puerto Ricans (1900–1921), Koreans (1903–1905), Spaniards (1907–1913), Filipinos (1907–1946), and others—creating the multicultural melting pot we have today.

As with all immigrants, who seem alien when they first arrive, they eventually blended in with their adopted communities and became outstanding members of Hawai'i's society. Now Hawai'i has one of the most diverse populations in the world, and people, for the most part, are very accepting of each other. I have seen nothing like it anywhere else. There is still some racism and prejudices here but not like on the mainland or in other countries.

Here, having a varied population actually makes life more interesting. It's easy to learn about and enjoy the better aspects of other cultures. You can even get saimin and kalo pies at McDonald's. And the Chinese lion and dragon dancers are definitely worth seeing. Hawai'i is moving toward having the best of all worlds. This was one of the positive things to arise from sugar.

By the 1950s and 1960s, the sugar industry began to fail because sugar could be produced cheaper elsewhere. Plantation land began being turned into residential subdivisions, resorts, and shopping centers. Most of the plantations closed by the 1990s, and the last one shut down in 2016 on Maui. Pineapple exports are also almost gone. Now, far and away Hawai'i's largest crop is genetically modified corn, which is grown to be sold as seeds to farmers.

Tropical Plantations

While on Maui, Twain visited many of its plantations. One of these was Rose Ranch (now called 'Ulupalakua Ranch), which, with 1,000 acres, was the largest sugar plantation in Hawai'i, although the Wailuku Plantation was the most productive. It was owned by James Makee, a former whaling captain who was severely injured in 1843 when, after denying his steward shore leave in Lāhainā, the steward hit him twice in the head with an axe. After recovering, he remained in Hawai'i and bought 'Ulupalakua, renaming it Rose Ranch. It was up on the slope of Haleakalā five miles from Mākena Harbor (now Mākena Landing) in south Maui. His remote plantation was equipped with guest cottages, a tennis court, a billiard room, a bowling alley, and a flock of peacocks.

Makee's son was married to the sister of Twain's friend Charles Warren Stoddard, from whom Twain no doubt had a very warm letter of introduction. Stoddard might have even been there at that time since later in the month, the two got together to journey to Kīlauea, the Big Island's most active volcano.

Seven years later, Twain mentioned Rose Ranch when discussing sugar in an 1873 article for the *New York Tribune*.

The most of the belt of sloping land that borders the sea and rises toward the bases of the mountains, is rich and fertile. There are only 200,000 acres of this productive soil, but only think of its capabilities! In Louisiana, 200,000 acres of sugar land would only yield 50,000 tons of sugar per annum, and possibly not so much; but in the Sandwich Islands, you could get at least 400,000 tons out of it. This is a good, strong statement, but it is true, nevertheless. Two and a half tons to the acre is a common yield in the Islands; three and a half tons is by no means unusual; five tons is frequent; and I can name the man who took fifty tons of sugar from seven acres of ground, in one season.

This cane was on the mountainside, 2,500 feet above sea level, and it took it three years to mature. Address your inquiries to Capt. Mckee, Island of Maui, S. I. Few plantations are stuck up in the air like that, and so twelve months is ample time for the maturing of cane down there.

And I would like to call attention to two or three exceedingly noteworthy facts. For instance, there you do not hurry up and cut your cane when it blossoms, but you just let it alone and cut it when you choose— no harm will come of it. And you do not have to keep an army of hands to plant in the planting season, grind in the grinding season, and rush in frantically and cut down the crop when a frost threatens. Not at all. There is no hurry. You run a large plantation with but a few hands, because you plant pretty much when you please, and you cut your cane and grind it when it suits your convenience. There is no frost, and the longer the cane stands the better it grows. Sometimes—often, in fact— part of your gang are planting a field, another part are cutting the crop from an adjoining field, and the rest are grinding at the mill.

You only plant once in three years, and you take off two ratoon crops without replanting. You may keep on taking off ratoon crops about as long as you please, indeed; every year the bulk of the cane will be smaller, but the juice will grow regularly denser and richer, and so you are all right. I know of one lazy man who took off sixteen rattoon crops without replanting!

What fortunes those planters made during our war, when sugar went up into the twenties! It had cost them about ten or eleven cents a pound, delivered in San Francisco, and all charges paid.

Now if anyone desires to know why these planters would probably like to be under our flag, the answer is simple: We make them pay us a duty of four cents a pound on refined sugars at present; brokerage, freights and handling (two or three times), costs three cents more; rearing the cane, and making the sugar, is an item of five cents more—total, 12 cents a pound, or within a cent of it, anyhow. And today refined sugar is only worth about 12 1/2 cents (wholesale) in our markets. Profit—none worth mentioning. But if we were to annex the Islands and do away with that crushing duty of four cents a pound, some of those heavy planters who can hardly keep their heads above water now, would clear $75,000 a year and upward. Two such years would pay for their plantations, and all their stock and machinery. It is so long since I was in the Islands that I feel doubtful about swearing that the United States duties on their sugars was four cents a pound, but I can swear it was not under three.[11]

YOU CAN VISIT 'ULUPALAKUA RANCH

'Ulupalakua Ranch abandoned sugarcane in 1883 after a severe drought, but it's still a cattle ranch, a vineyard, and the MauiWine Winery, complete with a wine tasting room, gift shop, and deli. 'Ulupalakua Ranch, 14815 Pi'ilani Highway, Kula, HI 96790. Mailing address: HC 1 Box 953, Kula, HI 96790, (808) 878-6058, ulupalakuaranch.com and mauiwine.com.

[May 3, 1866:]

Twain set off from 'Ulupalakua Ranch in the south for the Waihe'e Plantation in the north—a distance of twenty-five miles—but he didn't make it. When it got dark, he had to stop at the Waikapū Plantation (now called the Maui Tropical Plantation) for the night.

That same evening, down near the equator, a ship named the *Hornet* caught fire and sank, leaving its crew adrift in three small boats. Twain would later write extensively of this incident after one of the boats with its starving seamen came ashore on the Big Island. It was perhaps his only major news story. More on that later.

A Horse, Marriage, and a Greased Pig
[May 4, 1866:]

The following day, Twain made it to the Wailuku Plantation, and that night, he wrote a letter to his mother and sister describing his movements and intentions.

―⤎

Eleven o'clock at night: This is the infernalest darkest country when the moon don't shine. I stumbled and fell over my horse's lariat a minute ago and hurt my leg, and so I must stay here tonight. I went to 'Ulapalakua Plantation (25 miles) a few days ago, and returned yesterday afternoon, to Mr. Cornwell's (Waikapū Plantation) and staid all night (it is two miles from here) and came here this evening to Mr. [Sherman] Peck's, (Honolulu

YOU CAN VISIT THE MAUI TROPICAL PLANTATION

The Maui Tropical Plantation features botanical gardens, a duck pond, a zip line, a restaurant, gift shops, coffee roasting, and a fruit and vegetable stand. Maui Tropical Plantation, 1670 Honoapi'ilani Highway, Waikapū, HI 96793, (808) 244-7643, mauitropicalplantation.com.

friends of mine) [a senior partner at Charles Brewer and Co., which had a controlling interest in the Waikapū, Wailuku, and Waiheʻe Plantations, in addition to an interest in Rose Ranch], and took tea, and we have been playing seven-up and whist (plenty of ladies in his family), but I only hitched that horse, intending to ride to the further sea-shore, (this is a narrow peninsula in the middle of the island), and stay all night at the Waiheʻe Plantation, five miles from here, but as I said, I couldn't even see the horse it was so dark when I came out of Mr. Peck's a while ago, and so I fell and hurt my leg.

I got the same leg hurt last week. I said I hadn't got hold of a spirited horse since I had been on the island, and one of the proprietors loaned me a big, vicious colt. He was altogether too spirited. I went to tighten the cinch before mounting him, when he let out with his left and kicked me across a ten-acre lot. A native rubbed and doctored me so well that I was able to stand on my feet in half an hour.

It was then half after four, and I had an appointment to go seven miles and get a girl and take her to a card party at five. If I hadn't had a considerable weakness for her she might have gone to the devil under the circumstances, but as it was, I went after her.

I got even with the colt. It was a very rough road, but I got there at five minutes past five, and then had to quit, my leg hurt me so. She was ready and her horse was saddled, but we didn't go. But I had a jolly time—played cribbage nearly all night. If I were worth even $5,000 I would try to marry that plantation—but as it is, I resign myself to a long and useful bachelordom as cheerfully as I may.

I had a pleasant time of it at ʻUlupalakua Plantation. It is three thousand feet [300 m] above the level of the sea (in plain sight from here, twenty-five miles [40 km]) two pretty and accomplished girls in the family and the plantation yields an income of $60,000 a year—chance for some enterprising scrub. [That's $15 million in today's dollars.]

I have been clattering around among the plantations for three weeks, now, and next week I am going to visit the extinct crater of Mount Haleakalā—the largest in the world. It is ten miles to the foot of the mountain. It rises ten thousand feet above the valley; the crater is twenty-nine miles in circumference and a thousand feet deep [actually 10,023 feet high (3 km), about twenty miles (32 km) in circumference, and 2,720 feet deep (830 m)]. Seen from the summit, the city of St. Louis would look like a picture in the bottom of it.

As soon as I get back from Haleakalā (pronounced Hally-ekka-lah [actually Hallay-AH-kah-lah],) I will sail for Honolulu again and from thence to the Island of Hawai'i (pronounced HAH-WY-ye,) to see the greatest active volcano in the world—that of Kīlauea (pronounced Kee-low-WAY-ah)—and from thence back to San Francisco—and then, doubtless, to the States. I have been on this trip two months, and it will probably be two more before I get back to California.[12]

—<

[May 7, 1866:]

Twain probably made it to the Waihe'e Plantation but was back at the Wailuku Plantation by May 7, where he wrote a letter to his "first, and oldest, and dearest friend," steamboat captain William Bowen. He and Bowen had attended school together in Hannibal, Missouri, and on two occasions, they had piloted a riverboat together in 1859. The characters Tom Sawyer and Joe Harper in *Tom Sawyer* and *Huckleberry Finn* were partly inspired by Bowen.

—<

Dear Bill,

I have been mad at you so long [possibly from a disagreement while piloting or regarding a loan he made to Bowen in 1861] that the old anger has about spent itself and I begin to feel friendly again. But you ought to have your damned neck broken anyhow, my boy.

I expected to be in the States long before this but things fell out otherwise. I contracted with the *Sacramento Union* to go wherever they chose and correspond for a few months. And I had a sneaking notion that they would start me east—but behold how fallible is human judgment!—they sent me to the Sandwich Islands. I look for a recall by the next mail, though, because I have written them that I cannot go all over the eight inhabited islands of the group in less than five months and do credit to myself and them, and I don't want to spend so much time. I have been here two months and yet have only "done" the island of O'ahu and part of this island of Maui . . .

and it is going to take me two weeks more to finish this one and at least a month to "do" the island of Hawai'i and the great volcanoes—and by that time, surely, I can hear from them.

But I have had a gorgeous time of it so far. I wish you and Sam [Bowen's younger brother] were here. We would sail from island to island for a year and have a merry hell of a time. We would get more invitations from sea captains. Honolulu is a great stopping point for ships, and during the month I was there I was invited to go to every blamed place on the habitable globe, I think. The last was from the captain of a fine ship—he was going round the world—and if either of you bilks had been here I would have thrown up my berth and gone with him.

I have seen a fellow here that you and I knew in Hannibal in childhood—named [Daniel] Martin—he was a carpenter; he came here busted a year ago and called himself the Wizard of the East [and Martin the Wizard] and gave a sleight of hand entertainment—and it was the damnedest sleight of hand entertainment you ever heard of. He tried to shoot a pocket handkerchief into a closed oyster-can, and he pretty nearly shot the damned head off of a Kanaka spectator. None of his apparatus would work.

He had a learned pig, which he gave out could speak seven languages too—a striped learned pig. He told me he caught that hog in the extinct crater of Haleakalā, 10,000 feet above the level of the sea, where the son of a seahorse had been running wild for three generations; he brought him down here into the valley, shaved him close, painted stripes on him with iodine and then greased him, and advertised that he would give any person in the audience ten dollars who would come into the ring and catch the pig and hold him two minutes.

A big brawny Kanaka and a gigantic Missourian each got the hog by a hind leg, and the brute held on, notwithstanding the grease, but the hog turned and bit a square meal out of the Kanaka and made him let go, and then started, and took the bold Missourian straight through the audience, squealing, and upsetting people and benches, and raising more hell, and scaring women to death, and broke for high ground on Haleakalā, and neither he nor the Missourian were ever heard of afterwards—and Martin wasn't for some time, for in the melee he took his little cash-box and "shoved."

He says he likes to live here "because," says he, "when I'm busted I can go through a Kanaka lord of the soil; and when I can't do that, I can always rig a purchase to swindle one of them damned missionaries." I am of the opinion that Mr. Martin is a brick [meaning he's the best].

I wouldn't write you so much about Martin, only I haven't anything else to write about—except the Islands, and that is cash, you know, and goes in the *Union*.[13]

—⚡—

On one of his visits to Lāhainā, he rode horseback up over the side of the West Maui Mountains—which are actually a single mountain—on his way to either Waikapū or Wailuku. This trail rises up almost 1,600 feet (nearly 550 m) and comes back down near the small port of Maʻalaea. Twain's friend Henry Whitney described it as "a dusty and fatiguing ride of four or five hours" but warned that one occasionally had to "look out that the bridle does not blow off the horse, or the hat and coat from his rider."[14]

"Maʻalaea, an invention of the devil," wrote the author—and Twain's friend from San Francisco—Charles Warren Stoddard, "a necessary evil, and perhaps the least of two of them; for if one bound for Waihae [agricultural] lands on this side of the island [Maui's central valley], he may, indeed, enter the paradise of Lāhainā [by ship]; but after that follow the ascent and descent of a mountain trail more bleak, windy and treacherous than any I wot of elsewhere in this much traveled globe."[15]

(Remember Stoddard's name. He was a good friend of Twain's from his San Francisco days who also became a well-known author in the late 1800s. He will reappear periodically throughout this book. He and Twain visited the volcano Kīlauea together, and he also acted as Twain's secretary when Twain was lecturing in the United Kingdom. They remained good friends throughout their lives.)

Back to Stoddard's trail from hell: I've twice hiked the upper branch of this trail to the peak from the Maʻalaea side, and it is steep and rocky. I wouldn't want to ride a horse over it. It is very windy, and there are now thirty-four power-generating wind turbines along the ridge. Once when I was there, the rain was flying sideways. While the trail is a bit bleak—similar to desert—the view is wonderful. And Maʻalaea is now a rather charming harbor with a wonderful aquarium.

In one of his lectures, Twain spoke of the trail, saying,

> I once rode over a mountain in Maui with a white man whose horse was so lean and spiritless and worthless that he could not be persuaded or spurred out of a walk, and he kept going to sleep, besides—at least he seemed to. But the man said that when he got to Maʻalaea Bay he would find one of his own horses there—a blooded animal that could outstrip the wind.
>
> He got his blooded animal, and gave the slow horse to a Kanaka boy and told him to follow. Then he put his blooded steed to his utmost speed to show him off. But the Kanaka, without spur or whip, or scarcely any appearance of urging, sailed by us on the old plug, and stayed ahead, and in eight miles he beat us out of sight. I never could understand how those savages managed to make those wretched horses travel so. They are wild, free riders, and perfectly at home in the saddle—they call it a saddle, a little vile English spoon of a thing with a girth that never is tight enough to touch the horse and sometimes without any girth at all. With their loose ideas, they never cinch a Californian's horse tight enough to suit him.[16]

YOSEMITE OF THE PACIFIC
The Impressive ʻIao Valley

While Twain was staying in Wailuku, he visited ʻIao Valley and was very impressed. Wailuku sits at the entrance to this five-mile-long, two-mile-wide, 3,000-foot-deep valley (8-km-long, 3-km-wide, 900-m-deep valley). The valley cuts into the West Maui Mountains, which are actually the single volcano Mauna Kahalawai. Some say Mark Twain dubbed it the "Yosemite of Hawaiʻi," but he didn't. The earliest mention of that appellation I've found is from 1892.

—✒—

I still remember, with a sense of indolent luxury, a picnicking excursion up a romantic gorge there, called the ʻIao Valley. The trail lay along the edge of a brawling stream in the bottom of the gorge—a shady route, for it was well roofed with the verdant domes of forest trees. Through openings in

'Īao Valley in an illustration from the first edition of Mark Twain's *Roughing It* and as it is today. The 'Īao Needle looks like a pinnacle, but it's actually the end of a tall, thin ridge.
(RIGHT) AUTHOR'S PHOTO

the foliage we glimpsed picturesque scenery that revealed ceaseless changes and new charms with every step of our progress. Perpendicular walls from one to three thousand feet high guarded the way, and were sumptuously plumed with varied foliage, in places, and in places swathed in waving ferns. Passing shreds of cloud trailed their shadows across these shining fronts, mottling them with blots; billowy masses of white vapor hid the turreted

YOU CAN VISIT THE 'ĪAO NEEDLE

There are two parks in 'Īao Valley, and both are worth seeing. Kepaniwai Park and Heritage Gardens honors Maui's multicultural history. The 'Īao Valley State Monument features the noted landmark—the 'Īao Needle. 'Īao Valley State Monument, Division of State Parks, Maui District Office, 54 South High St., Rm. 101, Wailuku, HI 96793, (808) 984-8109, dlnr.hawaii.gov/dsp/parks/maui/iao-valley-state-monument.

summits, and far above the vapor swelled a background of gleaming green crags and cones that came and went, through the veiling mists, like islands drifting in a fog; sometimes the cloudy curtain descended till half the canyon wall was hidden, then shredded gradually away till only airy glimpses of the ferny front appeared through it—then swept aloft and left it glorified in the sun again.

Now and then, as our position changed, rocky bastions swung out from the wall, a mimic ruin of castellated ramparts and crumbling towers clothed with mosses and hung with garlands of swaying vines, and as we moved on they swung back again and hid themselves once more in the foliage. Presently a verdure-clad needle of stone, a thousand feet high, stepped out from behind a corner, and mounted guard over the mysteries of the valley.[17]

Maui's Volcanoes
[April 26, 1866:]

Jumping back in time a week or so from Twain's pig letter, Twain sent the following note to brothers William and Warren Kimball, who had sailed to Hawai'i with Twain on the *Ajax*. Twain wanted to ride up to the summit of Haleakalā ("the House of the Sun"), the third-largest volcano in the Islands and one of the two volcanos that form Maui, but he needed a guide and wanted company.

> Wailuku, April 26
> Messrs. Kimball,
>
> Gentlemen—Don't you think for a moment of going up on Haleakalā without giving me an opportunity of accompanying you! I have waited for and skirmished after some company for some time without avail, and now I hear that you will shortly be at Ha'ikū [on the north shore]. So I shall wait for *you*.
>
> Cannot you let me know just as soon as you arrive, and give me a day or two (or more, even, if possible) to get there with my horse? Because I am told the distance hence to Ha'ikū is 15 miles—to prosecute which will be a matter of time to my animal, and possibly

a matter of eternity. His strong suit is grace and personal comeliness rather than velocity.

Yours Very Truly,
Sam L. Clemens
(Or "Mark Twain," if you have forgotten my genuine name.)

My address is "Wailuku Plantation."

I shall send two or three notes by different parties for fear one might misfire—an idea suggested by my own native sagacity.

It was a couple weeks before they made the journey up Haleakalā. To get to Ha'ikū, Twain had to ride through windswept sand dunes past the port of Kahului, from which Maui's freight and produce were shipped. These dunes were the burying grounds of the ancient Hawaiians, and their bones were often visible. He would have followed a road along the north shore until he entered the beginning of the windward jungles, then traced the road up the hill to the small town of Ha'ikū. Today this town is commonly called Haiku with the Japanese pronunciation, "HI-koo," like the poems.

It was more than eleven days before they made the journey up Haleakalā. Twain's notes say, "Brown calls his horse Haleakalā—[an] extinct volcano—because if [there had] ever been any fire in him [it was] all gone out before he came across him."[18]

Haleakalā, at 10,020 feet (3 km), is the largest of Maui's two volcanoes. It's still an active volcano, even though the last time lava flowed from it was between the years 1480 and 1600. It has erupted more than ten times in the past 1,000 years and is expected to erupt again.

Each of the Hawaiian islands is formed by one or more volcanoes. They are shield volcanoes, which tend to form slowly from fluid lava flows and are rarely explosive like the famous cone-shaped stratovolcanoes, except for the spouts that form the relatively small tuff cones. These fountains can hurl lava bombs great distances. These, as well lava splatters, can burn you to the bone, but most of the time, the lava creeps along at the slow pace of about four feet per minute (a meter per minute). Usually, you can easily outwalk it, so it's rarely deadly.

People rarely die from Hawai'i's volcanoes. An explosive period in 1790 killed more than eighty Hawaiians on the Big Island, but these days, the park rangers are good at keeping people safe. It's usually those who ignore warnings and barriers and try to get close to the lava who are killed—generally by breathing deadly volcanic gases, which can suddenly suffocate you before you even reach the lava. An eruption can be accompanied by earthquakes, mudslides, and tidal waves, which can be deadly.

Amazingly, three volcanologists survived falling up to their knees in liquid lava that was fourteen times hotter than boiling water. You can read their first-hand accounts in *The Hawai'i Bathroom Book*—a book I highly recommend—since I wrote it myself.

Altogether, Hawai'i has five active volcanoes, although two of these haven't erupted in more than 100 years. Haleakalā is active, as are three of the Big Island's five volcanoes. The fifth active volcano is Lōʻihi—an underwater seamount off the Big Island's southeast coast, which is expected to become a new Hawaiian island sometime between 10,000 and 100,000 years from now. Only one of these volcanoes currently has active lava flows—Kīlauea, which forms the southeastern corner of the Big Island. This makes Kīlauea a huge tourist attraction, one that drew Mark Twain there, as we will see a bit later in this book.

The Hawaiian Islands are part of a chain of more than 130 volcanoes that extend northwest to Alaska's Aleutian Islands and Russia's Kamchatka Peninsula. They are a result of the Earth's crust slowing moving over a hot spot that currently is under the Big Island. In other words, every one of those volcanos and seamounts were once where the Big Island is now. They moved off the hot spot, and their volcanoes have been wearing away ever since and sinking further into the ocean floor.

This makes the eight main Hawaiian Islands and its twenty volcanoes the newest volcanoes in the chain. The oldest, near Alaska and Russia, is 81 million years old. It took that long for that volcano to be slowly dragged from where the Big Island is now, moving at roughly twice the rate that your fingernails grow.

It takes about 300,000 years for one of Hawai'i's volcanoes to grow from the ocean floor to the ocean's surface and then another 300,000 years to reach its maximum height. Then they begin to deteriorate. Most of the volcanoes beyond the fifteen newest have eroded so much that they're now below the surface of the Pacific Ocean.

Climbing the House of the Sun

[Sometime during May 7–12, 1866:]

Twain said they climbed 1,000 feet the first day and 8,000 the second. If they started at Haʻikū, the first day's climb would have put them in the town of Makawao. Henry Whitney's *The Hawaiian Guide Book for Travelers* (1875) says that from Makawao to the summit was fifteen miles and took four or five hours on horseback. The narrow track soon turned into numberless cattle tracks. He added that it's "often covered with snow" in the winter, but this is rare now. He also said in July there were wild strawberries that completely circled the mountain at a certain elevation. You advance into the clouds around 6,000 feet and rise above them at about 8,000 feet. From that point, there is little vegetation. The summit and the crater look a lot like Mars. From the summit, you can see about 100 miles in every direction, and when it's clear, you can see six of the Hawaiian Islands from the Big Island to Oʻahu.

—◁

But the chief pride of Maui is her dead volcano of Haleakalā—which means, translated, "the house of the sun." We climbed a thousand feet up the side of this isolated colossus one afternoon; then camped, and next day climbed the remaining nine thousand feet, and anchored on the summit, where we built a fire and froze and roasted by turns, all night.

With the first pallor of dawn we got up and saw things that were new to us. Mounted on a commanding pinnacle, we watched Nature work her silent wonders. The sea was spread abroad on every hand, its tumbled surface seeming only wrinkled and dimpled in the distance. A broad valley below appeared like an ample checker-board, its velvety green sugar plantations alternating with dun squares of barrenness and groves of trees diminished to mossy tufts. Beyond the valley were mountains picturesquely grouped together; but bear in mind, we fancied that we were looking *up* at these things—not down. We seemed to sit in the bottom of a symmetrical bowl ten thousand feet deep, with the valley and the skirting sea lifted away into the sky above us!

It was curious; and not only curious, but aggravating; for it was having our trouble all for nothing, to climb ten thousand feet toward heaven and then have to look up at our scenery. However, we had to be content with it

The top image looks down into Maui's central valley toward the West Maui Mountains, with Lanaʻi and Oʻahu on the horizon to the left. The lower picture is a side view of some of the tuff cones in the crater. At least one of these is taller than Diamond Head.
AUTHOR'S PHOTOS

and make the best of it; for, all we could do we could not coax our landscape down out of the clouds.

Formerly, when I had read an article ["The Balloon Hoax" from 1844] in which [Edgar Allan] Poe treated of this singular fraud perpetrated upon the eye by isolated great altitudes, I had looked upon the matter as an invention of his own fancy.

[Jack London described this illusion in even more detail when he visited Haleakalā, but I've never come across anyone who has seen it. I wonder if we're immune because we've often seen the landscapes from the high altitudes of airplanes and in photographs. I suspect Poe, Twain, and London had never before looked down on clouds, so looking down the mountain was like looking across a plain and valley floor below appearing to be the side of a mountain rising into the sky, with the clouds above it.]

I have spoken of the outside view—but we had an inside one, too. That was the yawning dead crater, into which we now and then tumbled rocks, half as large as a barrel, from our perch, and saw them go careering down the almost perpendicular sides, bounding three hundred feet at a jump; kicking up cast-clouds wherever they struck; diminishing to our view as they sped farther into distance; growing invisible, finally, and only betraying their course by faint little puffs of dust; and coming to a halt at last in the bottom of the abyss, two thousand five hundred feet down from where they started! It was magnificent sport. We wore ourselves out at it.

Looking down into the crater from the rim.
AUTHOR'S PHOTO

In his notebook, Twain commented, "Fun to roll rocks—or rather, fun to see able-bodied Kānaka do it at 50¢ a day."[19] This, of course, is illegal today.

The crater of Vesuvius, as I have before remarked, is a modest pit about a thousand feet deep and three thousand in circumference; that of Kīlauea is somewhat deeper, and *ten miles* in circumference. But what are either of them compared to the vacant stomach of Haleakalā? I will not offer any figures of my own, but give official ones—those of Commander Wilkes, U.S.N., who surveyed it and testifies that it is *twenty-seven miles in circumference!* If it had a level bottom it would make a fine site for a city like London. It must have afforded a spectacle worth contemplating in the old days when its furnaces gave full rein to their anger.

Presently vagrant white clouds came drifting along, high over the sea and the valley; then they came in couples and groups; then in imposing squadrons; gradually joining their forces, they banked themselves solidly together, a thousand feet under us, and *totally shut out land and ocean*—not a vestige of *anything* was left in view but just a little of the rim of the crater, circling away from the pinnacle whereon we sat (for a ghostly procession of wanderers from the filmy hosts without had drifted through a chasm in the crater wall and filed round and round, and gathered and sunk and blended together till the abyss was stored to the brim with a fleecy fog). Thus banked, motion ceased, and silence reigned. Clear to the horizon, league on league, the snowy floor stretched without a break—not level, but in rounded folds, with shallow creases between, and with here and there stately piles of vapory architecture lifting themselves aloft out of the common plain—some near at hand, some in the middle distances, and others relieving the monotony of the remote solitudes.

For natural beauty and wonder the nature-lover may see dissimilar things as great as Haleakalā, but no greater, while he will never see elsewhere anything more beautiful or wonderful.
—JACK LONDON, AUTHOR OF *THE CALL OF THE WILD* AND *WHITE FANG*[20]

Above is a sunrise over the crater, while below is a sunset from the summit with some of the astronomy observatories on the left.

(TOP) AUTHOR'S PHOTO; (BOTTOM) ELAINE MOLINA STEPHENS

There was little conversation, for the impressive scene overawed speech. I felt like the Last Man, neglected of the judgment, and left pinnacled in mid-heaven, a forgotten relic of a vanished world.

While the hush yet brooded, the messengers of the coming resurrection appeared in the east. A growing warmth suffused the horizon, and soon the sun emerged and looked out over the cloud-waste, flinging bars of ruddy light across it, staining its folds and billow-caps with blushes, purpling the shaded troughs between, and glorifying the massy vapor-palaces and cathedrals with a wasteful splendor of all blendings and combinations of rich coloring.

It was the sublimest spectacle I ever witnessed, and I think the memory of it will remain with me always.[21]

[Almost a year later, Twain wrote to Alice Hyde in St. Louis, Missouri. Alice was about age twenty-two when she and her mother sailed to Hawai'i on the *Ajax* with Twain.]

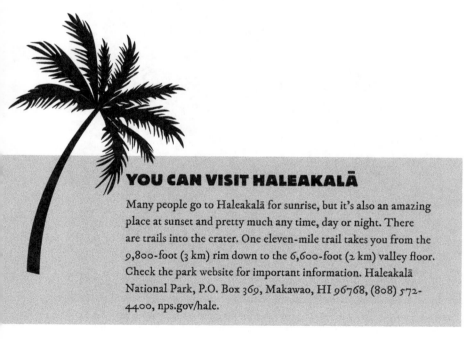

YOU CAN VISIT HALEAKALĀ

Many people go to Haleakalā for sunrise, but it's also an amazing place at sunset and pretty much any time, day or night. There are trails into the crater. One eleven-mile trail takes you from the 9,800-foot (3 km) rim down to the 6,600-foot (2 km) valley floor. Check the park website for important information. Haleakalā National Park, P.O. Box 369, Makawao, HI 96768, (808) 572-4400, nps.gov/hale.

There are three species of silverswords—one each on Maui's Haleakalā and the Big Island's Maunakea and Maunaloa. They live between fifteen and sixty years. At the end of their lives, they shoot their only flowers up to six feet high (2 m), after which the plant dies. This one is at Haleakalā's summit.

AUTHOR'S PHOTO

You remember I promised you, a long time ago in the Sandwich Islands, that I would be sure to get you a silversword when I ascended Haleakalā. I got it *away down in the old crater*, and used to try to think to send it to you, but always recollected it at some unseasonable hour.

> Packing my trunk tonight (for I leave tomorrow for New York, and, I suppose, for Europe a month later), I came across the old swords, and hasten to send them, begging at the same time that you will excuse my characteristic negligence. I had to send them—I wouldn't consider the island trip complete with so chivalrous a promise, so knightly a deed as the disarming of a crater many times larger than myself and the laying of his weapons at the feet of a lady, unaccomplished. How's that? I think I'll put that in my lecture.[22]

BACK ON O'AHU

THE KING'S GOVERNMENT

[MAY 22, 1866:]

Twain arrived back in Honolulu from Kahului aboard the interisland schooner *Ka Mōʻī* (the King). Once ensconced in his room, he wrote a letter to his brother's wife, Mollie Clemens, in Carson City, Nevada.

> I have just got back from a sea voyage—from the beautiful island of Maui, I have spent five weeks there, riding backwards and forwards among the sugar plantations—looking up the splendid scenery and visiting the lofty crater of Haleakalā. It has been a perfect jubilee to me in the way of pleasure.
>
> I have not written a single line, and have not once thought of business, or care or human toil or trouble or sorrow or weariness. Few such months come in a lifetime.
>
> I set sail again a week hence for the island of Hawaiʻi to see the great active volcano of Kīlauea. I shall not get back here for four or five weeks, and shall not reach San Francisco before the latter part of July. [. . .]
>
> If I were in the east now, I could stop the publication of a piratical book which has stolen some of my sketches.[1]

That was *Beadle's Dime Book of Fun No. 3*, which included three of his stories.

Explanatory

[May 23–25, 1866:]

It has been six weeks since I touched a pen. In explanation and excuse I offer the fact that I spent that time (with the exception of one week) on the island of Maui. I only got back yesterday. I never spent so pleasant a month before, or bade any place goodbye so regretfully. I doubt if there is a mean person there, from the homeliest man on the island (Lewers) down to the oldest (Tallant). I went to Maui to stay a week and remained five. I had a jolly time. I would not have fooled away any of it writing letters under any consideration whatever. It will be five or six weeks before I write again. I sail for the island of Hawaiʻi tomorrow, and my Maui notes will not be written up until I come back. [Actually, it was about five years before he wrote up some of his Maui notes.]

Hawaiian Legislature

I have been reporting the Hawaiian Legislature all day. [. . .]

The Legislature meets in the Supreme Courtroom, an apartment which is larger, lighter, and better fitted and furnished than any court-room in San Francisco. A railing across the center separates the legislators from the visitors.

When I got to the main entrance of the building, and was about to march boldly in, I found myself confronted by a large placard, upon which was printed:

> No Admittance by this Entrance Except to Members of the Legislature and Foreign Officials.

It shocked my republican notions somewhat, but I pocketed the insinu-ation that I was not high-toned enough to go in at the front door, and went around and entered meekly at the back one. If ever I come to these islands again I will come as the Duke of San Jose, and put on as many frills as the best of them. [. . .]

The King is invested with very great power. But he is a man of good sense and excellent education, and has an extended knowledge of business, which he acquired through long and arduous training as Minister of the Interior under the late king, and therefore he uses his vast authority wisely and well.[2]

Under other monarchies the male line takes precedence of the female in tracing genealogies, but here the opposite is the case—the female line takes precedence. Their reason for this is exceedingly sensible, and I recommend it to the aristocracy of Europe: They say it is easy to know who a man's mother was, but, etc., etc.[3]

The christianizing of the natives has hardly even weakened some of their barbarian superstitions, much less destroyed them. I have just referred to one of these. It is still a popular belief that if your enemy can get hold of any article belonging to you he can get down on his knees over it and *pray you to death.* Therefore many a native gives up and dies merely because he *imagines* that some enemy is putting him through a course of damaging prayer. This praying an individual to death seems absurd enough at a first glance, but then when we call to mind some of the pulpit efforts of certain of our own ministers the thing looks plausible.

—⋖

Previously, it was the priests of the old religion who did this to punish criminals, and there are stories of some withering away and dying from a guilty conscience and fear of the gods. Even today, people die of psychosomatic illnesses.

After the priesthood was abolished, the Hawaiians still believed prayer was the cause of disease, and ex-priests—retaining their role as doctors—did what they could to ward off the effects of these malicious prayers. It's more likely the patients were suffering from a disease and just thought it was from a prayer. Epidemics *were* killing them left and right.

Additional Spouses

In former times, among the islanders, not only a plurality of wives was customary, but a *plurality of husbands* likewise. Some native women of noble rank had as many as six husbands. A woman thus supplied did not reside with all her husbands at once, but lived several months with each in turn. An understood sign hung at her door during these months. When the sign was taken down, it meant "*Next.*" [. . .]

—⋖

The Hawaiians were very egalitarian, and both women and men could have multiple spouses, although calling them spouses is a bit of a misnomer. Couples just moved in together. If things didn't work out, one of them moved away. Among the chiefs, some unions were prearranged—sometimes before they were born—in order to produce offspring with high mana (spiritual power), thus maintaining their social standing. It didn't matter whether one was old and one was young. The important thing was the genealogy.

Other casual relationships came and went. There were few restrictions on relationships, although jumping from relationship to relationship was frowned upon. For chiefs, once a prearranged marriage produced heirs, they were pretty much free to do as they liked. King Kamehameha's wife, Queen Keōpūolani, who was the mother of his royal heirs, later took several other husbands, but he remained closest to his earlier favorite wife, Queen Ka'ahumanu. The relationships of the commoners tended to be more stable than those of the chiefs, and many couples stayed together for life. There was some jealousy, but generally, this was considered disgraceful and bad manners because it could be harmful to the children, who were very highly valued.

When it came to taking on additional wives or additional husbands, usually this had to be approved by the first spouse, although generally, it was the first spouse who suggested it, bringing their friends or relatives into family. Families thus became like small communities.

There were also group marriages, where sisters who lived together as a family would share their husbands. The same could apply to a family of brothers, although this was rare since men usually went to live with the woman's family. If a man wanted a relationship with a woman, he would go to the head of her family—usually her parents or grandparents—and ask for permission to move in with them. Because of this custom, Hawaiian parents preferred to give birth to girls because they would bring boys into the family that would take care of them into their old age. Boys born into the family would end up leaving. There was an old saying, "A boy supports his parents-in-law." But overall, the Hawaiians tended to treat everyone as one huge family, and they all helped take care of each other.

Hawai'i's conversion to Christianity put an end to this to some extent, and in his notes, Twain wrote that the king refused to let the Mormons practice polygamy, even though they claimed to have 5,000 converts in the Islands.

The Mormons originally had a colony on Lā'na'i, but they had to move Lāie on O'ahu's northeast shore after the leader of the colony stole their land. They are still at Lā'ie, with their temple, college, and the Polynesian Cultural Center, which is worth visiting. Alcohol can't be sold there, but it is available just a couple miles from town.

———

All the natives are Christians, now, but many of them still desert to the Great Shark God for temporary succor in time of trouble. [There were many shark gods—most were ancestral guardian spirits—but he's probably talking about Kamohoali'i, Pele's brother. Twain probably got this information from the missionaries. The Hawaiians were pretty much all Christians by his time and didn't worship a Great Shark God.] An eruption of the great volcano of Kīlauea, or an earthquake, always brings a deal of latent loyalty to the Great Shark God to the surface. It is common report that the King, educated, cultivated and refined Christian gentleman as he undoubtedly is, still turns to the idols of his fathers for help when disaster threatens. A planter caught a shark, and one of his Christianized natives testified his emancipation from the thrall of ancient superstition by assisting to dissect the shark after a fashion forbidden by his abandoned creed. But remorse shortly began to torture him. He grew moody and sought solitude; brooded over his sin, refused food, and finally said he must die and ought to die, for he had sinned against the Great Shark God and could never know peace any more. He was proof against persuasion and ridicule, and in the course of a day or two took to his bed and died, although he showed no symptom of disease. His young daughter followed his lead and suffered a like fate within the week.[4]

A word about Twain's sources: Twain was spending most of his time with Americans, many of them missionaries and their families. David Lawrence Gregg, the US commissioner to the Hawaiian Kingdom, wrote in his diary in 1858, "Thus it is always with Honolulu society. It is full of jealousies and scandals. No one can live in it without subjecting his character to the severest test. The Missionaries are the worst gossips and the most inveterate scandal-mongers. Their wives and daughters are far beyond anything St. Paul ever condemned in the way of tittle-tattle and mischief making."[5] Twain wrote something similar in his notebook: "The missionary—I should say preacher—feature of insincerity and hypocrisy makes the atmosphere of the place." Still, he seemed to be unaware of their influence on him because Hawaiian culture was a subject where he had little firsthand knowledge or experience.

And it was even worse when it came to the missionaries' perception of the natives, whom they sometimes treated as slaves. Herman Melville, the author of *Moby Dick*, was one of those who saw hypocrisy in what they were doing. Writing in the early 1840s, he said,

> Look at Honolulu, the metropolis of the Sandwich Islands! A community of disinterested merchants, and devoted self-exiled heralds

of the Cross, located on the very spot that twenty years ago was defiled by the presence of idolatry. What a subject for an eloquent Bible-meeting orator!

Nor has such an opportunity for a display of missionary rhetoric been allowed to pass by unimproved! But when these philanthropists send us such glowing accounts of one half of their labors, why does their modesty restrain them from publishing the other half of the good they have wrought?

Not until I visited Honolulu was I aware of the fact that the small remnant of the natives had been civilized into draught-horses, and evangelized into beasts of burden. But so it is. They have been literally broken into the traces, and are harnessed to the vehicles of their spiritual instructors like so many dumb brutes![6]

This was true. For a number of years, the missionaries, their families, and their visitors were hauled around in carts or on palanquins by native Hawaiians, usually without reward other than a blessing. Those Hawaiians working in the cane fields didn't fare much better. They were required to sign one-year contracts for minimal wages, and if they refused to work or abandoned their jobs for any reason, an 1850 law said they "could be committed to prison at hard labor until he consented to serve, and the costs of court action were assessed against him."[7] This was still going on after Twain's visit.

Some missionaries cared very deeply about the Hawaiians, but others who became businessmen and plantation owners viewed them very differently. This was a period when slavery was still legal in the United States and then had just ended. Some of the tactics Hawai'i's plantation owners used to keep their field hands in line were later used in the South after slavery was abolished, particularly when it came to preventing them from voting or forcing them to vote for a particular candidate.

Part of all this insinuated that the Hawaiians were ingrained savages and could never be changed, that they were child-like and were incorrigibly lazy. These racist ideas and others have long been refuted and were obviously wrong even at that time, especially since Hawaiians were prized workers and highly sought after. They were also competent politicians and rulers.

—

Rocks wrapped in ti leaves are still left as offerings. This is at the Rainbow Man petroglyph in ʻĪao Valley. Some believe he's a reminder that we need to protect the environment, among other things. Here he has a double rainbow on his shoulders.

Superstition is ingrained in the native blood and bone, and it is only natural that it should crop out in time of distress. Wherever one goes in the Islands, he will find small piles of stones by the wayside, covered with leafy offerings, placed there by the natives to appease evil spirits or honor local deities belonging to the mythology of former days.

The Latest Fashions

In the rural districts of any of the Islands, the traveler hourly comes upon parties of dusky maidens bathing in the streams or in the sea without any clothing on and exhibiting no very intemperate zeal in the matter of hiding their nakedness. When the missionaries first took up their residence in Honolulu, the native women would pay their families frequent friendly visits, day by day, not even clothed with a blush. It was found a hard matter to convince them that this was rather indelicate. [Actually, they were naked in public only when in the water or when apologizing to someone.]

Finally the missionaries provided them with long, loose calico robes, and that ended the difficulty—for the women would troop through the town, stark naked, with their robes folded under their arms, march to the missionary houses and then proceed to dress!—The natives soon manifested a strong proclivity for clothing, but it was shortly apparent that they only wanted it for grandeur.

The missionaries imported a quantity of hats, bonnets, and other male and female wearing apparel, instituted a general distribution, and begged the people not to come to church naked, next Sunday, as usual. And they did not; but the national spirit of unselfishness led them to divide up with neighbors who were not at the distribution, and next Sabbath the poor preachers could hardly keep countenance before their vast congregations. In the midst of the reading of a hymn a brown, stately dame would sweep up the aisle with a world of airs, with nothing in the world on but a "stovepipe" hat and a pair of cheap gloves; another dame would follow, tricked out in a man's shirt, and nothing else; another one would enter with a flourish, with simply the sleeves of a bright calico dress tied around her waist and the rest of the garment dragging behind like a peacock's tail off duty; a stately "buck" Kanaka would stalk in with a woman's bonnet on, wrong side before—only this, and nothing more; after him would stride his fellow,

VISITING THE MISSIONARIES.

This happened for only a short time until the Hawaiians learned the rules of Western fashion.
The illustration is from *Roughing It*.

with the legs of a pair of pantaloons tied around his neck, the rest of his person untrammeled; in his rear would come another gentleman simply gotten up in a fiery necktie and a striped vest.

The poor creatures were beaming with complacency and wholly unconscious of any absurdity in their appearance. They gazed at each other with happy admiration, and it was plain to see that the young girls were taking note of what each other had on, as naturally as if they had always lived in a land of Bibles and knew what churches were made for; here was the evidence of a dawning civilization.

The spectacle which the congregation presented was so extraordinary and withal so moving, that the missionaries found it difficult to keep to the text and go on with the services; and by and by when the simple children of the sun began a general swapping of garments in open meeting and produced some irresistibly grotesque effects in the course of re-dressing, there was nothing for it but to cut the thing short with the benediction and dismiss the fantastic assemblage.[8]

Pompous Circumstance

[. . .] I will now shovel in some information as to how this toy realm, with its toy population, is governed. By a constable and six policemen? By a justice of the peace and a jury? By a mayor and a board of aldermen? Oh, no. But by a King—and a Parliament—and a Ministry—and a Privy Council—and a standing army (200 soldiers)—and a navy (steam ferry-boat and a raft)—and a grand bench of supreme justices—and a lord high sheriff on each island. That is the way it is done. It is like propelling a sardine dish with the *Great Eastern's* machinery. [The SS *Great Eastern* was at that time the world's largest steamship.][9]

In our country, children play "keep house"; and in the same high-sounding but miniature way the grown folk here, with the poor little material of slender territory and meagre population, play "empire." There is his royal Majesty the King, with a New York detective's income of thirty or thirty-five thousand dollars a year from the "royal civil list" and the "royal domain." He lives in a two-story frame "palace."

King Kalākaua with government officials on the steps of the 'Iolani Palace in 1882.

And there is the "royal family"—the customary hive of royal brothers, sisters, cousins, and other noble drones and vagrants usual to monarchy—all with a spoon in the national pap-dish, and all bearing such titles as his or her Royal Highness the Prince or Princess So-and-so. Few of them can carry their royal splendors far enough to ride in carriages, however; they sport the economical Kanaka horse or "hoof it" with the plebeians.

Then there is his Excellency the "royal Chamberlain"—a sinecure, for his majesty dresses himself with his own hands, except when he is ruralizing at Waikīkī and then he requires no dressing. [. . .]

[Twain goes on to list a number of high-titled, high-paying positions, including at least one he invented.]

Imagine all this grandeur in a playhouse "kingdom" whose population falls absolutely short of sixty thousand souls!

The people are so accustomed to nine-jointed titles and colossal magnates that a foreign prince makes very little more stir in Honolulu than a Western Congressman does in New York.

And let it be borne in mind that there is a strictly defined "court costume" of so "stunning" a nature that it would make the clown in a circus look tame and commonplace by comparison; and each Hawaiian official dignitary has a gorgeous vari-colored, gold-laced uniform peculiar to his office—no two of them are alike, and it is hard to tell which one is the "loudest." The King had a "drawing-room" at stated intervals, like other monarchs, and when these varied uniforms congregate there—weak-eyed people have to contemplate the spectacle through smoked glass.

Is there not a gratifying contrast between this latter-day exhibition and the one the ancestors of some of these magnates afforded the missionaries the Sunday after the old-time distribution of clothing? Behold what religion and civilization have wrought![10]

In Session—Bill Ragsdale

At 11 a.m. His Royal Highness the President called the House to order. The roll call was dispensed with for some reason or other, and the chaplain, a venerable looking white man, offered up a prayer in the native tongue; and I must say that this curious language, with its numerous vowels and its entire absence of hissing sounds, fell very softly and musically from his lips.

A white chief clerk read the journal of the preceding day's proceedings in English, and then handed the document to Bill Ragsdale, a "half white" (half white and half Kanaka), who translated and clattered it off in Kanaka with a volubility that was calculated to make a slow-spoken man like me distressingly nervous.

[Bill Ragsdale made a tremendous impression on Twain, so much that Twain based the leading character of his Hawai'i novel on him. There's more about him later.]

Bill Ragsdale stands up in front of the speaker's pulpit, with his back against it, and fastens his quick black eye upon any member who rises, lets him say half-a-dozen sentences and then interrupts him, and repeats his speech in a loud, rapid voice, turning every Kanaka speech into English and every English speech into Kanaka, with a readiness and felicity of language that are remarkable—waits for another installment of talk from the member's lips and goes on with his translation as before. His tongue is in constant motion from eleven in the forenoon till four in the afternoon, and why it does not wear out is the affair of Providence, not mine.

There is a spice of deviltry in the fellow's nature and it crops out every now and then when he is translating the speeches of slow old Kānakas who do not understand English. Without departing from the spirit of a member's remarks, he will, with apparent unconsciousness, drop in a little voluntary contribution occasionally in the way of a word or two that will make the gravest speech utterly ridiculous. He is careful not to venture upon such experiments, though, with the remarks of persons able to detect him.

I noticed when he translated for His Excellency David Kalākaua, who is an accomplished English scholar, he asked, "Did I translate you correctly, your Excellency?" or something to that effect. The rascal. [. . .][11]

A CORRECTION

Speaking of the King reminds me of something which ought to be said and might as well be said in this paragraph. Some people in California have an idea that the King of the Sandwich Islands is a man who spends his time idling about the town of Honolulu with individuals of questionable respectability, and drinking habitually and to excess. This impression is wrong.

Before he ascended the throne he was "faster" than was well for him or for his good name, but, like the hero of Agincourt, he renounced his bad habits and discarded his Falstaffs when he became king, and since that time has conducted himself as becomes his high position. He attends closely to his business, makes no display, does not go about much, and in manners and habits is a thorough gentleman. He only appears in the streets when his affairs require it, and then he goes well mounted or in his carriage, and decently and properly attended.[12]

Whiskey's Antidote

[Regarding drinking and royalty, elsewhere Twain wrote:]

I have suggested that William [Lunalilo, who later became king] drinks. That is not an objection to a Sandwich Islander. Whiskey cannot hurt them; it can seldom even tangle the legs or befog the brains of a practiced native. It is only water with a flavor to it to Prince Bill; it is what cider is to us. Poi is the all-powerful agent that protects the lover of whiskey. Whoever eats it habitually may imbibe habitually without serious harm. The late king and his late sister Victoria both drank unlimited whiskey, and so would the rest of the natives if they could get it.

The native beverage, 'awa [kava], is so terrific that mere whiskey is foolishness to it. It turns a man's skin to white fish-scales that are so tough a dog might bite him, and he would not know it till he read about it in the papers. It is made of a root of some kind. The "quality" drink this to some extent, but the excise law has placed it almost beyond the reach of the plebeians. After 'awa, what is whiskey?

Many years ago the late King and his brother visited California, and some Sacramento folks thought it would be fun to get them drunk. So they gathered together the most responsible soakers in the town and began to fill up royalty and themselves with strong brandy punches. At the end of two or three hours the citizens were all lying torpid under the table and the two princes were sitting disconsolate and saying what a lonely, dry country it was! I tell it to you as it was told to me in Sacramento.[13]

[Returning to his *Sacramento Daily Union* letter:]

The present palace is to be pulled down and a new one erected. The Legislature has just made an appropriation of $40,000 to begin the work and carry it on for the next two years. There was nothing said about what it is ultimately to cost—wherefore I surmise that it is the design of the government to build a palace well worthy of the name.[14]

—

Altogether it cost more than $360,000—roughly $35 million in today's dollars.

The second 'Iolani Palace was in use from 1882 until the overthrow of the monarchy in 1893.
AUTHOR'S PHOTO

THE BIG ISLAND

A ROUGH JOURNEY

Horrible Conditions

On May 26, Twain caught an interisland schooner to the Big Island, accompanied by his friend, twenty-two-year-old Charles Warren Stoddard, who was one of Twain's friends in San Francisco. Stoddard at that time was considered a poet, but he was also an excellent writer who became very well known in the later part of the century. He is now remembered mainly for his travel books on Polynesia and for being an accomplished gay author. He accompanied Twain on the first half of Twain's trip around the Big Island. They remained close friends and corresponded until late in their lives. One of Twain's letters to Stoddard appears later in this book.

Twain, in his writings, uses the fictional Mr. Brown as his traveling companion. Some Twain biographers thought Brown might be based on Stoddard and/or Twain's later fellow traveler, Edward Howard, but I don't see any trace of either.

Travel author Charles Warren Stoddard in the 1860s and in 1903.

Brown is practically the opposite of both Stoddard and Howard. I think Brown was based primarily on a riverboat pilot named William Brown whom Twain had the misfortune of apprenticing under, along with a heavy dose of his imagination to make the character more sympathetic.

Whenever Twain thought of his steamboat days, the first figure who always came to mind was that pilot. "He was a middle-aged, long, slim, bony, smooth-shaven, horse-faced, ignorant, stingy, malicious, snarling, fault-hunting, mote-magnifying tyrant."[1] Every night after working with Brown, Twain would go to sleep imagining numerous exotic ways of killing him. This Brown made a huge impression, and Twain probably toned him down when creating his traveling companion. Mr. Brown appears in Twain's *Union* letters and in some later writings, but in *Roughing It*, he is called "Billings" and is reduced to only three brief mentions.

Twain and Stoddard took the *Emeline*, captained by Ezra Crane, to the Big Island. The schooner was scheduled to stop at Kailua-Kona and Ka'alu'alu Bay in the Ka'ū district at the southern end of the island. Kailua-Kona was once the capital of the Kingdom of Hawai'i and the largest town on the island. (Hilo is now the largest.) Ka'alu'alu Bay was in Twain's time the western landing point for travelers going to the volcano and was a spot for shipping sugarcane and cattle. Twain and Stoddard apparently talked Captain Crane into also stopping to pick them up at Kealakekua Bay.

For the first section of the trip, Twain changed the name of the ship to the *Boomerang* and its captain to Captain Kangaroo (although he later got confused and called the ship the *Kangaroo*). He did this so he'd have the freedom to write some negative things, exaggerations, and some fiction about the ship without offending the captain. He then switches back to the real names and highly praises both the captain and the ship.

Captain Crane's son later recalled that Twain approached his father at the Honolulu dock, asking where his ship was going and whether it took passengers. Twain later showed up with a double-handled carpet bag and booked passage.[2]

At Sea Again

Bound for Hawai'i (a hundred and fifty miles distant), to visit the great volcano and behold the other notable things which distinguish that island above the remainder of the group, we sailed from Honolulu on a certain Saturday afternoon, in the good schooner *Boomerang*.

The *Boomerang* was about as long as two streetcars and about as wide as one. She was so small (though she was larger than the majority of the interisland coasters) that when I stood on her deck I felt but little smaller than the Colossus of Rhodes must have felt when he had a man-of-war under him. I could reach the water when she lay over under a strong breeze. When the captain and Brown and myself and four other persons were all assembled on the little after portion of the deck which is sacred to the cabin passengers, it was full—there was not room for any more quality folks. Another section of the deck, twice as large as ours, was full of natives of both sexes, with their customary dogs, mats, blankets, pipes, calabashes of poi, fleas, and other luxuries and baggage of minor importance. As soon as we set sail the natives all lay down on the deck [. . .] and smoked, conversed, spit on each other, and were truly sociable.

[The trip could last for more than a week because of the lack of wind and the strong currents, and the Hawaiians had to spend the entire time exposed to the sun and rain, day and night, on the ship's deck, sometimes so crammed together that they couldn't even lie down, but conditions for the first-class passengers weren't exactly comfortable.]

The little low-ceiled cabin below was rather larger than a hearse, and as dark as a vault. It had two coffins on each side—I mean two bunks— though Mr. Brown, with that spirit of irreverence which is so sad a feature of his nature, preferred to call the bunk he was allotted his shelf. A small table, capable of accommodating three persons at dinner, stood against the forward bulkhead, and over it hung the dingiest whale-oil lantern that ever peopled the obscurity of a dungeon with grim and ghostly shapes. The floor room unoccupied was not extensive. One might swing a cat in it, perhaps, but then it would be fatal to the cat to do it.

The hold forward of the bulkhead had but little freight in it, and from morning till night a portly old rooster, with a voice like Baalam's ass, and the same disposition to use it, strutted up and down in that part of the vessel and crowed. He usually took dinner at six o'clock, and then, after an hour devoted to meditation, he mounted a barrel and crowed a good part of the night. He got hoarser all the time, but he scorned to allow any personal consideration to interfere with his duty, and kept up his labors in defiance of threatened diphtheria.

Sleeping was out of the question when he was on watch. He was a source of genuine aggravation and annoyance. It was worse than useless to shout at him or apply offensive epithets to him—he only took these things for applause, and strained himself to make more noise. Occasionally, during the day, I threw potatoes at him through an aperture in the bulkhead, but he only dodged and went on crowing.

The first night, as I lay in my coffin, idly watching the dim lamp swinging to the rolling of the ship, and snuffing the nauseous odors of bilge water, I felt something gallop over me. Lazarus did not come out of his sepulcher with a more cheerful alacrity than I did out of mine. However, I turned in again when I found it was only a rat.

Presently something galloped over me once more. I knew it was not a rat this time, and I thought it might be a centipede, because the captain had killed one on deck in the afternoon. I turned out. The first glance at the pillow showed me a repulsive sentinel perched upon each end of it— cockroaches as large as peach leaves—fellows with long, quivering antennae and fiery, malignant eyes. They were grating their teeth like tobacco worms, and appeared to be dissatisfied about something.

I had often heard that these reptiles were in the habit of eating off sleeping sailors' toenails down to the quick, and I would not get in the bunk anymore. I lay down on the floor. But a rat came and bothered me, and shortly afterward a procession of cockroaches arrived and camped in my hair. In a few moments the rooster was crowing with uncommon spirit and a party of fleas were throwing double somersaults about my person in the wildest disorder, and taking a bite every time they struck. I was beginning to feel really annoyed. I got up and put my clothes on and went on deck.

The above is not overdrawn; it is a truthful sketch of interisland schooner life. There is no such thing as keeping a vessel in elegant condition, when she carries molasses and Kānakas.

—⚓—

While Twain implies the Hawaiians were not very clean, this was definitely not the case, although it would be difficult for anyone to stay clean living on the deck of a ship for days. But under normal conditions, the Hawaiians kept themselves much cleaner than Americans and Europeans. While they considered nudity and bodily functions to be completely normal, not keeping clean was very shameful to them. Speaking of the women, sailor Ebenezer Townsend Jr. wrote in 1798 that "they are certainly the most cleanly people that I have ever seen. They bathe a number of times every day. They do nothing scarcely without bathing after it; they bathe immediately after every repast [meal]."[3] And Scottish seaman Archibald Campbell, who was there in 1809–1810, noted, "All ranks pay the utmost attention to personal cleanliness."[4]

Today, there's only one interisland ferry left, and it travels between Maui and Lāna'i. Unless you have a personal boat, the only way to get to another island is by plane or helicopter.

"Roll On, Silver Moon"

It was compensation for my sufferings to come unexpectedly upon so beautiful a scene as met my eye—to step suddenly out of the sepulchral gloom of the cabin and stand under the strong light of the moon—in the center, as it were, of a glittering sea of liquid silver, to see the broad sails straining in the gale, the ship keeled over on her side, the angry foam hissing past her lee bulwarks, and sparkling sheets of spray dashing high over her bows and raining upon her decks; to brace myself and hang fast to the first object that presented itself, with hat jammed down and coat tails whipping in the breeze, and feel that exhilaration that thrills in one's hair and quivers down his backbone when he knows that every inch of canvas is drawing and the vessel cleaving through the waves at her utmost speed.[5]

There was no darkness, no dimness, no obscurity there. All was brightness, every object was vividly defined. Every prostrate Kanaka; every coil of rope; every calabash of poi; every puppy; every seam in the flooring; every bolthead; every object, however minute, showed sharp and distinct in its every outline; and the shadow of the broad mainsail lay black as a pall upon the deck, leaving Brown's white upturned face glorified and his body in a total eclipse.[6]

[Twain goes on to describe how he attempted to entertain the seasick Mr. Brown by roughly paraphrasing as poetry Polonius's advice to his son from Shakespeare's *Hamlet*, which promptly cures Brown by making him vomit.]

MT. EVEREST IS *NOT* THE WORLD'S TALLEST MOUNTAIN

[MAY 28, 1866:]

On reaching the Big Island, the first things he saw were Hualālai and Maunaloa—two of the five volcanoes that form the Big Island, the others being Kohala, Maunakea, and Kīlauea.

Both Hualālai and Maunaloa are considered to be active. Hualālai (8,275 feet or 2,523 m tall) historically erupts two or three times every 1,000 years. Its last eruption was in 1801. Maunaloa has erupted at least thirty-eight times since 1832—the last in 1984.

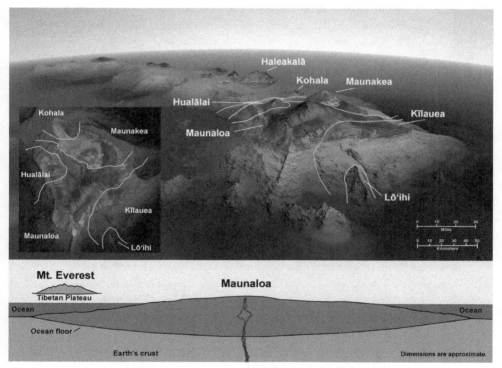

These maps show Hawai'i's newer volcanoes both above and below sea level. The inset is a satellite photograph of the Big Island. The lower diagram shows the relative sizes of Maunaloa and Mt. Everest.
AUTHOR'S GRAPHIC, INCORPORATING THE LARGER MAP FROM GERMANY'S SPACE AGENCY DLR AND AN INSERTED SATELLITE IMAGE FROM THE HAWAI'I STATE OFFICE OF PLANNING. THE LOWER IMAGE CONTAINS SOME ELEMENTS FROM A US GEOLOGIC SURVEY DIAGRAM.

YOU CAN VISIT THE MAUNALOA AND MAUNAKEA SUMMITS

Some dangers are involved in visiting the summits, so check the websites for warnings. Conditions can be severe, and you're pretty much on your own.

The Maunaloa and Maunakea roads are about 1,000 feet apart (300 m). To get to Maunaloa, on Saddle Road (Route 200) near mile marker 28, once you reach the Maunaloa Observatory Road turnoff, it's a seventeen-mile drive up to the Maunaloa Observatories at an elevation of 11,141 feet. From there, you can hike six miles to the summit, or if you have a four-wheel-drive vehicle, you can drive to within half a mile of summit as long as the gate is unlocked. Hawai'i Volcanoes National Park, PO Box 52, Hawai'i National Park, HI 96718, (808) 985-6178, nps.gov/havo/planyourvisit/hike_maunaloa.htm. Also check out nps.gov/havo/planyourvisit/20130113_hike_journal_dean.htm.

To Maunakea, from Saddle Road (Route 200) near mile marker 28, turn onto Mauna Kea Access Road. After about an hour, at 9,200 feet (2.8 km), you'll reach the Visitor Information Station. Spend at least half an hour here to acclimatize. To go farther, a four-wheel-drive vehicle with a low gear is recommended, as the next five miles (8 km) are on a steep gravel road that will take about an hour to drive. Only the Subaru telescope is open to the public, subarutelescope.org/Information/Tour/Summit/index.html. The hiking trail starts near the Visitor Information Station. It's six miles (9.7 km) to the summit and takes experienced hikers about eight hours. Hiking to the true summit is discouraged since it's considered a sacred site, and the culture of the Hawaiians deserves respect. Be sure to check out the rules and warnings at ifa.hawaii.edu/info/vis/visiting-mauna-kea/hiking.html. Maunakea Observatories Support Services, 177 Maka'ala St., Hilo, HI 96720-5108, (808) 934-4550, road conditions: (808) 935-6268, ifa.hawaii.edu/info/vis.

Chances are you didn't know that Maunaloa is the tallest mountain in the world. Most people think Mt. Everest is, but it's not. The confusion is caused because we don't normally measure mountains by how tall they are; we measure how high they rise above sea level—that is, where the sea level used to be, as it has risen since the standards were set and/or when the measurements were taken.

Mt. Everest sits on the Tibetan Plateau, while Maunaloa sinks into the ocean's floor. Like an iceberg, Maunaloa is mostly underwater. Measuring from the lowest point of base of each mountain, Everest itself is only 15,260 feet high (4.65 km), but it's boosted up by the Tibetan Plateau, so that its summit reaches about 29,032 feet (8.85 km) above sea level. Maunaloa, on the other hand, is about 56,000 feet tall (17 km)—13,678 feet (4 km) above sea level, about 16,400 feet (5 km) underwater, and approximately 26,000 feet (8 km) below the ocean floor. Maunaloa beats out Everest by more than 40,000 feet (12 km).

Relative to sea level, the nearby Big Island volcano Maunakea is 114 feet (35 m) higher than Maunaloa, but it's a smaller mountain, so it doesn't sink as far into the ocean floor; still, it's taller than Everest and is the world's second-tallest mountain. Even Maui's Haleakalā is about 675 feet (206 m) taller than Everest.

While Everest is a bit of the Earth's crust that was lifted up by the collusion of two tectonic plates, Maunakea is a volcano—it's a huge pile of lava that rose as magma from deep within the Earth. Maunakea last erupted about 4,500 years ago, but it's very likely it will erupt again, although probably not in our lifetimes.

Not only is Maunaloa the tallest mountain in the world, it is also the world's second largest volcano. The largest is Pūhāhonu, which is also in Hawai'i. It's mostly underwater, rising slightly above the surface of the ocean as the Gardner Pinnacles.

The Zones of the Earth Concentrated

Monday morning we were close to the island of Hawai'i. Two of its high mountains were in view—Maunaloa and Hualālai. The latter is an imposing peak, but being only ten thousand feet high is seldom mentioned or heard of. Maunaloa is fourteen thousand feet high. The rays of glittering snow and ice, that clasped its summit like a claw, looked refreshing when viewed from the blistering climate we were in.[7]

The climate is simply delicious—never cold at the sea level, and never really too warm, for you are at the half-way house—that is, twenty degrees above the equator. But then you may order your own climate for this reason: the eight inhabited islands are merely mountains that lift themselves out of the sea—a group of bells, if you please, with some (but not very much) "flare" at their bases. You get the idea.

Well, you take a thermometer, and mark on it where you want the mercury to stand permanently forever (with not more than 12 degrees [7°C] variation) winter and summer. If 82 [28°C] in the shade is your figure (with the privilege of going down or up 5 or 6 degrees [3°C] at long intervals), you build your house down on the "flare"—the sloping or level ground by the sea-shore—and you have the deadest surest thing in the world on that temperature. And such is the climate of Honolulu, the capital of the Kingdom.

If you mark 70 [21°C] as your mean temperature, you build your house on any mountain side, 400 or 500 feet [120 to 150 m] above sea level. If you mark 55 or 60 [13°C to 16°C], go 1,500 feet higher [0.5 km]. If you mark for wintry weather, go on climbing and watching your mercury. If you want snow and ice forever and ever, and zero and below, build on the summit of Maunakea, 16,000 feet [13,803 feet, or 4.207 km] up in the air. If you must have hot weather, you should build at Lāhainā, where they do not hang the thermometer on a nail because the solder might melt and the instrument get broken; or you should build in the crater of Kīlauea, which would be the same as going home before your time.

You cannot find as much climate bunched together anywhere in the world as you can in the Sandwich Islands. You may stand on the summit of Maunakea, in the midst of snow-banks that were there before Capt. Cook was born, maybe, and while you shiver in your furs you may cast your eye down the sweep of the mountain side and tell exactly where the frigid zone ends and vegetable life begins; a stunted and tormented growth of trees shades down into a taller and freer species, and that in turn, into the full foliage and varied tints of the temperate zone; further down, the mere ordinary green tone of a forest washes over the edges of a broad bar of orange trees that embraces the mountain like a belt, and is so deep and dark a green that distance makes it black; and still further down, your eye rests upon the levels of the sea-shore, where the sugar-cane is scorching in the sun, and the feathery coconut palm glassing itself in the tropical waves; and where you know the sinful natives are lolling about in utter nakedness and never knowing or caring that you and your snow and your chattering teeth are so close by.

So you perceive, you can look down upon all the climates of the earth, and note the kinds and colors of all the vegetations, just with a glance of the eye—and this glance only travels over about three miles as the bird flies, too.[8]

In case you didn't catch this, when he was talking about the various temperature ranges on the Islands and he said if desired hot weather, "you should build in the crater of Kīlauea, which would be the same as going home before your time," he was saying it would be the same as going to hell.

AUTHOR'S GRAPHIC, WITH A NOAA COASTAL SERVICES CENTER SATELLITE IMAGE AND AN INSERT OF THE ISLANDS FROM THE HAWAI'I STATE OFFICE OF PLANNING

The Big Island has one of the most diverse climates in the world. It has four of the five major climate zones and ten of the fourteen climate subgroups. The only climates the Big Island doesn't have are the Polar Ice Cap subcategory of Ice Climates (you have to go to the Arctic or Antarctica for that) and the Cold Continental Climates category with its three subcategories (such as at Fairbanks in Alaska, Fargo in North Dakota, or Pyongyang in North Korea). The summit of Haleakalā sometimes gets a little snow a few days a year. Maunaloa and Maunakea have snow much longer.

Twain and Stoddard disembarked from the *Emeline* at Kailua-Kona, a town that was in its heyday the capital of Hawai'i from 1812 to 1820. The capital moved to Lāhainā, Maui, because of the whaling trade and because King Kamehameha II (Liholiho) thought it might be safer for him after he brought the state religion to an end.

The Sleepiest Town

We landed at Kailua (pronounced Ki-LOO-ah), a little collection of native grass houses reposing under tall coconut trees—the sleepiest, quietest, Sundayest looking place you can imagine. Ye weary ones that are sick of the labor and care, and the bewildering turmoil of the great world, and sigh for a land where ye may fold your tired hands and slumber your lives peacefully away, pack up your carpet sacks and go to Kailua! A week there ought to cure the saddest of you all.

An old ruin of lava-block walls down by the sea was pointed out as a fort built by John Adams for Kamehameha I, and mounted with heavy guns—some of them 82-pounders—by the same sagacious Englishman.[9]

[John Adams was not an Englishman. He was John Adams Ki'iapalaoku Kuakini, who was Queen Ka'ahumanu's brother and a close advisor to Kamehameha. After the missionaries arrived, Hawaiians were encouraged to adopt Western names. When Kuakini took his Western name, John Quincy Adams was president of the United States. He became the royal governor of Hawai'i Island and O'ahu. Rev. William Ellis wrote in 1823 that Kuakini built the fort for Liholiho (Kamehameha II) on the ruins of Kamehameha's 'Ahu'ena Heiau. Three of the temple's tikis were placed on the wall with the cannons facing the sea.]

Top: Kailua-Kona in 1852, showing Hulihe'e Palace with the red roof—which was the vacation home of King Kalākaua and Queen Kapi'olani—and the Moku'aikaua Church, with the
volcano Hualalai in the background. Bottom: In 1908, Kailua-Kona was still a sleepy town.
(TOP) JAMES GAY SAWKINS; (BOTTOM) RAY JEROME BAKER

I was told that the fort was dismantled a few years ago, and the guns sold in San Francisco for old iron—which was very improbable. I was told that an adjacent ruin was old Kamehameha's sleeping-house; another, his eating-house; another, his god's house; another, his wife's eating-house—for by the ancient tabu system, it was death for man and woman to eat together. [Twain used "tabu," which is the alternate spelling of taboo, but as "kapu" is now more common in Hawai'i, I've changed it throughout.]

Every married man's premises comprised five or six houses. This was the law of the land. It was this custom, no doubt, which has left every pleasant valley in these islands marked with the ruins of numerous house enclosures, and given strangers the impression that the population must have been vast before those houses were deserted; but the argument loses much of its force when you come to consider that the houses absolutely necessary for half-a-dozen married men were sufficient in themselves to form one of the deserted "villages" so frequently pointed out to the "Californian" (to the natives all whites are haoles—how-ries [now pronounced "HOW-lees," as there is no longer an "r"-sound in Hawaiian]—that is, strangers, or, more properly, foreigners; and to the white residents all white newcomers are "Californians"—the term is used more for convenience than anything else).

—⋞

While the chiefs had that many grass huts, some commoners only had one, which they used for storage and as shelter in bad weather. Sometimes several families lived together sharing one or more huts. When there was more than one, they served the function of different rooms. One was for sleeping, one the men's eating hut, another eating hut for women, there was one for menstruating women, one for mat weaving, and one for the family's shrine where the head of the household would pray to the family's gods and guardian spirits.

Except for a few huts where animals were kept, they were generally described as being very clean and airy. John Ledyard, a Yankee sailor who sailed under Captain Cook, said that "the ground within being hard and dry is covered with thick coarse grass, dried plantain and palm-tree-leaves, over which they spread large well-wrought mats, which makes the house cleanly, and gives it an air of elegance and comfort."[10] There was also a raised area that was thick with mats,

'Ahu'ena Heiau. Top: An illustration from the narrative of Captain Otto von Kotzebue's visit in 1816. Bottom: This is how the reconstructed temple appears now from a different angle.

which served as a large bed shared by the family. Huts in drier areas sometimes lacked sides, while those in stormier areas were sealed up tighter.

I was told, also, that Kailua was old Kamehameha's favorite place of residence, and that it was always a favorite place of resort with his successors. Very well, if Kailua suits these kings—all right. Every man to his taste; but, as Brown observed in this connection, "You'll excuse *me*."[11]

From this compound, Kamehameha ruled his kingdom during the peaceful years following his uniting of the Islands, and almost every night, the king met with his kāhuna (priestly advisors) at the ʻAhuʻena Heiau (Temple of the Burning Altar). Only the heiau of the ruling chief had an oracle tower, which was wrapped in kapa cloth. It was here that the chief and his highest kahuna would receive advice from the gods. In Kamehameha's time, the ʻAhuʻena Heiau was considered the most powerful temple in Hawaiʻi. Human sacrifices were offered here to Kū, the war god, when Kamehameha was trying to gain control over the Big Island. On his return in 1812 after uniting all the Islands, Kona was suffering from a famine, so Kamehameha rebuilt this heiau and dedicated it to Lono, the god of agriculture, healing, and prosperity.

In Hawaiʻi, human sacrifices weren't nearly as common as with the Aztecs or other ancient cultures and generally were not as gruesome. Ritual human sacrifices were done primarily in privacy just outside of the heiaus (temples) on special occasions, such as during the building of a heiau, at the death of a chief, or before and after battles. Women were never sacrificed. Usually, it was criminals or captured warriors from the opposing side. In the case of a chief's death, often his closest associates volunteered, which is similar to Viking funerals, except the Vikings often sacrificed women. And there were also individuals of the small outcast caste who were designated for it from birth, knowing that their life would end along with that of their chief.

Criminals, even unwitting ones who accidentally broke a kapu, were occasionally executed or were prayed to death by the priests—who were the primary law enforcers—but there were methods by which their transgressions could be forgiven, and by King Kamehameha's time, if not earlier, the kapus weren't as strictly enforced. Their executions didn't gather huge crowds of observers like those in America and Europe at that time, and they weren't nearly as bloody as Britain's disembowelings or being drawn and quartered, especially since their religious sacrifices of enemy warriors had to be bloodless.

Russian explorer Captain Otto von Kotzebue wrote of his 1816 visit to 'Ahu'ena Heiau, "Kamehameha's first walk was to the morai [temple]; he embraced one of the statues, which was hung round more than the others, with fruits and pieces of a sacrificed hog, saying, 'These are our gods, whom I worship; whether I do right or wrong, I do not know; but I follow my faith, which cannot be wicked, as it commands me never to do wrong.' This declaration from a savage, who had raised himself by his own native strength of mind to this degree of civilization, indicated much sound sense, and inspired me with a certain emotion."

Kamehameha remained at this royal property until his death in 1819. A few months later, it was here that Kamehameha II broke the kapu when he sat down to eat with his mother, Keōpūolani—along with his sisters and Queen Ka'ahumanu— putting an end to the ancient Hawaiian religion. Shortly after that, it was here that the first wave of missionaries was given permission to land.

YOU CAN VISIT KAMEHAMEHA'S COMPOUND

Kamehameha's royal compound in Kailua-Kona was at the northern end of Kailua Bay, and the land is now part of the grounds of the Courtyard Mariott King Kamehameha's Kona Beach Hotel, or Kona Beach Hotel for short.

You can wander the royal grounds for free, but you can't go out to the heiau. The current heiau grounds are now just a third of the original size and have been altered by tsunamis. The heiau itself is a ⅔-scale replica.

Kona Beach Hotel, 755660 Palani Rd., Kailua-Kona, (808) 329-2911. See also ahuena-heiau.org.

EXPLORING KONA
Enduring Effects of the Voyage

I was told a good many other things concerning Kailua—not one of which interested me in the least. I was weary and worn with the plunging of the *Boomerang* in the always stormy passages between the Islands; I was tired of hanging on by teeth and toenails and, above all, I was tired of stewed chicken. All I wanted was an hour's rest on a foundation that would let me stand up straight without running any risk—but no information; I wanted something to eat that was not stewed chicken—I didn't care what—but no information. I took no notes, and had no inclination to take any.

Now, the foregoing is nothing but the feverish irritability of a short, rough sea-voyage coming to the surface—a voyage so short that it affords no time for you to tone down and grow quiet and reconciled, and get your stomach in order, and the bad taste out of your mouth, and the unhealthy coating off your tongue.

I snarled at the old rooster and the cockroaches and the national stewed chicken all the time—not because these troubles could be removed, but only because it was a sanitary necessity to snarl at something or perish. One's salt-water spleen must be growled out of the system—there is no other relief.

I pined—I longed—I yearned to growl at the captain himself, but there was no opening. The man had had such passengers before, I suppose, and knew how to handle them, and so he was polite and painstaking and accommodating—and most exasperatingly patient and even-tempered.

So I said to myself, "I will take it out of your old schooner, anyhow; I will blackguard the *Boomerang* in the public prints, to pay for your shameless good-nature when your passengers are peevish and actually need somebody to growl at for very relief!"

But now that I am restored by the land breeze, I wonder at my ingratitude; for no man ever treated me better than Captain Kangaroo [Crane] did on board his ship.

As for the stewed chicken—that last and meanest substitute for something to eat—that soothing rubbish for toothless infants—that diet for cholera patients in the rice-water stage—it was of course about the best food we could have at sea, and so I only abused it because I hated it as I do sardines or tomatoes, and because it was stewed chicken, and because it was such a relief to abuse somebody or something.

But Kangaroo—I never abused Captain Kangaroo. I hope I have a better heart than to abuse a man who, with the kindest and most generous and unselfish motive in the world, went into the galley, and with his own hands baked for me the worst piece of bread I ever ate in my life. His motive was good, his desire to help me was sincere, but his execution was damnable.

You see, I was not sick, but nothing would taste good to me; the Kanaka cook's bread was particularly unpalatable; he was a new hand—the regular cook being sick and helpless below—and Captain Kangaroo, in the genuine goodness of his heart, felt for me in my distress and went down and made that most infernal bread. I ate one of those rolls—I would have eaten it if it had killed me—and said to myself, "It is on my stomach; 'tis well; if it were on my conscience, life would be a burden to me."

I carried one up to Brown and he ate a piece, but declined to experiment further. I insisted, but he said no, he didn't want any more ballast.

When the good deeds of men are judged in the Great Day that is to bring bliss or eternal woe unto us all, the charity that was in Captain Kangaroo's heart will be remembered and rewarded, albeit his bread will have been forgotten for ages.[12]

—⋞—

In his notebook, Twain wrote that Hawai'i's chickens were the "most tasteless chickens in the world," which was why they stewed them. He also noted that the only "dish meaner than stewed chicken" was grasshopper pie.

Regarding the "portly old rooster, with a voice like Baalam's ass," the *Pacific Commercial Advertiser* reported on January 26, 1867, "Mark Twain will be interested to learn that the rooster, whose unintermitting crowing, on board the *Emeline* while Mark was a passenger, so annoyed that gentleman, has at length gone the way of all roosters. He mysteriously disappeared between two days, and has probably ere this figured conspicuously in a pot-pie or a curry, and Capt. Crane feels lonesome."[13]

The Famous Orange and Coffee Region

It was only about fifteen miles from Kailua to Kealakekua Bay, either by sea or land, but by the former route there was a point to be weathered where the ship would be the sport of contrary winds for hours, and she would probably occupy the entire day in making the trip, whereas we could do it on horseback in a little while and have the cheering benefit of a respite from the discomforts we had been experiencing on the vessel.

We [he and Stoddard] hired horses from the Kānakas, and miserable affairs they were, too. They had lived on meditation all their lives, no doubt, for Kailua is fruitful in nothing else. I will mention, in this place, that horses are plenty everywhere in the Sandwich Islands—no Kanaka is without one or more—but when you travel from one island to another, it is necessary to take your own saddle and bridle, for these articles are scarce. It is singular baggage for a sea voyage, but it will not do to go without it.

[After hiring their horses, Twain and Stoddard rode off for Kealakekua Bay, where Captain Cook met his end, about fifteen miles to the south.]

The ride through the district of Kona to Kealakekua Bay took us through the famous coffee and orange section. I think the Kona coffee has a richer flavor than any other, be it grown where it may and call it by what name you please.

At one time it was cultivated quite extensively, and promised to become one of the great staples of Hawaiian commerce; but the heaviest crop ever raised was almost entirely destroyed by a blight, and this, together with heavy American customs duties, had the effect of suddenly checking enterprise in this direction. For several years the coffee growers fought the blight with all manner of cures and preventives, but with small success, and at length some of the less persevering abandoned coffee-growing altogether and turned their attention to more encouraging pursuits.

The coffee interest has not yet recovered its former importance, but is improving slowly. [. . .] The coffee plantations we encountered in our short journey looked well, and we were told that the crop was unusually promising.[14]

There are no finer oranges in the world than those produced in the district of Kona; when new and fresh they are delicious. The principal market for them is California, but of course they lose much of their excellence by so long a voyage. [. . .] The orange culture is safe and sure, and is being more and more extensively engaged in every year. We rode through one orange grove that had ten thousand trees in it! They were all laden with fruit.

There are many species of beautiful trees in Kona—noble forests of them—and we had numberless opportunities of contrasting the orange with them. The verdict rested with the orange. Among the varied and handsome foliage of the kou, koa, kukui, breadfruit, mango, guava, peach, citron, ʻōhiʻa and other fine trees, its dark, rich green cone was sure to arrest the eye and compel constant exclamations of admiration. So dark a green is its foliage, that at a distance of a quarter of a mile the orange tree looks almost black.[15]

—⟋

Kona oranges are from seeds that Captain George Vancouver gave to King Kamehameha in 1792, which he brought from the Cape of Good Hope. They were Kona's primary export for several decades—particularly during the Gold Rush—until California became the major orange producer. California production later diminished as Florida took over. As far as I can tell, Kona oranges are no longer produced commercially, although there are still some Kona trees that continue producing oranges.

Kona coffee is a different story. It turns out that Kona's climate is ideal for growing coffee beans. It was about the time that Mark Twain was there that coffee began taking off, so that within forty years there were more than three million coffee trees covering six thousand acres in Kona. It is also grown in the nearby Kaʻū district, as well as on the opposite side of the island along the Hamakua Coast. Today there are more than 600 small coffee farms on the Big Island. Coffee from the Big Island is very popular and is considered among the best in the world.

You can sample it in Big Island cafés, restaurants, and at roadside fruit stands. Some coffee farms give tours. The Kaʻū district has an annual week-long coffee festival in early May, while Kona has one in early November.

As you move farther south along the Kona coast, the coffee farms fade away, being replaced by macadamia nut farms. Macadamia nuts arrived in Hawaiʻi in 1881. Coffee eventually reappears on the south side in the Kaʻū district. Macadamia orchards can also be found on the windward side of the island along the Hamakua Coast.

The ride from Kailua to Kealakekua Bay is well worth taking. The trail passes along on high ground—say a thousand feet above sea level—and usually about a mile distant from the ocean, which is always in sight, save that occasionally you find yourself buried in the forest in the midst of a rank, tropical vegetation and a dense growth of trees, whose great bows overarch the road and shut out sun and sea and everything, and leave you in a dim, shady tunnel, haunted with invisible singing birds and fragrant with the odor of flowers.

It was pleasant to ride occasionally in the warm sun, and feast the eye upon the ever-changing panorama of the forest (beyond and below us), with its many tints, its softened lights and shadows, its billowy undulations sweeping gently down from the mountain to the sea.

It was pleasant also, at intervals, to leave the sultry sun and pass into the cool, green depths of this forest and indulge in sentimental reflections under the inspiration of its brooding twilight and its whispering foliage.

The jaunt through Kona will always be to me a happy memory.[16]

At one farmhouse we got some large peaches of excellent flavor. This fruit, as a general thing, does not do well in the Sandwich Islands. It takes a sort of almond shape, and is small and bitter. It needs frost, they say, and perhaps it does; if this be so, it will have a good opportunity to go on needing it, as it will not be likely to get it.

The trees from which the fine fruit I have spoken of came, had been planted and replanted sixteen times, and to this treatment the proprietor of the orchard attributed his success.

We passed several sugar plantations—new ones and not very extensive. The crops were, in most cases, third rattoons. (*Note.*—The first crop is called "plant cane"; subsequent crops which spring from the original roots, without replanting are called "rattoons.") [...]

We stopped some time at one of the plantations, to rest ourselves and refresh the horses.[17]

⤙

This plantation was owned by the Lacks in Hōlualoa. In 1916, Frances Lack Nicoll Coon, whose father owned the plantation, told Mark Twain's cousin Mildred Leo Clemens:

A gentleman who gave his name as Clemens had come to the plantation and after the custom of those days had asked if he might stay there for a time. He was most welcome and proved a delightful guest. But father was Scotch and essentially practical and farming on a recent lava flow was 'hard diggings.' Our guest took life a little too easily, I suppose, and one day father said to mother, somewhat testily, "I wonder who that duffer is? He's too lazy to hoe a row of potatoes."

After a while Mr. Clemens (for such he had introduced himself) went away, without having reformed. One day there came an autographed copy of an article by "Mark Twain" acknowledging our hospitality and giving a beautiful description of our place which he called "an oasis in the desert."

Father scratched his head when he saw the signature, then said, much mollified. "So that was Mark Twain!" (for that name did mean something to us), then added, with the old spirit, "Well, anyhow, he was too lazy to hoe a row of potatoes!"[18]

In central Kona there is but little idle cane land now, but there is a good deal in north and south Kona. There are thousands of acres of cane land unoccupied on the island of Hawaiʻi, and the prices asked for it range from one dollar to a hundred and fifty an acre. It is owned by common natives, and is lying "out of doors." They make no use of it whatever, and yet, here lately, they seem disinclined to either lease or sell it. I was frequently told this. In this connection it may not be out of place to insert an extract from a book of Hawaiian travels recently published by a visiting minister of the gospel . . .

"Well, now, *I* wouldn't, if I was you."

"Brown, I *wish* you wouldn't look over my shoulder when I am writing and I wish you would indulge yourself in some little respite from my affairs and interest yourself in your own business sometimes."

"Well, I don't care. I'm disgusted with these mush-and-milk preacher travels, and I wouldn't make an extract from one of them. Father Damon has got stacks of books shoemakered up by them pious bushwhackers from America, and they're the flattest reading—they are sicker than the smart things children say in the newspapers. Every preacher that gets lazy comes to the Sandwich Islands to 'recruit his health,' and then he goes back home and writes a book. And he puts in a lot of history, and some legends, and some manners and customs, and dead loads of praise of the missionaries for civilizing and Christianizing the natives, and says in considerable chapters how grateful the savage ought to be; and when there is a chapter to be filled out, and they haven't got anything to fill it out with, they shovel in a lot of Scripture—now *don't* they? You just look at Rev. Cheever's book and Anderson's—and when they come to the volcano, or any sort of heavy scenery, and it is too much bother to describe it, they shovel in another lot of Scripture, and wind up with 'Lo! what God hath wrought!' Confound their lazy melts! [Literally, a melt is a spleen, particularly of a cow or pig.] Now, I wouldn't make extracts out of no such bosh."

"Mr. Brown, I brought you with me on this voyage merely because a newspaper correspondent should travel in some degree of state, and so command the respect of strangers; I did not expect you to assist me in my literary labors with your crude ideas. You may desist from further straining your intellect for the present, Mr. Brown, and proceed to the nearest depot and replenish the correspondent fountain of inspiration."

"Fountain dry now, of course. Confound me if I ever chance an opinion but I've got to trot down to the soda factory and fill up that cursed jug again. It seems to me that you need more inspiration . . ."

"Good afternoon, Brown."

The extract I was speaking of reads as follows:

"We were in north Kona. The arable uplands in both the Konas are owned chiefly by foreigners. Indeed the best of the lands on all the Islands appear to be fast going into foreign hands; and one of the allegations made to me by a foreign resident against the missionaries was that their influence was against such a transfer. The Rev. Mr. _____ told me, however, that to prevent the lands immediately about him, once owned by the admirable Kapi'olani, from going to strangers he knew not who, he had felt obliged to invest his own private funds in them."

We naturally swell with admiration when we contemplate a sacrifice like this. But while I read the generous last words of that extract, it fills me with inexpressible satisfaction to know that the Rev. Mr. _____ had his reward. He paid $1,500 for one of those pieces of land; he did not have to keep it long; without sticking a spade into it he sold it to a foreigner for $10,000 in gold. Yet there be those among us who fear to trust the precious promise, "Cast thy bread upon the waters and it shall return unto thee after many days."

I have since been told that the original $1,500 belonged to a ward of the missionary, and that inasmuch as the latter was investing it with the main view to doing his charge the best service in his power, and doubtless would not have felt at liberty to so invest it merely to protect the poor natives, his glorification in the book was not particularly gratifying to him. The other missionaries smile at the idea of their tribe "investing their own private funds" in this free and easy, this gay and affluent way—buying $1,500 worth of land at a dash (salary $400 a year), and merely to do a trifling favor to some savage neighbor.[19]

Taking Hawai'i

Most Americans at that time supported the work of the missionaries as being the most effective way to raise "savages" out of evil and transform them into good people. They expected the Puritan spirit would subdue the Islands, carrying on the work that had been done on the American continent subduing the Native Americans and making it safe for the influx of businesses and residents.

This fit in with the belief in Manifest Destiny—that God intended the United States to spread across the continent from coast to coast (and up into Canada, before the failure to take Canada in the War of 1812 put an end to that part of the idea). Gaining the land from coast to coast was accomplished by 1850, and people were beginning to look westward to Hawai'i for expansion. This was going on when Twain arrived. There were several failed movements to annex Hawai'i before it became a US territory in 1898.

Twain doesn't appear to have believed in Manifest Destiny, but initially, he agreed with the American residents he was hanging out with, who thought that Hawai'i should become part of the United States, but this opinion soon changed, as we shall see.

Traditionally, no one owned land in Hawai'i, although the royalty, chiefs, and priests had areas that were kapu to everyone else. It was thought that the land belonged to the gods and was administered by the king since he was the closest to the gods. Since everyone needed the land to survive, it was there for everyone to share, but certain people did have rights to the land under their care. Under the king were land managers who were each in charge of a large district. These districts were divided into smaller sections.

The commoners could move freely between sections and shared with people inside and outside of their area, but wherever they were, they had to pass a large portion of what they produced up the ladder through the land managers to the chiefs and priests. Only rare items, such as yellow feathers, were controlled. When someone needed something—such as uplanders needing fish or lowlanders needing produce—they'd light a fire for others to see.

When the ruling chief died, his or her successor would redistribute the districts among the other chiefs. The same thing happened on a lower chief's death. They saw themselves as temporary custodians, preserving the land of their ancestors for their descendants. Ultimately, they considered the land to be their ancestor—a divine ancestor. They revered the land and sea as the source of life and the source of everything they needed to live.

The missionaries, on the other hand, stressed the importance of landownership and insisted the lack of it was the primary cause of the decline in Hawai'i's population, adding that landownership would foster hard work, increase the population, and put underutilized land into productive use. Newly arrived foreigners wanted land for themselves so they could build their fortunes. They were investing money developing properties and wanted to be able to pass them on to their families. This was especially a huge issue for the ranch and sugar plantation owners, who needed vast tracts of land and foreign investment.

They finally convinced the king, and in 1848, the Great Māhele was instituted to begin landownership in the Islands. Missionary William Richards was put in charge of the commission for dividing up the land. Two years later, they persuaded the king to allow foreigners to own land in order to encourage foreign investment and expand capitalism. They said it would also prevent Hawai'i from being taken over by the British, French, or Americans—a very real threat since British Lord George Paulet took over the government for five months in 1843 and the French invaded Honolulu in 1948, while the Americans were starting to push for annexation.

The Māhele was supposed to benefit the common Hawaiians by giving them land of their own, but it turned out to be a disaster for them. Owning land was an alien concept to them, rather like owning the air or the sunshine. Since all

Hawaiians used the land and needed it to live, to them, it was a basic necessity for everyone. They just didn't understand how the land and its resources could be considered commodities.

Under the Māhele, Hawaiians could apply for the land they lived on or could buy available land that was not given to the chiefs and royalty, but most Hawaiians didn't understand the application process and didn't even know what a deed was. And most certainly couldn't afford to buy land. Some who started the process never completed it. Others just decided to continue living the way they had, outside of the landowning and work-for-wages system.

The non-Hawaiians, on the other hand, did understand the system and used it to their advantage. Some of the largest businesses and businessmen—some of whom were missionaries or descendants of missionaries—scooped up a lot of the land. Many took advantage of the Hawaiians, some even swindling them. Today, the courts are still sorting out conflicting claims.

After a group of American businessmen overthrew the Hawaiian government in 1893, 90 percent of the land was owned or controlled by foreigners through the boards of large chiefly trusts and the crown lands commission.[20] Just 1 percent was owned by common Hawaiians.

Lava Flows

At four o'clock in the afternoon we were winding down a mountain of dreary and desolate lava to the sea, and closing our pleasant land journey. This lava is the accumulation of ages; one torrent of fire after another has rolled down here in old times, and built up the island structure higher and higher.

Underneath, it is honeycombed with caves [lava tubes]; it would be of no use to dig wells in such a place; they would not hold water—you would not find any for them to hold, for that matter. Consequently, the planters depend upon cisterns.[21]

The last lava flow occurred here so long ago that there are none now living who witnessed it. In one place it enclosed and burned down a grove of coconut trees, and the holes in the lava where the trunks stood are still visible; their sides retain the impression of the bark; the trees fell upon the burning river, and becoming partly submerged, left in it the perfect counterpart of every knot and branch and leaf, and even nut, for curiosity seekers of a long distant day to gaze upon and wonder at.

A six-foot-wide stream of fire hose lava pouring from a lava tube in 2005.
KELLY WOOTEN, USGS AND HVO

There were doubtless plenty of Kānaka sentinels on guard hereabouts at that time, but they did not leave casts of their figures in the lava as the Roman sentinels at Herculaneum and Pompeii did. It is a pity it is so, because such things are so interesting, but so it is. They probably went away. They went away early, perhaps. However, they had their merits—the Romans exhibited the higher pluck, but the Kānakas showed the sounder judgment.

As usual, Brown loaded his unhappy horse with fifteen or twenty pounds of "specimens," to be cursed and worried over for a time, and then discarded for new toys of a similar nature. He is like most people who visit these islands; they are always collecting specimens, with a wild enthusiasm, but they never get home with any of them.

BURNING DOWN THE HOUSE

The Field of the Vanquished Gods

Only a mile or so from Kealakekua Bay is a spot of historic interest—the place where the last battle was fought for idolatry. Of course we visited it and came away as wise as most people do who go and gaze upon such mementoes of the past when in an unreflective mood.

While the first missionaries were on their way around the Horn, the idolatrous customs which had obtained in the Islands as far back as tradition reached were suddenly broken up. Old Kamehameha I was dead, and his son, Liholiho, the new king, was a free liver, a roistering, dissolute fellow, and hated the restraints of the ancient kapu. [This is a one-sided portrayal emphasizing the negative.] His assistant in the government, Ka'ahumanu, the Queen Dowager, was proud and high-spirited, and hated the kapu because it restricted the privileges of her sex and degraded all women very

King Kamehameha II (Liholiho) in the early 1820s.

nearly to the level of brutes. So the case stood. Liholiho had half a mind to put his foot down, Ka'ahumanu had a whole mind to badger him into doing it, and whiskey did the rest. It was probably the first time whiskey ever prominently figured as an aid to civilization.

Liholiho came up to Kailua as drunk as a piper, and attended a great feast; the determined Queen [assisted by his mother and sisters] spurred his drunken courage up to a reckless pitch, and then, while all the multitude stared in blank dismay, he moved deliberately forward and sat down with the women! They saw him eat from the same vessel with them, and were appalled!

Terrible moments drifted slowly by, and still the King ate, still he lived, still the lightnings of the insulted gods were withheld! Then conviction came like a revelation—the superstitions of a hundred generations passed from before the people like a cloud, and a shout went up, "The kapu is broken! the kapu is broken!"

Thus did King Liholiho and his dreadful whiskey preach the first sermon and prepare the way for the new gospel that was speeding southward over the waves of the Atlantic.[22]

—

Kamehameha was in his thirties when he married Ka'ahumanu—almost twice as old as her—but the marriage was primarily a political one to cement ties between the rulers of Maui and the Big Island. She went on to become his favorite wife and was the most powerful of his estimated twenty to thirty wives when he died in 1819. It was Kamehameha's wish that his twenty-two-year-old son by his highest-ranking wife become king but that she also become kuhina nui, or chief advisor, to co-rule with him. She was queen regent during the reign of Kamehameha III up until she died. Ka'ahumanu was the one primarily responsible for converting the Kingdom of Hawai'i into a Christian country and for encouraging Hawaiians to get an education, focusing particularly on literacy. It's also said she was an excellent surfer.

At the time the kapu ended, Ka'ahumanu was not the highest-born Hawaiian or the highest ranking, but she was the most influential and the most powerful.

Violating the Rules of Etiquette

Mixed-gender meals don't seem like a big deal to us, but it was one of the many kapus that held up the state religion, with all its priests and temples. The Hawaiians believed the kapus were commandments from the gods and if someone didn't obey one of the kapus, then the community would be punished with diseases or natural disasters, but through their contact with explorers, traders, and whalers, they had already seen that these visitors violated the kapus without suffering the wrath of the gods. Some women, including Queens Keōpūolani and Ka'ahumanu, sometimes ate with the sailors, including foods that were denied to women because of the foods' association with certain gods, and the gods hadn't punished them for it. Also, the people had already been decimated by diseases during the reign of Kamehameha, one of their greatest and most religious rulers, prompting some to question whether the gods really existed.

Over the centuries, the kapu system had become increasingly complex and burdensome to the people, including the royalty. There were kapus for everything. Some restrictions applied only to certain people and things—such as women and specific foods, like bananas, coconuts, and pork. Others applied to everyone for short periods of time. Then there were kapus that would come and go depending on the time of year. For example, 'ōpelu (mackerel scads) were kapu only from roughly January through July, while ula (lobster) and moi (threadfish) were kapu from sometime in May through sometime in August, and aku (skipjack tuna) were kapu from roughly June through January. While these were excellent environmental practices and we could learn a lot from them about protecting the environment, the punishments were severe. Violators were often killed, even if they broke a kapu by accident.

Some think that the kapu system may have begun as a way to define gender roles, but it gradually evolved to delineate the classes, giving privileges to those with rank and status and keeping the rest of the people in their place. Ancient Hawaiian society was divided into four classes—the ali'i (royalty and chiefs), kāhuna (holy men and master craftsman), maka'āinana (your average Joe, just about everyone), and a very few kauwā (outcasts, similar to India's untouchables).

By eating with the women, Liholiho was undermining his own claim to power, which they believed came from the gods. But he didn't do this because he was drunk and too lazy to perform all the rituals, although he did get drunk to do it since he thought the gods might strike him dead. Even though he knocked the royals down quite a few pegs by giving up their divine status, there were some advantages. The one that was probably foremost in his mind was recalling what had happened when his grandfather died. Kamehameha's father had made his highest-ranking son, Kiwalaʻō, the ruling chief of the Big Island, while the lower-ranked Kamehameha inherited the feathered war god, Kūkāʻilimoku, or "Kū, the snatcher of islands." The two then fought a number of battles for control before Kamehameha eventually won. This was about to repeat.

When Kamehameha died, Liholiho inherited the Kingdom, but his six-foot-six-inch-tall cousin—a priest named Keaoua Kekuaokalani—inherited Kamehameha's feathered war god. The twenty-two-year-old Liholiho lacked the support his father had and wasn't much of a warrior. It was his powerful aunt, Queen Kaʻahumanu—with her Maui and Big Island connections—who held the Kingdom together, but even she was nearly overthrown a number of years later.

It's likely Kekuaokalani was Liholiho's biggest threat, and by abolishing the state religion, he pulled the rug out from under his rival. Kekuaokalani lost his position as a priest to the god of war and many of his followers, along with much of his power and authority, and the feathered war god became a historical relic, which, since the Islands were united, Liholiho didn't need anyway.

—◁

The kapu broken and destruction failing to follow the awful sacrilege, the people, with that childlike precipitancy which has always character-ized them, jumped to the conclusion that their gods were a weak and wretched swindle, just as they formerly jumped to the conclusion that Captain Cook was no god, merely because he groaned, and promptly killed him without stopping to inquire whether a god might not groan as well as a man if it suited his convenience to do it [it was actually his behavior that did it for many of the natives]; and satisfied that the idols were powerless to protect themselves they went to work at once and pulled them down—hacked them to pieces—applied the torch—anni-hilated them![23]

The pagan priests were furious. And well they might be; they had held the fattest offices in the land, and now they were beggared; they had been great—they had stood above the chiefs—and now they were vagabonds.

They raised a revolt; they scared a number of people into joining their standard, and Kekuaokalani, an ambitious offshoot of royalty, was easily persuaded to become their leader.

In the first skirmish the idolaters triumphed over the royal army sent against them, and full of confidence they resolved to march upon Kailua.

The King sent an envoy to try and conciliate them, and came very near being an envoy short by the operation; the savages not only refused to listen to him, but wanted to kill him. So the King sent his men forth under Major General [William Pitt] Kalanimoku and the two hosts met at Kuamo'o.

The battleground and burial ground at Kuamo'o. The warriors of both sides are buried in the terraces. For some reason, the Hawaiians preferred fighting their battles on rough 'a'ā lava that you can barely walk on.
AUTHOR'S PHOTO

The battle was long and fierce—men and women fighting side by side, as was the custom—and when the day was done the rebels were flying in every direction in hopeless panic, and idolatry and the kapu were dead in the land!

The royalists marched gayly home to Kailua glorifying the new dispensation. "There is no power in the gods," said they; "they are a vanity and a lie. The army with idols was weak; the army without idols was strong and victorious!"

The nation was without a religion.[24]

⟶

For the king to violate a basic kapu like that meant that either thumbing his nose at the gods would rain destruction down on him and his people or that the gods didn't really exist and the entire kapu system was a sham. Amazingly the royalty, along with highest priest, took the latter position and began dismantling the state religion. Many others sided with the gods, including many priests who suddenly found themselves without work or status. They raised an army to battle it out with the royal warriors. Both sides had muskets, but the royal army, led by Kalanimoku, had a cannon. The religious army lost, and Kekuaokalani and his wife were killed. Altogether, more than 300 warriors were killed.

The Hawaiians didn't believe the gods would help them in battle, but they thought the feathered god—that one aspect of Kū—would instill fear in their enemies, taking away their courage. And they thought the gods would punish the army of irreligious kapu breakers. Since this didn't happen here or at a few other smaller battles, it was a clear indication that the gods didn't exist, and the state religion collapsed.

By ending the kapus, Liholiho forced his cousin's hand and was ready for him. This was the great test as to whether the religion was real. It was a fight between the religious and the nonreligious, and by winning, the unbelievers proved the religion to be false. Still, some things didn't happen immediately. It wasn't until after Queen Ka'ahumanu became a Christian several years later that she ordered the destruction of the tikis and heiaus and ended the priesthood, forcing the few remaining to operate in secret.

Liholiho had other reasons, too, for eating with the women. He wanted to improve the lives of women, and he wanted to release the commoners from time-consuming religious activities so they could harvest sandalwood and produce more food and items for trade with the foreign ships. And the royals wanted to deflect blame for their inability to get the gods to protect the people from the ravaging diseases that were killing them off.

But even after winning the battle, he was still on shaky ground, so he moved the Kingdom's capital to Lāhainā, Maui, where he was safer, and then later went on a world tour. William Pitt Kalanimoku, who commanded the royal forces at this battle, later said, "The King should not have so suddenly annihilated all that they held sacred. As a first consequence, he has been obliged to seek for safety in a foreign country."[25] Unfortunately both the king and the queen died in London from measles. His reign lasted only five years.

It was about six months after Kamehameha's death that Liholiho sat down to eat with women and pulled down their religion. A month later, the decisive battle was fought, essentially settling the matter.

YOU CAN VISIT KUAMOʻO BATTLEGROUND

The Kaumoʻo Battleground, also known as the Lekeleke Burial Grounds, is at the end of Aliʻi Drive where it turns into Māmalahoa Bypass Road on Keauhou Kainaliu Beach Road, Kailua-Kona, Hawaiʻi.

The state religion was gone, as were most of the kapus, but people's belief in their guardian gods and ancestral spirits continued. These beliefs predated the state religion, and some continue to believe them today.

The missionaries reached Kailua-Kona around three months after the battle. This seemingly minor event had an even greater influence on Hawaiian history and society. The missionaries quickly set about teaching the Hawaiians a whole new set of kapus.

—⌇

The missionary ship arrived in safety shortly afterward, timed by providential exactness to meet the emergency, and the gospel was planted as in a virgin soil.

—⌇

Three years later, the king's mother, Queen Keōpūolani, while on her deathbed, became the first royal to become a Christian. Queen Kaʻahumanu joined the church in 1825, then enthusiastically promoted it, touring all the Islands several times. Her sister, Queen Lydia Nāmāhāna Kekuaipiʻia, also joined that same year. She explained her reasoning to Captain Otto von Kotzebue, and he wrote, "She now informed me with much self-gratulation that she was a Christian, and attended the prayer-meeting several times every day. Desirous to know how far she had been instructed in the religion she professed, I inquired through Marini the grounds of her conversion. She replied that she could not exactly describe them, but that the missionary [Rev. Hiram] Bingham, who understood reading and writing perfectly well, had assured her that the Christian faith was the best; and that, seeing how far the Europeans and Americans, who were all Christians, surpassed her compatriots in knowledge, she concluded that their belief must be the most reasonable. 'If, however,' she added, 'it should be found unsuited to our people, we will reject it, and adopt another.'"[26]

CAPTAIN COOK WAS HERE
Rainbows in Moonlight

Twain and Stoddard moved on and soon reached Mauna ʻAlani (Orange Hill), the home of missionary Rev. John Paris Sr., which is now at the top of Nāpōʻopoʻo Road, about 100 feet east of the beginning of the hiking trail to Captain Cook's monument. At this house is an orange tree grown from one of the seeds Captain Vancouver gave to Kamehameha in 1792, and it's still producing oranges. In 1934, his daughter, Ella Paris, recalled Twain visiting her father, describing him as being dressed "like a traveler, a little rough looking."[27]

—

Shortly we came in sight of that spot whose history is so familiar to every schoolboy in the wide world—Kealakekua Bay—the place where Captain Cook, the great circumnavigator, was killed by the natives nearly a hundred years ago.

The setting sun was flaming upon it, a summer shower was falling, and it was spanned by two magnificent rainbows. [Double rainbows—one above the other—are common in Hawaiʻi.] Two men who were in advance of us rode through one of these, and for a moment their garments shone with a more than regal splendor.

AUTHOR'S GRAPHIC, MODIFIED FROM GOOGLE. DATA LDEO-COLUMBIA, NSF, NOAA. DATA MBARI, DATA SIO, NOAA, US NAVY, NGA, GEBCO, DATA SOEST/UHM, LANDSAT/COPERNICUS, WITH THE BIG ISLAND SATELLITE IMAGE FROM THE HAWAIʻI STATE OFFICE OF PLANNING

Why did not Captain Cook have taste enough to call his great discovery the Rainbow Islands? These charming spectacles are present to you at every turn; they are common in all the Islands; they are visible every day, and frequently at night also—not the silvery bow we see once in an age in the States, by moonlight, but barred with all bright and beautiful colors, like the children of the sun and rain.

I saw one of them a few nights ago. What the sailors call "rain-dogs"— little patches of rainbow—are often seen drifting about the heavens in these latitudes, like stained cathedral windows.

Kealakekua Bay is a little curve like the last kink of a snail shell, winding deep into the land, seemingly not more than a mile wide from shore to shore. It is bounded on one side—where the murder was done—by a little flat plain, on which stands a coconut grove and some ruined houses; a steep wall of lava, a thousand feet high at the upper end and three or four hundred at the lower, comes down from the mountain and bounds the inner extremity of it.

From this wall the place takes its name, Kealakekua, which in the native tongue signifies "The Pathway of the Gods." They say (and still believe, in spite of their liberal education in Christianity), that the great god Lono, who used to live upon the hillside, always traveled that causeway when urgent business connected with heavenly affairs called him down to the seashore in a hurry.

As the red sun looked across the placid ocean through the tall, clean stems of the coconut trees, like a blooming whiskey bloat through the bars of a city prison, I went and stood in the edge of the water on the flat rock pressed by Captain Cook's feet when the blow was dealt which took away his life, and tried to picture in my mind the doomed man struggling in the midst of the multitude of exasperated savages—the men in the ship crowding to the vessel's side and gazing in anxious dismay toward the shore . . . the . . . But I discovered that I could not do it.

It was growing dark, the rain began to fall, we could see that the distant *Boomerang* was helplessly becalmed at sea, and so I adjourned to the cheerless little box of a warehouse and sat down to smoke and think, and wish the ship would make the land—for we had not eaten much for ten hours and were viciously hungry.[28]

Cook's Goose Is Cooked

Plain unvarnished history takes the romance out of Captain Cook's assassination, and renders a deliberate verdict of justifiable homicide. Wherever he went among the Islands he was cordially received and welcomed by the inhabitants, and his ships lavishly supplied with all manner of food. He returned these kindnesses with insult and ill-treatment.

When he landed at Kealakekua Bay, a multitude of natives, variously estimated at from 10,000 to 15,000, flocked about him and conducted him to the principal temple with more than royal honors—with honors suited to their chiefest god, for such they took him to be.

They called him Lono—a deity who had resided at that place in a former age, but who had gone away and had ever since been anxiously expected back by the people. When Cook approached the awe-stricken people, they prostrated themselves and hid their faces. His coming was announced in a loud voice by heralds, and those who had not time to get out of the way after prostrating themselves, were trampled underfoot by the following throngs.

Arriving at the temple, he was taken into the most sacred part and placed before the principal idol, immediately under an altar of wood on which a putrid hog was deposited. "This was held toward him while the priest repeated a long and rapidly enunciated address, after which he was led to the top of a partially decayed scaffold. Ten men, bearing a large hog and bundles of red cloth, then entered the temple and prostrated themselves before him. The cloth was taken from them by the priest, who encircled Cook with it in numerous folds, and afterward offered the hog to

Captain James Cook, 1775–1776.
NATHANIEL DANCE

Top: Cook's ships arrive in Kealakekua Bay in 1879. The Hikiau Heiau is near the palm trees, and where Cook died is behind his ships. Bottom: A roasted pig is offered to Captain Cook at the Hikiau Heiau on January 16, 1879, by the voyage's artist.
JOHN WEBBER

him in sacrifice. Two priests, alternately and in unison, chanted praises in honor of Lono, after which they led him to the chief idol, which, following their example, he kissed."

He was anointed by the high priest—that is to say, his arms, hands and face, were slimed over with the chewed meat of a coconut; after this nasty compliment, he was regaled with 'awa manufactured in the mouths of attendants and spit out into a drinking vessel; "as the last most delicate attention, he was fed with swine-meat which had been masticated for him by a filthy old man."

These distinguished civilities were never offered by the islanders to mere human beings. Cook was mistaken for their absent god; he accepted the situation and helped the natives to deceive themselves. His conduct might have been wrong, in a moral point of view, but his policy was good in conniving at the deception, and proved itself so; the belief that he was a god saved him a good while from being killed—protected him thoroughly and completely, until, in an unlucky moment, it was discovered that he was only a man. His death followed instantly.

Jarves, from whose history, principally, I am condensing this narrative, thinks his destruction was a direct consequence of his dishonest personation of the god, but unhappily for the argument, the historian proves, over and over again, that the false Lono was spared time and again when simple Captain Cook of the Royal Navy would have been destroyed with small ceremony.

The idolatrous worship of Captain Cook, as above described, was repeated at every heathen temple he visited. Wherever he went the terrified common people, not being accustomed to seeing gods marching around of their own free will and accord and without human assistance, fled at his approach or fell down and worshipped him. A priest attended him and regulated the religious ceremonies which constantly took place in his honor; offerings, chants and addresses met him at every point. "For a brief period he moved among them an earthly god—observed, feared and worshipped."

During all this time the whole island was heavily taxed to supply the wants of the ships or contribute to the gratification of their officers and crews, and, as was customary in such cases, no return expected. "The natives rendered much assistance in fitting the ships and preparing them for their voyages."

At one time the king of the island laid a kapu upon his people, confining them to their houses for several days. This interrupted the daily supply of vegetables to the ships; several natives tried to violate the kapu, under threats made by Cook's sailors, but were prevented by a chief, who, for thus enforcing the laws of his country, had a musket fired over his head from one of the ships. This is related in Cook's *Voyages*. The kapu was soon removed, and the Englishmen were favored with the boundless hospitality of the natives as before, except that the Kānaka women were interdicted from visiting the ships; formerly, with extravagant hospitality, the people had sent their wives and daughters on board themselves.

—⚞—

Cook had strict rules to prevent his sailors from having sex with the natives of all the islands he went to, but they found ways to do it without him finding out, thus infecting the islanders with venereal diseases with disastrous consequences, such as reducing the population by preventing many births.

Social status among the Hawaiians was largely determined by genealogy. Moving up the social ladder usually involved having sex with someone of higher status, so when Cook arrived and was thought to be Lono—a god of cosmic reproduction—women flocked to his ships. The Hawaiians were very free with their sexuality, but this also had to do with their generosity, and with their religion, as some of these women were probably devotees of the goddess Laka, who was Lono's wife and a goddess of hula. To the Hawaiians, sex was sacred and a part of their religion.

—⚞—

The officers and sailors went freely about the island, and were everywhere laden with presents. The King visited Cook in royal state, and gave him a large number of exceeding costly and valuable presents—in return for which the resurrected Lono presented His Majesty a white linen shirt and a dagger—an instance of illiberality in every way discreditable to a god.

> On the 2d of February, at the desire of his commander, Captain King proposed to the priests to purchase for fuel the railing which surrounded the top of the temple of *Lono!* In this Cook manifested as little respect for the religion in the mythology of which he figured so conspicuously, as scruples in violating the divine precepts of his own.
>
> Indeed, throughout his voyages a spirit regardless of the rights and feelings of others, when his own were interested, is manifested, especially in his last cruise, which is a blot upon his memory.

Cook desecrated the holy places of the temple by storing supplies for his ships in them, and by using the level grounds within the enclosure as a general workshop for repairing his sails, etc.—ground which was so sacred that no common native dared to set his foot upon it.

[John] Ledyard, a Yankee sailor, who was with Cook, and whose journal is considered the most just and reliable account of this eventful period of the voyage, says two iron hatchets were offered for the temple railing, and when the sacrilegious proposition was refused by the priests with horror and indignation, it was torn down by order of Captain Cook and taken to the boats by the sailors, and the images which surmounted it removed and destroyed in the presence of the priests and chiefs.

The abused and insulted natives finally grew desperate under the indignities that were constantly being heaped upon them by men whose wants they had unselfishly relieved at the expense of their own impoverishment, and angered by some fresh baseness, they stoned a party of sailors and drove them to their boats.

From this time onward Cook and the natives were alternately friendly and hostile until Sunday, the 14th [February 1779], whose setting sun saw the circumnavigator a corpse.

Ledyard's account and that of the natives vary in no important particulars. A Kanaka, in revenge for a blow he had received at the hands of a sailor (the natives say he was flogged), stole a boat from one of the ships and broke it up to get the nails out of it. Cook determined to seize the King and remove him to his ship and keep him a prisoner until the boat was restored.

[The Kanaka mentioned was a chief named Palea, who had been a very friendly and accommodating to Cook's men. What happened is that a native stole a chisel and a pair of tongs from the *Discovery*. After giving so much, they probably felt they deserved something in return. The native escaped, but Cook's men tried to seize Chief Palea's canoe, and they knocked him out with a paddle; they were then pelted with stones by Palea's attendants. The items were later returned, probably by Palea, but as a reprisal for his mistreatment, one or more of Palea's men stole the ship's large cutter. It's not known whether Palea was involved, but the cutter was essential to Cook for ferrying his men ashore. He couldn't afford to lose it.]

By deception and smoothly worded persuasion he got the aged monarch to the shore, but when they were about to enter the boat a multitude of natives flocked to the place and one raised a cry that their king was going to be taken away and killed.

Great excitement ensued, and Cook's situation became perilous in the extreme. He had only a handful of marines and sailors with him, and the crowd of natives grew constantly larger and more clamorous every moment.

The Exploit Runs Awry

Cook opened the hostilities himself. Hearing a native make threats, he had him pointed out, and fired on him with a blank cartridge [or a barrel loaded with bird shot]. The man, finding himself unhurt, repeated his threats, and Cook fired again and wounded him mortally. A speedy retreat of the English party to the boats was now absolutely necessary; as soon as it was begun Cook was hit with a stone, and discovering who threw it, he shot the man dead.

The officer in the boats observing the retreat, ordered the boats to fire— this occasioned Cook's guard to face about and fire also, and then the attack became general. Cook and Lieutenant Phillips were together a few paces in the rear of the guard, and perceiving a general fire without orders, quitted the King and ran to the shore to stop it; but not being able to make themselves heard, and being close pressed upon by the chiefs, they joined the guard, who fired as they retreated.

Cook's death by the voyage's artist. Actually, the mountain wouldn't be visible from this angle. The mountain runs north to south, not east to west.
JOHN WEBBER

Cook having at length reached the margin of the water, between the fire and the boats, waved with his hat for them to cease firing and come in; and while he was doing this a chief stabbed him from behind with an iron dagger (procured in traffic with the sailors), just under the shoulder blade, and it passed quite through his body. Cook fell with his face in the water and immediately expired.

The native account says that after Cook had shot two men, he struck a stalwart chief with the flat of his sword, for some reason or other; the chief seized and pinioned Cook's arms in his powerful grip, and bent him backward over his knee (not meaning to hurt him, for it was not deemed possible to hurt the god Lono, but to keep him from doing further mischief) and this treatment giving him pain, he betrayed his mortal nature with a groan!

It was his death warrant. The fraud which had served him so well was discovered at last. The natives shouted, "He groans!—he is not a god!" and instantly they fell upon him and killed him.[29]

His flesh was stripped from the bones and burned (except nine pounds of it which were sent on board the ships). The heart was hung up in a native hut, where it was found and eaten by three children, who mistook it for the heart of a dog. One of these children grew to be a very old man, and died in Honolulu a few years ago. Some of Cook's bones were recovered and consigned to the deep by the officers of the ships.

Small blame should attach to the natives for the killing of Cook. They treated him well. In return, he abused them. He and his men inflicted bodily injury upon many of them at different times, and killed at least three of them before they offered any proportionate retaliation.[30]

The story of the heart is extremely unlikely. Warriors were allowed to take trophies from those they killed in battle, and Cook's hands were taken to be dried and used as flyswatters, but these were later returned to Cook's men. There are several different versions of the heart story, with some saying it was the small intestines, but Hawaiian dogs were small—about the size of an average terrier—and there's no way anyone could confuse a human heart or intestines with those of a poi dog. The organs would be about a third the size of the entire dog. Perhaps it's just an early urban legend, or maybe someone invented it to please the missionaries. I think a brother or relative may have made up the story to tease the children—the Hawaiians are always joking around—and never told the kids the story was fake.

Still, Cook was cooked. His body was taken to a special preparation area near the north end of the top of the cliffs, where it was roasted so the flesh could be removed and the bones extracted. Since they believed the mana, or spirit, was housed in certain bones such as the femurs, those are the only parts they were interested in. This was the method the Hawaiians used for preparing the bones of the chiefs who were the closest to the gods. So in spite of Cook's atrocious behavior, they still treated his corpse—after the war trophies were taken—with the highest respect. The priests of Lono still believed he *was* Lono and for many years carried some of his bones around as Lono's.

There is a bit more that Twain apparently wasn't aware of. Most of what follows comes from Cook's own men, particularly John Ledyard and the *Discovery's* surgeon, David Samwell, who interviewed many of those involved, with a few particulars from Hawaiian sources.

At around 7 a.m.—about an hour before his death—Cook went ashore with a group of armed marines and sailors manning the boats. He intended to get the Big Island's ruling chief (Twain and others call him a king, but there was no kingdom yet) and some other important people out onto one of his ships where he would hold them as hostages until the cutter was returned—a ploy that had worked for him in the past. He also placed some boats evenly spaced across the entrance of the bay to prevent any canoes from leaving that might be carrying news of Cook's actions and summoning reinforcements, but the Hawaiians knew something was up from the movement of the boats and Cook's coming ashore with an armed guard, which he hadn't done before. They immediately sent the women and children up the mountain, while the men monitored the situation from a distance. The ruling chief, Kalani'ōpu'u, remained in his compound with his wives and children.

Cook and his marines marched through the village, which appeared to be abandoned, up to Kalani'ōpu'u's residence. Meanwhile, at the mouth of the bay, Cook's men saw an outrigger heading out, so they shot and killed one of the men in it—a chief named Kalimu.

Kalani'ōpu'u agreed to go with Cook, but as they were headed toward shore, Kalimu's brother brought news of his murder, and a crowd of 300 or 400 people, half of whom were chiefs, surrounded Cook and the ruling chief. The crowd thought Cook might be planning to kill Kalani'ōpu'u, and they suddenly became very hostile. They and one of his wives began pleading with the ruling chief not

Chief Kana'ina, also known as Kalanimanookaho'owaha, before Captain Cook slashed his face with a sword. The *Discovery's* surgeon, David Samwell, said Kana'ina was killed in the fighting that day, but that might be wrong. He and Palea were the first two chiefs to greet Cook on his arrival.

JOHN WEBBER

to go, so he sat down on the ground. Cook was very insistent and tried to take him by the hand, but Chief Kana'ina put his club between them. Cook took this as an aggressive movement and slashed Kana'ina's face from temple to cheek with a sword.

Heavily outnumbered, Cook abandoned the ruling chief and tried to escape. The Hawaiians began making threatening gestures, and Cook fired the first shot. A sergeant of the marines may have fired the one or both of the second two. The Hawaiians began using their slings to hurl rocks at the marines, prompting the marines and the men in the boats and the ship to open fire. Four marines were killed, along with an unknown number of natives.

It was Chief Kana'ina who clubbed Cook. After staggering a bit, he fell on his hand and one knee. As he rose, someone stabbed him in the neck or upper shoulder, running him through. This was either a chief named Koho or one of Kalani'ōpu'u's attendants named Nuaa, possibly using the swordfish dagger that is now at the Bishop Museum. Cook fell into knee-deep water, and some men tried to hold Cook's head under. He got his head up, so they pulled him into deeper water. He was able to get free and was getting up by supporting himself on the rock when he was struck again by a club and fell back into the water. This killed him. The infuriated natives then took turns stabbing his corpse.

Ebenezer Townsend Jr. noted in his diary in 1798, "The man who killed Capt. Cook was alongside of us. He is not blamed by the natives, and I believe ought not to be, but the circumstance has been so much regretted among themselves, as well as on board every vessel that ever stops there, that he really feels not as though he had done wrong but a regret at having done it; he never visits on board, but goes alongside with what he may have to sell, and on shore again as soon as it is disposed of."[31]

When Rev. William Ellis later asked why they stole the cutter in the first place since they greatly preferred their own canoes and didn't need another boat, they replied that they broke up the boat that day to extract the nails so they could turn them into fishhooks.

It seems to me Cook could have avoided all this if he had treated the Hawaiians better and had rewarded their extreme generosity by just giving them a keg of nails.

The Revered Coconut Palm Stump

When I digressed from my personal narrative to write about Cook's death I left myself, solitary, hungry and dreary, smoking in the little warehouse at Kealakekua Bay. Brown was out somewhere gathering up a fresh lot of specimens, having already discarded those he dug out of the old lava flow during the afternoon. I soon went to look for him.

He had returned to the great slab of lava upon which Cook stood when he was murdered, and was absorbed in maturing a plan for blasting it out and removing it to his home as a specimen.

Deeply pained at the bare thought of such a sacrilege, I reprimanded him severely and at once removed him from the scene of temptation. We took a walk then, the rain having moderated considerably. We clambered over the surrounding lava field, through masses of weeds, and stood for a moment upon the doorstep of an ancient ruin—the house once occupied by the aged king of Hawai'i—and I reminded Brown that that very stone step was the one across which Captain Cook drew the reluctant old king when he turned his footsteps for the last time toward his ship.

I checked a movement on Mr. Brown's part. "No," I said, "let it remain; seek specimens of a less hallowed nature than this historical stone."

We also strolled along the beach toward the precipice of Kealakekua and gazed curiously at the semicircular holes high up in its face—graves, they are, of ancient kings and chiefs—and wondered how the natives ever managed to climb from the sea up the sheer wall and make those holes and deposit their packages of patrician bones in them.[32]

Tramping about in the rear of the warehouse, we suddenly came upon another object of interest. It was a coconut stump, four high, and about a foot in diameter at the butt. It had lava boulders piled around its base to hold it up and keep it in its place, and it was entirely sheathed over, from top to bottom, with rough, discolored sheets of copper, such as ships' bottoms are coppered with. Each sheet had a rude inscription scratched upon it—with a nail, apparently—and in every case the execution was wretched.[33]

It was almost dark by this time, and the inscriptions would have been difficult to read even at noonday, but with patience and industry I finally got them all in my notebook. They read as follows:

"Near this spot fell CAPTAIN JAMES COOK The Distinguished Circumnavigator Who Discovered these Islands A.D. 1778. His Majesty's Ship *Imogene*, October 17, 1837."

"Parties from HM ship *Vixen* visited this spot Jan. 25 1858."

"This sheet and capping put on by *Sparrowhawk* September 16, 1839, in order to preserve this monument to the memory of Cook."

"Captain Montressor and officers of HMS *Calypso* visited this spot the 13th of October, 1858."

"This tree having fallen, was replaced on this spot by HMSV *Cormorant*, G. T. Gordon, Esq., Captain, who visited this bay May 18, 1846."

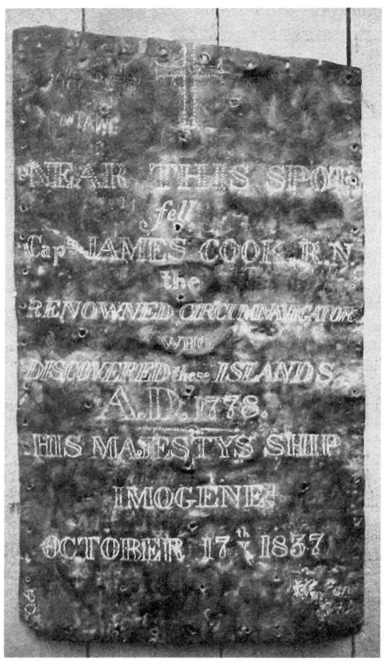

Twain made a slight mistake in copying the copper plate's inscription. This plate is at the Bishop Museum. Someone said they saw one of the others in San Francisco.

WILLIAM ALANSON BRYAN

Top: Cook's monument was built by British sailors in November 1874 on land donated by Princess Likelike. Two years later, four old cannons from HMS *Fantome* were imbedded breech downward in the concrete to support the chain in front of the monument. In the distance, the lava tubes in the cliff face of Pali Kapu o Keōua (the Forbidden Cliffs of Keōua) still hold the bones of chiefs and royalty. Bottom: A plaque marks the area where Captain Cook died. It is underwater at high tide because the land has subsided. There is also a small X carved in the lava.

(TOP) AUTHOR'S PHOTO; (BOTTOM) HAWAI'I'S DEPARTMENT OF LAND AND NATURAL RESOURCES

"This bay was visited, July 4, 1843, by HMS *Carysfort*, the Right Honorable Lord George Paulet, Captain, to whom, as the representative of Her Britannic Majesty Queen Victoria, these islands were ceded, February 25, 1843."

After Cook's murder, his second-in-command, on board the ship, opened fire upon the swarms of natives on the beach, and one of his cannon balls cut this coconut tree short off and left this monumental stump standing.[34]

It looked sad and lonely enough to us out there in the rainy twilight. But there is no other monument to Captain Cook. True, up on the mountain side we had passed by a large enclosure like an ample hog-pen, built of lava blocks [Puhina o Lono], which marks the spot where Cook's flesh was stripped from his bones and burned; but this is not properly a monument, since it was erected by the natives themselves, and less to do honor to the circumnavigator than for the sake of convenience in roasting him.[35]

A thing like a guideboard was elevated above this pen on a tall pole and formerly there was an inscription upon it describing the memorable occurrence that had there taken place; but the sun and the wind have long ago so defaced it as to render it illegible.

YOU CAN VISIT COOK'S MONUMENT AND PLAQUE

To get there by water, you can take a charter snorkeling boat or rent a kayak. The only other way to the monument is by the Ka'awaloa Trail, either hiking in or on horseback. The trail begins on Nāpō'opo'o Road (160) about 500 feet from the junction of Mamalahoa Bypass Road and Hawai'i Belt Road (Highway 11). The six-mile round-trip hike takes from two to four hours. Be aware that it gets very hot during the middle of the day, especially during summer. If it's raining or wet, don't attempt it, as the rocks in and on the trail will be slippery and can shift under your feet. There are no facilities—not even trash cans.

When you reach the shore, turn left when you see the marker 8 sign to get to the monument or go straight to get to the spot where Cook died. Cook's plaque is to the right of the kayak landing area and sometimes is underwater. Also, when going back up the mountain, be sure to take the right side of the fork in the trail. At an elevation of about 525 feet—just to the north of the second turn in the trail—are the ruins of Puhina o Lono ("Burning Lono"), the site where the Captain Cook's flesh was removed from his bones.

SENTIMENTAL MEDITATION
"Music Soothes the Sad and Lonely"

The sky grew overcast, and the night settled down gloomily. Brown and I went and sat on the little wooden pier, saying nothing, for we were tired and hungry and did not feel like talking. There was no wind; the drizzling, melancholy rain was still falling, and not a sound disturbed the brooding silence save the distant roar of the surf and the gentle washing of the wavelets against the rocks at our feet. We were very lonely. No sign of the vessel. She was still becalmed at sea, no doubt.

After an hour of sentimental meditation, I bethought me of working upon the feelings of my comrade. The surroundings were in every way favorable to the experiment. I concluded to sing—partly because music so readily touches the tender emotions of the heart, and partly because the singing of pathetic ballads and such things is an art in which I have been said to excel.

In a voice tremulous with feeling, I began:

> Mid pleasures and palaces though we may roam, Be it ever so humble there's no place like home; H-o-m-e . . . ho-home . . . sweet, swe-he-he . . .

My poor friend rose up slowly and came and stood before me and said, "Now look a-here, Mark—it ain't no time, and it ain't no place, for you to be going on in that way. I'm hungry, and I'm tired, and wet; and I ain't going to be put upon and aggravated when I'm so miserable. If you was to start in on any more yowling like that, I'd shove you overboard—I would, by geeminy."

Poor vulgar creature, I said to myself, *he knows no better. I have not the heart to blame him. How sad a lot is his, and how much he is to be pitied, in that his soul is dead to the heavenly charm of music. I cannot sing for this man; I cannot sing for him while he has that dangerous calm in his voice, at any rate.*

We spent another hour in silence and in profound depression of spirits; it was so gloomy and so still, and so lonesome, with nothing human anywhere near save those bundles of dry kingly bones hidden in the face of the cliff.

Finally Brown said it was hard to have to sit still and starve with plenty of delicious food and drink just beyond our reach—rich young coconuts!

I said, "what an idiot you are not to have thought of it before. Get up and stir yourself; in five minutes we shall have a feast and be jolly and contented again!"

The thought was cheering in the last degree, and in a few moments we were in the grove of coco palms, and their ragged plumes were dimly visible through the wet haze, high above our heads. I embraced one of the smooth slender trunks, with the thought of climbing it, but it looked very far to the top, and of course there were no knots or branches to assist the climber, and so I sighed and walked sorrowfully away.

"Thunder! what was that!"

It was only Brown. He had discharged a prodigious lava-block at the top of a tree, and it fell back to the earth with a crash that tore up the dead silence of the palace like an avalanche.

As soon as I understood the nature of the case I recognized the excellence of the idea. I said as much to Brown, and told him to fire another volley. I cannot throw lava-blocks with any precision, never having been used to them, and therefore I apportioned our labor with that fact in view, and signified to Brown that he would only have to knock the coconuts down—I would pick them up myself.

Brown let drive with another boulder. It went singing through the air and just grazed a cluster of nuts hanging fifty feet above ground.

"Well done!" said I; "try it again."

He did so. The result was precisely the same.

"Well done again!" said I; "move your hindsight a shade to the left, and let her have it once more."

Brown sent another boulder hurling through the dingy air—too much elevation—it just passed over the coconut tuft.

"Steady, lad," said I; "you scatter too much. Now—one, two, fire!" and the next missile clove through the tuft and a couple of long, slender leaves came floating down to the earth. "Good!" I said, "depress your piece a line."

Brown paused and panted like an exhausted dog; then he wiped some perspiration from his face—a quart of it, he said—and discarded his coat, vest and cravat.

The next shot fell short. He said, "I'm letting down; them large boulders are monstrous responsible rocks to send up there, but they're rough on the arms."

He then sent a dozen smaller stones in quick succession after the fruit, and some of them struck in the right place, but the result was—nothing. I said he might stop and rest awhile.

"Oh, never mind," he said, "I don't care to take any advantage—I don't want to rest until you do. But it's singular to me how you always happen to divide up the work about the same way. I'm to knock 'em down, and you're to pick 'em up. I'm of the opinion that you're going to wear yourself down to just nothing but skin and bones on this trip, if you ain't more careful. Oh, don't mind about me resting—I can't be tired—I ain't hove only about eleven ton of rocks up into that liberty pole."

"Mr. Brown, I am surprised at you. This is mutiny."

"Oh, well, I don't care what it is—mutiny, sass or what you—please—I'm so hungry that I don't care for nothing."

It was on my lips to correct his loathsome grammar, but I considered the dire extremity he was in, and withheld the deserved reproof.

After some time spent in mutely longing for the coveted fruit, I suggested to Brown that if he would climb the tree I would hold his hat.

His hunger was so great that he finally concluded to try it. His exercise had made him ravenous. But the experiment was not a success. With infinite labor and a great deal of awkwardly constructed swearing, he managed to get up some thirty feet, but then he came to an uncommonly smooth place and began to slide back slowly but surely. He clasped the tree with his arms and legs, and tried to save himself, but he had got too much sternway, and the thing was impossible; he dragged for a few feet and then shot down like an arrow.

"It is kapu," he said, sadly. "Let's go back to the pier. The transom to my trousers has all fetched away, and the legs of them are riddled to rags and ribbons. I wish I was drunk, or dead, or something—anything so as to be out of this misery."

I glanced over my shoulders, as we walked along, and observed that some of the clouds had parted and left a dim lighted doorway through to the skies beyond; in this place, as in an ebony frame, our majestic palm stood up and reared its graceful crest aloft; the slender stem was a clean, black line; the feathers of the plume—some erect some projecting horizontally, some drooping a little and others hanging languidly down toward the earth—were all sharply cut against the smooth gray background.

"A beautiful, beautiful tree is the coco palm!" I said, fervently.

"I don't see it," said Brown, resentfully. "People that haven't clumb one are always driveling about how pretty it is. And when they make pictures of these hot countries they always shove one of the ragged things into the foreground."

Perceiving that Brown's mutilated pantaloons were disturbing his gentle spirit, I said no more.

Toward midnight a native boy came down from the uplands to see if the *Boomerang* had got in yet, and we chartered him for subsistence service. For the sum of twelve and a half cents in coin he agreed to furnish coconuts enough for a dozen men at five minutes' notice. He disappeared in the murky atmosphere, and in a few seconds we saw a little black object, like a rat, running up our tall tree and pretty distinctly defined against the light place in the sky; it was our Kanaka, and he performed his contract without tearing his clothes—but then he had none on, except those he was born in.

He brought five large nuts and tore the tough green husks off with his strong teeth, and thus prepared the fruit for use. We perceived then that it was about as well that we failed in our endeavors, as we never could have gnawed the husks off. I would have kept Brown trying, though, as long as he had any teeth.

We punched the eye-holes out and drank the sweet (and at the same time pungent) milk of two of the nuts, and our hunger and thirst were satisfied. The boy broke them open and we ate some of the mushy, white paste inside for pastime, but we had no real need of it.[36]

After a while a fine breeze sprang up and the schooner soon worked herself into the bay and cast anchor. The boat came ashore for us, and in a little while the clouds and the rain were all gone. The moon was beaming tranquilly down on land and sea, and we two were stretched upon the deck sleeping the refreshing sleep and dreaming the happy dreams that are only vouchsafed to the weary and the innocent.[37]

[May 29, 1866:]

Although it's difficult to tell, it seems to me Twain wrote more about this day's excursions than of any other of his days in Hawai'i. This day was certainly eventful for him with a wide variety of new experiences.

The Temple Ruins

When I woke up on the schooner's deck in the morning, the sun was shining down right fervently, everybody was astir, and Brown was gone—gone in a canoe to Captain Cook's side of the bay, the captain said. I took a boat and landed on the opposite shore, at the port of entry. There was a house there—I mean a foreigner's house—and near it were some native grass huts. The collector of this port of entry not only enjoys the dignity of office, but has emoluments also. That makes it very nice, of course.

He gets five dollars for boarding every foreign ship that stops there, and two dollars more for filling out certain blanks attesting such visit. As many as three foreign ships stop there in a single year, sometimes. Yet, notwithstanding this wild rush of business, the late collector of the port committed suicide several months ago.

The foreign ships which visit this place are whalers in quest of water and potatoes. The present collector lives back somewhere—has a den up the mountain several thousand feet—but he comes down fast enough when a ship heaves in sight.

I found two Washoe men at the house. But I was not surprised; I believe if a man were to go to perdition itself he would find Washoe men there, though not so thick, maybe, as in the other place.

Two hundred yards from the house was the ruins of the pagan temple of Lono, so desecrated by Captain Cook when he was pretending to be that deity. Its low, rude walls look about as they did when he saw them, no doubt. In a coconut grove near at hand is a tree with a hole through its trunk, said to have been made by a cannon ball fired from one of the ships at a crowd of natives immediately after Cook's murder. It is a very good hole.

—⚓

While the chiefs lived across the bay at Ka'awaloa—where Cook was killed—the kāhuna, or priests, lived along the shore and around the lake near Lono's temple—the Hikiau Heiau. Other chiefs lived nearby. Commoners also lived in the area, supplying food and goods to the chiefs and kāhuna. There were about 10,000 people there at the time, although many were probably there for the Makahiki festival.

Three days after Cook's death, the *Discovery's* men had to go ashore to fill their barrels with water. They did this at a spring near the pond next to the Hikiau Heiau, but the Hawaiians prevented it by throwing stones at them, injuring several. The outraged crowd followed Cook's men to the beach, so the ship fired two cannons at them, killing three men and taking a woman's arm off.

Cook's men regrouped at the ship and tried again, but this time, they were armed with pistols, cutlasses, hand grenades, and torches. They lured the natives into a trap and fired the cannons at them, while one group of seamen snuck around and set the priests' village on fire. Some Hawaiians rushed into the houses, probably to retrieve valuables, and were burned alive.

The following day, Cook's men tried again, but this time, the Hawaiians were at the top of the cliff above the spring and rolled boulders down on them. They cut off the heads of two Hawaiians and placed them on poles to scare the natives away. In all, they killed between 200 and 300 Hawaiians, including 30 chiefs.

After three days of fighting, a priest surrounded by boys and girls carrying white flags and green branches brought them fruit and were soon followed by townspeople bringing supplies and pigs. Peace was declared. On going aboard the ship, one of the chiefs was shocked and horrified to see the two heads on the deck and talked Captain Clerke into throwing them overboard.

This was the terrible end to what had been a promising beginning.

The Hikiau Heiau was a temple dedicated to Kū for nine lunar months of the year. Then it was primarily used for funeral services and ceremonies related to war. People were sacrificed to Kū here. But during the Makahiki festival—their harvest and New Year's festival—Kū would lose his power, and the temple would be devoted to the peaceful, fun-loving agricultural god, Lono. It was party time. War was outlawed, work was abandoned, worship was reduced, and everyone got together to socialize, play games, have sex, feast, compete in sports, consume 'awa

Above is a somewhat romanticized view looking across Kealakekua Bay toward the village of Ka'awaloa in the 1820s. Below is the same view from a lower viewpoint. The Hikiau Heiau was restored in 1917. The kāhuna had their houses to the right of the heiau around a pond. The low peninsula in the distance is where Cook died.
AUTHOR'S PHOTO

(kava, an intoxicating drink with effects similar to alcohol), and generally cele-brate and be merry. It was like Christmas or Hanukkah, New Year's, the World Series, the Super Bowl, and everyone's birthdays, all rolled into one—and it lasted for four lunar months. Not surprisingly, Lono was almost everyone's favorite god.

MOVING ON
The Hero of the Sunday School Books

The high chief cook of this temple—the priest who presided over it and roasted the human sacrifices—was uncle to Obookia [Henry ʻŌpūkahaʻia], and at one time that youth was an apprentice-priest under him.[38]

Obookia was a young native of fine mind, who, together with three other native boys, was taken to New England by the captain of a whaleship during the reign of Kamehameha I, and they were the means of attracting the attention of the religious world to their country. This resulted in the sending of missionaries there.

And this Obookia was the very same sensitive savage who sat down on the church steps and wept because his people did not have the Bible. That incident has been very elaborately painted in many a charming Sunday School book—aye, and told so plaintively and so tenderly that I have cried over it in Sunday School myself, on general principles, although at a time when I did not know much and could not understand why the people of the Sandwich Islands needed to worry so much about it as long as they did not know there was a Bible at all.

This was the same Obookia—this was the very same old Obookia—so I reflected, and gazed upon the ruined temple with a new and absorbing interest. Here that gentle spirit worshipped; here he sought the better life, after his rude fashion; on this stone, perchance, he sat down with his sacred lasso, to wait for a chance to rope in some neighbor for the holy sacrifice; on this altar, possibly, he broiled his venerable grandfather, and presented the rare offering before the high priest, who may have said, "Well done, good and faithful servant." It filled me with emotion.

Kanui the Unfortunate

Obookia was converted and educated, and was to have returned to his native land with the first missionaries, had he lived. [He died of typhoid at age twenty-six.] The other native youths made the voyage, and two of them did good service, but the third, William Kanui, fell from grace afterward, for a time, and when the gold excitement broke out in California he journeyed thither and went to mining, although he was fifty years old. He succeeded pretty well, but the failure of Page, Bacon & Co. relieved him of $6,000, and then, to all intents and purposes, he was a bankrupt community.[39]

Thus, after all his toils, all his privations, all his faithful endeavors to gather together a competence, the blighting hand of poverty was laid upon him in his old age and he had to go back to preaching again. One cannot but feel sad to contemplate such afflictions as these cast upon a creature so innocent and deserving.

And finally he died—died in Honolulu in 1864. The Rev. Mr. Damon's paper [*The Friend*], referring—in the obituary notice—to Page-Bacon's unpaid certificates of deposit in the unhappy man's possession, observes that "he departed this life leaving the most substantial and gratifying evidence that he was prepared to die."

And so he was, poor fellow, so he was. He was cleaned out, as you may say, and was prepared to go. He was all ready and prepared—Page-Bacon had attended to that for him. All he had to do was to shed his mortal coil. Then he was all right. Poor, poor old fellow. One's heart bleeds for him.

For some time after his bereavement in the matter of finances, he helped Rev. M. Rowell to carry on the Bethel Church in San Francisco and gave excellent satisfaction for a man who was so out of practice. Sleep in peace, poor tired soul!—you were out of luck many a time in your long, checkered life, but you are safe now where care and sorrow and trouble can never assail you anymore.[40]

How to Build an Effective Temple

Quite a broad tract of land near the temple, extending from the sea to the mountain top, was sacred to the god Lono in olden times—so sacred that if a common native set his sacrilegious foot upon it, it was judicious for him to make his will because his time had come.

He might go around it by water, but he could not cross it. It was well sprinkled with pagan temples and stocked with awkward, homely idols carved out of logs of wood. There was a temple devoted to prayers for rain—and with fine sagacity it was placed at a point so well up on the mountain side that if you prayed there twenty-four times a day for rain you would be likely to get it every time. You would seldom get to your amen before you would have to hoist your umbrella.

Phantom Construction Company

And there was a large temple near at hand which was built in a single night, in the midst of storm and thunder and rain, by the ghastly hands of dead men!

Tradition says that by the weird glare of the lightning a noiseless multitude of phantoms were seen at their strange labor far up the mountain side at dead of night—flitting hither and thither and bearing great lava-blocks clasped in their nerveless fingers—appearing and disappearing as the pallid luster fell upon their forms and faded away again.

Even to this day, it is said, the natives hold this dread structure in awe and reverence, and will not pass by it in the night.[41]

[Many structures—heiaus, dams, canals, fishponds—are said to have been constructed in this manner, but these days they are attributed to the menehune, who were very short, hairy, and potbellied, with supernatural powers.]

Twain Finds a Nude Beach and Studies Anatomy

At noon I observed a bevy of nude native young ladies bathing in the sea, and went and sat down on their clothes to keep them from being stolen. I begged them to come out, for the sea was rising and I was satisfied that they were running some risk. But they were not afraid, and presently went on with their sport. They were finished swimmers and divers, and enjoyed themselves to the last degree.

They swam races, splashed and ducked and tumbled each other about, and filled the air with their laughter. It is said that the first thing an islander learns is how to swim; learning to walk being a matter of smaller consequence, comes afterward. One hears tales of native men and women swimming ashore from vessels many miles at sea—more miles, indeed, than I dare vouch for or even mention. And they tell of a native diver who went down in thirty or forty-foot waters and brought up an anvil! I think he swallowed the anvil afterward, if my memory serves me. However I will not urge this point.[42]

That is the more polished account that he wrote for his book *Roughing It*. His original version that appeared in the *Sacramento Daily Union* portrays the Hawaiian ladies and himself in a different light.

Venus at the Bath

At noon I observed a bevy of nude native young ladies bathing in the sea, and went down to look at them. But with a prudery which seems to be characteristic of that sex everywhere, they all plunged in with a lying scream, and when they rose to the surface they only just poked their heads out and showed no disposition to proceed any further in the same direction.

I was naturally irritated by such conduct, and therefore I piled their clothes up on a boulder in the edge of the sea and sat down on them and kept the wenches in the water until they were pretty well used up. I had them in the door, as the missionaries say. I was comfortable, and I just let them beg. I thought I could freeze them out, maybe, but it was impracticable. I finally gave it up and went away, hoping that the rebuke I had given them would not be lost upon them.

Mahulualani (pronounced Ma-hulu-a-lani, meaning; "bright feathers of heaven") our nurse, used to take us children down with her for a swim. Wally was then the baby a few weeks old and brother Bert was past his second birthday. I was amused to see Mahulualani, while sitting in the creek, throw the baby out into the water, four or five feet away from her and the little shaver would come swimming back to her, as happy as possible, paddling for all the world like a puppy dog. I asked her if she did the same with us when we were little and she said, "Of course," and pointed out how well we could swim. We were, in fact all ducks in the water equal to the natives.
—FRANKLIN AUSTIN, WHO WAS RAISED NEAR HILO ON THE BIG ISLAND IN THE MID-1800S [43]

I have seen this done today in the ocean and it is an unsettling sight, but seems to be perfectly safe.

I went and undressed and went in myself. And then they went out. I never saw such singular perversity. Shortly a party of children of both sexes came floundering around me, and then I quit and left the Pacific Ocean in their possession.[44]

—⚋

Actually, in Twain's time, pretty much all of Hawai'i's beaches were nude beaches—at least for the vast majority of the population. Even though the missionaries were very powerful, they weren't powerful enough to end this traditional Hawaiian form of recreation. That took the influx of Americans and tourists about half a century later.

Since the 1960s, there have been unofficially designated nude beaches, and partly because of the many European visitors, a few women go topless on even the most crowded beaches, while the bikinis are rapidly shrinking. And it's common to see naked children frolicking in the sand and surf. So far, Hawai'i's courts continue to find in favor of nude bathing.

When Twain was here, wearing nothing was still the most common form of swimming attire, but it was something Twain hadn't been exposed to before. The Hawaiians had been doing it for centuries. Part of the reason was that the men's loincloths and the women's dresses were made from bark and would tear if they got wet. Up through Kamehameha's day, there was a kapu against wearing wet clothes in the presence of a chief or near his house that was punishable by death, which was strong incentive for people not to wear clothes when swimming.

Another factor was that, unlike the Americans and other foreigners, the Hawaiians did not think of their genitals as something that needed to be hidden. The Hawaiians didn't wear clothes out of modesty, shame, or self-consciousness; they felt their genitals were their prized possessions and wore clothes to protect them.

Plundering the Islands
I got uneasy about Brown finally, and as there were no canoes at hand I got a horse whereon to ride three or four miles around to the other side of the bay and hunt him up.

As I neared the end of the trip, and was riding down the "pathway of the gods" toward the sea in the sweltering sun I saw Brown toiling up the hill in the distance, with a heavy burden on his shoulder, and knew that canoes were scarce with him, too.

I dismounted and sat down in the shade of a crag, and after a while—after numerous pauses to rest by the way—Brown arrived at last, fagged out, and puffing like a steamboat, and gently eased his ponderous burden to the ground—the coconut stump all sheathed with copper memorials to the illustrious Captain Cook.

"Heavens and earth!" I said, "what are you going to do with that?"

"Going to do with it! . . . lemme blow a little . . . lemme blow . . . it's monstrous heavy, that log is; I'm most tired out . . . going to do with it! Why, I'm going to take her home for a specimen."

"You egregious ass! March straight back again and put it where you got it. Why, Brown, I am surprised at you—and hurt. I am grieved to think that a man who has lived so long in the atmosphere of refinement which surrounds me can be guilty of such vandalism as this.

"Reflect, Brown, and say if it be right—if it be manly—if it be generous—to lay desecrating hands upon this touching tribute of a great nation to her gallant dead? Why, Brown, the circumnavigator Cook labored all his life in the service of his country—with a fervid soul and a fearless spirit, he braved the dangers of the unknown seas and planted the banner of England far and wide over their beautiful island world. His works have shed a glory upon his native land which still lives in her history today; he laid down his faithful life in her service at last and unforgetful of her son, she yet reveres his name and praises his deeds—and in token of her love, and in reward for the things he did for her, she had reared this monument to his memory—this symbol of a nation's gratitude—which you would defile with unsanctified hands. Restore it—go!"

"All right, if you say so; but I don't see no use of such a spread as you're making. I don't see nothing so very high-toned about this old rotten chunk. It's about the orneryest thing for a monument I've ever struck yet. If it suits Cook, though, all right; I wish him joy; but if I was planted under it I'd heist it, if it was the last act of my life.

"Monument! It ain't fit for a dog. I can buy dead loads of just such for six bits. She puts this over Cook—but she put one over that foreigner—what was his name?—Prince Albert—that cost a million dollars—and what did *he* do?

"Why, he never done anything—never done anything but lead a gallus, comfortable life, at home and out of danger, and raise a large family for government to board at £300,000 a year apiece.

"But with this fellow, you know, it was different. However, if you say the old stump's got to go down again, down she goes. As I said before, if it's your wishes, I've got nothing to say. Nothing only this—I've fetched her a mile or a mile and a half, and she weighs a hundred and fifty I should judge, and if it would suit Cook just as well to have her planted up here instead of down there, it would be considerable of a favor to me."

I made him shoulder the monument and carry it back, nevertheless. His criticisms on the monument and its patron struck me, though, in spite of myself. The creature has got no sense, but his vaporings sound strangely plausible sometimes.

In due time we arrived at the port of entry once more.[45]

[Five years later when writing about Maui's 'Īao Needle, Twain added:]

It seemed to me that if Captain Cook needed a monument, here was one ready-made—therefore, why not put up his sign here, and sell out the venerable coconut stump?[46]

Lono Goes Crazy

I have spoken several times of the great god Lono and Captain Cook's impersonation of him. Now, while I am here in Lono's home, upon ground which his terrible feet have trodden in remote ages—unless these natives lie, and they would hardly do that, I suppose—I might as well tell who he was.

The idol the natives worshipped for him was a slender, unornamented staff twelve feet long. Tradition says he was a favorite god on the island of Hawai'i—a great king who had been deified for meritorious services—just our own fashion of rewarding heroes, with the difference that we would have made him a postmaster instead of a god, no doubt.

In an angry moment he slew his wife, a goddess named Kaikilani Aliʻi.

—◁—

Twain's joke about making him postmaster refers to nineteenth-century political tradition where a newly elected US president would reward his top political supporters by appointing them as postmaster of a state or district. It was a high-paying government job with good benefits and absolutely no work to do. The position was ceremonial and consisted primarily of things like ribbon cutting. In other words, it was the ideal job that everyone aspired to.

Kaikilani was a human who on marrying the god became the goddess Kaikilani-aliʼi-o-Puna (Royal-Kaikilani-from-the-Puna-district). Overall, Lono was a very good god. He was fun-loving, with a passion for surfing and other sports, but jealousy and a flash temper were the failings that destroyed his life.

—◁—

Remorse of conscience drove him mad, and tradition presents us the singular spectacle of a god traveling "on the shoulder"; for in his gnawing grief he wandered about from place to place boxing and wrestling with all whom he met. Of course this pastime soon lost its novelty, inasmuch as it must necessarily have been the case that when so powerful a deity sent a frail human opponent "to grass" he never came back anymore. Therefore, he instituted games called Makahiki, and ordered that they should be held in his honor, and then sailed for foreign lands on a three-cornered raft, stating that he would return some day, and that was the last of Lono. He was never seen any more; his raft got swamped, perhaps. But the people always expected his return, and thus they were easily led to accept Captain Cook as the restored god.[47]

—◁—

The games aren't called Makahiki. Makahiki is a harvest and New Year's festival that features many games and sporting events.

The Poetic Tradition

But there is another tradition which is rather more poetical than this bald historical one. Lono lived in considerable style up here on the hillside. His wife was very beautiful, and he was devoted to her.

One day he overheard a stranger proposing an elopement to her, and without waiting to hear her reply he took the stranger's life and then upbraided Kaikilani so harshly that her sensitive nature was wounded to the quick. She went away in tears, and Lono began to repent of his hasty conduct almost before she was out of sight.

He sat him down under a coconut tree to await her return, intending to receive her with such tokens of affection and contrition as should restore her confidence and drive all sorrow from her heart. But hour after hour winged its tardy flight and yet she did not come. The sun went down and left him desolate. His all-wise instincts may have warned him that the separation was final, but he hoped on, nevertheless, and when the darkness was heavy he built a beacon fire at his door to guide the wanderer home again, if by any chance she had lost her way. But the night waxed and waned and brought another day, but not the goddess.

Lono hurried forth and sought her far and wide, but found no trace of her. At night he set his beacon fire again and kept lone watch, but still she came not; and a new day found him a despairing, broken-hearted god. His misery could no longer brook suspense and solitude, and he set out to look for her. He told his sympathizing people he was going to search through all the island world for the lost light of his household and he would never come back anymore till he found her.

The natives always implicitly believed that he was still pursuing his patient quest and that he would find his peerless spouse again someday, and come back; and so, for ages they waited and watched in trusting simplicity for his return. They gazed out wistfully over the sea at any strange appearance on its waters, thinking it might be their loved and lost protector. But Lono was to them as the rainbow-tinted future seen in happy visions of youth—for he never came.

Some of the old natives believed Cook was Lono to the day of their death; but many did not, for they could not understand how he could die if he was a god.

Journey to the City of Refuge

At noon, we hired a Kanaka to take us down to the ancient ruins at Hōnaunau in his canoe—price two dollars—reasonable enough, for a sea voyage of eight miles, counting both ways.

The native canoe is an irresponsible looking contrivance. I cannot think of anything to liken it to but a boy's sled runner hollowed out, and that does not quite convey the correct idea. It is about fifteen feet long, high and pointed at both ends, is a foot and a half or two feet deep, and so narrow that if you wedged a fat man into it you might not get him out again.[48]

It sits on top of the water like a duck, but it has an outrigger and does not upset easily if you keep still. This outrigger is formed of two long bent sticks, like plow handles, which project from one side, and to their outer ends is bound a curved beam composed of an extremely light wood, which skims along the surface of the water and thus saves you from an upset on that side, while the outrigger's weight is not so easily lifted as to make an upset on the other side a thing to be greatly feared.

Still, until one gets used to sitting perched upon this knife-blade, he is apt to reason within himself that it would be more comfortable if there were just an outrigger or so on the other side also.

Sleepy Scenery

I had the bow seat, and Brown sat amidship and faced the Kanaka, who occupied the stern of the craft and did the paddling. With the first stroke the trim shell of a thing shot out from the shore like an arrow.

There was not much to see. While we were on the shallow water of the reef, it was pastime to look down into the limpid depths at the large bunches of branching coral—the unique shrubbery of the sea.

We lost that, though, when we got out into the dead blue water of the deep. But we had the picture of the surf, then, dashing angrily against the crag-bound shore and sending a foaming spray high into the air.

There was interest in this beetling border, too, for it was honeycombed with quaint caves and arches and tunnels, and had a rude semblance of the dilapidated architecture of ruined keeps and castles rising out of the restless sea.

When this novelty ceased to be a novelty, we turned our eyes shoreward and gazed at the long mountain with its rich green forests stretching up into the curtaining clouds, and at the specks of houses in the rearward distance and the diminished schooner riding sleepily at anchor.[49]

And when these grew tiresome we dashed boldly into the midst of a school of huge, beastly porpoises [spinner dolphins] engaged at their eternal game of arching over a wave and disappearing, and then doing it over again and keeping it up—always circling over, in that way, like so many well-submerged wheels. But the porpoises wheeled themselves away, and then we were thrown upon our own resources.

It did not take many minutes to discover that the sun was blazing like a bonfire, and that the weather was of a melting temperature. It had a drowsing effect, too, and when Brown attempted to open a conversation, I let him close it again for lack of encouragement. I expected he would begin on the Kanaka, and he did:

"Fine day, John."

"A'ole iki."

(I took that to mean "I don't know," and as equivalent to "I don't understand you.")

"Sorter sultry, though."

"A'ole iki."

"You're right—at least I'll let it go at that, anyway. It makes you sweat considerable, don't it?"

"A'ole iki."

"Right again, likely. You better take a bath when you get down here to Hōnaunau—you don't smell good, anyhow, and you can't sweat that way long without smelling worse."

"A'ole iki."

"Oh, this ain't any use. This Injun don't seem to know anything but 'Owry ikky,' and the interest of that begins to let down after it's been said sixteen or seventeen times. I reckon I'll bail out a while for a change."

I expected he would upset the canoe, and he did. It was well enough to take the chances, though, because the sea had flung the blossom of a wave into the boat every now and then, until, as Brown said in a happy spirit of exaggeration, there was about as much water inside as there was outside.

There was no peril about the upset, but there was a very great deal of discomfort. [. . .][50]

Mark Twain Goes Surfing

In one place we came upon a large company of naked natives, of both sexes and all ages, amusing themselves with the national pastime of surf-bathing. Each heathen would paddle three or four hundred yards out to sea, (taking a short board with him), then face the shore and wait for a particularly prodigious billow to come along; at the right moment he would fling his board upon its foamy crest and himself upon the board, and here he would come whizzing by like a bombshell! It did not seem that a lightning express train could shoot along at a more hair-lifting speed.

I tried surf-bathing once, subsequently, but made a failure of it. I got the board placed right, and at the right moment, too; but missed the connection myself. The board struck the shore in three quarters of a second, without any cargo, and I struck the bottom about the same time, with a couple of barrels of water in me. None but natives ever master the art of surf-bathing thoroughly.[51]

Yes, they really did call it "surf-bathing" back then. It's not something Twain came up with. It was also called "surf playing" and "surf-riding."

The Hawaiians have chants about surfing dating back to 1500. When the Europeans were still off fighting in the Crusades, the Hawaiians were surfing. It's thought the Western Polynesians began surfing more than 3,000 years ago, so it may have been brought to Hawai'i with the first Polynesian migration here. The sport then spread around the world in the early twentieth century.

In ancient times up through the 1850s, all Hawaiians surfed—royalty, chiefs, priests, and commoners. They rode on long boards and short boards, bodysurfed, and even rode the waves in outrigger canoes—some still do. Children rode sections of banana stalks. When the surf was up, all work was abandoned.

The missionaries tried to suppress it, considering it a waste of time and because it encouraged the intermingling of naked or scantily clad men and women and because the Hawaiians liked to gamble on the sport. It was suppressed during the latter half of the 1800s but remained popular in rural areas until it rose in popularity again around 1900.

Of course, surfing remains immensely popular and is just one of the many sports and activities that locals and tourists enjoy. Since Twain's time, the types

SURF-BATHING—SUCCESS.

Hawaiian girls and Mark Twain demonstrate the art of surfing, from his book *Roughing It*.

SURF-BATHING—FAILURE.

of activities have broadened considerably and now include stand-up paddleboarding, boogie boarding, windsurfing, kitesurfing, parasailing, canoeing, kayaking, and jet skiing. There's also swimming, snorkeling, scuba diving, and spear fishing. There's fishing from the shore, fishing from a boat, whale watching, dolphin watching, sunset cruises, dinner cruises, and helicopter tours. There's hiking, biking, horseback riding, zip lines, camping, golfing, and tennis. On the

Big Island, there's skiing and snowboarding for very adventurous experts. (The summits of both Maunaloa and Maunakea are covered with snow in winter, but there are no ski lifts or facilities of any kind.) And there's shopping, restaurants, luaus, hula shows, and lounging at pools or near beaches with Mai Tais, Blue Hawaiians, and Lava Flows.

There's also much more, but these are the main activities here. Surfing is probably the fourth most popular after swimming, shopping, and lounging.

ESCAPING DEATH . . . OR NOT
The Ruined City of Refuge
At the end of an hour we had made the four miles, and landed on a level point of land, upon which was a wide extent of old ruins, with many a tall coconut tree growing among them. Here was the ancient City of Refuge—a vast enclosure, whose stone walls were twenty feet thick at the base, and fifteen feet high; an oblong square, a thousand and forty feet one way, and a fraction under seven hundred the other. Within this enclosure, in early times,

This is the end of the short leg of the 1,000-foot (305 m) wall separating the royal compound from the City of Refuge. This wall was built ca. 1550—around the same time Copernicus explained that the Earth was revolving around the sun. The Hawaiians still construct walls that look like this although not nearly so wide.
AUTHOR'S PHOTO

has been three rude temples; each was two hundred and ten feet long by a hundred wide, and thirteen high.

In those days, if a man killed another anywhere on the island the relatives were privileged to take the murderer's life; and then a chase for life and liberty began—the outlawed criminal flying through pathless forests and over mountain and plain, with his hopes fixed upon the protecting walls of the City of Refuge, and the avenger of blood following hotly after him!

Sometimes the race was kept up to the very gates of the temple, and the panting pair sped through long files of excited natives, who watched the contest with flashing eye and dilated nostril, encouraging the hunted refugee with sharp, inspiriting ejaculations, and sending up a ringing shout of exultation when the saving gates closed upon him and the cheated pursuer sank exhausted at the threshold.

But sometimes the flying criminal fell under the hand of the avenger at the very door, when one more brave stride, one more brief second of time would have brought his feet upon the sacred ground and barred him against all harm. Where did these isolated pagans get this idea of a City of Refuge—this ancient Oriental custom?

This old sanctuary was sacred to all—even to rebels in arms and invading armies. Once within its walls, and confession made to the priest and absolution obtained, the wretch with a price upon his head could go forth without fear and without danger—he was kapu, and to harm him was death.

The routed rebels in the lost battle for idolatry fled to this place to claim sanctuary, and many were thus saved.[52]

—⸲—

Once there, a kahuna pule (priest) would perform a ritual for them, and in a matter of hours or days, they would be absolved and free to go. It was a safe haven for kapu breakers, defeated warriors, deserters, and old men, women and children who sought protection during a war. The cities of refuge weren't actually cities. They were more like protected church grounds.

Each of the Big Island's ten districts had a place of refuge, although this one in the Kona district was the largest in all the Islands. During times of war, women, children, and the elderly would go here for protection. They would soon be followed by retreating warriors of the defeated side, even if the losing side was from another island and, had they won, might have killed the women, children, infirm, and elderly who hadn't made it to the refuge. Criminals and kapu breakers could also be forgiven by the gods here. If a safe haven wasn't nearby, a kapu high chief could also offer forgiveness.

Twain among the Tikis

This refuge, called Pu'uhonua o Hōnaunau, was closely connected with the Kamehamehas since the bones of around twenty-three of the Kamehameha ancestors were kept in the Hale o Keawe Heiau, many of which were in wicker containers shaped like human torsos with heads. British captain Lord George Byron (cousin of the poet) described the interior in 1825, saying, "On entering the morai [heiau] we saw on one hand a line of deities made of wicker-work, clothed in fine kapa, now nearly destroyed by time, and adorned with feathered helmets and masks, made more hideous by rows of sharks' teeth, and tufts of human hair; each differing a little from the other, but all preserving a strong family likeness. Under these

The top picture is from inside of the royal compound looking west toward the huge wall, with the Hale o Keawe Heiau between the wall and the royal canoe landing area. The bottom picture looks east toward Pu'uhonua o Hōnaunau. The platform in the center is the second heiau platform. Behind it, under the complete length of the row of palm trees (excluding the group of trees at the right), is the wall, with the Hale o Keawe at its left end.
AUTHOR'S PHOTOS

The caskets of Līloa and Lonoikamakahiki from Hale o Līloa, at a city of refuge on the Big Island's north shore. Līloa ruled the Big Island in the late fifteenth century and his great-grandson Lonoikamakahiki ruled it around 1700. Both caskets were stolen from the Bishop Museum in 1994, hopefully to give them a proper internment, as these were two of the most important items in Hawaiian culture.
HAWAIIAN HISTORICAL SOCIETY

the bones of the ancient kings of the Island are said to be deposited; and near them the favorite weapons of deceased chiefs and heroes, their ornaments, and whatever else might have been pleasing to them while alive."[53]

Of the City's three heiaus, all that remains of the first and oldest are scattered stones. It was replaced by a second, much larger heiau that was built sometime before 1550. This very large platform was abandoned as a heiau and used as a hula stage after Hale o Keawe was built in about 1650. That third heiau was originally known as Ka Iki ʻĀleʻaleʻa, or "Little Light of Joy," which seems odd considering the human sacrifices that were made at each stage of building it in order to increase its mana, or spiritual power.

Today's Hale o Keawe is too small to be a working heiau. It lacks the oracle tower, altar, and other buildings. Only the royal mausoleum has been re-created. So the platform must have been much larger back in Kamehameha's time.

Technically, people didn't really worship tikis in Hawaiʻi, any more than Christians worship crosses. There were different types of tikis or, more properly, "kiʻi," meaning "images." The images that could be seen by the public around heiaus were there to instill a sense of awe, similar to stained-glass windows depicting biblical scenes, and since it was the god's house, they wanted to make it look good for when he came to visit. These images weren't considered to be sacred—just decoration—so the public was allowed to see them. Once the ceremonial period was over, many of the images would be cast aside or even burnt as firewood in the temple fires. New ones would be created when the heiau came into use again.

The sacred ones were carved from wood or stone or were wicker work covered with feathers. These were conduits for communicating with the gods and something to focus on, much like the crucifixes in churches. After infusing them with mana, they were consulted, and then the applicant would wait for some sign that they could interpret as an answer. And like crucifixes, they would also pray to them, trusting their god would receive the message. When not in use, they would be hidden away. No one knelt to them, although Kamehameha did hug one, and Lono's priests had Captain Cook kiss one.

Generally, only the chiefs and priests saw these images. When being transported, they were usually covered. If anyone was near, they had to strip off their clothes, except for their loincloths, and lie down on their backs until the procession had passed. This was not worship but was done to protect themselves from the image's powerful mana. Even the king had to stoop around the kapu chiefs, including his wife Keōpūolani, who were considered closest to the gods, for the same reason.

Worship by the congregation was conducted with ceremonies and prayers by the priests and chiefs outside the heiau. No images were used. The commoners did have their own images at home to represent their family's god and their guardian spirits, but these were generally used in the same manner as the temple images.

The Place of Execution

Close to the corner of the great enclosure is a round structure of stone, some six or eight feet high, with a level top about ten or twelve in diameter. This was the place of execution. A high palisade of coconut piles shut out

Hale o Keawe, then and now. This engraving was based on an 1822 or 1823 drawing by missionary Rev. William Ellis. The photograph is of the reconstructed heiau, which includes an offering tower that is not shown in the engraving.

(TOP) WILLIAM ELLIS AND J. ARCHER; (BOTTOM) AUTHOR'S PHOTO

the cruel scenes from the vulgar multitude. Here criminals were killed, the flesh stripped from the bones and burned, and the bones secreted in holes in the body of the structure. If the man had been guilty of a high crime, the entire corpse was burned.[54]

The round stone structure is long gone. It may have been used as Twain says, but the description sounds similar to the place where Captain Cook's bones were removed from his body and the flesh burned. Criminals and human sacrifices were executed outside of the heiau, then the body was left on the main altar for two days. On the third day, the body was moved just outside the temple to a flat stone where the flesh was stripped from the bones, and both were washed in the ocean. The flesh was then burned to ash behind the altar, while certain bones—which were then considered to be infused with mana (spirit)—were tied in bundles.

Human Sacrifices

We discussed human sacrifices earlier in the book. Criminals could also be executed for their crimes, although Hawaiian society was so dominated by religion that we can't really separate human sacrifice from capital punishment since the sentence of death for crimes was because they believed the offender had incurred the wrath of the gods which would be taken out on the population in general. Thus, the criminal had to die in order to appease the gods, which in turn would rescue the people from the effect of his or her crime.

> Rev. William Ellis spoke with Chief Kamakau at Ka'awaloa, where Cook's monument is, and noted, "On his being asked why he had worshipped that log of wood? He answered, because he was afraid he would destroy his coconuts."[55]

John Ledyard, a sailor from the British colony of Connecticut who was with Captain Cook on his final voyage, wrote,

> [...] the chiefs condemn and they make the body of the people exe-cute. The criminal in this case is bound to a stake. The chiefs cast the first stone, and then the spectators at large until the malefactor expires, and there is a particular spot of ground where his body is afterwards disposed of; but I believe this last circumstance respects the chiefs only. A condemned malefactor of an inferior class, we gen-erally understood was preserved as a sacrifice to the god of war, pro-vided they were not then possessed of any prisoners of war. In matters not capital the offender seems to be disregarded as an object not mer-itorious of public notice, and is generally well threshed or kicked by some of the chiefs, or by all of them whenever they know his demerits and happen to meet him. We could not learn that they had any other method of punishing capital or inferior crimes.[56]

These were presumably criminals who weren't able to make it to a refuge. While we now refer to it as a "city," Puʻuhonua o Hōnaunau was just a place of protection. People stayed there only during a military invasion or for as long as it took to obtain forgiveness.

There were other types of refuges, and most of these didn't have walls. During Kamehameha's reign, all the lands associated with his feathered god Kūkāʻil-imoku were refuges, as was Queen Kaʻahumanu and her lands. She could pardon just about anyone. According to Samuel Kamakau—who personally knew the Queen—Kamehameha "treated her as if she were a goddess."[57] Because of her lineage, the people believed she was the closest to actually being one. She is cred-ited with saving many people's lives after they suffered defeat in battles against her husband.

Not all crimes were punishable by death. Kamehameha instituted lesser pen-alties for many crimes. Theft was sometimes a capital crime, depending on what was stolen and whether it was from a chief. Still, the punishment could be severe, such as gouging out the thief's eyes. And this is one reason why thefts were prac-tically unknown in the Islands.

I find it very interesting that when the royal descendant and future king, Liholiho, arrived on Kauaʻi, the people expressed their loving respect and praise by shouting, "Here comes the son of our lord; he alone has the right to gouge out our eyes!"[58] Not that they expected him to actually do it.

It should be noted that thefts didn't become a problem for Captain Cook until after the Hawaiians were mistreated by him and his men. Also, the lure of metal proved a bit overwhelming for the natives. In addition, the chiefs were used to taking what they wanted, and it's possible they thought some of the items were gifts or had been abandoned. Cook on his final voyage had Polynesians flogged or cut off their ears for theft, while Captain Vancouver hanged two Hawaiians in Waikīkī for the same crime to set an example.

Tales of Two Rocks

Outside of these ancient walls lies a sort of coffin-shaped stone eleven feet four inches long and three feet square at the small end (it would weigh a few thousand pounds), which the high chief [Keōua] who held sway over this district many centuries ago brought thither on his shoulder one day to use as a lounge!

Keōua's stone is on the north side of the second heiau platform.
AUTHOR'S PHOTO

This circumstance is established by the most reliable traditions. He used to lie down on it, in his indolent way, and keep an eye on his subjects at work for him and see that there was no "soldiering" done. And no doubt there was not any done to speak of, because he was a man of that sort of build that incites to attention to business on the part of an employee.

He was fourteen or fifteen feet high. When he stretched himself at full length on his lounge, his legs hung down over the end, and when he snored he woke the dead.

These facts are all attested by irrefrangible tradition.

Brown said, "I don't say anything against this Injun's inches, but I copper his judgment [meaning he doubts it]. He didn't know his own size. Because if he did, why didn't he fetch a rock that was long enough, while he was at it?"[59]

Most of the chiefs were very tall—well over six feet—and they were bulky and very strong—at least the men were, as the women were protected from physical exertion. The commoners, on the other hand, tended to be a lot smaller and thinner. This prompted at least one early visitor to think they might be different races. It probably also reinforced the idea that they were more closely related to the gods. No doubt the tallest and strongest men became successful warriors, moving up in the ranks through genealogy or marriage, until their descendants made up most of the chiefly class.

Ka'ahumanu's Rock

On the other side of the [second] temple is a monstrous seven-ton rock, eleven feet long, seven feet wide and three feet thick. It is raised a foot or a foot and a half above the ground, and rests upon half-a-dozen little stony pedestals. The same old fourteen-footer brought it down from the mountain, merely for fun (he had his own notions about fun), and propped it up as we find it now and as others may find it a century hence, for it would take a score of horses to budge it from its position.

They say that fifty or sixty years ago the proud Queen Ka'ahumanu used to fly to this rock for safety, whenever she had been making trouble with her fierce husband, and hide under it until his wrath was appeased. But these Kānakas will lie, and this statement is one of their ablest efforts—for

Queen Ka'ahumanu in 1816 and two views of her stone, which is on the south side of the second heiau platform. I wonder whether this or Keōua's stone could have been execution places.
(TOP RIGHT) PORTRAIT BY LOUIS CHORIS: BOTH PHOTOGRAPHS BY AUTHOR

Ka'ahumanu was six feet high—she was bulky—she was built like an ox—and she could no more have squeezed herself under that rock than she could have passed between the cylinders of a sugar mill.

What could she gain by it, even if she succeeded? To be chased and abused by a savage husband could not be otherwise than humiliating to her high spirit, yet it could never make her feel so flat as an hour's repose under that rock would.[60]

The guardians of the Hale o Keawe at the City of Refuge.
Author's photo

The story is that Kamehameha and Ka'ahumanu had an argument, and she fled
to the City of Refuge, hiding under this stone, but her poi dog's barking gave her
away. Ka'ahumanu's father arranged for her to marry Kamehameha when she was
about eighteen (some say thirteen), so she may have still been a teenager when she
hid there. There is also a similar version of this story that involves her hiding in
a cave instead of under this rock.[61] I wonder whether that cave could have been a
lava tube Mark Twain explored and which he will tell us about shortly, as it seems
to be one of the nicest caves in the area.

YOU CAN VISIT THE CITY OF REFUGE

Take Mamalahoa Highway (Highway 11)—also known as Hawai'i Belt Road—to near mile marker 104. Turn onto Ke Ala o Keawe Road (Highway 160) and then Honaunau Beach Road, which ends in the park's parking lot. Pu'uhonua o Hōnaunau National Historical Park, PO Box 129, Hōnaunau, HI 96726, (808) 328-2326, nps.gov/puho/index.htm.

While the tikis at the park are reproductions, you can see many of the originals at the Bishop Museum, 1525 Bernice St., Honolulu, HI 96817, (808) 847-3511, bishopmuseum.org.

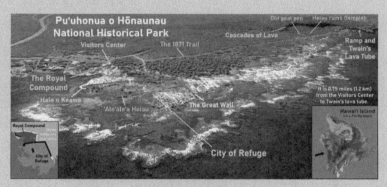

AUTHOR'S GRAPHIC, MODIFIED FROM GOOGLE, WITH THE BIG ISLAND SATELLITE IMAGE FROM THE HAWAI'I STATE OFFICE OF PLANNING

We're Off to See the Lava

On leaving the City of Refuge, Twain, probably accompanied by Stoddard, hiked south to see some other interesting features of the area that are rarely visited today.

We walked a mile over a raised macadamized road of uniform width; a road paved with flat stones and exhibiting in its every detail a considerable

Top: A cascade of lava into ‘Alo‘i Crater in 1969. Bottom: Lava, frozen in time, cascades all along Keanae‘e Pali (cliff). This lava flowed 750 to 1,500 years ago. There are about a dozen lava tubes in the escarpment, but this is a protected area, and visitors are not allowed to leave the 1871 trail. Near the far end of the cliff toward the City of Refuge are the walls of an old goat pen, and a bit closer are ruins of a heiau, but these aren't visible here. The entrance to Mark Twain's lava tube is to the right near the top of the ramp, facing back toward the cascades.

(TOP) D. A. SWANSON, USGS: (BOTTOM) AUTHOR'S PHOTO

degree of engineering skill. Some say that that wise old pagan Kamehameha I planned and built it, but others say it was built so long before his time that the knowledge of who constructed it has passed out of the traditions. In either case, however, as the handiwork of an untaught and degraded race it is a thing of pleasing interest. The stones are worn and smooth, and pushed apart in places, so that the road has the exact appearance of those ancient paved highways leading out of Rome which one sees in pictures.

The object of our tramp was to visit a great natural curiosity at the base of the foothills—a congealed cascade of lava. Some old forgotten volcanic eruption sent its broad river of fire down the mountain side here, and it poured down in a great torrent from an overhanging bluff some fifty feet high to the ground below. The flaming torrent cooled in the winds from

Top left: The longer lava tube Twain mentions is on the left near the top of the ramp, which was built after Twain was there. The pyramid is probably under the ramp. Right: The tunnel curves around to the right and exits on the ocean-side cliff. Sunlight can be seen shining on the wall of the curve about twenty feet from the exit. The cave is quite dark when unilluminated by the flash. Lower left: Looking in from the ramp side, you can see light from the ocean side down the tunnel. The tube has a steel grate at both ends to keep vandals out; unfortunately, park employees store things in it.
AUTHOR'S PHOTOS

the sea, and remains there today, all seamed, and frothed and rippled—a petrified Niagara.

It is very picturesque, and withal so natural that one might almost imagine it still flowed. A smaller stream trickled over the cliff and built up an isolated pyramid about thirty feet high, which has the semblance of a mass of large gnarled and knotted vines and roots and stems intricately twisted and woven together.

We passed in behind the cascade and the pyramid, and found the bluff pierced by several cavernous tunnels, whose crooked courses we followed a long distance, but with no notable result, save that we made a discovery that may be of high interest to men of science.

We discovered that the darkness in there was singularly like the darkness observable in other particularly dark places—exactly like it, I thought. I am borne out in this opinion by my comrade, who said he did not believe there was any difference, but if there was, he judged it was in favor of this darkness here.

Two of these winding tunnels stand as proof of Nature's mining abilities. Their floors are level, they are seven feet wide, and their roofs are gently arched. Their height is not uniform, however. We passed through one a hundred feet long, which leads through a spur of the hill and opens out well up in the sheer wall of a precipice whose foot rests in the waves of the sea.

The ceiling of Twain's lava tube.
AUTHOR'S PHOTO

It is a commodious tunnel, except that there are occasional places in it where one must stoop to pass under. The roof is lava, of course, and is thickly studded with little lava-pointed icicles an inch long, which hardened as they dripped. They project as closely together as the iron teeth of a corn-sheller, and if one will stand up straight and walk any distance there, he can get his hair combed free of charge.

Brown tried to hurry me away from this vicinity by saying that if the expected land breeze sprang up while we were absent, the *Boomerang* would be obliged to put to sea without waiting for us; but I did not care; I knew she would land our saddles and shirt-collars at Ka'ū, and we could sail in the superior schooner *Emeline*, Captain Crane, which would be entirely to my liking. Wherefore we proceeded to ransack the country for further notable curiosities.[62]

YOU CAN VISIT CASCADE AND LAVA TUBES

The cascades and lava tubes Mark Twain explored are in the Pu'uhonua o Hōnaunau National Historical Park, but the entrances to the tubes are blocked with metal grid-like gates. You can look into them but can't go inside. You'll have to go to another lava tube to comb your hair. And there are many more of them on the Islands. The Hawaiian Volcano Observatory has reports of more than 250 of them. Some are cavernous and more than a mile in length. Others are short, and you have to crawl into them. Some are free, but the nicer ones generally have an entrance fee, with tours that can vary from half an hour to a couple of hours. There are also some at Volcanoes National Park, which Twain will take us to shortly.

Here's Another Fine Mess You've Gotten Us Into

Leaving the caves and tunnels, we returned to the road and started in a general direction [back] toward Hōnaunau but were presently attracted by a number of holes in a bluff not more than three or four hundred yards from the place we had just left.

We concluded to go up and examine them. Our native boatman, who had faithfully followed us thus far, and who must have been bearing the chief part of the heat and burden of the day, from the amount of perspiring he was doing looked a little discouraged, I thought and therefore we signified to him, in elaborate pantomime, that he might sit down and wait till we came back. We scrambled through a tangle of weeds which concealed great beds of black and wrinkled lava, and finally reached the low bluff. But the holes were just high enough to be out of reach. I bent a little below the lower one and ordered Brown to mount my shoulders and enter it. He said he could hold me easier than I could hold him, and I said he was afraid to go in that dark cavern alone. He used some seditious language of small consequence and then climbed up and crawled in.

I suppose the fellow felt a little nervous, for he paused up there on his hands and knees and peered into the darkness for some minutes with nothing of him visible in the face of the precipice but his broad boot soles and a portion of his person which a casual acquaintance might not have recognized at a cursory glance. Then he and his boot soles slowly disappeared.

I waited a minute in a state of lively curiosity; another minute with flagging curiosity as regarded the cave, but with a new born attention to the pelting sun; another long minute with no curiosity at all—I leaned drowsily against the wall. And about this time the investigator backed suddenly out of the hole and crushed me to the earth. We rolled down the slight declivity and brought up in a sitting posture face to face. I looked astonished, maybe, but he looked terrified.

"It's one of them infernal old ancient graveyards!" he said.

"No? This is why the superstitious Kanaka stayed behind then?"

"Yes, likely. I suppose you didn't know that boneyard was there, else you'd have gone in yourself, instead of me. Certainly you would—oh, of course."

"Yes, you are right—but how is it in there, Brown? Compose yourself, lad—what did you find?"

"Oh, it's easy enough to talk, but I'm not going to prospect any more of them holes, not if I know myself, I ain't, and I think I do; it ain't right, anyway, to be stirring up a dead man that's done his work and earned his rest, and besides it ain't comfortable."

"But what did you see, Brown—what did you see?"

"I didn't see anything, at first—I only felt. It was dark as the inside of a whale in there, and I crawled about fifteen feet and then fetched up against something that was wood with my nose and skinned the end of it a little where you notice it's bloody. I felt of it with my hand, and judged it to be a canoe, and reached in and took out something and backed out till it was light enough, and then I found it was a withered hand of one of them rusty old kings. And so I laid it down and come out."

"Yes, you did 'come out'—and you 'come out' in something of a hurry, too. Give me a light."

I climbed in and put the relic back into the canoe, with its fellows, and I trust the spirit of the deceased, if it was hovering near, was satisfied with this mute apology for our unintentional sacrilege.

A burial cave, probably near Honolulu, ca. 1898, that looks like it has been ransacked.
W. A. BRYAN

And thus another item of patiently acquired knowledge grew shaky. We had learned, early, that the bones of great chiefs were hidden, like those of Kamehameha the Great; the information was accepted until we learned that it was etiquette to convey them to the volcano and cast them into the lakes of fire; that was relied on till we discovered that the legitimate receptacle for them was the holes in the precipice of Kealakekua; but now found that the walls of the City of Refuge contain orifices in which the bones of the great chiefs are deposited, and lo! here were more in this distant bluff!—and bones of great chiefs, too—all bones of great chiefs. The fact is, there is a lie out somewhere. [63]

―◡

These were probably the bones not of chiefs but of the local families that lived near the cliffs. The remains of chiefs would have been taken three miles away to Pali Kapu o Keōua (the Forbidden Cliffs of Keōua) at Kealakekua Bay.

They had different ways of dealing with bodies, depending on the person's class. Royalty had the flesh stripped, and the bones—along with favorite possessions and items considered kapu—were placed in heiaus or lava tubes or hidden in secret locations.

According to Rev. Ellis in 1825, the bodies of lower-ranking priests and chiefs were laid out straight, wrapped in kapa, and then buried. Others had a rope passed under their knees and around the back of their neck, pulling them into a fetal position with their chin resting on their hands, which were in turn on their knees. Some were then wrapped in many kapas forming a circular shape. Others were wrapped in one rough kapa. They were then buried—often in sand dunes—or placed on lava tubes.

Some corpses were placed in areas surrounded by high rock walls, although whether this was temporary or permanent is unclear since some were left to rot in caves or remote huts. Eventually, the family would carefully clean the bones, wrap them up, and place the bundle in the family's lava tube or burial place. Some select relatives were wrapped in red kapa and tossed into the ocean for the sharks, believing the deceased's spirit would take over the shark and would protect the relatives from shark attacks. On the Big Island, some bones were thrown into the volcano in the belief that their relative's spirit would join the volcano goddess Pele and would protect them from lava.

Funerals were conducted at night because, if seen, their neighbors would throw rocks at them in anger that the funeral procession was passing by their house, believing the spirit of the dead would periodically retrace the route to return home.

THE JOURNEY CONTINUES
A Torch on a Stormy Sea
[May 30, 1866:]
Here Twain drops the pseudonyms he used for Captain Crane and the *Emeline* and begins referring to them by their actual names.

As we expected, there was no schooner *Kangaroo* at Kealakekua when we got back there, but the *Emeline* was riding quietly at anchor in the same spot so lately occupied by our vessel, and that suited us much better. We waited until the land breeze served, and then put to sea. The land breeze begins to blow soon after the sun sets and the earth has commenced cooling; the sea breeze rushes inland in the morning as soon as the sun has begun to heat the earth again.

All day we sailed along within three to six miles of the shore. The view in that direction was very fine. We were running parallel with a long mountain that apparently had neither beginning nor end. It rose with a regular swell from the sea till its forests diminished to velvety shrubbery and were lost in the clouds. If there were any peaks we could not see them. The white mists hung their fringed banners down and hid everything above a certain well-defined altitude. The mountain side, with its sharply marked patches of trees; the smooth green spaces and avenues between them; a little white habitation nestling here and there; a tapering church-spire or two thrust upward through the dense foliage; and a bright and cheerful sunlight over all—slanted up abreast of us like a vast picture, framed in between ocean and clouds. It was marked and lined and tinted like a map. So distinctly visible was every door and window in one of the white dwellings, that it was hard to believe it was two or three miles from our ship and two thousand feet above the level of the sea. Yet it was—and it was several thousand feet below the top of the mountain, also.

Inherent Unselfishness of the Natives

The night closed down dark and stormy. The sea ran tolerably high and the little vessel tossed about like a cork. About nine or ten o'clock we saw a torch glimmering on the distant shore, and presently we saw another coming toward us from the same spot; every moment or so we could see it flash from the top of a wave and then sink out of sight again. From the speed it made I knew it must be one of those fleet native canoes.

I watched it with some anxiety, because I wondered what desperate extremity could drive a man out on such a night and on such a sea to play with his life—for I did not believe a canoe could live long in such rough water. I was on the forecastle. Pretty soon I began to think maybe the fellow stood some chance; shortly I almost believed he would make the trip, though his light was shooting up and down dangerously; in another minute he darted across our bow and I caught the glare from his torch in my face. I sprang aft then to get out of him his dire and dreadful news. [. . .]

—⋖

It was a swindle. It was one of those simple natives risking his life to bring the captain a present of half-a-dozen chickens.

"He has got an ax to grind." I spoke in that uncharitable spirit of the civilized world which suspects all men's motives—which cannot conceive of an unselfish thought wrought into an unselfish deed by any man whatsoever, be he pagan or Christian.

"None at all," said the captain; "he expects nothing in return—wouldn't take a cent if I offered it—wouldn't thank me for it, anyway. It's the same instinct that made them load Captain Cook's ships with provisions. They think it is all right—they don't want any return. They will bring us plenty of such presents before we get to Ka'ū."

I saw that the Kanaka was starting over the side again.

I said, "Call him back and give him a drink anyhow; he is wet—and dry also, maybe."

"Pison him with that Jamaica rum down below," said Brown.

"It can't be done—five hundred dollars fine to give or sell liquor to a native."

The captain walked forward then to give some orders, and Brown took the Kanaka downstairs and "pisoned" him. He was delighted with a species of rum which Brown had tried by mistake for claret during the day, and had afterwards made his will, under the conviction that he could not survive it.

They are a strange race, anyhow, these natives. They are amazingly unselfish and hospitable. To the wayfarer who visits them they freely offer their houses, food, beds, and often their wives and daughters. If a Kanaka who has starved two days gets hold of a dollar he will spend it for poi, and then bring in his friends to help him devour it. When a Kanaka lights his pipe he only takes one or two whiffs and then passes it around from one neighbor to another until it is exhausted.

The example of white selfishness does not affect their native unselfishness any more than the example of white virtue does their native licentiousness. Both traits are born in them—are in their blood and bones and cannot be educated out.

—‹—

It's probably cultural rather than genetic or instinctual. Experts on Hawaiian culture, E. S. Craighill Handy and Mary Kawena Pukui, noted, "Inhospitality was so rare that a case would be discussed with horror for years. Nevertheless, there were of course some who were stingy and avaricious. [. . .] Being so seldom met with, when a case of inhospitality was found, it was noised abroad and discussed with derision."[64]

In those days, the spirit of aloha went far beyond anything that can be found in Christianity or other religions, except for those rare cases like St. Damien. It is difficult for a giving culture to survive when infused in a taking culture, but while the Hawaiians haven't been able to remain as generous as in the past for various reasons, by Western standards, they are still very generous today. I often see Hawaiians go out of their way to help people and refuse any gift or compensation. It's refreshing, and I try to follow their example.

Twain's comments about alcohol refer to laws preventing the sale of alcohol to Hawaiians in an attempt to prevent alcoholism. When he was in Honolulu, he wrote in his notebook, "In Honolulu, you can treat a Kanaka as much as you please, but he cannot treat you. No one is allowed to sell liquor to the natives, and an infraction of this law is visited with a heavy penalty. It is evaded by using back doors, as is the custom in civilized countries."

History has shown us that prohibition of things like alcohol, drugs, surfing, and hula tend to meet with limited success and sometimes cause more harm than good, such as the rise of organized crime during the Prohibition of the 1920s and 1930s that still plagues us today.

—⟋—

In Distress

[May 31, 1866:]

By midnight we had got to within four miles of the place we were to stop at—Kaʻū—but to reach it we must weather a point which was always hard to get around on account of contrary winds.

The ship was put about and we were soon standing far out to sea. I went to bed. The vessel was pitching so fearfully an hour afterward that it woke me up.

—⟋—

First of all, the Hawaiʻi-born, unlike the Californian, does not talk big. "When you come down to the Islands you must visit us," he will say; "we'll give you a good time." That's all. No swank. Just like an invitation to dinner. And after the visit is accomplished you will confess to yourself that you never knew before what a good time was, and that for the first time you have learned the full alphabet of hospitality. There is nothing like it. The Hawaiʻi-born won't tell you about it. He just does it.[65]

—JACK LONDON, AUTHOR, 1916

The distance from Kealakekua Bay to the landing in Ka'alu'alu Bay is roughly eighty miles (130 km) by sea and about fifty miles (80 km) by land. While they were able to cover that distance in just a few hours, the currents, winds, and a storm delayed them from going the last four miles by thirty-six hours.

Twain went on to say that the captain summoned him to the deck, where Mr. Brown was seasick again and begging for poetry, so Twain obliges him by reading him alternate lines from "The Burial of Sir John Moore" and "The Destruction of the Sennacherib," again achieving the desired result. Brown vomited.

Ka'ū and Wai'ōhinu

All day the next day we fought that treacherous point—always in sight of it but never able to get around it. At night we tacked out forty or fifty miles, and the following day at noon we made it and came in and anchored.[66]

Back in Paradise

[June 1, 1866:]

They anchored at Ka'alu'alu, a tiny port on the southeast coast of the Big Island in the Ka'ū district.

—⤢

We went ashore in the first boat and landed in the midst of a black, rough, lava solitude, and got horses and started to Wai'ōhinu, six miles distant, bending our way over the summer-clad mountain-terraces, toward the great volcano of Kīlauea (Ke-low-way-ah). We made nearly a two days' journey of it, but that was on account of laziness. The road was good, and our surroundings fast improved. We were soon among green groves and flowers and occasional plains of grass.

There are a dozen houses at Wai'ōhinu, and they have got sound roofs, which is well, because the place is tolerably high upon the mountain side and it rains there pretty much all the time. The name means "sparkling water," and refers to a beautiful mountain stream there, but they ought to divide up and let it refer to the rain also.

A sugar plantation has been started at Wai'ōhinu, and 150 acres planted, a year ago, but the altitude ranges from 1,800 to 2,500 feet above sea level, and it is thought it will take another year for the cane to mature.[67]

Twain and Stoddard stopped at that plantation, which was run by Captain Charles Spencer and Captain Nelson Haley, whose wives were sisters. Twain asked if there were any hotels in the area. May Rothwell recalled,

> "Why, there are no hotels in all the district of Ka'ū," laughed my father, Captain Nelson Haley. "But please dismount. We will be glad to have you stay with us as long as you like."
>
> "My name is Samuel Clemens, and I'm sort of knocking about, seeing the country." [. . .]
>
> My father, being of a merry turn of mind and somewhat of a raconteur himself, delighted in the companionship of Mr. Clemens. Together they rode over the hills of Ka'ū. They discussed cattle, volcanoes and sugarcane growing—an industry then in its infancy in the Islands. [. . .]
>
> Sometimes the stranger talked of his travels. At other times he sat in the garden busy with pen and paper.
>
> "Letters to his family," thought my mother.
>
> Afterwards she knew he must have been writing some of those delightful and whimsical accounts of his wanderings.[68]

Once again, it was not until after he was long gone that they discovered his identity, probably from his *Union* articles, but they apparently never realized that another soon-to-be-famous author, Stoddard, was with him.

We had an abundance of mangoes, papayas, and bananas here, but the pride of the Islands, the most delicious fruit known to men, cherimoya, was not in season. It has a soft pulp, like a papaw or pawpaw and is eaten with a spoon. The papaya looks like a small squash, and tastes like a pawpaw.

In this rainy spot trees and flowers flourish luxuriantly, and three of those trees—two mangoes and an orange—will live in my memory as the greenest, freshest, and most beautiful I ever saw—and withal, the stateliest and most graceful.

One of those mangoes stood in the middle of a large grassy yard, lord of the domain and incorruptible sentinel against the sunshine. When one passed within the compass of its broad arms and its impenetrable foliage he was safe from the pitiless glare of the sun—the protecting shade fell everywhere like a somber darkness.

The Cistern Tree

Speaking of trees reminds me that a species of large-bodied tree grows along the road below Wai'ōhinu whose crotch is said to contain tanks of fresh water at all times; the natives suck it out through a hollow weed, which always grows near. As no other water exists in that wild neighborhood, within a space of some miles in circumference, it is considered to be a special invention of Providence for the behoof [use] of the natives. I would rather accept the story than the deduction, because the latter is so manifestly but hastily conceived and erroneous. If the happiness of the natives had been the object, the tanks would have been filled with whiskey.[69]

Mark Twain's Monkeypod

While Twain was there, Captain Spencer—who went on to become the minister of the interior under King Kalākaua—began planting several trees, and Twain offered to help. While Spencer planted one at the north corner of the property near the street just inside a low rock wall, Twain planted a monkeypod, also known as saman or rain trees, at the south corner. At least two people said they watched him do it, and one of them—a Hawaiian boy—claimed he handed Twain the shovel.

Many years later, these old trees were cut down, but townspeople prevented the removal of Twain's tree. The cottage he stayed in was just to the north of the tree and back a bit from the road, but the roof caved in around 1900, and it was demolished.

The monkeypod grew to be twelve feet tall, with a one-hundred-foot diameter, before strong winds knocked it over on December 1, 1956. The limbs and trunk were cut up into 5,000 board feet of lumber, and the six-foot-wide stump was then pushed back into the ground by the woodcutters, and within nine months,

Mark Twain's monkeypod.
AUTHOR'S PHOTO

it had sprouted a number of shoots from which grew the current tree. This sometimes happens to trees. As the root structure is the most important part, the trunk can grow back, and it will still be the same tree. It's a bit more severe than losing a limb but not as drastic as what you can do to a planarian—a type of flatworm—which can regrow its head and most of its body after you cut it off. For trees that can live for hundreds of years, it was just a temporary flesh wound.

The wood was used to make calabashes (gourd-shaped containers), bowls, and trays, with 2,000 board feet saved for the proposed Skipper Kent's Kona Hawaiian Hotel in Kona. During the tiki craze of the 1940s, 1950s, and 1960s, Frank "Skipper" Kent was the owner or part owner of six tiki-style restaurants and lounges—Skipper Kent's (San Francisco), The Skipper (Berkeley), the Zombie Village (Oakland, California), The West Indies (Reno, Nevada), and the Polynesian Rooms (Chicago and Boston). It's said the hotel was never built because a heiau and other ancient Hawaiian artifacts were found on the land, so perhaps he used the wood in his Kona house.[70]

Because Twain spent the night in Wai'ōhinu, the town also has a Mark Twain Street, Mark Twain Square, and the Mark Twain Estates residential area, in addition to his historic 150-plus-year-old tree.

This beautiful tree is a fitting monument to America's greatest author and one that would have probably pleased him immensely. His cousin Mildred Clemens wrote, "While trailing Mark Twain over three continents I have seen many monuments erected to his memory, but none, it seems, would please him quite like that spreading Monkeypod Tree in the land, to him always, Paradise!"[71]

I imagine that just the thought of the small sapling that he planted so long ago, still growing in that picturesque corner of Hawai'i and now commemorated to him, would have thrilled him to no end. And I'm confident he'd think it's considerably finer than Cook's monument.

YOU CAN VISIT TWAIN'S MONKEYPOD

Take Mamalahoa Highway (Highway 11)—also known as Hawai'i Belt Road—to the town of Wai'ōhinu. Twain's tree is located on the east side of the bend in the road between mile markers 65 and 66 and has a historical marker sign in front of it. You can park in the lot on the south side of the tree.

[June 2, 1866:]

At 9 a.m., Twain and Stoddard proceeded on their journey to the volcano's crater.

The Procession Moveth Again

Brown bought a horse from a native at Wai'ōhinu for twelve dollars, but happening to think of the horse jockeying propensities of the race, he removed the saddle and found that the creature needed "half-soling," as he expressed it. Recent hard riding had polished most of the hide off his back. He bought another and the animal went dead lame before we got to the great volcano, forty miles away. I bought a reckless little mule for fifteen dollars, and I wish I had him yet. One mule is worth a dozen horses for a mountain journey in the Islands.

The first eighteen miles of the road lay mostly down by the sea, and was pretty well sprinkled with native houses. The animals stopped at all of them—a habit they had early acquired; natives stop a few minutes at every shanty they come to, to swap gossip, and we were forced to do likewise—but we did it under protest.

Brown's horse jogged along well enough for sixteen or seventeen miles [25 km], but then he came down to a walk and refused to improve on it. We had to stop and intrude upon a gentleman who was not expecting us, and who I thought did not want us, either, but he entertained us handsomely, nevertheless, and has my hearty thanks for his kindness.

⤙

This gentleman was missionary Frederick Lyman, whose house was in Pāhala. They had gone twenty-four miles and had about sixteen to go. Lyman later wrote,

> One Saturday afternoon after work was done and we had had our supper, two travelers rode up to our front door and asked if we could lodge them overnight on their way to the volcano. We recommended them to go four miles further on to where travelers usually stopped, to the Kapāpala Ranch, but they begged to stay; they were so tired and it was so late.
>
> We finally consented, Bella [Isabella, his wife] and her native boy cooked supper for them. She made one of her elegant short cakes

[cornbread, she wrote in her diary] and other things. They introduced themselves as Mr. Clemens and Mr. Stoddard. They enjoyed the supper very much and seemed very grateful for our hospitality.

After supper they laid themselves out to entertain us, especially Mr. C. with his slow drawling way. He kept us in roars of laughter. We had not then heard of Mark Twain, but later on found that Mr. C. was the veritable "Mark Twain" of later days. In his book published later, he mentioned his visit with us and said the lady was not very glad to see them, but she did not lock up her silver while they were there.

Twain wrote that that evening,

We looked at the ruddy glow cast upon the clouds above the volcano, only twenty miles away, now (the fires had become unusually active a few days before) for a while after supper, and then went to bed and to sleep without rocking.

[June 3, 1866:]

Mr. Lyman continued, "The next morning, Sun., after breakfast and family prayers Mr. C. made comments on the scriptures read, which amused the children very much."[72]

Then they rode the four miles to Kapāpala Ranch, also known as Reed's Ranch, where they stopped to hire a guide. This was owned by cousins Charles and Julius Richardson, who also owned the Volcano House—the hotel where Twain and Stoddard stayed while inspecting the crater.

We stopped a few miles further on, the next morning, to hire a guide, but happily were saved the nuisance of traveling with a savage we could not talk with. The proprietor and another gentleman intended to go to the volcano the next day, and they said they would go at once if we would stop and take lunch. We signed the contract, of course. It was the usual style. We had found none but pleasant people on the island, from the time we landed at Kailua.

To get through the last twenty miles, guides are indispensable. The whole country is given up to cattle ranching, and is crossed and recrossed by a riddle of "bull paths" which is hopelessly beyond solution by a stranger.

MAGMA ON MY MIND
Like the Path to Mordor

Portions of that little journey bloomed with beauty. Occasionally we entered small basins walled in with low cliffs, carpeted with greenest grass, and studded with shrubs and small trees whose foliage shone with an emerald brilliancy. One species, called the māmane, with its bright color, its delicate locust leaf, so free from decay or blemish of any kind, and its graceful shape, chained the eye with a sort of fascination. The rich verdant hue of these fairy parks was relieved and varied by the splendid carmine tassels of the 'ōhi'a tree. Nothing was lacking but the fairies themselves.

The Kingdom of Desolation

As we trotted up the almost imperceptible ascent and neared the volcano, the features of the country changed. We came upon a long dreary desert of black, swollen, twisted, corrugated billows of lava—blank and dismal desolation! Stony hillocks heaved up, all seamed with cracked wrinkles and broken open from center to circumference in a dozen places, as if from an explosion beneath. There had been terrible commotion here once, when these dead waves were seething fire; but now all was motion less and silent—it was a petrified sea!

The narrow spaces between the upheavals were partly filled with volcanic sand, and through it we plodded laboriously. The invincible 'ōhi'a struggled for a footing even in this desert waste, and achieved it—towering above the billows here and there, with trunks flattened like spears of grass in the crevices from which they sprang.

Toward sunset on the second day [June 3], we reached an elevation of some four thousand feet above sea level, and as we picked our careful way through billowy wastes of lava long generations ago stricken dead and cold in the climax of its tossing fury, we began to come upon signs of the near presence of the volcano—signs in the nature of ragged fissures that discharged jets of sulfurous vapor into the air, hot from the molten ocean down in the bowels of the mountain. We came at last to the summit of the mountain, and these tokens warned us that we were nearing the palace of the dread goddess Pele—the crater of Kīlauea.[73]

Kīlauea, being the youngest of the Big Island's volcanoes, is also its smallest, at only 4,008 feet tall (1,222 m), which makes it look like it's just a bump on the side of Maunaloa, but it is a separate volcano. Despite being the smallest, it is still forty miles (65 km) wide above water and about seventy miles (110 km) across at its base.

For scientists, "Kīlauea" refers to the entire volcano, but for Hawaiians—and just about everyone else—it's just the caldera at the top, which is the home of the volcano goddess, Pele (PEH-leh, usually mispronounced as PAY-lay as in the great soccer superstar). It's one of the world's most active volcanoes and might even be the *most* active, drawing tourists—including Twain—from all around the world. While it occasionally has explosive eruptions, usually the lava gently flows slower than you can walk, but like a blazing hot bulldozer from hell, it's still incredibly destructive, setting trees, houses, and cars on fire as it mows them down.

While the Hawaiians treat Pele with respect because of her fiery temper and regal bearing, they love her anyway, and she's one of the most popular of the Hawaiian gods. She is merciless and exacting, attractive and courageous. Not only is she the goddess of fire and lava, she *is* the lava. And she is hot—2,140°F (1,170°C), to be exact.

The Great Volcano of Kīlauea

Shortly the crater came into view. I suppose no man ever saw Niagara for the first time without feeling disappointed. I suppose no man ever saw it the fifth time without wondering how he could ever have been so blind and stupid as to find any excuse for disappointment in the first place. I suppose that any one of nature's most celebrated wonders will always look rather insignificant to a visitor at first, but on a better acquaintance will swell and stretch out and spread abroad, until it finally grows clear beyond his grasp—becomes too stupendous for his comprehension. I know that a large house will seem to grow larger the longer one lives in it, and I also know that a woman who looks criminally homely at a first glance will often so improve upon acquaintance as to become really beautiful before the month is out.

Kīlauea's crater.
AUTHOR'S PHOTO

I was disappointed when I saw the great volcano of Kīlauea (Ke-low-way-ah) today for the first time. It is a comfort to me to know that I fully expected to be disappointed, however, and so, in one sense at least, I was not disappointed.

As we "raised" the summit of the mountain and began to canter along the edge of the crater, I heard Brown exclaim, "There's smoke, by George!" (poor infant—as if it were the most surprising thing in the world to see smoke issuing from a volcano), and I turned my head in the opposite direction and began to crowd my imagination down. When I thought I had got it reduced to about the proper degree, I resolutely faced about and came to a dead halt.

"Disappointed, anyhow!" I said to myself. "Only a considerable hole in the ground—nothing to Haleakalā—a wide, level, black plain in the bottom of it, and a few little sputtering jets of fire occupying a place about as large as an ordinary potato-patch, up in one corner—no smoke to amount to anything. And these 'tremendous' perpendicular walls they talk about, that enclose the crater! they don't amount to a great deal, either; it is a large cellar—nothing more—and precious little fire in it, too."

So I soliloquized. But as I gazed, the "cellar" insensibly grew. I was glad of that, albeit I expected it. I am passably good at judging of heights and distances, and I fell to measuring the diameter of the crater. After considerable deliberation I was obliged to confess that it was rather over three miles, though it was hard to believe it at first.

It was growing on me, and tolerably fast. And when I came to guess at the clean, solid, perpendicular walls that fenced in the basin, I had to acknowledge that they were from six hundred to eight hundred feet high, and in one or two places even a thousand, though at a careless glance they did not seem more than two or three hundred. The reason the walls looked so low is because the basin enclosed is so large.

The place looked a little larger and a little deeper every five minutes, by the watch. And still it was unquestionably small; there was no getting around that. About this time I saw an object which helped to increase the size of the crater.

Perched upon the edge of the crater, at the opposite end from where we stood, was a small lookout house—say three miles away. It assisted us, by comparison, to comprehend and appreciate the great depth of the basin—it looked like a tiny martin-box clinging at the eaves of a cathedral! That wall appeared immensely higher after that than it did before.[74]

When writing about a year later, he said that "the Vesuvius of today is a very poor affair compared to the mighty volcano of Kīlauea, in the Sandwich Islands."[75]

Then writing about four years after that in *Roughing It*, he added,

> I have seen Vesuvius since, but it was a mere toy, a child's volcano, a soup-kettle, compared to this. Mount Vesuvius is a shapely cone thirty-six hundred feet high; its crater an inverted cone only three hundred feet deep, and not more than a thousand feet in diameter, if as much as that; its fires meagre, modest, and docile.—But here was a vast, perpendicular, walled cellar, nine hundred feet deep in some places, thirteen hundred in others, level-floored, and *ten miles in circumference!* Here was a yawning pit upon whose floor the armies of Russia could camp, and have room to spare.[76]

Continuing on with his narrative,

—⟡—

I reflected that night was the proper time to view a volcano, and Brown, with one of those eruptions of homely wisdom which rouse the admiration of strangers, but which custom has enabled me to contemplate calmly, said five o'clock was the proper time for dinner, and therefore we spurred up the animals and trotted along the brink of the crater for about the distance it is from the Lick House, in San Francisco, to the Mission, and then found ourselves at the Volcano House.

On the way we passed close to fissures several feet wide and about as deep as the sea, no doubt, and out of some of them steam was issuing. It would be suicidal to attempt to travel about there at night.

As we approached the lookout house I have before spoken of as being perched on the wall, we saw some objects ahead which I took for the brilliant white plant called the "silversword," but they proved to be "buoys"— pyramids of stones painted white, so as to be visible at night, and set up at intervals to mark the path to the lookout house and guard unaccustomed feet from wandering into the abundant chasms that line the way.

By the path it is half-a-mile from the Volcano House to the lookout house. [There were grass huts at the caldera long before the Volcano House, but the one built in 1846 was the first to have that name. Just three months before Twain arrived there, it was rebuilt or expanded so that it contained

The Volcano House in 1870 and the ad that Mark Twain would have seen right before he sailed to the Big Island, from the *Pacific Commercial Advertiser*, May 19, 1866. Note how the hotel image in the ad doesn't quite match the real thing.

four rooms for visitors to sleep in. It was a larger grass hut.] After a hearty supper we waited until it was thoroughly dark and then started to the crater.

The first glance in that direction revealed a scene of wild beauty. There was a heavy fog over the crater and it was splendidly illuminated by the glare from the fires below. The illumination was two miles wide and a mile high, perhaps; and if you ever, on a dark night and at a distance beheld the light from thirty or forty blocks of distant buildings all on fire at once, reflected strongly against overhanging clouds, you can form a fair idea of what this looked like.

The Vision of Hell and Its Angels

Arrived at the little thatched lookout house, we rested our elbows on the railing in front and looked abroad over the wide crater and down over the sheer precipice at the seething fires beneath us. The view was a startling improvement on my daylight experience.

I turned to see the effect on the balance of the company and found the reddest-faced set of men I almost ever saw. In the strong light every countenance glowed like red-hot iron, every shoulder was suffused with crimson and shaded rearward into dingy, shapeless obscurity! The place below looked like the infernal regions and these men like half-cooled devils just come up on a furlough.

Pele's House

I turned my eyes upon the volcano again. The "cellar" was tolerably well lighted up. For a mile and a half in front of us and half a mile on either side, the floor of the abyss was magnificently illuminated; beyond these limits the mists hung down their gauzy curtains and cast a deceptive gloom over all that made the twinkling fires in the remote corners of the crater seem countless leagues removed—made them seem like the camp-fires of a great army far away. [. . .]

Here and there were gleaming holes a hundred feet in diameter, broken in the dark crust, and in them the melted lava—the color a dazzling white just tinged with yellow—was boiling and surging furiously; and from these holes branched numberless bright torrents in many directions, like the spokes of a wheel, and kept a tolerably straight course for a while and then swept round in huge rainbow curves, or made a long succession of sharp worm-fence angles, which looked precisely like the fiercest jagged lightning. These streams met other streams, and they mingled with and crossed and recrossed each other in every conceivable direction, like skate tracks on a popular skating ground.

Sometimes streams twenty or thirty feet wide flowed from the holes to some distance without dividing—and through the opera-glasses we could see that they ran down small, steep hills and were genuine cataracts of fire, white at their source but soon cooling and turning to the richest red, grained with alternate lines of black and gold.

Every now and then masses of the dark crust broke away and floated slowly down these streams like rafts down a river. Occasionally the molten lava flowing under the superincumbent crust broke through—split a dazzling streak, from five hundred to a thousand feet long, like a sudden flash of lightning, and then acre after acre of the cold lava parted into fragments, turned up edgewise like cakes of ice when a great river breaks up, plunged downward and were swallowed in the crimson cauldron. Then the wide expanse of the "thaw" maintained a ruddy glow for a while, but shortly cooled and became black and level again. [. . .]

Through the glasses, the little fountains scattered about looked very beautiful. They boiled, and coughed, and spluttered, and discharged sprays of stringy red fire—of about the consistency of mush, for instance—from ten

Halemaʻumaʻu crater's lava lake in 2012.
USGS AND NPS

to fifteen feet into the air, along with a shower of brilliant white sparks—a quaint and unnatural mingling of gouts of blood and snowflakes! [. . .]

I forgot to say that the noise made by the bubbling lava is not great, heard as we heard it from our lofty perch. It makes three distinct sounds—a rushing, a hissing, and a coughing or puffing sound; and if you stand on the brink and close your eyes it is no trick at all to imagine that you are sweeping down a river on a large low-pressure steamer, and that you hear the hissing of the steam about her boilers, the puffing from her escape pipes and the churning rush of the water abaft her wheels. The smell of sulfur is strong, but not unpleasant to a sinner.

Toasted Mostly

We left the lookout house at ten o'clock in a half-cooked condition because of the heat from Pele's furnaces, and wrapping up in blankets (for the night was cold) returned to the hotel.

After we got out in the dark we had another fine spectacle. A colossal column of cloud towered to a great height in the air immediately above the crater, and the outer swell of every one of its vast folds was dyed with a rich crimson luster, which was subdued to a pale rose tint in the depressions between. It glowed like a muffled torch and stretched upward to a dizzy height toward the zenith. I thought it just possible that its like had not been seen since the children of Israel wandered on their long march through the desert so many centuries ago over a path illuminated by the mysterious "pillar of fire." And I was sure that I now had a vivid conception of what the majestic "pillar of fire" was like, which almost amounted to a revelation.[77]

—

[June 4, 1866:]

The next night was appointed for a visit to the bottom of the crater, for we desired to traverse its floor and see the "North Lake" (of fire) which lay two miles away, toward the further wall. After dark half a dozen of us set out, with lanterns and native guides, and climbed down a crazy, thousand-foot pathway in a crevice fractured in the crater wall, and reached the bottom in safety.

The eruption of the previous evening had spent its force and the floor looked black and cold; but when we ran out upon it we found it hot yet, to the feet, and it was likewise riven with crevices which revealed the underlying fires gleaming vindictively. A neighboring cauldron was threatening to overflow, and this added to the dubiousness of the situation. So the native guides refused to continue the venture, and then everybody deserted except a stranger named [probably Charles W.] Marlette. He said he had been in the crater a dozen times in daylight and believed he could find his way through it at night. He thought that a run of three hundred yards would carry us over the hottest part of the floor and leave us our shoe-soles.

His pluck gave me backbone. We took one lantern and instructed the guides to hang the other to the roof of the lookout house to serve as a beacon for us in case we got lost, and then the party started back up the precipice and Marlette and I made our run. We skipped over the hot floor and over the red crevices with brisk dispatch and reached the cold lava safe but with pretty warm feet.

Then we took things leisurely and comfortably, jumping tolerably wide and probably bottomless chasms, and threading our way through picturesque lava upheavals with considerable confidence. When we got fairly away from the cauldrons of boiling fire, we seemed to be in a gloomy desert, and a suffocatingly dark one, surrounded by dim walls that seemed to tower to the sky. The only cheerful objects were the glinting stars high overhead.

By and by Marlette shouted "Stop!" I never stopped quicker in my life. I asked what the matter was. He said we were out of the path. He said we must not try to go on till we found it again, for we were surrounded with beds of rotten lava through which we could easily break and plunge down a thousand feet. I thought eight hundred would answer for me, and was about to say so when Marlette partly proved his statement by accidentally crushing through and disappearing to his arm-pits.

He got out and we hunted for the path with the lantern. He said there was only one path and that it was but vaguely defined. We could not find it. The lava surface was all alike in the lantern light. But he was an ingenious man. He said it was not the lantern that had informed him that we were out of the path, but his *feet*. He had noticed a crisp grinding of fine lava-needles under his feet, and some instinct reminded him that in the path these were all worn away. So he put the lantern behind him, and began to search with his boots instead of his eyes. It was good sagacity. The first time his foot touched a surface that did not grind under it he announced that the trail was found again; and after that we kept up a sharp listening for the rasping sound and it always warned us in time.

It was a long tramp, but an exciting one. We reached the North Lake between ten and eleven o'clock, and sat down on a huge overhanging lava-shelf, tired but satisfied. The spectacle presented was worth coming double the distance to see. Under us, and stretching away before us, was a heaving sea of molten fire of seemingly limitless extent. The glare from it was so blinding that it was some time before we could bear to look upon it steadily. It was like gazing at the sun at noon-day, except that the glare was not quite so white.

At unequal distances all around the shores of the lake were nearly white-hot chimneys or hollow drums of lava, four or five feet high, and up through them were bursting gorgeous sprays of lava-gouts and gem spangles, some white, some red and some golden—a ceaseless bombardment, and one that fascinated the eye with its unapproachable splendor. The mere distant jets, sparkling up through an intervening gossamer veil of vapor, seemed miles away; and the further the curving ranks of fiery fountains receded, the more fairy-like and beautiful they appeared.

Now and then the surging bosom of the lake under our noses would calm down ominously and seem to be gathering strength for an enterprise; and then all of a sudden a red dome of lava of the bulk of an ordinary dwelling would heave itself aloft like an escaping balloon, then burst asunder, and out of its heart would flit a pale-green film of vapor, and float upward and vanish in the darkness—a released soul soaring homeward from captivity with the damned, no doubt. The crashing plunge of the ruined dome into the lake again would send a world of seething billows lashing against the shores and shaking the foundations of our perch.

By and by, a loosened mass of the hanging shelf we sat on tumbled into the lake, jarring the surroundings like an earthquake and delivering a suggestion that may have been intended for a hint, and may not. We did not wait to see.

We got lost again on our way back, and were more than an hour hunting for the path. We were where we could see the beacon lantern at the lookout house at the time, but thought it was a star and paid no attention to it. We reached the hotel at two o'clock in the morning pretty well fagged out.

Kīlauea never overflows its vast crater, but bursts a passage for its lava through the mountain side when relief is necessary, and then the destruction is fearful. About 1840 it rent its overburdened stomach and sent a broad river of fire careering down to the sea, which swept away forests, huts, plantations and everything else that lay in its path. The stream was *five miles broad*, in places, and *two hundred feet deep*, and the distance it traveled was forty miles. It tore up and bore away acre-patches of land on its bosom like rafts—rocks, trees and all intact. At night the red glare was visible a hundred miles at sea; and at a distance of forty miles fine print could be read at midnight. The atmosphere was poisoned with sulfurous vapors and choked with falling ashes, pumice stones and cinders; countless columns of smoke rose up and blended together in a tumbled canopy that hid the heavens and glowed with a ruddy flush reflected from the fires below; here and there jets of lava sprung hundreds of feet into the air and burst into rocket-sprays that returned to earth in a crimson rain; and all the while the

Top: A Hawaiian Volcano Observatory (HVO) geologist is shown collecting splatter samples in 2011. Bottom: Another HVO geologist took a close look at a bank of ʻaʻā lava that was moving toward Hilo in 1984 at a rate of fifty-five yards (50 m) per hour.
(TOP) MATTHEW R. PATRICK, USGS; (BOTTOM) P. W. LIPMAN, USGS

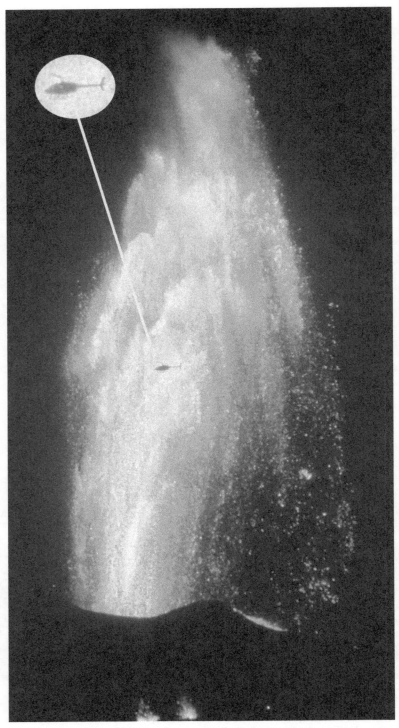

In 1985, the Puʻu Ōʻō fountain shot lava 1,500 feet (460 m) into the air.
MARDIE LANE. NPS

laboring mountain shook with Nature's great palsy and voiced its distress in moanings and the muffled booming of subterranean thunders.

Fishes were killed for twenty miles along the shore, where the lava entered the sea. The earthquakes caused some loss of human life, and a prodigious tidal wave swept inland, carrying everything before it and drowning a number of natives. The devastation consummated along the route traversed by the river of lava was complete and incalculable. Only a Pompeii and a Herculaneum were needed at the foot of Kīlauea to make the story of the eruption immortal.[78]

Accommodations for Man and Beast

It is only at very long intervals that I mention in a letter matters which properly pertain to the advertising columns, but in this case it seems to me that to leave out the fact that there is a neat, roomy, well-furnished and well-kept hotel at the volcano would be to remain silent upon a point of the very highest importance to anyone who may desire to visit the place. The surprise of finding a good hotel in such an outlandish spot startled me considerably more than the volcano did. The house is new—built three or four months ago—and the table is good.

One could not easily starve here even if the meats and groceries were to give out, for large tracts of land in the vicinity are well-paved with excellent strawberries. One can have as abundant a supply as he chooses to call for. There has never heretofore been anything in this locality for the accommodation of travelers but a crazy old native grass hut, scanty fare, hard beds of matting and a Chinese cook.[79]

—⚊

The Volcano House has been rebuilt several times. In 1877, the four-bedroom grass hut that Twain and Stoddard stayed in was torn down and replaced with a frame house that had six bedrooms, a dining room, and a parlor. After a few more rebuildings, it burned down in 1940, and a larger structure was built on the other side of the road.

YOU CAN VISIT (AND STAY AT) THE VOLCANO HOUSE

While Twain's Volcano House is long gone, you can stay near that spot. Other notable guests were Robert Louis Stevenson, Jack London, French microbiologist Louis Pasteur, President Franklin D. Roosevelt, and aviator Amelia Earhart. Volcano House Hotel, 1 Crater Rim Dr., Hawaiʻi Volcanoes National Park, HI 96718, (844) 569-8849, (808) 756-9625, frontdesk@hawaiivolcanohouse.com, hawaiivolcanohouse.com.

Lava flowing toward the Royal Gardens subdivision in 2008.
TIM R. ORR. USGS

The Mystery of Great Kammy's Bones

"Kammy," by the way, is how some people affectionately referred to the great king in Twain's time, and Twain himself used that in one of his notes.

A story by Twain was published in the *New York Saturday Press* that takes place in the caldera. Here is a short excerpt:

> Towards eleven o'clock, it was suggested that the character of the night was peculiarly suited to viewing the mightiest active volcano on the earth's surface in its most impressive sublimity. There was no light of moon or star in the inky heavens to mar the effect of the crater's gorgeous pyrotechnics.
>
> In due time I stood, with my companion, on the wall of the vast cauldron which the natives, ages ago, named Halema'uma'u—the abyss wherein they were wont to throw the remains of their chiefs, to the end that vulgar feet might never tread above them.
>
> We stood there, at dead of night, a mile above the level of the sea, and looked down a thousand feet upon a boiling, surging, roaring ocean of fire!—shaded our eyes from the blinding glare, and gazed far away over the crimson waves with a vague notion that a supernatural fleet, manned by demons and freighted with the damned, might presently sail up out of the remote distance; started when tremendous thunder-bursts shook the earth, and followed with fascinated eyes the grand jets of molten lava that sprang high up toward the zenith and exploded in a world of fiery spray that lit up the somber heavens with an infernal splendor.

A native Hawaiian then tells him how Kamehameha's funeral procession brought the bones down into the caldera, but Pele and her ghostly retinue took them away before they could throw them into the crater. It was later found that the secret location of the sacred relics—or potential fishhooks, depending on your point of view—would be revealed after a couple of things happened, adding that those things had just occurred, so all the Hawaiians were excited with expectation.

Later that evening, Twain reads a book about how the solutions to mysteries are often revealed in dreams and then falls asleep. He dreams he is hiking across the caldera when he encounters a spectral figure who leads him into a cave where a large boulder hides the king's grave.

After waking and falling back asleep a couple of times, he retraces his steps, convinced it is a supernatural revelation, and ends up back at the boulder, where he succeeds in pushing it over, only to discover the bones aren't there.

> I just said to myself, "Well, if this ain't the blastedest, infernalest swindle that ever I've come across yet, I wish I may never!"
>
> And then I scratched out of there, and marched up here to the Volcano House, and got out my old raw-boned fool of a horse, "Oahu," and "lammed" him till he couldn't stand up without leaning against something.
>
> You cannot bet anything on dreams.[80]

The story was dated April 1 at the Volcano House—April Fool's Day. That was about the time he was on his "tour around the island" of O'ahu, but it's not necessarily the day he wrote it. The story was published in the *New York Saturday Press* on June 2, but he didn't arrive at the caldera until June 3, so he must have written it in O'ahu or on Maui or somewhere in between. Perhaps it was inspired by a real dream he had. He was fascinated by dreams and always wrote his down. If not, then he probably wrote this ghost story to take a poke at those who believe in the supernatural.

Growing up, his mother gullibly believed in the latest health fads, patent medicines, and things like phrenology, which was the pseudoscientific nonsense of determining a person's personality by the lumps on their skull. She was the model for Tom Sawyer's Aunt Polly, who insisted on giving Tom an obnoxious medicine, which on one occasion he gave to the cat, that instantly shot around the room like a frenzied rocket, knocking over things and causing general mayhem until it shot out of the window. No doubt his mom's belief in such things contributed to Twain's becoming a skeptic.

As a reporter in San Francisco, he wrote several skeptical investigative articles on spiritualism, séances, and ghosts. This story is also reminiscent of his Nevada Territory satire about the discovery of a petrified man.

Where'd They Go?

People have long speculated as to where King Kamehameha's bones were hidden. There are many rumors, speculations, theories, and fictions. The only people who really knew the secret were the king's two closest friends and trusted advisors who hid his bones for him, probably in a spot that he requested, or disposed of them, if they were thrown into the Halemaʻumaʻu volcano crater. The two people tasked with the job were his advisor Hoʻolulu and his half brother Ulumāheihei Hoapili. Hoapili then married two of Kamehameha's widows—Keōpūolani and Kalakua. Hoʻolulu's descendants continue to be responsible for guarding royal remains, and since 1893, one of them has lived in a caretaker's house—Hale Hoʻolulu (or Hoʻolulu's House)—at the Royal Mausoleum in Honolulu.

It's said that Kamehameha's bones were hidden not because he was afraid they might be made into fishhooks but because he was afraid they'd be desecrated or stolen by rival chiefs or by foreigners, as anthropologists and tourists—like Mark Twain and his friends—were doing.

There are many possible locations. On Maui, his bones may be in a long-lost or possibly mythical royal burial cave in ʻĪao Valley or at Kamehameha III's royal compound on Lāhainā's Mokuʻula Island in the grotto of Kihawahine—a half-woman, half-dragon goddess. There was a place for royal remains on the island. The island and its surrounding lake were buried in the early twentieth century and are now under Lāhainā's Maluʻuluolele Park.

On the Big Island, it's said they're in an underwater cave in the side of Kaloko Fishpond, which is about two miles (3 km) south of the Kona International Airport, in another cave in Kalako, or in one farther inland. An 1819 survey map indicates the bones are at Thurston's Point in Kailua Bay.[81]

Some believe King David Kalākaua retrieved the bones from one of those places and put them in the Royal Mausoleum at Nuʻuanu Valley on Oʻahu.

One person who is most likely to have some knowledge on the subject is Bill Kaiheʻekai Maiʻoho, a descendent Hoʻolulu and caretaker of the Royal Mausoleum. The information passed down through his family is that the great king's bones were bound in a sinnet casket with mother-of-pearl eyes and the king's own teeth around the mouth. The flesh was consigned to the deep far out at sea. Then one moonless night, Hoʻolulu, accompanied by Hoapili and Queen Keōpūolani, took the casket from the 'Ahu'ena Heiau at the City of Refuge, then paddled their canoe to a cave accessible only at low tide and buried the casket in the sand. Under these conditions and because of the way coastal sand washes out each winter and back in each spring and with the time that's passed, the casket and bones probably disintegrated long ago, and the teeth were well dispersed.[82] And perhaps this lends a touch of credibility to the 1819 map.

Or this could just be a story they tell tourists and newspaper reporters in order to keep Kammy's bones safely at rest and the secret secure.

Adventures at the Crater

[June 7, 1866:]

On Twain's final day at the caldera, he wrote a note in the Volcano House's Register. This was a logbook where visitors could write down significant conditions at the volcano for future research, but some people used it like a guest book, noting all sorts of irrelevant information and frivolous personal stuff, so Twain decided to make fun of some of these entries.

Like others who came before me, I arrived here. I traveled the same way I came—most of the way. But I knew there was a protecting Providence over us all, and I felt no fear.

We have had a good deal of weather; some of it was only so-so (and to be candid the remainder was similar). But, however, details of one's trifling experiences during his journey hither may not always be in good taste in a book designed as a record of volcanic phenomena; therefore let us change to the proper subject.

We visited the crater, intending to stay all night, but the bottle containing the provisions got broke and we were obliged to return.

But while we were standing near the south lake—say 250 yards distant—we saw a lump of dirt about the size of a piece of chalk. I said, "In a moment there is something unusual going to happen."

We stood by for a surge and waited, but nothing happened—not at that time. But soon afterwards we observed another clod of dirt about the same size. It hesitated, shook, then let go and fell into the lake. Oh, God! It was awful!

We then took a drink.

Few visitors will ever achieve the happiness of having two such experiences as the above in succession.

While we lay there, a puff of gas came along, and we jumped up and galloped over the rough lava in the most ridiculous manner, leaving our blankets behind. We did it because it is fashionable, and because it makes one appear to have had a thrilling adventure.

We then took another drink, after which we returned and camped a little closer to the lake.

I mused and said, "How the stupendous grandeur of this magnificently terrible and sublime manifestation of celestial power doth fill the poetic soul with grand thoughts and grander images, and how the overpowering solemnity . . ."

Here the gin gave out. In the careless hands of Brown the bottle broke.[83]

YOU CAN VISIT THE VOLCANO

There are many things to see and do at Hawai'i Volcanoes National Park. Most people start at the large Kīlauea Visitor Center, which features many displays. Then there are lava tubes, steam vents, sulfur banks, caldera overlooks, and lots of hiking trails to check out. You should also drive Chain of Craters Road, which takes you down through the lava fields to the ocean.

The National Park Service has done a lot to prevent people from doing the dangerous things that could kill them, but there are still things you should be aware of, so be sure to check out their website. Hawai'i Volcanoes National Park, PO Box 52, Hawai'i National Park, HI 96718, (808) 985-6101, nps.gov/havo/index.htm.

VARIEGATED VAGABONDIZING

TWAIN STAYED AT THE CALDERA FROM JUNE 3 TO JUNE 7, and after writing his note in the *Register*, he headed off toward Hilo on the east side on his way around the island. Stoddard left him by this time, and Twain convinced an Englishman named Edward Howard to join him. Franklin Austin, at whose home the pair later stayed, described him as being "tall and athletic, fully six feet, light sandy mustache, blond hair and blue eyes."[84] The two didn't get along very well. Twain later called him "Ned," but during the trip, he referred to him as "Mr. Brown." Apparently, Howard hadn't read Twain's *Union* articles, so he didn't get the joke. Howard didn't understand Twain's sense of humor and thought he was silly, while Twain thought Howard was cold and unemotional.

Several years later, Twain later wrote in a letter, "Tastes differ, and 200 miles muleback in company is the next best thing to a sea-voyage to bring a man's worst points to the surface. [...] I would as soon think of embracing a fish, or an icicle, or any other particularly cold and unemotional thing—say a dead stranger, for instance."[85]

From the Volcano House to Hilo was about thirty miles and normally took about eight hours on horseback, passing through thick jungle most of the way. At the halfway point, there was the appropriately named Half Way House at ʻŌlaʻa. This was just a small group of grass huts where people could stay if they wished.

Franklin Austin later wrote out Howard's description of the journey.

—⸰—

"I fell in with him at the Volcano House and he seemed to take a fancy to me—showed me on a map where he was going to, some part on the other side of the island (I can't pronounce its name) [Kawaihae] and he showed me no end of letters of introduction. As I am going to cross America on my way home to England, I thought I would have an excellent opportunity of getting acquainted with and studying the ways of a typical American beforehand, and I had failed to get letters although I have many English friends in Honolulu. But, my eyes, I am sure I cannot imagine what is to become of us.

"In the first place the man cannot seem to remember my name—always calls me Brown. I labored with him about this but to no purpose; and then, he talks all the time, telling no end of silly stories. If America is so full of half the perils he tells about, perhaps, I had better keep away from there. Howard, Howard," he repeated pathetically, solemnly appealing to Miss E.[tta, Austin's schoolteacher, as he was a boy at the time]; "Do you think that a hard name to remember?"

It was difficult for Miss E. or me to stifle a laugh in the interests of good breeding. It seemed incredible that anyone could be so lacking in the sense of humor.

"Before leaving the Volcano," he continued, "I suggested that we have a guide. He wouldn't hear of it, said the trail was so plainly worn on the rocks that we couldn't miss it, but before noon we were lost in the forest, following goat and cattle trails in every direction, riding around great cracks, some of which we nearly fell into. My word, what great tree ferns there were, twenty and thirty feet high.

"When it came night, even he thought we had better not go on for fear of falling into a lava crack. He pulled his saddle off his horse and made a pillow of it after scraping up some leaves, as if he were used to this sort of thing, and put his raincoat over him. Even then the man wanted to tell me a story that he was reminded of, hungry as we were. This most improvident man had thrown our lunch away that had been given us at the Volcano House early in the day; said we'd be at the Half Way House before noon.

[June 8, 1866:] "Next morning, fortunately, a native came along with a gun, hunting goats, and we persuaded him to lead us to the Half Way House. It was only a few miles away. Here we got something to eat and the native who fed us on roast pig and boiled kalo and some nasty paste he called 'poi' which Sam seemed to relish, guided us to a wide, well-marked road through the Hilo forest which he said led into town and couldn't be missed [. . .]"

"Where did you stop in Hilo?" asked Miss E.

"We came into town through a native village a wide street and turned down to the waterfront, then turned to the left passing some Chinese stores until we came to a drug store. I was for going to a hotel and went in to inquire. A little freckled-faced girl, who walked lame, came out of the backroom behind the counter and laughed when I asked for a hotel.

"'There is no hotel,' she said, 'but if you are strangers, if you will wait until my father, the doctor comes in I will take you home and you can stay with us as long as you please.'

Top: The road from Kīluaea to Hilo, ca. 1890s. Bottom: Hilo Bay, with Coconut Island on the right, ca. 1890.

"My word; no introduction—didn't know who we were, our names even, and seemed disappointed because we didn't wait and let her take us home; bright faced girl, too, even if she did have freckles."

Miss E. laughed, "A hotel couldn't live a minute in Hilo. When a vessel comes in with passengers those dear people go down to the boat landing and fight to see who's going to get the strangers for guests. Of course, if they have a letter to one of them that settles it."

"How extraordinary! Sam had followed me in to the store and pulling a lot of letters from his pocket asked the girl where he could find Captain Thomas Spencer. She told us that his was the next store in the long building but that we would probably not find him there but by turning the corner, the street ran right into his place, a large house on the hill."

Miss E. was being very much amused by this Englishman and with a twinkle in her eyes, asked, "What do you think of Americans anyway as far as you have gone?"

"Sam Clemens is a most curious sort of chap, always telling silly stories and everybody seems to be laughing at him, so much so, in fact, that I sometimes feel sorry for him, but, nevertheless, he is a very gentlemanly fellow and a good sport. But Captain Spencer is a very vulgar sort of a man—has an awful voice and bellows like a bull, but, my word, what a sport he is and knows how to live too. He and Sam got on well together. You could have heard him laugh and give orders to his servants, I daresay, blocks away."[86]

Captain Thomas Spencer was the brother of Captain Charles Spencer for whom Twain planted the monkeypod tree. Both were former whaling captains and came from a family of whaling captains. Franklin Austin said that Captain Thomas Spencer called Hilo the Crescent City of Churches, and Austin thought the place would have just been "a hum-drum missionary town" if it wasn't for the captain. Besides his large store, Spencer had a 3,000-acre sugar plantation and a mill within the town's limits.

While Twain said he spent three days with Sheriff John Coney, he might still have stayed at Spencer's. Or he may have been at Hilo for more than three days and stayed at both places. The time line is a bit hazy at this point.

Up in Smoke

[Probably June 11, 1866:]

From Hilo, Twain and Howard rode six miles to the Onomea Sugar Plantation, which was cofounded by Judge Stafford Austin, the father of Franklin Austin, who at that time was a boy with an excellent memory. Again, they didn't know he was Mark Twain until later on. He recalled that late in the afternoon, two strangers rode up—an immaculately dressed Englishman in riding breeches, pigskin leggings, and brass spurs and a slouchily dressed American wearing a native laulala straw hat with large, jingling Mexican spurs.

After reading the letter father held out his hand and smiling said: "I am glad to see you Mr. Clemens. You are welcome anyway as all strangers are, but with this letter from my old friend, you are doubly welcome." [. . .]

Clemens then turned to the Englishman, "This is my friend Brown, Judge Austin."

"My name is not Brown. It is Howard," hastily interposed the Englishman in some vexation as he shook hands. "My traveling companion persists in calling me Brown."

"Well, it's easier to remember," drawled Mr. Clemens.

Father looked first at the vexed Englishman's face, then caught a teasing twinkle in the eyes of the shorter man, and laughed, "Oh well, what's in a name," and led the way up the slate blue walk through the garden to the house [. . .]

[After being shown their quarters and refreshing, they gathered for dinner, along with the plantation's overseers and mechanics.]

Samuel Clemens (Mark Twain) from the start dominated the conversation, keeping the table in roars of laughter with anecdotes and jokes, so much so, in fact, that father could hardly carve the roast and had to stand up to his job, while mother nearly spilled the vegetables she dished out. He seemed pleased with his seat at the head of the table where he could see all of the faces and note the effect of his jokes. The only one who did not seem to appreciate the fun was Howard, the Englishman, who wore a bored expression. I may be mistaken, but I imagined that Clemens was a little annoyed that he could not make "his friend Brown" laugh. His slow, drawling voice for which he became famous, was too funny for anything. [. . .]

After the most hilarious and enjoyable dinner in my memory, at Onomea, we retired to the parlor while the men filed out to their lodgings. The first thing Clemens did was to slap father on the back in a familiar way and remark, "Now Judge, I want your strongest pipe and strongest tobacco."

Father was startled. He was a very dignified man, tall, an inch over six feet, weighing two hundred and forty pounds, and no one ever took such liberties with him. But a twinkle came into his eyes and I was sure he meant mischief—to have revenge on this fresh and familiar young man.

"Wait just a few minutes until I have my man cut up some tobacco and we will retire to my smoking room and enjoy smoking to our hearts' content," father said.

Mahulualani [the children's nursemaid] had just come in with the baby for mother to nurse before putting it to bed and father told her to call Kekau. When his servant answered the call he instructed him to cut up a lot of the "paka eleele" (black tobacco). A few weeks before this some naval officers had visited Onomea from an American man-of-war visiting Hilo Bay for a time (I think it was Capt. Kempt and his officers from the old gunboat *Adams*) and they had given father—several long plugs of black navy tobacco. He also had a large meerschaum pipe, with a long stem, that was so strong that even he could not smoke it. [...]

Kekau reported the tobacco cut and we all adjourned to the smoking room. Father handed Clemens the big pipe, which he raved over, and the box of tobacco Kekau had just cut up.

"Where did you get that Navy Plug?" he exclaimed, "It can't be bought."

Father explained how he got it and gave him a piece. Mother did not like tobacco smoke, but she braved it. She saw that father had some joke up his sleeve and did not want to miss it or Mr. Clemens' stories. She knew at once what father was up to when he brought out the big pipe and shook her head smiling. Howard filled himself pipe of milder tobacco and kept on talking to Miss E. with whom he seemed to be getting on very well. [...] As soon as Mr. Clemens had filled the big meerschaum and settled himself comfortably in one of father's easy rocking chairs, he began his stories and jokes again. After smoking his pipe out Mr. Howard excused himself and said he would retire.

"Don't hurry in the morning," father called. "We never have family breakfast until eight o'clock."

Miss E. began also to see what father was driving at when she saw Mr. Clemens with the big pipe, for it was a standing joke that at last Judge Austin had got a pipe too strong for him. But it did not phase Sam Clemens a bit. He filled pipeful after pipeful and kept us laughing until two o'clock in the morning.[87]

—⸝

The practical joker was doomed to disappointment. Twain was a devoted smoker who smoked like a blast-furnace chimney almost constantly up until he got married in 1870, and even then, he would smoke on those occasions when he could, and he resumed again after she died. He once said, "I have made a rule never to smoke but one cigar at a time. [. . .] As an example to others, and not that I care for moderation myself, it has always been my rule never to smoke when asleep, and never to refrain when awake. It is a good rule."[88]

The Missing Twain

[Probably June 12, 1866:]

In the morning, Franklin recalled he woke up late to a great commotion. Twain had gone missing, and Howard was pacing back and forth saying, "The man has lost himself again—lost again." Etta was trying to calm him, while the Judge sent out people to search for him. Twain was finally found about four hours later. He was out in the cane fields with one of the work parties, sitting on a pile of sugarcane near a flume, making sketches. Franklin added,

> Of course, I did not appreciate it at the time, but in looking backward to this incident I cannot help remarking the strange, apparently hypnotic influence this man's personality shed about him upon everyone, for sheer joy, happiness and gladness by simply being in his presence.
>
> Even Howard, who utterly failed to appreciate his humor, was nevertheless, drawn to him in his matter-of-fact way as if he were, in fact irresponsible and needed his protection and guardianship; even the tall, handsome athletic Kanaka, who had just guided him out of the canefields, with bright happy eyes, and who could not understand what he said, just laughed from sheer joy when he looked at him, and Kekau, the faithful and solemn, would look at him,

lingeringly, with his one bright eye and, as was his nature, in his doglike way, would surely have cheerfully laid down his life for him if he had ever been in a fix. He seemed to have a personal and voiceless affinity for all things natural and human.[89]

On the Road Again
[Probably June 12 to 15, 1866:]

After lunch, Twain insisted they move on in spite of the Judge's pleas that they remain until the following day, but time was short since the pair had to make it over some rough terrain to reach Kawaihae on the other side of the island in order to catch the steamship back to Oʻahu, a distance of about sixty-seven miles (108 km). The Hamakua Coast is on the rainy side of the island, so is thick jungle with lots of gulches that they would have to ride down into on switchbacks and ford streams and rivers at the bottom and then ride back up. They made it only four miles (6 km) that afternoon and probably the following day reached Laupāhoehoe, where we know they stayed a night. That would have left them less than two days to get to Kawaihae—about fifty-one miles (82 km) at that time—to catch the steamer or wait another week. My guess is they spent the next night at Parker Ranch in Waimea—one of the oldest ranches in the United States and the largest in Hawaiʻi, reaching their destination the following day.

This was a very rough journey, and Twain should have taken it slowly. As a result, he ended up with severe saddle boils—infected saddle sores—that incapacitated him for quite some time.

Twain doesn't mention it, but there were three heiaus in Kawaihae that he would have found very interesting. Perhaps he was too sore and exhausted or just didn't have the time to wander over to see them. But even then, he must have seen two of them from a distance.

The largest of the three, Puʻukoholā Heiau, is the second-largest heiau in the Islands. It's on a hill overlooking the bay and was built by Kamehameha for his war god in preparation for his attack on Maui and then Oʻahu. Originally, it had more than forty colossal tikis and an altar on which victims who had been stoned to death or strangled were placed. Below that is an older heiau, and out in the bay, was the smallest of the three heiaus. It's said this one was dedicated to one or more of the local shark gods. Once the corpses of middle

Hale o Kapuni
Heiau
(approximate location, now gone)

Stone Leaning Post

Pu'ukoholā
Heiau

Mailekini
Heiau

Top: Kamehameha built Pu'ukoholā Heiau and dedicated it to his war god Kūkā'ilimoku—or "Kū, the snatcher of islands"—before he set out to conquer the other islands. Bottom: Pu'ukoholā Heiau is on top of the hill, above the older Mailekini Heiau. The purpose of the older heiau is unknown. Out in the bay is the site where the Hale o Kapuni Heiau was. Its stones have been scattered, probably by several tsunamis. Its remnants were last seen in the 1950s. Dedicated to sharks, this apparently was a personal temple for the district chief's family gods, believing his ancestors could manifest themselves through the sharks. Tales say this chief murdered people whom he or his priests captured along the trails in order to feed them to the sharks. Sharks—especially the black-tipped reef sharks—are most often seen in this bay between February and April.

(TOP) AUTHOR'S PHOTO; (BOTTOM) AUTHOR'S GRAPHIC USING A PHOTOGRAPH BY S. BERGFELD, DLNR, AND A SATELLITE IMAGE OF THE BIG ISLAND FROM THE HAWAI'I STATE OFFICE OF PLANNING

heiau's sacrificial victims began to rot, they were placed in the bay's heiau, where sharks could come in and eat them, but more often, they fed the sharks pigs and chickens. That heiau is now gone, and its stones are scattered across the bay floor. Onshore is a large cylindrically shaped rock against which a chief sat while watching the sharks in the bay. Unfortunately, someone accidentally shortened the stone by backing a truck into it, but the stone and two of the pieces that were knocked off are still there, although they have been moved a bit farther from the shore.

—✍

[Probably June 15, 1866:]

Twain, Howard, and five other cabin passengers, along with sixty deck passengers, all took the steamship *Kīlauea*, which was owned by the Hawaiian government, back to Honolulu. Twain was on the Big Island for two weeks, not counting the two-day voyage from Kealakekua to Ka'ū.

YOU CAN VISIT THE SITE OF THE SHARK TEMPLE

Pu'ukoholā Heiau is King Kamehameha's war temple, Mailekini Heiau is the older temple, and Hale o Kapuni was the shark heiau. Pu'ukoholā Heiau National Historic Site, 62-3601 Kawaihae Rd., Kawaihae, HI 96743, (808) 882-7218 x1014, nps.gov/puhe/index.htm.

RETURNING TO
OʻAHU

CASUALTIES AND SURVIVORS

"Home Again"

[June 16, 1866:]

I have just got back from a three weeks' cruise on the island of Hawai'i and an eventful sojourn of several days at the great volcano. But of that trip I will speak hereafter. I am too badly used up to do it now. I only want to write a few lines at present by the *Live Yankee*, merely to keep my communications open, as the soldiers say.[1]

﹏

On returning to Honolulu, Twain went back to the American House to recuperate from his saddle boils. Six years later, Twain received a letter from a close friend that reminded him of his confinement in the American House.

> I received a letter from the Reverend Doctor Rising, who had been rector of the Episcopal church in Virginia City in my time, in which letter Doctor Rising made reference to certain things which had happened to us in the Sandwich Islands six years before; among other things he made casual mention of the Honolulu hotel's poverty in the matter of literature.
>
> At first I did not see the bearing of the remark; it called nothing to my mind. But presently it did—with a flash! There was but one book in Mr. Kirchhof's hotel [the American House], and that was the first volume of Doctor [Oliver Wendell] Holmes's blue-and-gold series. I had had a fortnight's chance to get well acquainted with its contents, for I had ridden around the Big Island (Hawai'i) on horseback and had brought back so many saddle boils that if there had been a duty on them it would have bankrupted me to pay it.
>
> They kept me in my room, unclothed and in persistent pain, for two weeks, with no company but cigars and the little volume of poems. Of course I read them almost constantly; I read them

from beginning to end, then read them backwards, then began in the middle and read them both ways, then read them wrong end first and upside down. In a word, I read the book to rags, and was infinitely grateful to the hand that wrote it.[2]

I wonder why he didn't spend the time writing. But then, poetry did have a recuperative effect on Mr. Brown when he was seasick.

The Passing of a Princess

A couple of weeks earlier, while Twain was visiting the site of Captain Cook's death, the king's sister and presumptive heir to the throne suddenly died at the age of twenty-seven. When Twain returned to O'ahu, he arrived in the middle of the monthlong mourning period, the center of which was the 'Iolani Palace—just two blocks from Twain's hotel. Princess Victoria Kamāmalu Ka'ahumanu was the granddaughter and last female descendant of Kamehameha.

—❧—

The natives have always been remarkable for the extravagant love and devotion they show toward their chiefs—it almost amounts to worship. When Victoria was a girl of fifteen she made an excursion through the island of Hawai'i (the realm of the ancient founders of her race), with her guardian and a retinue of servants, and was everywhere received with a wild enthusiasm by her people.

In Hilo [on the east side of the Big Island], they came in multitudes to the house of the reverend missionary, where she was stopping, and brought with them all manner of offerings—poi, kalo, bananas, pigs, fowls—anything they could get hold of which was valuable in their eyes—and many of them stinted and starved themselves for the time being, no doubt, to do this honor to a princess who could not use or carry away the hundredth part of what they lavished upon her. And for hours and even days together the people thronged around the place and wept and chanted their distressing songs, and wailed their agonizing wails; for joy at the return of a loved one and sorrow at his death are expressed in precisely the same way with this curious people. [. . .]

Mourning for the Dead

The Princess died on Tuesday, May 29th, and on Wednesday the body was conveyed to the King's palace, there to lie in state about four weeks, which is royal custom here. [. . .]

Outside, on the broad verandahs and in the ample palace yard, a multitude of common natives howl and wail, and weep and chant the dreary funeral songs of ancient Hawai'i, and dance the strange dance for the dead. Numbers of these people remain there day after day and night after night, sleeping in the open air in the intervals of their mourning ceremonies. [. . .]

Twain went on to further describe the traditional Hawaiian activities during this period of mourning and how the missionaries strongly objected to them.

—≈

[June 16–17, 1866:]

On the night of his return to O'ahu, Twain went to the outskirts of the Palace grounds to hear the singing of the mourners. He said some of it "was exceedingly plaintive and beautiful," while he described other parts as "distressing noise." It was 2 a.m. on the 17th when he returned to his hotel room.[3]

—≈

[June 21, 1866:]

In a letter to his mother and sister, Twain wrote,

—≈

I have just got back from a hard trip through the Island of Hawaii, begun on the 26th of May and finished on the 18th [16th] of June—only six or seven days at sea—all the balance horseback, and the hardest mountain roads in the world. I staid at the volcano about a week [four days at the caldera] and witnessed the greatest eruption that has occurred for years. I lived well there. They charge $4 a day for board, and a dollar or two extra for guides and horses. I had a pretty good time. They didn't charge me anything. I have got back sick—went to bed as soon as I arrived here—shall not be strong again for several days yet. I rushed too fast. I ought to have taken five or six weeks on that trip.

A week hence I start for the Island of Kaua'i, to be gone three weeks and then I go back to California.

The Crown Princess is dead and thousands of natives cry and wail and dance the dance for the dead, around the King's palace all night and every night. They will keep it up for a month and then she will be buried.

I've Got Friends in Low Latitudes

Hon. Anson Burlingame, U.S. Minister to China, and Gen. Van Valkenburgh, Minister to Japan, with their families and suits, have just arrived here enroute. They were going to do me the honor to call on me this morning, and that accounts for my being out of bed now. You know what condition my room is always in when you are not around—so I climbed out of bed and dressed and shaved pretty quick and went up to the residence of the American Minister and called on them.

Mr. Burlingame told me a good deal about Hon. Jere Clemens and that Virginia [Sherrard] Clemens who was wounded in a duel. He was in Congress years together with both of them. [They were Twain's third cousins. Both Burlingame and Van Valkenburgh were former congressmen, and Burlingame had been minister to China since 1861.]

Mr. B. sent for his [eighteen-year-old] son [Edward, who years later became the editor of *Scribner's Magazine*], to introduce him—said he could tell that frog story of mine as well as anybody. I told him I was glad to hear it for I never tried to tell it myself without making a botch of it. At his request I have loaned Mr. Burlingame pretty much everything I ever wrote. I guess he will be an almighty wise man by the time he wades through that lot.

If the new United States Minister to the Sandwich Islands (Hon. Edwin McCook,) were only here now, so that I could get his views on this new condition of Sandwich Islands politics, I would sail for California at once. But he will not arrive for two weeks yet and so I am going to spend that interval on the island of Kaua'i.

I stopped three days with Hon. Mr. [John] Coney, Deputy Marshal of the Kingdom, at Hilo, Hawai'i, last week and by a funny circumstance he knew everybody that ever I knew in Hannibal and Palmyra. We used to sit up all night talking and then sleep all day. He lives like a Prince.

Confound that Island! I had a streak of fat and a streak of lean all over it—got lost several times and had to sleep in huts with the natives and live like a dog. Of course I couldn't speak fifty words of the language.

Take it altogether, though, it was a mighty hard trip.[4]

⸺

According to the *Pacific Commercial Advertiser*, "He learned a few Kānaka words and his droll use of them caused any amount of fun for the natives."[5]

Sadly, Twain didn't make it to Kaua'i because of a shipwreck, his developing friendship with Burlingame, and his saddle boils.

Living Skeletons Wash Ashore

[Probably June 23, 1866, although Twain's letter is dated the 25th:]
On June 15th, a longboat was brought ashore at the Big Island's small northeastern town of Laupāhoehoe, containing the starving survivors of a sunken ship.

⸺

A letter arrived here yesterday morning [June 22] giving a meager account of the arrival on the island of Hawai'i of nineteen [fifteen] poor starving wretches, who had been buffeting a stormy sea in an open boat for forty-three days! Their ship, the *Hornet*, from New York, with a quantity of kerosene on board, had taken fire and burned in lat. 2 degrees north and long. 135 degrees west.

Think of their sufferings for forty-three days and nights, exposed to the scorching heat of the center of the torrid zone, and at the mercy of a ceaseless storm! When they had been entirely out of provisions for a day or two and the cravings of hunger became insupportable, they yielded to the shipwrecked mariner's final and fearful alternative, and solemnly drew lots to determine who of their number should die to furnish food for his comrades—and then the morning mists lifted and they saw land. They are being cared for at Sanpohoihoi [Laupāhoehoe], a little seaside station I spent a night at two weeks ago.

This boatload was in charge of the captain of the *Hornet*. He reports that the remainder of the persons in his ship (twenty in number) left her in two boats, under command of the first and second mates and the three boats kept company until the night of the nineteenth day, when they got separated. No further particulars have arrived here yet, and no confirmation of the above sad story.

Dinners to the Envoys

The American citizens of Honolulu, anxious to show to their distinguished visitors the honor and respect due them, have invited them to partake of a dinner upon some occasion before their departure. Burlingame and General Van Valkenburgh have accepted the invitation and will inform the Committee this evening what day will best suit their convenience.

—✎

There's a contrast for you. Starving men barely make it ashore as a banquet is planned. Some Twain scholars believe Twain put these two stories together on purpose to heighten the drama and to hold the readers' interest for his next *Union* letter.

The *Hornet*'s third mate and all but one of its sailors were taken to Hilo on June 18th. Captain Josiah Mitchell, passengers Samuel and Henry Ferguson, and seaman Antonio Cassero remained at Laupāhoehoe to continue recuperating.

—✎

[June 24–27, 1866:]

The third mate and ten of the sailors arrived at the hospital in Honolulu on June 24. Twain interviewed them for a letter to the *Sacramento Daily Union* that was dated June 25, so it's probable he interviewed them on that day.

In one of Twain's autobiographies, which wasn't published until after his death, he wrote,

—✎

When Mr. Burlingame arrived at Honolulu I had been confined to my room a couple of weeks—by night to my bed, by day to a splint-bottom chair, deep-sunk like a basket. There was another chair but I preferred this one, because my malady was saddle-boils.

When the boatload of skeletons arrived after forty-three days in an open boat on ten days' provisions—survivors of the clipper *Hornet* which had perished by fire several thousand miles away—it was necessary for me to interview them for the *Sacramento Union*, a journal which I had been commissioned to represent in the Sandwich Islands for a matter of five or six months. Mr. Burlingame put me on a cot and had me carried to the hospital, and during several hours he questioned the skeletons and I set down the answers in my notebook.[6]

Over the years, several of Twain's autobiographies have been published, along with many parts of autobiographies. A couple of burlesque autobiographies were published in 1871—one of which said in its entirety, "I was born November 30th, 1835. I continue to live, just the same." He added, "I could easily have made it longer, but not without compromising myself."[7]

The Twain family tree, from an illustration that appeared on the cover of *Mark Twain's (Burlesque) Autobiography*.

A Failed Grand Literary Debut

In 1899, Twain published an account of writing about the *Hornet* disaster in *The Century Magazine*, saying that it was chapter 14 from his unpublished autobiography.

The *Century* account was titled "My Début as a Literary Person" and is credited to "Mark Twain (formerly 'Mike Swain')." This is his best account of the disaster. In the following excerpts from it, I've retained only a few salient parts and those related to Hawai'i.

—◁—

In those early days I had already published one little thing ("The Jumping Frog") in an Eastern paper, but I did not consider that that counted. In my view, a person who published things in a mere newspaper could not properly claim recognition as a Literary Person: he must rise away above that; he must appear in a magazine. He would then be a Literary Person; also, he would be famous—right away.

These two ambitions were strong upon me. This was in 1866. I prepared my contribution, and then looked around for the best magazine to go up to glory in. I selected the most important one in New York [*Harper's New Monthly Magazine*]. The contribution was accepted. I signed it "Mark Twain"; for that name had some currency on the Pacific Coast, and it was my idea to spread it all over the world, now, at this one jump.

The article appeared in the December number, and I sat up a month waiting for the January number [since back then they didn't give the author credit with the article; they received credit in the year's index that came out in the January issue]; for that one would contain the year's list of contributors, my name would be in it, and I should be famous and could give the banquet I was meditating.

I did not give the banquet. I had not written the "Mark Twain" distinctly; it was a fresh name to Eastern printers, and they put it "Mike Swain" or "MacSwain," I do not remember which. At any rate, I was not celebrated and I did not give the banquet. I was a Literary Person, but that was all—a buried one; buried alive.

My article was about the burning of the clipper ship *Hornet* on the line, May 3, 1866. There were thirty-one men on board at the time, and I was in

Mark Twain's national literary debut in *Harper's New Monthly Magazine.*

Honolulu when the fifteen lean and ghostly survivors arrived there after a voyage of forty-three days in an open boat, through the blazing tropics, on *ten days' rations* of food. A very remarkable trip; but it was conducted by a captain who was a remarkable man, otherwise there would have been no survivors. He was a New Englander of the best sea-going stock of the old capable times—Captain Josiah Mitchell. [. . .]

I had been in the Islands several months when the survivors arrived. I was laid up in my room at the time, and unable to walk. Here was a great occasion to serve my journal, and I was not able to take advantage of it. Necessarily I was in deep trouble.

But by good luck his Excellency Anson Burlingame was there at the time, on his way to take up his post in China, where he did such good work for the United States. He came and put me on a stretcher and had me carried to the hospital where the shipwrecked men were, and I never needed to ask a question. He attended to all of that himself, and I had nothing to do but make the notes. It was like him to take that trouble. He was a great man and a great American, and it was in his fine nature to come down from his high office and do a friendly turn whenever he could.

We got through with this work at six in the evening. I took no dinner, for there was no time to spare if I would beat the other correspondents. I spent four hours arranging the notes in their proper order, then wrote all night and beyond it; with this result: that I had a very long and detailed account of the *Hornet* episode ready at nine in the morning, while the other correspondents of the San Francisco journals had nothing but a brief outline report—for they didn't sit up. The now-and-then schooner was to sail for San Francisco about nine; when I reached the dock she was free forward and was just casting off her stern-line. My fat envelope was thrown by a strong hand, and fell on board all right, and my victory was a safe thing.

All in due time the ship reached San Francisco, but it was my complete report which made the stir and was telegraphed to the New York papers by Mr. Cash; he was in charge of the Pacific bureau of the *New York Herald* at the time. [. . .]

The *Hornet* survivors reached the Sandwich Islands the 15th of June. They were mere skinny skeletons; their clothes hung limp about them and fitted them no better than a flag fits the flagstaff in a calm. But they were well nursed in the hospital; the people of Honolulu kept them supplied with all the dainties they could need; they gathered strength fast, and were presently nearly as good as new. Within a fortnight the most of them took ship for San Francisco; that is, if my dates have not gone astray in my memory. I went in the same ship, a sailing-vessel.[8]

—⸲—

Twain says that after the interviews, he stayed up all night writing so he could send his scoop off the next morning, but there was actually an extra day in there since the ship to San Francisco—the *Milton Badger*—didn't leave until June 27, so it probably took him longer to write it up than he remembered, or else he misdated his letter and interviewed them on June 26. It was published on the front page of the *Union* on July 19 and was the first detailed account of the disaster published in the States.

The *Union* article was based primarily on the third mate's account, enhanced with information from the other men. He later spent a lot of time interviewing Captain Mitchell and the two Fergusons, in addition to copying the diaries they kept during their forty-three days adrift. A few months later, he published an article in *Harper's New Monthly Magazine* that was almost entirely from the diaries kept by the captain and the passengers.

Twain wrote in *The Century Magazine* article, "Within ten days after the landing all the men but one were up and creeping about. In his notebook, he wrote that they were wandering the streets of Honolulu in eleven days.

In 1910, just after Twain's death, Bailey Millard—who beginning in the 1890s became an editor at the *San Francisco Daily Morning Call*, the *San Francisco Examiner*, and the *San Francisco Evening Bulletin*—wrote about Twain's *Hornet* article in the *Sacramento Daily Union*, saying, "This occasion was really the only one on which Mark Twain distinguished himself as a newsgatherer and some of the old timers in California are still wondering how he did it."[9]

Help from My Friends

[June 27, 1866:]

On the day the *Milton Badger* sailed off with Twain's scoop, Twain wrote a letter to his mother and sister in St. Louis. Unfortunately only the last part survives.

> I got the whole story from the third mate and two of the sailors. If my account gets to the *Sacramento Union* first, it will be published first all over the United States, France, England, Russia and Germany—all over the world, I may say. You will see it.
>
> Mr. Burlingame [. . .] hunted me up as soon as he came here, and has done me a hundred favors since, and says if I will come to China in the first trip of the great mail steamer next January and make his house in Peking [Beijing] my home, he will afford me facilities that few men can have there for seeing and learning. He will give me letters to the chiefs of the great Mail Steamship Company which will be of service to me in this matter. I expect to do all this, but I expect to go to the States first—and from China to the Paris World's Fair.[10]

Burlingame wanted Twain to go to China partly because he liked Twain but also because he wanted someone who could help promote trade with China back in the United States.

—⟨—

[June 29, 1866:]

In his notebook, Twain wrote, "Honolulu, June 29—visited the hideous Maʻi Pākē Hospital and examined the disgusting victims of Chinese Leprosy."[11] This is a bit of a misnomer because "maʻi Pākē" means "Chinese disease." At the time, it was thought that leprosy came to Hawaiʻi from China—maybe it did, but it didn't originate there. The oldest known case was in England between AD 415 and AD

545, and it turns out that several strains were being passed around in medieval Europe.[12] It was definitely not a Chinese disease.

Leprosy is now called Hansen's disease. It's not nearly as contagious as people once thought, and it can now be controlled with medications.

Apparently, he saw one or more people suffering from this disease when he first arrived in Honolulu. In at least two of his Sandwich Island lectures, he said, "Unfortunately, the first object I ever saw in the Sandwich Islands was a repulsive one. It was a case of Oriental leprosy, of so dreadful a nature that I have never been able to get it out of my mind since."[13] They had just begun transporting patients to an isolated community to die on the Kalapapua Peninsula on the north coast of Molokai.

Although he didn't write about visiting Honolulu's leprosy hospital, his visit seems to have affected him deeply. Two years later after visiting a poorhouse, he wrote in a letter, "After church, at noon today, I went with him to the alms house [...] I have not had anything touch me so since I saw the leper hospitals of Honolulu and Damascus."[14]

The King

[June 30, 1866:]

The princess's funeral was held on June 30, and Twain attended the procession from the 'Iolani Palace to the royal cemetery, writing about it at length. It was at the mausoleum that he finally got to see the king from afar.

—⊱

The King is thirty-four years of age, it is said, but looks all of fifty. He has an observant, inquiring eye, a heavy, massive face, a lighter complexion than is common with his race, tolerably short, stiff hair, a moderate

King Kamehameha V, also known as Lot Kapuāiwa, in 1865.
CHARLES WEED

mustache and imperial, large stature, inclining somewhat to corpulence (I suppose he weighs fully one hundred and eighty—maybe a little over), has fleshy hands, but a small foot for his size, is about six feet high, is thoughtful and slow of movement, has a large head, firmly set upon broad shoulders, and is a better man and a better looking one than he is represented to be in the villainous popular photographs of him, for none of them are good.[15]

A SOCIAL BUTTERFLY
Hobnobbing with High Society
[Still July 1, 1866:]

Gen. Van Valkenburgh has achieved a distinguished success as a curiosity finder—not hunter. Standing on the celebrated Pali, a day or two ago, and amusing himself by idly punching into the compact lava wall through which the road is cut, he crumbled away a chunk of it, and observing something white sticking to it, he instituted an examination, and found a sound, white, unmarred and unblemished human jaw-tooth firmly imbedded in the lava! Now the question is, how did it get there in the side—where a road had been cut in—of a mountain of lava seven hundred feet above the valley? A mountain which has been there for ages, this being one of the oldest islands in the group.

Burlingame was present, and saw the General unearth his prize. I have critically examined it, but, as I half expected myself, the world knows as much about how to account for the wonder now as if I had let it alone.[16]

[July 4, 1866:]

On the Fourth of July, Twain went to a "great luau" in Waikīkī hosted by David Kalākaua in honor of Burlingame and General Van Valkenburg, who were about to leave the Islands. Kalākaua would later become Hawai'i's last king. Twain, in his notebook, wrote, "Honolulu. Went to ball 8:30 p.m.—danced till 12:30—went home with M.C.—stopped at Gen. Van Valkenbergh's room and talked with him and Mr. Burlingame, Col. Rumsey and Ed Burlingame, until 3 a.m."

I don't know about you, but I have difficulty picturing Twain dancing since he was so slow and uncoordinated, giving the impression of being drunk.

At some point during their visit, General Van Valkenburg rather observantly said to Twain, "California is proud of Mark Twain, and someday the American people will be, too, no doubt."[17]

[July 5–18, 1866:]

Twain spent much of the remainder of his stay socializing and sightseeing, but he didn't really write about this period. Still, he seems to have had fun. He later wrote that he, Burlingame, and General Van Valkenburg "made Honolulu howl. I only got tight once, though. I know better than to get tight oftener than once in three months. It sets a man back in the esteem of people whose good opinions are worth having."[18]

Twain's visit to Kaua'i never came about. There are several things that may have caused him to decide to abandon this trip. One was probably his saddle sores. He was able to do some horseback riding but probably not enough to tour Kaua'i. Another reason may have been that he wanted to return with his friend Rev. Franklin Rising, who he had spent a lot of time with in the Nevada Territory and later wrote about in *Roughing It*. Then they probably delayed their return by a week so they would be on the same ship with Captain Mitchell and the Fergusons, as Twain wanted to copy their lifeboat diaries. And another consideration was that he was likely low on funds. The daughter of James Anthony, one of the *Sacramento Daily Union*'s three owners and publishers, wrote that Twain "squandered his means to such an extent—that they were obliged to pay his passage home."[19]

It's possible Twain considered remaining in Hawai'i. Twain's cousin Mildred Leo Clemens wrote in 1917, "They told me in Honolulu how Sam Clemens had been willing to take a steady job on the old *Pacific Commercial Advertiser*, but never got it."[20]

WHAT HE MISSED

Mark Twain didn't make it to Kauaʻi. This is some of what he missed.

Top: Looking down on Hanalei Valley from Princeville.

Middle: Waimea Canyon, the Grand Canyon of the Pacific.

Bottom: The Nāpali Coast and Kalalau Beach are accessible only by water or helicopter.

(TOP) AUTHOR'S PHOTO; (MIDDLE) TEAMHEALTHY808; (BOTTOM) PEXELS

[July 18, 1866:]

Preparing to sail back to the United States, Twain wrote in his notebook, "I got my passport from the royal damned Hawaiian collector of customs and paid a dollar for it, and tomorrow we sail for America in [the] good ship *Smyrnote*; we love it, Master—and I have got a devilish saddle boil to sit on for the first two weeks at sea."[21]

LEAVING
HAWAI'I

SAILING TOWARD THE GOLDEN GATE

[JULY 19, 1866:]

Twain was in Hawai'i from March 18 to July 1—four months and one day. He sailed out on the *Smyrniote*, along with Rev. Rising, and the captain and the two passengers from the *Hornet*. Two and a half hours earlier, the *Comet* set sail, carrying Edward Howard and the wife and daughters of Captain Thomas Spencer, whom Twain may have stayed with in Hilo.

The *Ajax* was a steamship, so it took only eleven days for him to get to Hawai'i. The return voyage from Hawai'i took twenty-five days because the *Smyrniote* had to use its sails against the wind, and it was becalmed half the time. It was slower, but it was steadier than a steamship in windy weather.

Becalmed

[July 24 to August 8, 1866:]

Five days into the voyage, both the *Smyrniote* and the *Comet* hit the doldrums and sat still, bobbing on the ocean, for two weeks.

After half a year's luxurious vagrancy in the Islands, I took shipping in a sailing vessel, and regretfully returned to San Francisco—a voyage in every way delightful, but without an incident: unless lying two long weeks in a dead calm, 1,800 miles from the nearest land, may rank as an incident.

Schools of whales grew so tame that day after day they played about the ship among the porpoises and the sharks without the least apparent fear of us, and we pelted them with empty bottles for lack of better sport. Twenty-four hours afterward these bottles would be still lying on the glassy water under our noses, showing that the ship had not moved out of her place in all that time.

The calm was absolutely breathless, and the surface of the sea absolutely without a wrinkle.[1]

Elsewhere, Twain described several silly games they came up with to relieve the boredom. In his notebook, he wrote, "This Brown told the girl her sweetheart had a glass eye and told the latter that the former had a glass eye."[2]

—✧—

[July 30, 1866:]
Twain wrote in a letter to his mother and sister,

—✧—

We left the Sandwich Islands eight or ten days—or twelve days ago—I don't know which, I have been so hard at work until today (at least part of each day), that the time has slipped away almost unnoticed. [. . .]

I suppose, from present appearances—light winds and calms—that we shall be two or three weeks at sea, yet—and I hope so—I am in no hurry to go to work.

East of the Sun, West of the Moon
[August 6, 1866:]
Sunday Morning, Aug. 6. This is rather slow. We still drift, drift, drift along—at intervals a spanking breeze and then—drift again—hardly move for half a day. But I enjoy it. We have such snowy moonlight, and such gorgeous sunsets. And the ship is so easy—even in a gale she rolls very little, compared to other vessels—and in this calm we could dance on deck, if we chose. You can walk a crack, so steady is she. Very different from the *Ajax*. My trunk used to get loose in the stateroom and rip and tear around the place as if it had life in it, and I always had to take my clothes off in bed because I could not stand up and do it.

—✧—

[August 10, 1866:]
Friday, Aug. 10—We have breezes and calms alternately. The brig is two miles to three astern, and just stays there. We sail directly east—this brings the brig, with all her canvas set, almost in the eye of the sun, when it sets— beautiful. She looks sharply cut and black as coal, against a background of fire and in the midst of a sea of blood.[3]

BACK IN SAN FRANCISCO

[AUGUST 13, 1866:]

In his notebook, he wrote, "San Francisco. Home again. No, not home again; in prison again, and all the wide sense of freedom gone. The city seems so cramped and so dreary with toil and care and business anxiety. God help me, I wish I were at sea again!"[4]

[August 20, 1866:]

[Continuing his letter to his mother and sister, Twain referred to his journal and quoted this note:] "Ashore again, and devilish sorry for it."

I have been up to Sacramento and squared accounts with the *Union*. They paid me a great deal more than they promised me. I suppose that means that I gave satisfaction, but they did not say so.[5]

[In his *Century Magazine* article, he wrote,]

When I returned to California by-and-by, I went up to Sacramento and presented a bill for general correspondence at twenty dollars a week. It was paid. Then I presented a bill for "special" service on the *Hornet* matter of three columns of solid nonpareil at *a hundred dollars a column*. The cashier didn't faint, but he came rather near it. He sent for the proprietors, and they came and never uttered a protest. They only laughed in their jolly fashion, and said it was robbery, but no matter; it was a grand "scoop" (the bill or my *Hornet* report, I didn't know which): "Pay it. It's all right."

The best men that ever owned a newspaper.[6]

Hawai'i's Response

Twain's *Union* articles were still being published and had seven more to go, some of which he wrote after his return.

Back in Hawai'i, the newspapers were reprinting excerpts, sometimes with comments. Surprisingly, they didn't say much, but overall the response was positive. Of course, there are always a few critics. Twain wrote in his notebook, "The mish's are outraged by the levity of my letters, and have so expressed themselves—but in sorrow, not in anger."[7] Of course it shouldn't be surprising the missionaries didn't like the humor.

Twain's friend Henry Whitney wrote, "His letters abound in genuine good humor and fun, though if he would stick a little closer to facts, they would be more reliable. In conversation he is courteous and inquisitive, but a peculiar manner that he possesses gives one the idea that he has just got up from the anxious seat—an idea which is very soon dissipated on hearing one of his "dry jokes," or reading a paragraph in his letters. [. . .] We half suspect he brought the cats with him, [. . .] as we haven't heard a cat for a [*sic*] twelve-month."[8]

And a couple months later, Whitney added, "though not always exactly correct, in facts and figures, are near enough for all practical purposes."

Now, criticism between editors and reporters was common at that time. Usually, they were inside jokes and just fun potshots between friends. But this was Hawai'i, which was nothing like Nevada, where Twain had years of practice. I'm sure Whitney wasn't prepared for Twain's response. He began by saying he was going to catch a ship to Honolulu.

> I am going chiefly, however, to eat the editor of the [*Pacific*] *Commercial Advertiser* for saying I do not write the truth about the Hawaiian Islands, and for exposing my highway robbery in carrying off Father Damon's book—*History of the Islands*. I shall go there mighty hungry.
>
> Mr. Whitney is jealous of me because I speak the truth so naturally, and he can't do it without taking the lockjaw. [. . .] if he sits down solemnly and takes one of my palpable burlesques and reads it with a funereal aspect, and swallows it as petrified truth—how am I going to help it? [. . .] But I am coming down there mighty hungry—most uncommonly hungry, Whitney.[9]

This was published in the *Daily Hawaiian Herald*, a new rival of Whitney's *Pacific Commercial Advertiser*. It was started by Colonel James Ayers, one of the founders and the editor of the *San Francisco Morning Call*. He had come to Honolulu on the first *Ajax* voyage to start the *Daily Hawaiian Herald*, which lasted only a few months. Interestingly, in San Francisco, Twain had sought work from Ayers at the *Morning Call*, but while Ayers thought Twain was a good reporter for the wilds of Nevada, he felt Twain wasn't what was needed in a "settled community" like San Francisco, where they wanted the "unvarnished truth."

Writing about one of Twain's *Union* articles, Ayers gave him something of a backhanded compliment, saying that Twain "blunders on so much truth that we have a notion to countermand our order for him to communicate with us."[10]

There were also more than half a dozen articles mentioning Twain and the purloined book, with some disagreement as to whether Twain stole it from Whitney or Rev. Damon. The day Twain left Hawai'i, he sent Damon a note explaining, "I 'cabbage' it by the strong arm, for fear you might refuse to part with it if I asked you. This is a case of military necessity, and is therefore admissible. The honesty of the transaction may be doubtful, but the policy of it is sound—sound as the foundation upon which the imperial greatness of America rests."

Twain returned the book the following year.

Having arrived back in San Francisco, Twain didn't know what to do. Being a reporter didn't appeal to him anymore, and he loved traveling, so he had two ideas—one was to take up Burlingame's offer of going to China, and the other was to seek out a newspaper that would send him on a tour of Europe, the Mediterranean, and the Holy Land. He opted for the latter, but that tour didn't start until the following year. He had to find something else to do in the meantime.

Then Hawai'i's Queen Emma arrived in San Francisco on September 24, 1866, stirring up interest in the Islands, and Twain began thinking of giving a lecture. Three days later, Twain's lecture ads began appearing.

SKYROCKETING TO STARDOM

I WAS HOME AGAIN, IN SAN FRANCISCO, without means and without employment. I tortured my brain for a saving scheme of some kind, and at last a public lecture occurred to me! I sat down and wrote one, in a fever of hopeful anticipation. I showed it to several friends, but they all shook their heads. They said nobody would come to hear me, and I would make a humiliating failure of it. They said that as I had never spoken in public, I would break down in the delivery, anyhow. I was disconsolate now.[11]

One of those whom Twain consulted was George Barnes, the editor of the *San Francisco Morning Call* who fired Twain by talking him into resigning as its reporter. He recalled,

The writer recollects the evening distinctly when he came to the *Call* editorial room to advise with the people there on the subject. It was raining heavily. Mr. Clemens entered in a sort of uncertain way, clad in a thin black frockcoat—his only protection from the storm. Buttoned up to the chin and soaked, he looked, and no doubt felt, as if he had just been fished out of the Dismal swamp.

Taking a mass of manuscript from out of the breast-pocket of his soddened garment, where it had only been imperfectly protected from the rain, he threw it on the desk before one of the editors and said, "I wish you'd read that and give me your opinion about it. I think it might do for a lecture."

"A lecture?"

"Yes; it's about the Islands. I've been to Bowman, and I've been to Harte and Stoddard, and the rest of the fellows, and they say, 'Don't do it, Mark; it will hurt your literary reputation.'"

The editor had glanced over some of the pages in the meantime, and found a well-constructed piece of work. Mr. Clemens stood with his back to the fire that was burning in the grate, half concealed in the vapory haze arising from his drying clothes, but waiting anxiously for the verdict.

"Mark," asked the editor, after a while, looking up from his manuscript, "which do you need most at present, money or literary reputation?"

"Money, by God!" We are sorry it is necessary to blank his full reply. Mr. Clemens could be profane, in those days, on occasion.

"Then go to [Thomas] Maguire, hire the Academy of Music on Pine Street, and there deliver this lecture. With the prestige of your recent letters from the Hawaiian islands, you will crowd the theater."[12]

[Returning to Twain:]

But at last an editor slapped me on the back and told me to "go ahead." He said, "Take the largest house in town, and charge a dollar a ticket." The audacity of the proposition was charming; it seemed fraught with practical worldly wisdom, however. The proprietor of the several theaters endorsed the advice, and said I might have his handsome new opera-house at half price—fifty dollars. In sheer desperation I took it—on credit, for sufficient reasons. In three days I did a hundred and fifty dollars' worth of printing and advertising, and was the most distressed and frightened creature on the Pacific Coast. I could not sleep—who could, under such circumstances?

Trouble on the Way

For other people there was facetiousness in the last line of my posters, but to me it was plaintive with a pang when I wrote it:

"Doors open at 7 1/2. The trouble will begin at 8."

That line has done good service since. Showmen have borrowed it frequently. I have even seen it appended to a newspaper advertisement reminding school pupils in vacation what time next term would begin.

—◅

For other lectures over the years, he used variations such as "The Wisdom will flow at 8, and not a drop should be lost," "The orgies to commence at 8 p.m.," "The Inspiration will begin to gush at 8," or "The doors will be besieged at 7 o'clock. The Insurrection will start at 8."

He also used, "For only one night! And only a portion of that!"[13] And "Mr. Mark Twain, the man who will lecture, has a very Large nose, and any one whose nose exceeds its measurements will be admitted free. All other noses must pay a dollar."[14] For a lecture during that same period but on a different topic, his ad said, "One Night Only. Farewell Benefit for the Future Widows and Orphans of Mark Twain."[15]

In a letter to an editor advertising church fund-raising lecture on the Sandwich Islands, he mentioned the results of a previous benefit, saying, "The proceeds enabled them to put a new roof on that church, and everybody said that that roof would cave in, sometime or other, and mash the congregation, because I was one of those sinful newspaper men, but it never did."[16]

On the left is the ad for his first lecture from the *Daily Alta California* of October 2, 1866, while on the right is for his lecture in Grass Valley, California, from the *Grass Valley Daily Union* of October 20, 1866.

For one in Brooklyn, New York, Twain said his Sandwich Island lecture was the best he'd ever written and was also the only one, adding that it was "an infallible cure for all bronchial afflictions, sore eyes, fever and ague, and warts."[17]

Returning to his first lecture, his friends began having fun with the idea. The *Alta California* said they doubted Twain would have a Hawaiian Hornpipe in the program but thought Mr. Brown would sing a song in the Hawaiian language, adding that the lecture would be "high toned" as long as Twain spoke loud enough. *The Californian* said the lecture would refute some stories that were circulating, such as those of his romantic interludes, including the one with a mermaid.

Meanwhile, Twain was having a rough time.

As those three days of suspense dragged by, I grew more and more unhappy. I had sold two hundred tickets among my personal friends, but I feared they might not come. My lecture, which had seemed "humorous" to me, at first, grew steadily more and more dreary, till not a vestige of fun seemed left, and I grieved that I could not bring a coffin on the stage and turn the thing into a funeral.

I was so panic-stricken at last that I went to three old friends, giants in stature, cordial by nature, and stormy-voiced, and said, "This thing is going to be a failure; the jokes in it are so dim that nobody will ever see them; I would like to have you sit in the parquet, and help me through."

They said they would. Then I went to the wife of a popular citizen [probably Mollie Low, the California governor's wife], and said that if she was willing to do me a very great kindness, I would be glad if she and her husband would sit prominently in the left-hand stage box, where the whole house could see them. I explained that I should need help, and would turn toward her and smile, as a signal, when I had been delivered of an obscure joke—"and then," I added, "don't wait to investigate, but respond!"

She promised. Down the street I met a man I never had seen before. He had been drinking, and was beaming with smiles and good nature.

He said, "My name's Sawyer. You don't know me, but that don't matter. I haven't got a cent, but if you knew how bad I wanted to laugh, you'd give me a ticket. Come, now, what do you say?"

"Is your laugh hung on a hair-trigger?—that is, is it critical, or can you get it off *easy*?"

My drawling infirmity of speech so affected him that he laughed a specimen or two that struck me as being about the article I wanted, and I gave him a ticket, and appointed him to sit in the second circle, in the center, and be responsible for that division of the house. I gave him minute instructions about how to detect indistinct jokes, and then went away, and left him chuckling placidly over the novelty of the idea.

I ate nothing on the last of the three eventful days—I only suffered. I had advertised that on this third day the box-office would be opened for the sale of reserved seats. I crept down to the theater at four in the afternoon to see if any sales had been made. The ticket seller was gone, the box-office was locked up. I had to swallow suddenly, or my heart would have got out.

"No sales," I said to myself; "I might have known it."

I thought of suicide, pretended illness, flight. I thought of these things in earnest, for I was very miserable and scared. But of course I had to drive them away, and prepare to meet my fate. I could not wait for half-past seven—I wanted to face the horror, and end it—the feeling of many a man doomed to hang, no doubt.

I went down back streets at six o'clock, and entered the theater by the back door. I stumbled my way in the dark among the ranks of canvas scenery, and stood on the stage. The house was gloomy and silent, and its emptiness depressing. I went into the dark among the scenes again, and for an hour and a half gave myself up to the horrors, wholly unconscious of everything else. Then I heard a murmur; it rose higher and higher, and ended in a crash, mingled with cheers. It made my hair raise, it was so close to me, and so loud.

There was a pause, and then another; presently came a third, and before I well knew what I was about, I was in the middle of the stage, staring at a sea of faces, bewildered by the fierce glare of the lights, and quaking in every limb with a terror that seemed like to take my life away. The house was full, aisles and all!

The tumult in my heart and brain and legs continued a full minute before I could gain any command over myself. Then I recognized the charity and the friendliness in the faces before me, and little by little my fright melted away, and I began to talk. Within three or four minutes I was comfortable, and even content.

My three chief allies, with three auxiliaries, were on hand, in the parquet, all sitting together, all armed with bludgeons, and all ready to make an onslaught upon the feeblest joke that might show its head. And whenever a joke did fall, their bludgeons came down and their faces seemed to split from ear to ear; Sawyer, whose hearty countenance was seen looming redly in the center of the second circle, took it up, and the house was carried handsomely. Inferior jokes never fared so royally before. [In the beginning, his friends thought it was funny to laugh and pound their clubs in the wrong parts of his speech.]

Presently I delivered a bit of serious matter with impressive unction (it was my pet), and the audience listened with an absorbed hush that gratified me more than any applause; and as I dropped the last word of the clause, I happened to turn and catch Mrs. _____'s intent and waiting eye; my conversation with her flashed upon me, and in spite of all I could do I smiled. She took it for the signal, and promptly delivered a mellow laugh that touched off the whole audience; and the explosion that followed was the triumph of the evening. I thought that that honest man Sawyer would choke himself; and as for the bludgeons, they performed like pile-drivers. But my poor little morsel of pathos was ruined. It was taken in good faith as an intentional joke, and the prize one of the entertainment, and I wisely let it go at that.[18]

—⚹—

Borrowing from an expression of that day, Twain tried it on the dog and, not only did the cur survive, he came out smelling like a rose. He continued giving lectures and dinner speeches until near the end of his life. His Hawai'i lecture seems to have been his favorite. He gave it almost a hundred times—more than any of his others—and it may have been his most popular lecture, at least, most of the time. Twain was constantly changing it, not always for the better.

Shock and Awe

Twain loved shocking his audience with the unexpected. Writing in the West was much more uninhibited than in the East, and Twain had taken full advantage of it and pushed the boundaries. In the 1860s and 1870s, his jokes about sex, nudity, vomiting, remnants of the dead, and cannibalism were considered crude, tasteless, and shocking by some. San Francisco's *Dramatic Chronicle* felt that some parts were "so nearly improper—not to say course—that they could not be heartily laughed at by ladies."[19] The *Sacramento Daily Union* thought his wit coarser than the audience was used to, but "many quiet lovers of a good joke were amazed and confounded at the impudence and freedom of this wild Californian."[20]

Shocking the audience remains an effective tool of many comedians. That's all a part of comedy. Still, he avoided obscenities and his usual cursing, so he avoided being accused of bad taste. In addition, Twain was doing more than crude jokes. He included some very intelligent humor that usually flew over the heads of most of his audience. Some of his material was darker than expected. That was him playing with contrasts and throwing the audience off balance, but he may have also done it to keep the audience from getting too exhausted from laughter—at least that's one reason why he did it in later years. And in spite of his reputation for lying and ludicrous exaggerations, he was also more honest than some liked, pointing out society's hypocrisy and prejudices.

The *San Francisco Examiner* said, "He is sometimes a little too rough; of that there can be no doubt. He verges, indeed, occasionally upon coarseness; but his roughness is the roughness of the crude diamond, through the opaque incrustation of which flashes ever and anew a ray of that fountain of light which is the essence of the gem."[21]

No one else was so candid with such an easygoing manner, and he could be really funny. He would have the crowds roaring with laughter. Because of this, he became wildly popular.

A Manner of Speaking

As with normal lectures, Twain's lecture was informative, but that was just incidental. It was actually more of a stand-up comedy routine. Oddly, many people didn't seem to realize that Twain wasn't giving a lecture—it was a parody of a lecture. Some critics even complained that his lecture was short on facts, so he added more—particularly before he went to England.

Twain was acting the part of a serious, highly sensitive, but bumbling and inept lecturer. His peculiar mannerisms, his forgetfulness, the mistakes, his unawareness of the humor, it was all carefully planned, rehearsed, and memorized. It was designed to generate sympathy for him and to disarm them for when suddenly he hit them with his zingers, which appeared to be unintended. As a prop, he usually came onstage with a crumpled pile of notes "under his arm, like a ruffled hen" and on rare occasions pretended to refer to them. At least once, he had huge sheets of butcher's paper containing his notes written in large letters with a brush, and, turning his back to the audience, he held the giant sheets up toward the light and proceeded to read his lecture from them.

Instead of appearing polished and authoritative, like most lecturers, he had a more intimate tone, trying to connect with his listeners by looking into their faces. He kneaded his hands, fiddled with his hair, rubbed his chin, and freely admitted his mistakes. When talking, he'd half close his eyes and wrinkle his nose. And he would never smile. The more the audience laughed, the more sorrowful and distressed he looked.

For his lectures, Twain had a very slow, deliberate way of talking, pausing between almost every word, putting the emphasis in the wrong place, and giving each of his vowels a "corkscrew twist that would make even the announcement of a funeral sound like a joke."[22] That, with his drawl, added to his uniqueness. Some reporters complained that he was dull, speaking in a "droning monotone" with complete indifference and a "rising inflection at the beginning, middle, and end of his sentences."[23] After one lecture, an old man asked him, "Be them your natural tones of eloquence?"[24]

One said he spoke at the rate of three words per minute. While that was exaggerated, he did speak painfully slowly, prompting his first audience to yell for him to talk faster. It was like he was either extremely tired or extremely lazy and "slightly inebriated." On the other hand, he gave the appearance of being very anxious and that it was painful for him to come up with his words.

In his lectures, the sophisticated journalist of the *Union* letters and the boorish Mr. Brown were gone, replaced by the awkward lecturer who seemed oblivious when he stumbled into the realm of what at that time was considered coarse humor. Of course, that was one of the things that struck audiences as being so funny. Here was a supposedly intellectual lecturer, with his slow, deliberate, deadpan delivery, unknowingly making abrupt vulgar and outlandish statements as though it was information you'd expect to hear in a normal lecture. He would then look confused or mystified when his listeners applauded or laughed.

Sometimes when the audience was roaring with laughter, he'd ask them what was so funny and wouldn't proceed until someone answered him. Even when the crowd knew something was coming, he was still able to catch them off guard. His act was completely unique. There was nothing else like him. San Francisco's *The Golden Era* observed, "Nature must have been in one of her funniest moods when she fashioned this mixture of the sublime and the ridiculous."[25]

No Introduction Necessary

Mark Twain gave nearly a hundred lectures on Hawai'i from 1866 to 1873. This made him famous throughout the United States. He was better known as a lecturer than as a writer for a while. His foreign tours lecturing on other topics brought him worldwide fame. While he enjoyed public speaking, he found the lecture tours grueling. Although he stopped occasionally, he continued to lecture and give dinner speeches until near the end of his life.

The title of his Hawai'i lectures varied over the years, such as "Kānakadom, or the Experiences of a Late Journey Through the Sandwich Islands," and "Sandwich Islands! A Serio-Humorous Lecture Concerning Kānakadom," but he seems to have preferred "Our Fellow Savages of the Sandwich Islands." He used that title more often, probably because some people found it offensive.

I have made the following reconstruction of his lecture by piecing together bits from a number of sources—mostly newspaper reviews of his lectures. Unfortunately, the reporters had to rely on their memories and notes when quoting Twain, so sometimes they weren't very accurate. And, sadly, much of what he said wasn't written down at all. Some of the reporters included the audiences' responses, others didn't. I've retained those when they were mentioned.

Twain constantly altered his lectures—throwing out parts and adding new ones—partly because newspapers kept quoting his punch lines. He also tended to change the order, so for the following reconstruction, I followed the list of the topics on an advertisement for his first New York lecture, although my reconstruction contains many bits that weren't in the New York lecture and is missing the parts of the New York lecture that were lost. And while he carefully memorized and practiced every word, he wasn't wedded to his script and would alter his wording and presentation on a whim. So, while he never actually gave the following reconstruction, it is a collection of the surviving high points of his Hawai'i lectures from throughout the seven-year period that he gave them.

For an entrance in his early lectures, he'd sometimes be playing a piano, singing a simple song, or wandering around aimlessly on the stage when the curtain was raised to reveal him. He'd then feign surprise, shock, and horror at his situation, unsure whether to retreat or face the crowd. He would stand for a minute with an idiotic look on his face, fidgeting, rubbing his hands together, shifting his shoulders, looking from side to side at the audience, sometimes shading his eyes with his hand as if searching for someone in particular. It was all part of his act as an incompetent lecturer.

In 1871, the *Chicago Evening Post* gave a good description of one of his entrances:

> The entertainment of the season thus far was the curious, disjointed, delightfully incoherent talk of Mark Twain (Clemens is his married name) [. . .]
>
> Every seat in the house, 400 chairs in the aisles, and standing room for 200 or 300 were crowded full, when the lank, lantern jawed, and impudent Californian bestrode the stage as if it were the deck of a steamboat, and getting to the middle of the front rubbed his bony hands and gazed around. A thin man of five-feet-ten, thirty-five or so, eyes that penetrate like a new gimlet [a nautical tool for boring holes], nasal prow projecting and pendulous, carroty curly hair and mustache, arms that are always in the way, expression dreadfully melancholy, he stares inquisitively here and there, and cranes his long neck round the house like a bereaved Vermonter who has just come from the death bed of his mother-in-law, and is looking for a sexton [a church official, one of whose duties is burying the dead]. [. . .]
>
> Now he snapped his fingers; now he rubbed his hands softly, like the catcher of the champion nine; now he caressed his palm with his dexterous fingers, like the end minstrel-man propounding a conundrum; now he put his arms akimbo, like a disgusted auctioneer; and now he churned the air in the vicinity of his imperiled head with his outspread hands, as if he was fighting mosquitoes at Rye Beach. Once he got his arms tangled so badly, that three surgeons were seen to edge their way toward the stage, expecting to be summoned; but he unwound himself during the next anecdote.[26]

And here's what he said:

⟋

Ladies and gentlemen. By request of the Chairman of the committee, who has been very busy, and is very tired, I suppose, I ask leave to introduce to you the lecturer of the evening, Mr. Samuel L. Clemens, otherwise known as Mark Twain, a gentleman whose great learning, aptness in philosophy, whose historical accuracy, whose devotion to science, and whose veneration for the . . . truth *(laughter)* are only equaled by his moral character and his majestic and imposing presence. *(Renewed laughter.)*

I . . . ah . . . refer . . . ah . . . indirectly to . . . to my-self! *(Shouts of laughter and applause.)*

I am a little opposed to the custom of ceremoniously introducing the lecturer to the audience, because it seems to me unnecessary where the man has been properly advertised *(laughter)*, and besides it is very uncomfortable for the lecturer. But where it is the custom, an introduction ought to be made, and I had rather make it myself in my own case, and then I can rely on getting in all the . . . facts! *(Continued laughter.)*

I always feel uncomfortable while undergoing this ordeal. It is not a simple introduction that I mind. I don't really care for that at all, but it is the compliments that sometimes go with it—that is what hurts. It would make anyone uncomfortable. You can fancy a young lady introduced to a parlor-full of company as the best conversationalist, the best model in every way in her section of the country. You might just as well knock her in the head. *(Laughter.)* She could not say a word the rest of the evening.

I never had but one public introduction that seemed exactly the thing; that seemed to be a very inspiration in the way of an introduction. I knew nothing of the man who introduced me [a big awkward miner in the small town of Red Dog], and he knew nothing concerning me. I requested him to leave out all compliments, and get me through as quickly as possible. Well, we went upon the platform and the man said, "Ladies and Gentlemen. I shall not waste any unnecessary time in the introduction. I don't know anything about this man. *[Laughter.]* At least I know only two things about him: one is that he has never been in the penitentiary, and the other is . . . I can't imagine why." *(Prolonged laughter and applause.)*

Now such an introduction puts a man right at ease. *(More applause.)*[27]

—

Another humorous introduction he received in Grass Valley, California, went, "Ladies and Gentlemen, this is the celebrated Mark Twain from the celebrated city of San Francisco, with his celebrated lecture about the celebrated Sandwich Islands."

Moving on to his lecture, the *Philadelphia Evening Telegraph* said his lecture "would not be nearly so funny to read as it is to hear from Mark Twain's lips."[28] Britain's *The Observer*, echoing this, said, "It is nothing less than a gross injustice to draw conclusions as to the matter and the quality of Mark Twain's lecture on the Sandwich Islands from a simple report; no matter how accurate, of what he says, eminently interesting and humorous though it be. The great enjoyment of the thing lies in seeing the man, and hearing from his own lips and in his own peculiarly eccentric style his reminiscences of what he saw and heard and experienced during his sojourn in the Sandwich Islands."[29]

Unfortunately we'll never be able to see and hear him perform. All we can do is read the reconstruction and use our imagination.

OUR FELLOW SAVAGES

AFTER COMING ON THE STAGE, he would spend a minute or so looking around at the audience, without saying anything. Then he would begin with his slow, monotone, anxious manner.

—⌐

Julius Caesar is dead, Shakespeare is dead, Napoleon is dead, Abraham Lincoln is dead, and I am far from well myself.

When in the course of human events it became necessary for him to have such an audience, they should learn to bear the affliction patiently.

The Sandwich Islands will be the subject of my lecture—when I get to it—and I shall endeavor to tell the truth as nearly as a newspaper man can. If I embellish it with a little nonsense, that makes no difference; it won't mar the truth; it is only as the barnacle ornaments the oyster by sticking to it.

To cut the matter short the Sandwich Isles are 2,100 miles southwest from San Francisco, but why they were put away out there in the middle of the Pacific, so far away from any place and in such an inconvenient

An illustration of Mark Twain lecturing from the December 16, 1885, issue of *Puck* magazine.
JOSEPH FERDINAND KEPPLER

out-of-the-way locality, is a thing . . . well, I never could find that out. *(Laughter.)* But it's no matter. It is no business of ours—it was the work of Providence and is not open to criticism. The subject is a good deal like many others we should like to inquire into, such as, "What mosquitoes were made for?," etc., but under the circumstances we naturally feel a delicacy about doing it.

The Islands are twelve in number—eight of them inhabited and four of them the most marvelously productive sugar land in the known world. And they have volcanoes—the largest dead volcanoes in the world. They are of volcanic origin; of volcanic construction, I should say. They are composed of lava harder than any statement I have made in fifteen years. There is not a spoonful of legitimate dirt in the whole group, unless it has been imported.

These islands were discovered some eighty or ninety years ago by Captain Cook, though another man came very near discovering them before, and he was diverted from his course by a manuscript found in a bottle. He wasn't the first man who has been diverted by suggestions got out of a bottle.

Eighty or ninety years ago they had a native population of full 400,000 souls, and they were comfortable, prosperous, and happy. But then the white people came, and brought complicated diseases, trade, and commerce, and education, and civilization, and all sorts of other calamities, and the consequence was the poor natives began to die off with wonderful rapidity. Forty years ago they were reduced to 200,000, and by the last census they had dwindled down to 55,000. Then the white people doubled the educational facilities; and it was just the same as turning the smallpox loose in a community that hadn't been vaccinated at all! If they start but a few more seminaries of learning there, it will surely finish them. *(Laughter.)*

It is not education or civilization that is doing this—it is the importation of disease. Owing to consumption [tuberculosis] and other reliable diseases, the natives are retiring from business very fast.

The natives of the Sandwich Islands of color are a rich dark brown. A very pleasing tint. The tropical sun and the easy-going ways inherited from their ancestors, have made them rather idle. They are a very excellent people.

I do not see where old Kamehameha got his fierce warriors. He was a great warrior, you know—a Kanaka Napoleon—and in the old times when the feudal system prevailed and the Islands were so divided up that there was an average of three kings to an acre, he held four aces once and took them all in and combined the whole concern under one sovereignty. He fought many great battles, but I cannot think where he got his fighting material, for certainly the Kānakas of the present day are the most peaceable, inoffensive, unwarlike creatures imaginable. One would as soon expect a rabbit to fight as one of these.

You often see them quarreling—doubling their fists and striking them together, and making frightful grimaces, and hurling curses and the deadliest insults at one another, even striking out savagely within an inch of one another's faces—and just as you think blood is going to flow, just as you think there is going to be a Kanaka for breakfast, it all ends in smoke. They go off growling and viciously shaking their heads.

The native women in the rural districts wear a single long, loose garment, but the men don't. *(Loud and continued applause.)* They don't wear anything to speak of. They would cheerfully wear a plug hat and a vest if they had them, but they haven't. . . . The men wear,—well, as a general thing, they wear—a smile, or a pair of spectacles,—or any little thing like that. *(Laughter.)* When the weather is inclement, men wear cotton in their ears—some little fancy article like that—further than this they have no inclination towards gorgeousness of costume. They don't seem to care anything for display at all. *(Laughter.)*

Guess I won't continue that subject any longer.

In former times the king's person was sacred, he was the supreme head of the church and state, he was the captain over all, the arbiter of fate, the lord of life. There was a law that if a man came to the king with a wet head, he should die; if any man's shadow fell on the king he had to die. If the king put his kapu on anyone there was no hope for him; (by the bye, from these we got our word "tabooed").

In former times the women were the abject slaves of the whole party. By the ancient kapu (law of the land), death was the punishment of a woman, who dared to sit at the same table with her husband, or to eat out of the same dish with him. If she ate choice fruit, she was to suffer the death penalty. And it is wisdom—unquestionably it is wisdom. Perhaps the men remembered the difficulty between another woman and some fruit some time back and didn't feel justified in taking any more chances. *(Laughter.)* Can't be too particular about fruit—with women.

I am not married, myself, but yet I have no right to advertise myself this way publicly.

Still . . . I am not married.

Now the Sandwich Islanders are the best educated of any people on the earth. And all this wonderful work was accomplished by our American missionaries. The missionaries set up schools and taught them to read and write with facility, in the native tongue, and there is not a single uneducated person above eight years of age in the Sandwich Islands! They are the best educated people in the world, I believe, not excepting some portions of the United States. I can testify to the zeal of the missionaries, and to their faith and devotion.

And what is curious further, this great work—extending over so many years and costing so much, was paid for in great part by the American Sunday School children with their pennies. We all took part in it. I know that I contributed. *(Laughter.)* I have had nearly two dollars invested there for thirty years. But I don't mind it. I don't care for the money *(laughter)*, if it has been doing good. I don't say this in order to show off. I only mention it as a gentle humanizing fact that may possibly have a beneficent effect upon some members of this audience. *(Laughter.)*

True, the system gave opportunities to bad boys. Though it is beyond all comprehension, many a bad little boy has reaped a lucrative income by confiscating the pennies given him for missionary contributions, dropping into the box such brass buttons as he could spare from his garments. But it is the proudest reflection of my life that I never did that . . . at least, not more than once or twice, anyhow.

These natives are an exceedingly hospitable people. Their nature is gentleness and kindness itself. If you want to stay two or three days and nights in a native cabin you will be welcome. They will make you feel entirely at home—for theirs is the freest hospitality in the world. They will do everything they possibly can to make you comfortable. They will feast you on raw salt pork, raw fish with the scales on, coconuts, plantains, baked dogs, and fricasseed cats—all the luxuries of the season. *(Laughter.)* Everything the human heart can desire they will set before you. *(Laughter.)*

Perhaps now, this isn't a captivating feast at first glance, but it is offered in all sincerity, and with the best motives in the world, and that makes any feast respectable whether it is palatable or not.

They have a dish called poi which they eat. Eating poi will cure a drunkard. In order to like poi, you must get used to it. It smells a good deal worse than it tastes, and it tastes a good deal worse than it looks. I am sending all my friends there.

It is said by some, and believed, that Kānakas won't lie, but I know they *will* lie—lie like auctioneers—lie like lawyers—lie like patent-medicine advertisements—they will *almost* lie like *newspaper* men. They will lie for a dollar when they could get a dollar and a half for telling the truth. They *never* tell a traveler the right road or right distance to a place. Christian Kānakas will go into court and swear on the Bible and then stand up and lie till the lights burn blue around them, and then go home and go through a lot of purifying idolatrous ceremonies and the thing is all straight.

There is only one way of getting them to tell the truth, on the stand or anywhere else—and that is to swear them on the Great Shark God, which seems to have been the most potent personage in their idolatrous mythology. In old times, when the priests fancied that the shark god was angry or out of sorts about anything and stood in need of a sacrifice to compose his spirits, they used to go forth and lasso a poor wretch of a plebeian native and cast him into the sea where the sharks could devour him. And to this day, in the island of Hawai'i, they fear and respect this deity, and when they swear by him they keep the oath and tell the truth. And yet the unsagacious judges go on swearing such witnesses on the Scriptures and refuse to profit by our keener judgment. When we have a Chinese witness on an important case we swear him on a butchered chicken.

But if you want to trade, that's quite another thing—that's business! And the Kanaka is ready for you. He is a born trader, and he will swindle you if he can. He will lie straight through from the first word to the last. Not such lies as you and I tell *(laughter)*, but gigantic lies, lies that awe you with their grandeur, lies that stun you with their imperial impossibility. He will sell you a mole-hill at the market price of a mountain and will lie it up to an altitude that will make it cheap at the money. *(Laughter.)* If he is caught he slips out of it with an easy indifference that has an unmistakable charm about it. *(Laughter.)*

All these natives have a great many mothers, not natural mothers, but adopted ones. It is perfectly easy for a native to have as many as 150 mothers if his affections are liberal and stretchy, and most of them are. They have a custom of calling any woman "mother"—without regard to her color or politics *(laughter)*—that they happen to take a particular liking to. [Now they call just about every woman older than themselves their auntie.]

This custom breeds some curious incidents among people who didn't know anything about it. A California gentleman who owned a sugar plantation hired one of these natives to work for him in the busy season. He soon came to ask leave to bury his mother. Shortly after he came again with the same request.

"I thought you buried her last week," said the gentleman.

"This is another one," said the native.

The Californian thought it strange, but said "Well, go and plant her."

Within a month the man wanted to bury some more mothers.

"Look here," said the planter, "I don't want to be hard on you in your affliction, but it appears to me that your stock of mothers holds out pretty well. It interferes with business, so clear out, and never come back until you have buried every mother you have in the world."

Those natives are strange folks. They are not afraid of death. They can die whenever they want to. *(Laughter.)* That's a fact. They don't mind dying any more than a jilted Frenchman does. When they take a notion to die, they die, and it doesn't make any difference whether there is anything the matter with them or not, and they can't be persuaded out of it—have got ready to die, made up their minds to die, and *will* die, in spite of all. When one of them makes up his mind to die, he just lies down and is just as certain to die as though he had all the doctors in the world hold of him! *(Laughter.)*

A gentleman in Hawai'i asked his servant if he wouldn't like to die and have a big funeral. He said yes, and looked happy, and the next morning the overseer came and said, "That boy of yours laid down and died last night and said you were going to give him a fine funeral."

They are more civilized and Christianized than they used to be, but still they believe an enemy can offer incantations to the idols and pray them to death. Three Kānakas on one whaleship that left the Islands last year died one after the other, from no apparent cause, and each said it was no use to try to save them, for they knew some enemy at home was praying them to death. I know there is something in it—albeit it is rank idolatry—and I sincerely feel for these poor creatures. Even in this Christian city I went to church last Sunday and came mighty near getting prayed to death myself.

Big funerals are their main weakness. Fine grave clothes, fine funeral appointments, and a long procession are things they take a generous delight in. They are fond of their chief and their king; they reverence them with a genuine reverence and love them with a warm affection, and often look forward to the happiness they will experience in burying them. They will beg, borrow, or steal money enough, and flock from all the Islands, to be present at a royal funeral on O'ahu. All they care for is a funeral. It makes but little difference to them whose it is; they would as soon attend their own funeral as anybody else's.

There are 3,000 white people in the Islands—mostly Americans—and they are still increasing. They own all the money, control all the commerce, and own all the ships. In fact they are the kings of the Sandwich Islands, the monarchy is not much more than a mere name. These people stand as high in the scale of character as any people in the world, and some of them who were born and educated in those islands don't even know what vice is.

A Kanaka or native is nobody unless he has a princely income of $75 annually, or a splendid estate worth $100. The country is full of office holders and office-seekers; there are plenty of such noble patriots. You can take a club and knock down three men, and the chances are that two of them are office-holders and the other an office-seeker.

In a little island, half the size of one of the wards of St. Louis, there are lots of noblemen, princes, and men of high degree, with grand titles, holding big offices, receiving immense salaries—such as ministers of war, secretaries of the navy, secretaries of state and ministers of justice. They make a fine display of uniforms, and are very imposing at a funeral.

The army consists of two hundred men, but it is not on a war footing, now, happily. Some of the muskets haven't got any locks to them, and the others haven't got any ramrods. The navy [has] no fleet except two fishing boats and a bathing machine. [There are] ministers of the interior, although you cannot go into the interior but a little ways without danger of falling overboard on the opposite side.

That's the country for a petty hero to go to; he would soon have the conceit taken out of him. There are so many of them, that a nobleman from any other country would be nobody.

Kānakas are fond of horses, and they have got plenty of them. They seldom walk anywhere; they nearly always ride. Whenever you see a lot of men and women at work in a sugar plantation, you will see as many horses hitched at hand for them to ride a quarter of a mile home on.

These are probably worth about seven dollars and a half—the scrubbiest lot of horses in the world. They have eleven distinct styles of gallop. When one of them gallops he mixes them all up at once, making it rather uncomfortable.

When a Kanaka rides through the country, he stops fifteen or twenty minutes at every single cabin he comes to, and has a chat. Consequently their horses early acquire an inveterate habit of stopping, and they cannot be cured of it. If you attempt to keep them in the road and go on about your business, they grow frantic and kick up and charge around fiercely, and finally take the bits in their mouths and carry you to the cabin by main force.

I rode Kānaka horses nearly altogether. When I made the tour of that pleasant country, I hadn't any business at any of the roadside cabins, but I stopped at them all. The horses wanted to stop, and I had to put up with it. That is how I happen to have such an intimate knowledge of the country and the people.

The Kānakas are passionately fond of dogs—not great, magnificent Newfoundlands or stately mastiffs or graceful greyhounds—but a species of little, puny, cowardly, sneaking, noisy cur. There is nothing attractive about these dogs. There is not a handsome feature about them, unless it is their bushy tales. A friend of mine said if he had one of those dogs, he would cut off his tail and throw the rest of the dog away.

They love these puppies better than they love one another—better than their children or their religion. They feed them—stuff them—with poi and fish, from their own calabashes when the supply is scanty, and even the family must go hungry. They sleep with them; they don't mind the fleas. Men and women carry these dogs in their arms, always. If they have got to walk a mile, the dog must be carried—or five miles, for that matter—while the little children walk. When the woman rides on horseback, she often carries the puppy in front of her on the horse; and when the man rides— they nearly always go in a keen gallop—the puppy stands up behind the saddle, "thortships," as a sailor would say, and sways gently to and fro to the motion of the horse. No danger of its falling; it is educated to ride thus from earliest puppyhood.

They passionately love and tenderly care for the puppy . . . pet him . . . feed him . . . caress him . . . fondle him, and when he has become fat, they cook him and eat him.

Now, I couldn't do that. *(Laughter.)* I'd rather go hungry for two days than devour an old personal friend in that way. *(Laughter.)* There's something sad about that. *(Laughter.)* But perhaps I ought to explain that these dogs are raised entirely for the table, and fed exclusively on a cleanly vegetable diet all their lives. Many a white citizen of those islands throws aside his prejudices and takes his dinner off one of those puppies—and after all, it is nothing but our cherished American sausage with the mystery removed. *(Laughter.)*

I did not eat any dog. I ate raw salt pork and poi, and that was bad enough, but I was lost in the woods and hungry.

In olden times it used to be popular to call the Sandwich Islanders cannibals, but that was a slander. They never were cannibals. That's amply proven. They didn't eat Captain Cook—or if they did, it was only for fun.

There was one there once, but he was a foreign savage, who opened his establishment there for a while and did quite a business while he stayed. He was a useful citizen, but had strong political prejudices, and used to save up a good appetite for just before election, so that he could thin out the Democratic vote. *(Laughter.)* [Democrats were the conservatives at that time, and they had just lost their fight in the Civil War to keep slaves.] By and by he got tired of his diet. Well, anybody would. So he undertook to eat a missionary with onions for breakfast. The change was too sudden, and he didn't survive very long afterward. He suffered. There is no telling how much he suffered. He lingered for a few days, and then died. He could not digest the old missionary no more than he could a keg of nails; he died—miserably died.

Let this be a warning to all of you.

I don't tell this on account of its value as a historical fact *(laughter)*, but only on account of the moral which it conveys. You don't appear to see the moral; but I know there must be a moral in it somewhere, because I have told it forty or fifty times and never got a moral out of it yet! *(Laughter.)*

(Mark Twain paused and said with an indescribable look:) At this point in my discourse, it is my custom to illustrate cannibalism before the audience; but I am a stranger here, and feel diffident about asking favors. However, if there is anyone present who is willing to contribute a baby for the purposes of the lecture, I should be glad to know it now. *(Laughter.)*

I will leave out that part of my program, though it is very neat and pleasant. Yet it is not necessary. I am not hungry.

In former times, when a great noble died, they bit pieces of their own bodies off. They used to tear and burn their flesh, or shave their heads, or pluck out their eyes, or knock out a couple of their front teeth, when a great chief died. And if their bereavement were particularly sore that they couldn't possibly bear it and they could get relief in no other way, they would go out and scalp a neighbor or burn his house down. There was no law against it. It was an excellent custom, too, for it gave everyone a good opportunity to square up old grudges. Pity we didn't have it here!

In the season of mourning for a great person they permit any crime that will best express great sorrow. The largest liberty in the matter of mourning was permitted. They would also kill now and then an infant—bury him alive sometimes. But the missionaries have done away with all that. The American missionaries are opposed to infanticide. . . . For my part, I can't see why.

Down there in the Islands they have exploded one of our most ancient and trusted maxims. It was a maxim that we have all of us implicitly believed in and revered—and now it turns out to be a swindling humbug. *Be virtuous and you will be happy.* The Kānakas are not virtuous—neither men, women, nor children—and yet they are the happiest creatures the sun shines on. They are as happy as the day is long.

They have some curious customs there; among others, if a man makes a bad joke they kill him. I can't speak from experience on that point, because I never lectured there.

I suppose if I had I should not be lecturing here.

The natives do everything wrong end foremost. The same word stands for "How d'ye do?" and "Goodbye," so that you never could tell whether you had just arrived or were going. When you meet one on horseback he turns out on the wrong side to let you go by; they cinch a horse on the wrong side and mount him from the wrong side; their lineage and rank come down from the female ancestor instead of the male; the women smoke more than the men; the natives' English "no" generally means "yes"; they eat their fish raw, and bathe in the middle of the day; instead of keeping it from a patient that he is likely to die, they tell him early; when they beckon to a person to come, they make a sign that with us is considered a repulsive motion; the only native bird that has handsome feathers has only two, and they are under its wings instead of on top of its head; frequently a native cat has a tail only two-inches long and has got a knot tied in the end of it; the native duck lives on the dry tops of mountains 5,000 feet high and never sees any moisture until it rains, and then it is the first to seek shelter; the natives always stew chickens instead of baking them; they dance at funerals; they sing a dismal heartbroken dirge and groan in a heart-broken way when they are particularly happy; they spit on a spoon when they want to clean it; and with atrocious perverseness they wash your shirts with a club and iron them with a brickbat.

In the noble, soul-inspiring game of Seven-Up, the dealer deals the cards to his right instead of to the left; and what is insufferably worse, the ten takes the ace! *(Prolonged laughter.)* Now, such abject ignorance as that is reprehensible, and for one, I am glad the missionaries have gone there. *(Laughter.)*

Now, you see what kind of voters you will have if you take these islands away from these people, as we are pretty sure to do someday. They will do everything wrong end first. They will make a deal of trouble here too. Instead of fostering and encouraging a judicious system of railway speculations, and all that sort of thing, they will elect the most incorruptible men to Congress. *(Prolonged laughter and applause.)* Yes, they will turn everything upside down.

It is a solemn pleasure to stand upon the summit of the extinct crater of Haleakalā, 10,000 feet above the sea, and gaze down into its awful crater, twenty-seven miles in circumference and 220 feet deep, and to picture to yourself the seething world of fire that once swept up out of the tremendous abyss ages ago.

The prodigious funnel is dead and silent now, and even has bushes growing far down in its bottom, where the deep-sea line could hardly have reached in the old times, when the place was filled with liquid lava. These bushes look like parlor shrubs from the summit where you stand, and the file of visitors moving through them on their mules is diminished to a detachment of mice almost; and to them you, standing so high up against the sun, two thousand feet above their heads, look no larger than a grasshopper.

This in the morning; but at three or four in the afternoon a thousand little patches of white clouds, like handfuls of wool, come drifting noiselessly, one after another, into the crater, like a procession of shrouded phantoms, and circle round and round the vast sides, and settle gradually down and mingle together until the colossal basin is filled to the brim with snowy fog and all its seared and desolate wonders are hidden from sight.

And then you may turn your back to the crater and look far away upon the broad valley below, with its sugar-houses glinting like white specks in the distance, and the great sugar-fields diminished to green veils amid the lighter-tinted verdure around them, and abroad upon the limitless ocean. But I should not say you look down; you look up at these things.

You are ten thousand feet above them, but yet you seem to stand in a basin, with the green islands here and there, and the valleys and the wide ocean, and the remote snow-peak of Maunaloa, all raised up before and above you, and pictured out like a brightly tinted map hung at the ceiling of a room.

You look up at everything; nothing is below you. It has a singular and startling effect to see a miniature world thus seemingly hung in mid-air.

But soon the white clouds come trooping along in ghostly squadrons and mingle together in heavy masses a quarter of a mile below you and shut out everything—completely hide the sea and all the earth save the pinnacle you stand on. As far as the eye can reach, it finds nothing to rest upon but a boundless plain of clouds tumbled into all manner of fantastic shapes—a billowy ocean of wool aflame with the gold and purple and crimson splendors of the setting sun! And so firm does this grand cloud pavement look that you can hardly persuade yourself that you could not walk upon it; but if you stepped upon it you would plunge headlong and astonish your friends at dinner ten thousand feet below.

Standing on that peak, with all the world shut out by that vast plain of clouds, a feeling of loneliness comes over a man which suggests to his mind the last man at the flood, perched high upon the last rock, with nothing visible on any side but a mournful waste of waters, and the ark departing dimly through the distant mists and leaving him to storm and night and solitude and death!

(The view from Mount Haleakalā, on Maui, was described by him in the most sublime and thrilling language. The audience was perfectly fascinated and spellbound with the eloquence of the speaker, when, with unexampled diffidence, he pretended to forget a word—which would have finished his description—thereby spoiling the whole thing almost and losing that outburst of applause which certainly would have followed had he finished as he commenced. He made up for this seeming omission, however, by another gorgeous display of brilliant eloquence.[30])

The chief glory of the Sandwich Islands is their great volcano. The volcano Kīlauea['s crater] is 17,000 feet in diameter, and 700 to 800 feet deep. Vesuvius is nowhere. [sic] It is the largest live volcano in the world; shoots up flames tremendously high. You witness a scene of unrivaled sublimity, and witness the most astonishing sights.

When the volcano Kīlauea broke through a few years ago, lava flowed out of it for twenty days and twenty nights, and made a stream forty miles in length, till it reached the sea, tearing up forests in its awful fiery path, swallowing up huts, destroying all vegetation, rioting through shady dells and sinuous canyons. Amidst this carnival of destruction, majestic columns of smoke ascended, and formed a cloudy murky pall overhead. Sheets of green, blue, lambent flame were shot upwards and pierced this vast gloom, making all sublimely grand.

The natives are indifferent to volcanic terrors. During the progress of an eruption they ate, drank, bought, sold, planted, built, apparently indifferent to the roar of consuming forests, the sight of devouring fire, the startling detonations, the hissing of escaping steam, the rending of the earth, the shivering and melting of gigantic rocks, the raging and dashing of the fiery waves, the bellowings and unearthly mutterings coming up from a burning deep. They went carelessly on, amid the rain of ashes, sand, and fiery scintillations, gazing vacantly on the ever-varying appearance of the atmosphere, murky, black, livid, blazing, the sudden rising of lofty pillars of flame, the upward curling of ten thousand columns of smoke, and their majestic roll in dense and lurid clouds. All these moving phenomena were regarded by them as the fall of a shower or the running of a brook; while to others they were as the tokens of a burning world, the departing heavens, and a coming judge . . .

(After this burst of eloquence—delivered with perfect indifference and almost as if without an effort—he clapped his hands and the audience joined, making the vaulted roof of the Library Hall reverberate with the sound of enthusiastic applause. He paused for just an instant, and then said in the same passionless tone:)

There! I'm glad I've got that volcano off my mind.

(After another burst of eloquence about some perennial flower, he applauds himself; would repeat it again if requested to by the audience; the audience requests him to proceed, but the lecturer declines with such a comical gesture, that it sends the audience into convulsions.)

We can have any climate we want in the Sandwich Islands. On the summits, which are 16,000 feet above the level of the valley, whose tops are whitened by perpetual snow, we can have everlasting winter, and near the leeward shore everlasting summer. A single glance of the eye takes in all the climates on the earth. It was so cold on the tops of the mountains that I could not speak the truth, but on level ground I can speak the truth as well as any other man.

If you would see magnificent scenery—scenery on a mighty scale— and get scenery which charms with its softness and delights you with its unspeakable beauty, at the same moment that it deeply impresses you with its grandeur and its sublimity, you should go to the Islands.

Each island is a mountain—or two or three mountains. They begin at the seashore—in a torrid climate where the coconut palm grows, and the coffee tree, the mango, orange, banana, and the delicious cherimoya; they begin down there in a sweltering atmosphere, rise with a grand and gradual sweep till they hide their beautiful regalia of living green in the folds of the drooping clouds, and higher and higher yet they rise among the mists till their emerald forests change to dull and stunted shrubbery, then to scattering constellations of the brilliant silversword, then higher yet to dreary, barren desolation—no trees, no shrubs, nothing but torn and scorched and blackened piles of lava; higher yet, and then, towering toward heaven, above the dim and distant land, above the waveless sea, and high above the rolling plains of clouds themselves, stands the awful summit, wrapped in a mantle of everlasting ice and snow and burnished with a tropical sunshine that fires it with a dazzling splendor! Here one may stand and shiver in the midst of eternal winter and look down upon a land reposing in the loveliest hues of a summer that hath no end.

Such is Maunaloa—16,000 feet high by recent and accurate measurement, and such is Maunakea, 14,000 feet high. . . .

The land that I have tried to tell you about lies out there in the midst of the watery wilderness, in the very heart of the almost soilless solitudes of the Pacific. It is a dreamy, beautiful, charming land. I wish I could make you comprehend how beautiful it is. It is a land that seems ever so vague and fairy-like when one reads about it in books, peopled with a gentle, indolent, careless race. It is Sunday land. The land of indolence and dreams, where the air is drowsy and things tend to repose and peace, and to emancipation from the labor and turmoil and weariness and anxiety of life.

(At the close of the lecture Mr. Clemens went off the stage as he came on, with well-feigned awkwardness, and amid loud applause. Everyone retired highly delighted with the irrepressible Californian.)[31]

Critics

In the slang of the day, Twain tried it on the dog, and the cur survived. Actually, he came out smelling like a rose. Twain's Sandwich Islands lectures were well received, and while he gave lectures and speeches on many topics, this was the most popular and seems to have been his favorite.

Here are some reviews, notes, and comments regarding his Sandwich Island lectures over the years:

> there arose before the audience picture after picture of the gem-like isles, set in their verdant beauty in the midst of a silvery fringe of spray, low down near the equator, where the dawn comes unannounced, and where the day dies rapidly away to give place to soft nights, with great mellow stars burning like torches overhead; where the sea is ever beauteous, whether sparkling in the sun or purple beneath the storm
>
> —*Once a Week* (London).[32]

> one of the most interesting and amusing lectures ever given in this city
>
> —*The Evening Bulletin* (San Francisco).[33]

> one of the greatest successes of the season
>
> —*The Dramatic Chronicle* (San Francisco).[34]

> mixture of the sublime and the ridiculous
>
> —*The Golden Era* (San Francisco).[35]

> passages of drollest humor [. . .] and rising occasionally to lofty flights of descriptive eloquence
>
> —*The Daily Territorial Enterprise* (Virginia City).[36]

he is a word painter of no mean caliber.

—*Once a Week* (London).[37]

To use the expression of a rapt listener to the lecture, "He's lightnin'."

—*San Jose Mercury*.[38]

a tissue of nonsense from beginning to end, and his delivery is as disgusting as the lecture is foolish.

—*New Haven Daily Palladium*.[39]

The only remarkable feature about the matter was the sudden illness produced by the appearance of Mark's handbills on the members of the [Oakland, CA] City Council—they were to meet last evening—and their equally sudden convalescence about 8 o'clock p.m. Nearly the whole Council were to be seen at the lecture, apparently in the enjoyment of their usual good health.

—*The Evening-Bulletin* (San Francisco).[40]

the lecture was unanimously pronounced a brilliant success.

—*Daily Hawaiian Herald* (Honolulu).[41]

He has no elocution, but simply a style that knows no restraints

—*The Philadelphia Press*.[42]

for over an hour he kept his audience in a state varying from a gentle ripple to a loud storm of laughter, whose breakers rolled and dashed against the walls, to fall back in a very spray of mirth.

—*Once a Week* (London).[43]

—⚓—

Meeting "Mark" this morning on Montgomery Street, the following dialogue ensued:

"Mark"—Well, what do they say about my lecture?

We—Why, the envious and jealous say it was "a bilk" and a "sell."

"Mark"—All right. It's a free country. Everybody has a right to his opinion, [even] if he *is* an ass. Upon the whole, it's a pretty even thing. They have the consolation of abusing me, and I have the consolation of slapping my pocket and hearing their money jingle. They have their *opinions,* and I have their *dollars. I'm* satisfied.

—*The San Francisco Dramatic Chronicle.*[44]

Just a Minute

Okay. His lectures were a comedy routine, but there are a few things that could use some additional illumination.

While there were some racist jokes, again one needs to remember he was one of the most antiracist celebrities of his time, and people criticized him for *not* being racist at the time. A hundred years later, people were criticizing him for *being* racist. Times change, and the frame of reference shifts, turning an antiracist into a racist. I feel we should view him from his time, not ours, but we should also note what is no longer acceptable and is unjustified.

Now, regarding eating dogs: Before Western contact (I always hesitate to say "Western" since Western civilization came to Hawai'i from their east), the only land animals they had to eat were hogs, dogs, birds, bats, and rats, and I'm pretty sure they didn't eat bats or rats, so aside from sea creatures, there weren't many sources for meat. But I suspect the dogs kept as pets weren't eaten—only those raised for food.

Called poi dogs because they were only fed poi, they didn't bark and were small, short-legged, dim-witted, and sluggish, probably because of their vegetarian diet—primarily poi. But it's said they tasted quite good. Poi dogs, as a breed, vanished by the 1930s from interbreeding with imported dogs.

The ancient Hawaiians usually ate it only on special occasions. Their dogs were only fed poi and were served as part of the main course at luaus, where it was considered a delicacy. The Hawaiians baked the meat in the ground, just as they do kalua pork. Because of their religion, women were not allowed to eat pork, but they were allowed to eat dog meat.

In 1851, R. T. Macoun wrote, "I must say that the idea of eating dog was somewhat revolting to me at first, but seeing others partake with great relish, my curiosity got the better of my stomach, and as I thought in all probability it might be the only opportunity I would ever have of tasting such a delicacy, I soon had a goodly slice smoking on my plate. 'Ce n'est que le premier pas qui coûte' [It's only the first step that costs], for I soon found doggy very tender, very juicy, and most delightfully cooked."[45]

James Jackson Jarves noted in 1843, "All strangers profess to be desirous to taste dog, and they seldom leave disappointed. If they manifest any disapprobation, they are then helped to pig, alias a dog with a pig's head and feet ingeniously attached, which invariably is pronounced very fine. So much for the reputation of O'ahu poi-fed pork."[46]

But that was more than a century ago. Nobody eats dogs in Hawai'i anymore and haven't for a long time. And they never did eat fricasseed cats.

Still, the idea of eating dog meat is one of those things that tend to shock people in American society, which is why Twain liked to use it in his lectures. His matter-of-fact presentation of it kept his audience off balance, preparing them for his sideways discussion of cannibalism.

Twain's lecture relies on ethnic humor, but he sometimes flips things around to poke fun at his audience, making the Hawaiians the ones who were superior. And even though he was well aware the Hawaiians never were cannibals, he used this popular notion in his lectures and elsewhere because he knew his audience had very strong feelings against cannibalism, making it one of his favorite tools to unsettle them. And he would often comically include himself as one of the cannibals. He does something similar when titling some of his lectures "Our

Fellow Savages of the Sandwich Islands," which allowed him to joke about savagery by intimating that we are not much different and indicating that his lecture might also point out uncomfortable truths about his own culture.

In leading up to some of his cannibal jokes in his lectures, he'd say the Hawaiians "were never cannibals" or "It used to be said that the Kānakas were cannibals, but that was a slander." And sometimes he would point out that the cannibal in his tale was not Hawaiian. But his denials seem to have gone over the heads of some.

Even the *New York Times* had trouble transcribing his lecture. Where Twain subtly blamed the massive death toll of the Hawaiians on the Americans and missionaries, the *Times* flipped it around, as if it was a good thing, saying, "The visit of the whites introduced civilization and education and killed out the natives. The latest reliable information fixes the population at 50,000, and when the benevolent foreigners start a few more seminaries, it is to be hoped that that event will materially help to kill off the remainder of the native population."[47] Twain must have been horrified when he read that misquotation.

The *Boston Advertiser* decided to just shift the blame altogether, saying, "The European nations brought into the Islands their own diseases, together with civilization, education and other calamities. The effect of this had been to diminish the native population—education in particular, causing a frightful mortality as the facilities for learning were multiplied."[48] As the missionaries all sailed from Boston, this was probably one time when they were pleased that someone else was given credit for their work.

Perhaps the transcriptionists had trouble hearing because of all the laughter, but it makes me wonder how many other people in the audience misunderstood what he said or heard what they wanted to hear.

On the Road

With the success of his first lecture, Twain went on the road, giving his lectures. Recruiting his friend Denis McCarthy to manage the door, they set off to nearby towns. Previously, McCarthy was one of the owners of the *Daily Territorial Enterprise* and its shop foreman. Twain began working for him in 1862 on arriving in Virginia City and had continued until heading off to San Francisco. After touring through Sacramento and then to small towns in the

Sierra Nevada foothills, they headed up through mining towns, lecturing in such places as You Bet and Red Dog, before giving lectures in Nevada.

This was something of a triumphant return after having fled Virginia City under a cloud on May 29, 1864. It was here that some of his satires—such as the Petrified Man and the Empire City Massacre—became literary hoaxes when people thought the articles were real. It was also here that Twain said he almost had to fight a duel after a rival newspaper called him "an unmitigated *liar, a poltroon [coward], and a puppy.*"

The duel threats resulted from an 1864 satirical article Twain had written while drunk making fun of the ladies of Carson City who led a fund-raiser to help wounded Union soldiers, suggesting some of the funds were being diverted to support racially mixed marriages. That was Twain poking at society's sore spots. Twain, who was acting editor of the *Daily Territorial Enterprise*, never intended it to be published. After showing it to a friend and fellow journalist, he left it on the editing table. Later, it's likely the foreman, looking for additional material to fill the newspaper, picked it up and printed it.

This was during a war of words with a rival paper, and that paper immediately attacked Twain. He felt he couldn't reveal the error and had to brass it out, which led to a duel that was called off at the last minute. He printed a somewhat oblique apology, but things were so hot that he and Steve Gillis began preparing to go to California. He received four more challenges to duels from Carson City husbands, but these apparently faded on news he was leaving.

So one can understand why he was nervous about giving a lecture in Carson City. But all was forgiven, and some citizens sent him a public letter asking him to lecture there, and he made a public reply thanking them and promising to "disgorge a few lines and as much truth as I can pump out without damaging my constitution" and signing it as the "late Independent Opposition Missionary to the Sandwich Islands."[49] The lecture was a success.

Many years later, Twain's youngest daughter would call him "a contrary cuss and difficult to keep out of deadly indiscretions."[50]

Soon after this, his friends staged a holdup as a practical joke on Twain. The idea was to give Twain a financial incentive to do another lecture in Virginia City while also giving him the subject matter for the lecture. They had been trading practical jokes for a couple of weeks, but this was too much for Twain.

Furious, he canceled his remaining four lectures and headed back to San Francisco on November 12.

On his return, George Barnes, editor of the *San Francisco Morning Call*, asked him how it went. Twain replied that they did fairly well, adding they would have done much better if Denis McCarthy hadn't "mistook our trip for a spree."[51]

Torturing His Audience

Twain returned to San Francisco to give his second lecture there about a month and a half after the first. He felt he couldn't give the same lecture twice in the same town, so he drastically changed it. The first fifteen minutes of the new Sandwich Islands lecture wasn't humorous and wasn't about Hawai'i. He decided he would precede the lecture with something he thought would get them to laugh and gain him a connection with his audience. Somehow he got it into his head that he could make his audience laugh through mere repetition, so he flogged them with one of the lamest jokes ever told—one that they had all heard way too many times. This was the tall tale of journalist and editor Horace Greeley and stagecoach driver Hank Monk. San Francisco had been plagued by the joke for half a dozen years. Everyone was sick of it, but for some reason, it continued to circulate.

The story is a drawn-out account of how Greeley got on a stagecoach, telling Monk he needed to get to his destination quickly, so Monk got the horses going so fast over the bumpy road that the buttons came off Greeley's coat and his head went through the roof. Horace begged Monk to slow down. The punch line is, "But Hank Monk said 'Keep your seat, Horace, I'll get you there on time!'... and you bet he did, too, what was left of him!"

After Twain slowly repeated the story four or five times, acting like it was a funny story but pretending to not understand why the audience didn't get it, someone in the audience finally realized the absurdity of what he was doing and began laughing, with the rest of the audience joining in.

Years later, Twain did the same thing in New York when sharing the stage with poet James Russell Lowell. On telling Lowell beforehand what he was going to do, Lowell said, "I think you are dangerous company. I am going to move to the other end of this platform and get out of the way of the bricks."

Twain had to tell the tale five times before he got a "welcome crash." Lowell shook his hand, saying it was a "triumph of art," a "triumph of grit," and that he would rather "take my chances of a soldier's bloody death than try to duplicate that performance," adding that "he had never been so sorry for a human being before, and that he was cold all down his spine until the fifth repetition broke up the house and brought the blessed relief."[52]

Returning to that San Francisco lecture, after the Monk–Greeley story, Twain then tormented his audience some more by describing a few horrors that had little to do with Hawai'i. He began by mentioning leprosy, then moved on to a sculpture in Milan of a man without any skin, and then to his experience as a boy of finding a corpse late one night in his father's office. The idea was, no doubt, to create a stark contrast between the ugliness of death and disease with the beauty of the Islands. Finally, he began his humorous talk about Hawai'i but cut much of the informative material while adding more humor that some found offensive. He ended with an account of the staged robbery, prompting one woman in the audience to comment about his fright during the holdup that "she supposed he had never been robbed before."[53]

This revised lecture didn't go over very well. The audience didn't seem to get it, and the reviewers didn't like it, but that didn't bother Twain. He was particularly proud his Greeley joke finally got a laugh.

It was billed as a farewell lecture, but all the money he made was confiscated by the court.

You may recall that before Twain set off for Hawai'i, he had published a number of articles attacking the police and their chief, Martin Burke, and that they had thrown him in jail. Well, there was another incident in 1864 where Twain's friend, Steve Gillis—the *Daily Territorial Enterprise* compositor who went with Twain to San Francisco following the trouble with the duel— defended a man who was being beaten by barkeeper Big Jim Casey, a friend of Chief Burke. Gillis was arrested, and Twain signed a $500 bond for his release. Steve Gillis jumped bail, heading back to Virginia City. Twain didn't have the money, so he went with Gillis's brother Jim to Jackass Hill, about eight miles outside of Sonora in California's gold country. Twain insisted the hill had that name before he got there. Steve later joined them. It was the middle of winter, so they didn't do much prospecting. At nearby Angels Camp, Twain first heard the jumping-frog story and other tall tales that later appeared in his articles, books, and lectures.

This is why Twain's proceeds from that lecture were garnished to pay the bond, forcing him to continue lecturing and to do a second farewell lecture in San Francisco. It's another reason Twain disliked the police. Burke was voted out and became a realtor. Perhaps Twain's articles played a role in that.

He made three more lectures in the area before returning to San Francisco to redeliver his original lecture, promising "many uncommonly bad jokes."

About 2,000 people attended Twain's first lecture at fifty cents or a dollar per ticket, but he gave away quite a few tickets, so the total take was said to be either $1,200 or $1,400, depending on the source. He paid fifty dollars and half the take to the theater owner. He also spent $150 on advertising. It's thought he ended up with around $400—about $6,500 in today's dollars. For his fifteen West Coast lectures, Twain said he received half the take, which was $1,200 to $1,500. Since most were much smaller venues, there were some that he just broke even on.

In one of his autobiographies, Twain wrote that "in October 1866 I broke out as a lecturer, and from that day to this I have always been able to gain my living without doing any work; for the writing of books and magazine matter was always play, not work. I enjoyed it; it was merely billiards to me."[54]

Five days after his second farewell lecture, on December 15, 1866, he sailed for New York.

THE CANNIBAL AT HOME AND ABROAD

TWAIN HAD BEEN IN THE WEST FOR FIVE AND A HALF YEARS, and the East had drastically changed. The Civil War had littered the landscape with destruction and graves. Twain was a bit apprehensive.

He had gone out West as a printer and a riverboat pilot, taking a vacation until the river reopened. He came back as a journalist, travel writer, and humorist lecturer. He had some money and a little bit of fame. His *Harper's Magazine* article on the *Hornet* shipwreck, which was mainly the transcripts of the survivors' diaries, had just come out, and he wouldn't find out about the error in spelling his name until the following month.

A week or so earlier, he had decided not to go to China, writing to his family in St. Louis, "The China Mail Steamer is getting ready and everybody says I am throwing away a fortune in not going in her. I firmly believe it myself."[55]

He mainly wanted to visit his family, but he was also hoping to travel around the world to generate material for a travel book. He thought he might lecture a little on a small scale, and he was planning to prepare his *Sacramento Daily Union* letters for a book. In addition, he hoped to continue sending correspondence to the West Coast newspapers.

He left San Francisco on December 15 on board a steamer to Nicaragua, crossed over the isthmus, and caught another steamer to New York, arriving on January 12, 1867. During that second voyage, cholera broke out on the ship, and they were soon having one or more funerals each day. He was fortunate to survive.

Twain's Dreamland

Twain was going on sixty-three when he wrote an article or story or essay (it's a bit hard to categorize) titled "My Platonic Sweetheart" in 1898. It recounts a series of dreams he had over a forty-five-year period, but I am placing it here because it was in January 1867 that he had a dream set in Maui's ʻĪao Valley.

"My Platonic Sweetheart" is likely based on a girlfriend whom he lost in real life from his riverboat days on the Mississippi. They saw each other for about three months before they parted, but he was haunted by her memory for the rest of his life, and he often thought of her before he fell asleep.

What happened between them isn't clear, but apparently he asked her to marry him—or something of the sort—and she thought she should play hard to get, figuring he would continue to pursue her, but he took the rejection hard and left, never seeing her again—although they did exchange a few letters late in their lives. It's possible she was the inspiration or partial inspiration for many of the young female characters in his novels, including Becky Thatcher. It's not surprising that she would appear repeatedly in his dreams.[56]

Twain was very skeptical of the supernatural, but he had a strong interest in discovering the origins of dreams and kept a detailed record of all that he had. He said he could still vividly recall all of them.

Soon after arriving in New York, he dreamt he was in ʻĪao Valley with his dream sweetheart.

We wandered far up the fairy gorge, gathering the beautiful flowers of the ginger-plant and talking affectionate things, and tying and retying each other's ribbons and cravats, which didn't need it; and finally sat down in the shade of a tree and climbed the vine-hung precipices with our eyes, up and up and up toward the sky to where the drifting scarfs of white mist clove them across and left the green summits floating pale and remote, like spectral islands wandering in the deeps of space; and then we descended to earth and talked again.

The dream turned tragic when she is killed by a falling arrow fired from a gun. The ancient Hawaiian chiefs did have small bows and arrows, but they used them only to shoot at rats.[57] She continued to appear in later dreams none the worse for wear.

Fear and Loathing in New York City

Shortly after arriving in New York, Twain headed to St. Louis to see his mother and sister. He gave four lectures in the Midwest—including in his hometown of Hannibal, Missouri—before returning to New York in April.

While in St. Louis, he noticed an advertisement for an excursion around the Mediterranean, and the idea appealed to him immensely. He wrote, "Five months of utter freedom from care and anxiety of every kind, and in company with a set of people who will go only to enjoy themselves, and will never mention a word about business during the whole voyage."

Now, people take pleasure cruises all the time, but back then, this was one of the first—if not the first. Twain abandoned his around-the-world trip and convinced the *Alta California* to pay the $1,250 for his passage and $20 for each of his letters. There was an additional charge of $500 for side tours of Europe, but I'm not sure whether the *Alta California* paid for that. As a journalist and a popular humorist, he may have talked the organizers into comping it.

The cruise was a nonprofit venture, put together by Rev. Henry Ward Beecher's Plymouth Congregational Church in Brooklyn, and "the character and standing of every applicant for passage had to undergo the strictest assay by a Committee before his money would be received and his name booked. This was an appalling state of affairs." Since it was limited to 110 passengers, Twain was concerned about being accepted, so for his references: "Among others, I referred to Rev. Mr. Damon, of Honolulu, and it lies heavy on my conscience, because I stole a book from him, which I have not returned yet. For my other references I chose men of bad character, in order that my mild virtues might shine luminously by contrast with their depravity."[58]

On reaching New York, he was waiting in the booking office to find out whether he'd been accepted when he overheard a man ask which notable personalities were going. "A clerk, with evident pride, rattled off the names: 'Lieutenant-General Sherman, Henry Ward Beecher, and Mark Twain; also, probably, General Banks.'"[59]

Not only had his references worked, but he was pleased to find he was an attraction, even though he wasn't yet well known on the East Coast. The other notables didn't make it, so he was it. And they ended up with about sixty-six passengers, so they probably would have taken him without references. Of course, only the wealthy people who could spare the time were able to afford it, so the average age of the passengers he later estimated was about fifty. Being only thirty-one, he wrote that "the idea of those venerable fossils skipping forth on a six months' picnic seems exquisitely ludicrous."[60]

With two months before sailing, Twain focused on two projects, both of them managed by friends—getting a book published and setting up a lecture in New York City.

Charles Henry Webb, the founder and sometime editor of *The Californian*, moved to New York after the magazine failed. He had been trying to get Twain to put together a collection of his Nevada and California stories and sketches into a book. Twain loved the idea but didn't want to do the work, so Webb offered to do it all for him. After putting the book together, he shopped it around to several publishers, but as none were interested, Webb decided to publish the book himself. He released Twain's first book, *The Celebrated Jumping Frog of Calaveras County, and Other Sketches*, on May 1, 1867. While this book didn't sell well in the United States, two pirate editions of it sold very well in Britain.

In the meantime, Twain also sent a number of letters to the *Alta California* at $20 each and resold some of his Hawai'i *Union* letters to the *New York Weekly*. He was also trying to find an East Coast publication that would pay him for regular submissions.

At the same time, Twain tried to get a publisher for his Hawai'i book based on his *Union* letters, but after receiving one offer, he ended up withdrawing the manuscript, citing "dull publishing times."[61]

Twain's other major New York project was a Hawai'i lecture, and it was his friend Frank Fuller who was in charge of that. Twain said Fuller talked him into it, but Fuller said it was all Twain's idea. Fuller was the governor of Utah when he and Twain became friends, and in New York, he was the vice president and one of the directors of the Northern Pacific Railroad Company. He was also a physician, dentist, lawyer, reporter, author, lecturer, military organizer, and businessman. Fuller offered to cover any losses and to give Twain the profits. Fuller was very enthusiastic about the project and quickly rented a large hall that could seat 3,000, with room for another 1,500 or so standing. He set the day of the lecture for five days after the release of Twain's book. Twain wrote,

> There was something catching about that man's prodigious energy. For a moment he almost convinced me that New York was wild to hear me. I knew better. I was well aware that New York had never heard of me, was not expecting to hear of me, and didn't want to hear of me—yet that man almost persuaded me. I protested, as soon as the fire which he had kindled in me had cooled a little, and went on protesting. It did no good. Fuller was sure that I should make fame and fortune right away without any trouble. He said leave it to him—just leave everything to him—go to the hotel and sit down and be comfortable—he would lay fame and fortune at my feet in ten days.

Fuller later wrote,

> Mark was never a very fine dresser, and though his ordinary sack suit was good enough. I told him he must wear evening dress, and he said he never had had a claw-hammer coat in his life. [. . . During the fitting] he railed at the damned tailor who had sewed up the buttonholes so that he couldn't button his coat. I told him it was not customary to button a dress coat. [. . .] He then cut the stitches holding his buttonholes, buttoned his coat [. . .][62]

Twain was soon panicking. He wasn't that well known in New York and didn't have many friends there. He was also going up against a lot more competition for that evening's entertainment. Once again, he was afraid of facing an empty hall. As the day approached, Twain pleaded with Fuller to do anything to bring in an audience, so Fuller began sending out pairs of free tickets to schoolteachers, college professors, bankers, and everyone else he thought would make a good audience.

Twain continued,

But when I got near the building I found that all the streets for a quarter of a mile around were blocked with people, and traffic was stopped. I couldn't believe that those people were trying to get into Cooper Institute, and yet that was just what was happening. [. . .] [It's estimated there were 2,000 to 3,000 in the audience, and many more had to be turned away.]

I was happy, and I was excited beyond expression. I poured the Sandwich Islands out onto those people with a free hand, and they laughed and shouted to my entire content. For an hour and fifteen minutes I was in paradise. From every pore I exuded a divine delight—and when we came to count up we had thirty-five dollars in the house.

Fuller was just as jubilant over it as if it had furnished the fame and the fortune of his prophecy. [. . .]

"Oh," he said, "the fortune didn't come in—that didn't come in—that's all right. That's coming in later. The fame is already here, Mark. Why, in a week you'll be the best known man in the United States. This is no failure. This is a prodigious success." [. . .]

He was right about the fame. I certainly did get a working quantity of fame out of that lecture. The New York newspapers praised it. The country newspapers copied those praises. The lyceums of the country—it was right in the heyday of the old lyceum lecture system—began to call for me.[63]

Fuller added:

> The expense of the lecture was a little over $600; the receipts were not quite $300.
>
> Some twenty-five years later I asked Mark if he remembered the time when he only had $7, and wanted to "preach" in Cooper Union.
>
> "Seven dollars!" he exclaimed. "I had $700 in gold in old man Leland's safe at the hotel."
>
> "You did not tell me that, Mark," I responded.
>
> "Well," he drawled, "maybe I didn't bring out the second syllable quite plainly."[64]

While this lecture didn't make any money, it received rave reviews and made him quite popular in New York. Fuller thought it was a huge success, and Twain performed two more lectures in New York before sailing on the Mediterranean cruise. From this point on, there was constant demand for his lectures, and while the demands of touring were rough, causing him to give up lecturing on occasion, he returned to it when he needed money or for charity events.

The Writing on the Wall (Back in Jail)

Soon after his first New York lecture, he was arrested in the Five Points, New York City. He wrote about it in the *Alta California*:

—✕—

I have been in the Station House. I stayed there all night. I don't mind mentioning it, because anybody can get into the Station House here without committing an offence of any kind. And so he can anywhere that policemen are allowed to cumber the earth. I complimented this police force in a letter some time ago, and felt like a guilty, degraded wretch when I was doing it, and now I am glad I got into the Station House, because it will teach me never to so far forget all moral principle as to compliment a police force again.

I was on my way home with a friend a week ago—it was about midnight—when we came upon two men who were fighting. We interfered like a couple of idiots, and tried to separate them, and a brace of policemen came up and took us all off to the Station House. We offered the officers two or three prices to let us go (policemen generally charge $5 in assault and battery cases, and $25 for murder in the first degree, I believe), but there were too many witnesses present, and they actually refused. They put us in separate cells, and I enjoyed the thing considerably for an hour or so, looking through the bars at the dilapidated old hags, and battered and ragged bummers, sorrowing and swearing in the stone-paved hall, but it got rather tiresome after a while. [. . .]

At last I beheld a handwriting on the wall that made me start! I felt as if an accusing spirit had been raised up to mock me. The legend read (how familiar it was!) "The trouble will begin at eight o'clock!" How well I remembered inventing that sentence in the *Morning Call* office when I was writing the advertisement for my first lecture in San Francisco [seven months earlier]—and behold how little did I think then that I should live to see it inscribed upon the walls of a prison-house, many and many a hundred miles away!

I smiled at the conceit when I first wrote it, but when I thought how sad-hearted and how full of dreams of a happier time the poor fellow might have seen who scribbled it here, there was a touching pathos about it that I had never suspected it possessed before. I am not writing a fancy sketch, now, but simply jotting down things just as they occurred in that villainous receptacle for rascals and unfortunates downtown yonder.[65]

—

Mark Twain was quickly gaining fame.

Leaving New York on June 8, 1867, Twain set off on the pleasure cruise, and it would completely alter his life. Having learned from his Hawai'i travel letters and his experiences in New York, Twain wrote a series of humorous travel letters about the devout travelers on their six-month cruise, tramping around the Mediterranean on their way to the Holy Land, that were published in the *New York Herald* and then in July 1869 as *The Innocents Abroad, or The New Pilgrims' Progress*. Later in his lectures, he often referred to them as "vandals" rather than "innocents," and as religious groups are not usually partiers, he also noted that "the pleasure trip was a funeral excursion without a corpse."[66]

Mark Twain in 1867, taken in Constantinople (now Istanbul) while on his Mediterranean cruise.
ABDULLAH FRÈRES

This book was a huge best seller and gave him international fame. He had become a celebrity.

In a November 1869 letter to his sister, Twain wrote, "I get just about five hundred more applications to lecture than I can possibly fill—and in the West they say 'Charge all you please, but come.' [. . .] They flood me with high-priced invitations to write for magazines and papers, and publishers besiege me to write books. Can't do any of these things."[67]

But something even more significant happened on the cruise.

Twain became friends with eighteen-year-old Charles Langdon, who one day showed Twain a picture of his sister, Olivia. Twain was infatuated and met her soon after the end of the cruise. For their first date, they went to a reading by Charles Dickens. Her father was a very wealthy businessman involved in coal mining. He eventually won her and her father over, and they got married in 1870.

Twain's Cannibal Family

A humorous article promoting Twain's December 7, 1869, lecture in Philadelphia appeared in the *Philadelphia Bulletin*. Perhaps it was written by Twain himself— or maybe not.

⤙

Mark Twain, the well-known humorist, will lecture tomorrow night at the Academy of Music, upon the Sandwich Islands. Mr. Twain's reputation is so great that he does not need any special recommendation from us. He knows all about the Sandwich Islands, for he was born there. His ancestors were at one time kings of those islands, and for many years they gamboled upon the sunny savannah of their dominions attired in banana leaves and satiated upon a diet of their poor relations.

Love of their fellow men has always been a trait of the Twain family, and they never cared what their personal peculiarities were, so [long as] they were cooked with a crust on and were served up with gravy.

When Mr. Twain came away, the entire population shed tears at the wharf.

"Heaven bless you," they said. "Don't come back unless you grow fatter. Mark, we love you—we love you done rare, with the bones out"; and one woman, to whom he had given his heart's young affections, and with whom

Mark Twain as a cannibal in a *Minneapolis Journal* political cartoon from March 23, 1901.

he had wandered often, hand in hand, on starry nights, in glade and dell, while the balmy breath of the topics swept in from the murmuring sea and whispered to their enraptured souls of elysian joys—this young woman fell upon his neck and made him pledge to her his solemn promise that she should have his liver when he returned. The scene was very affecting; there was not a dry eye on the pier.

Mr. Twain's real name is Wam-pau-telli-macglaherty. He was converted by a Bohemian priest named O'Callahan. He speaks the English language fluently, and firmly believes that George Washington was an Irishman who discovered America and was rescued by Pocahontas from an awful death on Plymouth rock, after a perilous voyage in the Spanish Armada, which he saved from ruin by cutting down a mast with a little hatchet which had been given him by his father, who perished in the storm, and so could not give his son permission to leave a post which the heroic boy firmly refused to forsake without his father's orders.[68]

Dining with a Cannibal

In another of his comic stories—this one definitely by Twain—Twain interviews a refined and cultured cannibal over dinner. It is similar in style to the burlesques in his Sandwich Island letters. Unfortunately, I don't have room to reprint it, so I'll just give a synopsis.

The article says the cannibal is the king of Easter Island, but internal evidence suggests it actually takes place in Hawai'i. At least, Hawai'i is what Twain was familiar with, so he incorporated those elements into the story, but since he knew the Hawaiians weren't cannibals, he moved the scene to Easter Island—not that the Easter Islanders were cannibals either.

The interview begins with the king finishing a tale about how a girl saved a man from a shark by shoving her "Kaboosh" between its jaws. They continue with a discussion of various types of poi, when the king points out that the same girl improved the recipe by adding grasshoppers. The king notes that this special poi is so good that it's kapu to "the common herd." As Twain begins feeling a bit queasy, their conversation moves on to some bad press the islanders received about their mistreatment of the missionaries, whereupon the king insists the stories were biased, that it was natural his people should be curious and he had told them not to do anything cruel, so the Kānakas conducted only a few experiments in the interest of science, such as scorching and scalping them. The king added that he only killed one of them because he wanted to see how the missionaries would taste with onions.

At this point, they're served baked dog with yams, which the king explains is a national dish that's essential to every luau. The king then continues that it was one of the survivors who "sent home those damaging reports to your country, in which he spoke of the treatment of his brethren in a peevish, fault-finding spirit, ill becoming to his sacred calling. I suppose your people believed every word of it, and just jumped to the conclusion that we were a bad, inhospitable race."

Twain sympathizes with him, and the king offers him some Frenchman—formerly the king's brother-in-law—asking whether he'd prefer white or dark meat. As they continue to dine, the king is suddenly horrified to discover that the cook had fried the Frenchman, insisting he should have been baked, adding that in the morning he would take the cook and "fry *him*, and see how he likes it."

Then the king receives an even greater shock on discovering what he thought was the Frenchman was actually his long-lost twin brother. The king is carried off insensible, and Twain is left wondering what the Frenchman would have tasted like.

This story was very popular when it came out in 1870, and it was reprinted in newspapers throughout the country,[69] but the tale is long forgotten now.

The Good, the Bad, and the Ugly

From November 1869 through January 1870, Twain was on a major speaking tour, giving his Hawai'i lecture almost fifty times. It was an exhausting schedule.

Twain married Olivia—called Livy—in February 1870, and with Twain's book and lecture earnings, their lifestyle was lavish. This was new to Twain but not to Livy. Soon after the wedding, her father died. Then a friend of Livy's died in their house, and then their son—the first of four children—was born prematurely. Livy then caught typhoid fever. She always had poor health and was an invalid as a teenager with what is thought to be a rare form of tuberculosis that affects the bones, particularly the spine.

In December 1870, Twain wrote in a letter, "I love to see people from the Islands, notwithstanding I conducted myself so badly there and left behind me so unenviable a name." This sounds to me like he was suffering from depression. An odd characteristic of depression is that you remember only bad things and none of the good ones, and the bad ones often concern small things that everyone else has long forgotten. He probably didn't really conduct himself badly, but it's typical of depression that he unjustly thought so.

In the same letter, he adds, "I am under contract to write two more books the size of *Innocents Abroad* (600 pp., 8 vo.) and after that I am going to do up the Islands and Harris. They have 'kept' four years, and I guess they will keep two or three longer."[70]

Harris was a Kingdom of Hawai'i government official whom Twain really disliked and had gone at great lengths to criticize. I'll discuss him in a bit more detail later. The interesting thing here is Twain says he's going to "do up the Islands and Harris." He could be referring to his planned travel book based on his *Union* letters, but this might be an early reference to a novel about Hawai'i that he later worked on.

The first of the two books he was contracted to write was initially titled *The Innocents at Home*, but he changed it to *Flush Times in the Silver Mines* before changing it again to *Roughing It*, although the first title was kept for volume 2 of the British edition. It was a travel book prequel to *The Innocents Abroad*, focusing on his journey to the Nevada Territory and his experiences there and in California, including many of the sketches and tall tales he wrote for the West Coast newspapers and magazines.

The contracted books were required to be very long—about 170,000 words. (Most books are 100,000 to 120,000 words.) Twain's manuscript was about 140,000 words, and he needed another 30,000, so he decided to include material from his Hawai'i manuscript. Discarding the business letters and the material with Mr. Brown, he cut out more than two-thirds of his *Union* letters, rewriting bits of what he retained while adding newly written accounts of Maui's Haleakalā and 'Īao Valley.

Roughing It was published in 1872. The chapters on Hawai'i were deleted from later editions of the book to bring it down to a more normal size. But this is probably the reason the Hawai'i book was never published.

Many years after his death, the *Union* letters were reprinted in *Letters from the Sandwich Islands* and *Mark Twain's Letters from Hawaii*, while the Hawai'i chapters from *Roughing It* were reprinted as *Mark Twain in Hawaii*.

What Grandmother Taught Me

In a column of short miscellaneous items Twain wrote for *The Galaxy* magazine, he included these short pieces, which, although not strictly related to Hawai'i—other than that they were inspired by items in Honolulu's *Pacific Commercial Advertiser*, September 17, 1870—I trust you will find are still worth including.

History Repeats Itself

The following I find in a Sandwich Island paper which some friend has sent me from that tranquil far-off retreat. The coincidence between my own experience and that here set down by the late Mr. Benton is so remarkable that I cannot forbear publishing and commenting upon the paragraph. The Sandwich Island paper says:

> How touching is this tribute of the late Hon. T. H. Benton [a Whig senator from Missouri] to his mother's influence: "My mother asked me never to use tobacco; I have never touched it from that time to the present day. She asked me not to gamble, and I have never gambled. I cannot tell who is losing in games that are being played. She admonished me, too, against liquor-drinking, and whatever capacity for endurance I have at present, and whatever usefulness I may have attained through life, I attribute to having complied with her pious and correct wishes. When I was seven years of age she asked me not to drink, and then I made a resolution of total abstinence; and that I have adhered to it through all time I owe to my mother."

I never saw anything so curious. It is almost an exact epitome of my own moral career—after simply substituting a grandmother for a mother.

How well I remember my grandmother's asking me not to use tobacco, good old soul! She said, "You're at it again, are you, you whelp? Now don't ever let me catch you chewing tobacco before breakfast again, or I'll black-snake you within an inch of your life!" I have never touched it at that hour of the morning from that time to the present day.

She asked me not to gamble. She whispered and said, "Put up those wicked cards this minute!—two pair and a jack, you numskull, and the other fellow's got a flush!"

I never have gambled from that day to this—never once—without a "cold deck" in my pocket. I cannot even tell who is going to lose in games that are being played unless I deal myself.

When I was two years of age she asked me not to drink, and then I made a resolution of total abstinence. That I have adhered to it and enjoyed the beneficent effects of it through all time, I owe to my grandmother—let these tears attest my gratitude. I have never drunk a drop from that day to this of any kind of water. [. . .]

⸺

In a Sandwich Island paper [*The Pacific Commercial Advertiser*, September 24, 1870] just received by mail, I learn that some gentlemen of taste and enterprise, and also of Keokuk, Iowa, have named a fast young colt for me. Verily, one does have to go away from home to learn news. The cannibal paper adds that the colt has already trotted his mile, of his own accord, in 2:17 1/2. He was probably going to dinner at the time.

The idea of naming anything that is fast after me—except an anchor or something of that kind—is a perfect inspiration of humor. If this poor colt could see me trot around the course once, he would laugh some of his teeth out—he would indeed, if he had time to wait till I finished the trip.

I *have* seen slower people than I am—and more deliberate people than I am—and even quieter, and more listless, and lazier people than I am. But they were dead.[71]

⸺

In the item after this one, Twain says the same paper reported that his friend, Henry Whitney, was retiring as the editor of the *Pacific Commercial Advertiser*. Twain describes him as "one of the fairest-minded and best-hearted cannibals I ever knew" and adds, "I cannot think of Whitney without my mouth watering. We used to eat a great many people in those halcyon days, which shall come again, alas! nevermore."

Two weeks earlier the *Pacific Commercial Advertiser* described Twain during his Honolulu days as a "roving traveler, whom many of our readers will remember as a coarse and rather slovenly but good-natured fellow, with an everlasting cigar in his mouth, and his feet upon everybody's desk or table." They went on to quote an article noting how much he had changed after getting married a few months earlier, that he'd given up drinking and smoking, and that marriage "lends a finer quality of late to his humor, which used occasionally to have a touch of grossness in it."[72] Obviously people back then were much more sensitive than we are now. And perhaps they hadn't read his recent cannibal story.

Summarizing Hawai'i

Soon after *Roughing It* was published, tragedy again hit Twain's life when his nineteen-month-old son died from diphtheria. Twain blamed himself for taking his son out in cold weather before he became ill, saying, "Yes, I killed him." His actions probably had nothing to do with it, but Twain convinced himself that they did. Meanwhile, his daughter Olivia Susan (Suzy) was born.

At the end of 1872, the famous founder and editor of the *New York Tribune*, Horace Greeley, died, and his paper was bought by Whitelaw Reid, backed by some wealthy investors. On taking over, one of the first things he did was write to Twain asking him to supply an article on any topic he wanted, so Twain sent him two long articles on Hawai'i. The first article summarized his impressions of the Islands, while the second focused on the government and royalty. King Kamehameha V (Lot) had just died, and newspapers across the country were speculating on who would be chosen to replace him, usually, as Twain pointed out, ignoring Prince William Lunaliho. Twain was correct, and Lunaliho did become the next king.

For his summary, some of this he had said before in a different way, but he adds a bit to it here.

A Paradise for All Sorts

I spent several months in the Sandwich Islands, six years ago, and, if I could have my way about it, I would go back there and remain the rest of my days. It is paradise for an indolent man. If a man is rich he can live expensively, and his grandeur will be respected as in other parts of the earth; if he is poor he can herd with the natives, and live on next to nothing; he can sun himself all day long under the palm trees, and be no more troubled by his conscience than a butterfly would.

When you are in that blessed retreat, you are safe from the turmoil of life; you drowse your days away in a long deep dream of peace; the past is a forgotten thing, the present is heaven, the future you leave to take care of itself. You are in the center of the Pacific Ocean; you are two thousand miles from any continent; you are millions of miles from the world; as far as you can see, on any hand, the crested billows wall the horizon, and beyond this barrier the wide universe is but a foreign land to you, and barren of interest. [. . .]

About the Natives

The natives of the Islands number only about 50,000, and the whites about 3,000, chiefly Americans. According to Capt. Cook, the natives numbered 400,000 less than a hundred years ago. But the traders brought labor and fancy diseases—in other words, long, deliberate, infallible destruction; and the missionaries brought the means of grace and got them ready. [...]

I am truly sorry that these people are dying out, for they are about the most interesting savages there are. Their language is soft and musical; it has not a hissing sound in it, and *all* their words end with a vowel. They would call [robber baron] Jim Fisk "Jimmy Fikki," for they will even do violence to a proper name if it grates too harshly in its natural state. [...]

[This next bit is the exact opposite of what he wrote when he first arrived in the Islands and expressed the stereotypical view of ancient Hawai'i "whose ferocious inhabitants closed in upon the doomed and helpless Captain Cook and murdered him." This shows how much his views had changed.]

These natives are the simplest, the kindest-hearted, the most unselfish creatures that bear the image of the Maker. Where white influence has not changed them, they will make any chance stranger welcome, and divide their all with him—a trait which has never existed among any other people, perhaps. They live only for today; tomorrow is a thing which does not enter into their calculations.

I had a native youth in my employ in Honolulu, a graduate of a missionary college, and he divided his time between translating the Greek Testament and taking care of a piece of property of mine which I considered a horse. Whenever this boy could collect his wages, he would go and lay out the entire amount, all the way up from fifty cents to a dollar, in poi (which is a paste made of the kalo root, and is the national dish), and call in all the native ragamuffins that came along to help him eat it. And there, in the rich grass, under the tamarind trees, the gentle savages would sit and gorge till all was gone. My boy would go hungry and content for a day or two, and then some Kanaka he probably had never seen before would invite him to a similar feast, and give him a fresh start.

Curious Moral and Religious Aspects

The ancient religion was only a jumble of curious superstitions. The shark seems to have been the god they chiefly worshiped—or rather sought to propitiate. Then there was Pele, a goddess who presided over the terrible fires of Kīlauea; minor gods were not scarce.

The natives are all Christians, now—every one of them; they all belong to the church, and are fonder of theology than they are of pie; they will sweat out a sermon as long as the Declaration of Independence; the duller it is the more it infatuates them [...]

Sunday schools are a favorite dissipation with them, and they never get enough. If there was physical as well as mental intoxication in this limb of the service, they would never draw a sober breath. Religion is drink and meat to the native. He can read his neatly printed Bible (in the native tongue—every solitary man, woman, and little child in the Islands can), and he reads it over and over again. And he reads a whole world of moral tales, built on the good old Sunday-school book pattern exaggerated, and he worships their heroes—heroes who walk the world with their mouths full of butter, and who are simply impossibly chuckle-headed and pious. And he knows all the hymns you ever heard in your life, and he sings them in a soft, pleasant voice, to native words that make "On Jordan's stormy banks I stand" sound as grotesquely and sweetly foreign to you as if it were a dictionary grinding wrong end first through a sugar-mill.

Now you see how these natives, great and small, old and young, are saturated with religion—at least the poetry and the music of it. But as to the practice of it, they vary. Some of the nobler precepts of Christianity they have always practiced naturally, and they always will. Some of the minor precepts they as naturally do not practice, and as naturally they never will. The white man has taught them to lie, and they take to it pleasantly and without sin—for there cannot be much sin in a thing which they cannot be made to comprehend is a sin. Adultery they look upon as poetically wrong but practically proper.

These people are sentimentally religious—perhaps that describes it. They pray and sing and moralize in fair weather, but when they get into trouble, that is "business"—and then they are tolerably apt to drop poetry and call on the Great Shark God of their fathers to give them a lift. Their ancient superstitions are in their blood and bones, and they keep cropping out now and then in the most natural and pardonable way.

The natives make excellent seamen, and the whalers would rather have them than any other race. They are so tractable, docile and willing, and withal so faithful, that they rank first in the sugar-planters' esteem as laborers. Do not these facts speak well for our poor, brown Sunday-school children of the far islands?[73]

Twain, in the second of his *New York Tribune* articles, facetiously said the United States should annex the Islands. Unfortunately, some people missed the irony and thought he was in favor of annexation. They must not have read what he wrote.

Let us annex, by all means. We could pacify Prince Bill [William Lunalilo, who was about to become king] and other nobles easily enough—put them on a reservation. Nothing pleases a savage like a reservation—a reservation where he has his annual hoes [to farm with], and Bibles and blankets to trade for powder and whiskey—a sweet Arcadian retreat fenced in with soldiers. By annexing, we would get all those 50,000 natives cheap as dirt, with their morals and other diseases thrown in. No expense for education—they are already educated; no need to convert them—they are already converted; no expense to clothe them—for obvious reasons.

We *must* annex those people. We can afflict them with our wise and beneficent government. We can introduce the novelty of thieves, all the way up from street-car pickpockets to municipal robbers and government defaulters, and show them how amusing it is to arrest them and try them and then turn them loose—some for cash and some for "political influence." We can make them ashamed of their simple and primitive justice. We can do away with their occasional hangings for murder, and let them have Judge Pratt to teach them how to save imperiled assassins to society. We can give them some Barnards [corrupt judges] to keep their money corporations out of difficulties. We can give them juries composed entirely of the most simple and charming leatherheads. We can give them railway corporations who will buy their legislatures like old clothes, and run over their best citizens and complain of the corpses for smearing their unpleasant juices on the track.

In place of harmless and vaporing [Charles] Harris [a Hawai'i government official], we can give them [corrupt politician "Boss"] Tweed. We can let them have [corrupt politician] Connolly; we can loan them [corrupt politician] Sweeny; we can furnish them some Jay Goulds [robber barons] who will do away with their old-time notion that stealing is not respectable. [. . .] We can give them lecturers! I will go myself.

We can make that little bunch of sleepy islands the hottest corner on earth, and array it in the moral splendor of our high and holy civilization.[74]

When Twain went to the Islands, he was very patriotic and believed the United States had the best government in the world. By this point, he had reported on what was going on in Washington, D.C., and New York, and he had just returned from Britain. This had changed his views. In an unpublished cover letter to Reid, Twain wrote, "To speak truly, I would rather those islands remained under a native king, if I were there, but you can easily see that that won't suit those planters."[75]

Who Should Be the Next King?

With all the speculation around who would become the next king, Twain made it clear who he thought that should be. The *Sacramento Daily Union* reported, "Mark Twain has written a lecture—which he proposes to deliver at $200, or so, a night—on his rights to the Sandwich Islands throne."[76]

Twain Conquers England

In 1873, Twain gave four Sandwich Island lectures in New York and New Jersey, then returned to England for his second visit, performing six Hawai'i lectures in one week to sellout crowds in London's largest hall. Twain's books were already extremely popular in Britain, so his lecture was an even bigger hit here than back in the United States. Everybody was talking about him.

By this time Twain's anti-British sentiments had vanished. In *The Innocents Abroad*, he wrote, "Travel is fatal to prejudice, bigotry, and narrow-mindedness, and many of our people need it sorely on these accounts. Broad, wholesome, charitable views of men and things cannot be acquired by vegetating in one little corner of the earth all one's lifetime. He also wrote, "nothing so liberalizes a man and expands the kindly instincts that nature put in him as travel and contact with many kinds of people."[77]

Two months later, after taking his family back home, he returned to England and gave another seven lectures in one week at the same place. He also gave two in Liverpool in January 1874, which was the last known time that he gave his Sandwich Island lecture. Of course, he gave other lectures during the previous years and in England, but we're just interested in the one on Hawai'i.

During his time in England, his friend from San Francisco and Hawai'i, Charles Warren Stoddard, stayed with him acting as his secretary. Secretaries were often men in those days, although Twain said he actually hired him to keep him company. Stoddard came to London as a roving reporter for the *San Francisco Chronicle*. Twain's lecture manager was the same one Charles Dickens had.

To help publicize his first lecture, Twain wrote a letter to the editor of the *London Evening Standard*, which was reprinted in newspapers across the United States, saying,

> In view of the prevailing frenzy concerning the Sandwich Islands, and the inflamed desire of the public to acquire information concerning them, I have thought it well to tarry yet another week in England and deliver a lecture upon this absorbing subject. [. . .] I feel and know that I am equal to this task, for I can allay any kind of an excitement by lecturing upon it. I have saved many communities in this way. I have always been able to paralyze the public interest in any topic that I chose to take hold of and elucidate with all my strength.[78]

The *London Times* paraphrased Twain, saying, "In view of the liberality of England, who had sent to America all the lecturers that she could spare, he had felt it nothing but right and fair that the United States, in however imperfect a way, should reciprocate the compliment, and he had, therefore, voluntarily thrown himself into the breach. He was present that evening under those circumstances, but not in his own insignificant individual capacity, but as a representative and exponent of the gratitude of America, and so firmly was he impressed with the importance of his diplomatic mission that to make amends for past neglect he should insist on sending to Great Britain in future fourteen Yankee lecturers for everyone who left these shores."[79]

In the summer of 1874, Twain's second daughter Clara was born. Twain was thirty-eight years old at the time.

A Sighting in New York

A news article that was printed all across the country in 1875 said,

> From a New York correspondent.
>
> Coming out of the Erie Railway building, I yesterday saw Mark Twain, whom we used to know in the old 'Frisco days as Sam Clemens. He wears the same old brigand hat and cloak, and one is always sure when looking at him that he would rather look shabby than wear a pink overcoat with yellow buttons.
>
> It is now just ten years since I sat one day on the steps of the American House, in Honolulu, Sandwich Islands, with Clemens, and happened to mention that I was writing letters to the *New York Herald*. He was then unknown, except as an odd character in San Francisco, and as the writer of letters to the *Sacramento Union*, and he very timidly said he had received an offer from a musical monthly to write a page for it for six dollars. He wanted to know whether it would pay him to go on to New York. I had never read anything of his, and I told him that if he went on to New York he couldn't earn his salt.
>
> Yet there he stood yesterday, with his saucy mustache and gimlet eyes, as unconcerned as if he hadn't made $100,000 and hadn't married a girl with more salt lying around loose than would pickle all Honolulu.[80]

The date of this photograph is unknown. In 1878, Mark Twain wrote on his application for a German passport, "My description is as follows: Born 1835; 5 ft. 8 ½ inches tall; weight about 145 pounds . . . dark brown hair and red moustache, full face with very high ears and light gray beautiful beaming eyes and a damned good moral character."

At about the same time, newspapers across the country printed a blurb referring to Hawai'i saying, "Mark Twain has been there and says he is the only man who really understands the Sandwich Islands, and that the prevalent idea that these islands are real sandwiches is erroneous, for he has had pieces of them in his victuals while there and knows better."[81]

There were also reports that "Mark Twain is hashing up another play, said to be a dramatization of 'Roughing It in the Sandwich Islands.'"[82] Unfortunately, this never came to be.

The following year—1876—*The Adventures of Tom Sawyer* was published in Britain, and the American edition came out six months after that. In 1878 and 1879, Twain and his family moved to Germany to reduce their living expenses, and because he had become so famous, he needed a place where he would be left alone to write. They also traveled through central and southern Europe, and their experiences were published in 1880 as *A Tramp Abroad*. Soon after, Twain's third daughter Jane (called Jean) was born. Twain was forty-four.

Longing for an Incendiary Bomb

Twain, on receiving a postcard from Hawai'i written by his friend Charles Warren Stoddard, responded with this letter:

Hartford, Oct. 26 '81.

My Dear Charlie,

Now what have I ever done to you that you should not only slide off to Heaven before you have earned a right to go, but must add the gratuitous villainy of informing me of it? [. . .]

The house is full of carpenters and decorators; whereas, what we really need here, is an incendiary. If the house would only burn down, we would pack up the cubs and fly to the isles of the blest, and shut ourselves up in the healing solitudes of the crater of Haleakalā and get a good rest; for the mails do not intrude there, nor yet the telephone and the telegraph. And after resting, we would come down the mountain a piece and board with a godly, breech-clouted native, and eat poi and dirt and give thanks to whom all thanks belong, for these privileges, and never housekeep any more.

[. . .] I sigh for the incendiary. [. . .]

What I have always longed for, was the privilege of living forever away up on one of those mountains in the Sandwich Islands overlooking the sea.

Yours ever
Mark.

Then in a letter to his close friend and the editor of *The Atlantic Monthly*, William Dean Howells, in Boston, Twain wrote:

Hartford, Oct. 26 '81.

My Dear Howells,

[. . .] Charley Warren Stoddard has gone to the Sandwich Islands permanently. Lucky devil. It is the only supremely delightful place on earth. It does seem that the more advantages a body doesn't earn here, the more of them God throws at his head. This fellow's postal card has set the vision of those gracious islands before my mind, again, with not a leaf withered, nor a rainbow vanished, nor a sun-flash missing from the waves, and now it will be months, I reckon, before I can drive it away again. It is beautiful company, but it makes one restless and dissatisfied.

With love and thanks,
Yrs ever,
Mark.[83]

TWAIN'S LONG-LOST HAWAI'I NOVEL

IN 1884, *The Adventures of Huckleberry Finn*, which many consider to be his masterpiece, was published in Britain, with the American edition coming out the following year. This was also the year Twain completed his Hawai'i novel.

The novel was never published, and the manuscript has been lost. Only seventeen pages remain. The beginning segment describes the Islands:

> The date is 1840. Scene: the true Isles of the Blest; that is to say, the Sandwich Islands—to this day the peacefullest, restfullest, sunniest, balmiest, dreamiest haven of refuge for a worn and weary spirit the surface of the earth can offer. Away out there in the mid-solitudes of the vast Pacific, and far down in the edge of the tropics, they lie asleep on the waves, perpetually green and beautiful, remote from the workday world and its frets and worries, a bloomy, fragrant paradise, where the troubled may go and find peace, and the sick and tired find strength and rest. There they lie, the divine islands, forever shining in the sun, forever smiling out on the sparkling sea, with its soft mottlings of drifting cloud-shadows and vagrant cat's paws of wind; forever inviting you, never repulsing you; and whosoever looks upon them once, will never more get the picture out of his memory till he die. With him it will stay, and be always present; always present and always fresh; neither time nor distance can dim its features, or dull their charm, or reconcile him to the thought that he will never see that picture with his eyes of flesh again.
>
> The Islands are so beautiful! The richest fancy cannot imagine their beauty, and no brush can adequately paint it. Indeed, you move through a very paradise, and you say nothing, because you cannot put into words, even to yourself, the deep charm and solace and beauty of it. The skies do weep, there, but the leaves never fade—because the skies weep.[84]

Twain is expressing his own longing to return to the Islands, something he would do eleven years later.

His last line is an adaption of William Kennedy's lyrics to the 1838 song "Pirate's Serenade." Twain really liked these lyrics and wrote them down three times in his Hawai'i notebooks. He also used them elsewhere. Here is another of his variations of the lines:

> Oh, islands there are on the face of the deep
>
> Where the leaves never fade and the skies weep.

Kennedy's original lyrics end with "Where the leaves never change and the skies never weep," but Twain objected to the skies never weeping after experiencing Hawai'i's rains.

The novel covered two time periods with a break in between. It appears to start at the end, as 1840 appears to be the end of the second period. Twain's comments indicate the beginning of the first period would be in December 1819, although it makes sense that he would have actually started it a month earlier with the breaking of the kapus and the subsequent battle.

Bill Ragsdale

William "Bill" Ragsdale (1830s–1877) is the protagonist, but he's moved back in time about thirty-five years and combined with Obookia (Henry 'Ōpūkaha'ia), the Hawaiian who was taken with the missionaries to the East Coast, where he cried on the church steps because the Hawaiians didn't know about the Bible, inspiring a flood of donations to the missionaries. Ragsdale was the interpreter Twain saw at the Hawaiian legislature. He had been the editor of a Hawaiian-language newspaper published by Henry Whitney. He later became a lawyer and was living in Hilo when he discovered he had leprosy. He eventually died at the settlement on Molokai's Kalaupapa Peninsula. He arrived there about the same time as Father Damian and was appointed to be the overseer of the colony by the Board of Health.

Twain wanted to illustrate the sudden cultural changes with the arrival of the explorers, merchants, and missionaries, so he has a young Ragsdale who grew up under Kamehameha's rule. Like Obookia, who served at the Hikiau Heiau on Kealakekua Bay, the novel's Ragsdale character was devoted to the ancient Hawaiian religion. The book begins three months before the missionaries arrive. One surviving bit of dialogue involves the King Kamehameha II (Liholiho) questioning a boy (Ragsdale) about a girl who is about to be put to death, although it's unclear why since this was after the end of the kapus. Both are orphans. The king pardons her over the objections of a powerful priest and seems to have adopted them. Years later, the girl becomes Ragsdale's love interest, perhaps even fiancée, whom he is forced to abandon when he heads off to exile because of his leprosy. Leprosy first appeared in the Islands in 1835.

Another fragment has the priests and villagers in a tizzy because someone stole the king's spittoon, which could be used by his enemies to pray him to death. While we usually associate spittoons with the Wild West, they were common all over America at that time. The ancient Hawaiians had their own version of a spittoon that was used by the high chiefs. It was a calabash containing water with flowers floating in it.

A final fragment describes the comfort of a grass hut. In real life, many travel writers have commented on grass houses, usually describing them as airy, clean, comfortable, fragrant, and cool.

Twain explained a bit more about the novel to William Dean Howells, who was going to turn the book into a play.

> My billiard table is stacked up with books relating to the Sandwich Islands: the walls are upholstered with scraps of paper penciled with notes drawn from them. I have saturated myself with knowledge of that unimaginably beautiful land and that most strange and fascinating people. And I have begun a story.
>
> Its hidden motive will illustrate a but-little considered fact in human nature; that the religious folly you are born in you will die in, no matter what apparently reasonabler religious folly may seem to have taken its place meanwhile, and abolished and obliterated it.
>
> I start Bill Ragsdale at twelve years of age, and the heroine at four, in the midst of the ancient idolatrous system, with its picturesque and amazing customs and superstitions, three months before the arrival of the missionaries and the erection of a shallow Christianity upon the ruins of the old paganism. Then these two will become educated Christians, and highly civilized.
>
> And then I will jump fifteen years, and do Ragsdale's leper business. When we come to dramatize [it], we can draw a deal of matter from the story, already to our hand.[85]

Both the hero and the heroine are half Anglo and half Hawaiian. The real Ragsdale was the son of a Hawaiian lower chieftess and a plantation owner from Virginia, so it's likely his character in the book was too. The Twain's heroine, named Aloha, was the daughter of a Hawaiian woman and a Boston sailor. So both of them are bicultural. They embody the conflict of cultures and the bringing of them together.

You may recall that in one of his *Union* letters from Oʻahu, Twain called Ragsdale a rascal and said, "There is a spice of deviltry in the fellow's nature." It's also said he was something of a Casanova, but he was about to marry his Anglo-Hawaiian girlfriend when he discovered he had leprosy and went into exile. The *Daily Alta California*, in describing him, said, "No better-hearted man we ever met; a true Bohemian; he never was anybody's enemy but his own."[86]

Twain also told William Dean Howells that the novel would include Charles Harris—Twain's favorite punching bag from Hawai'i—partly because he hated mediocre people who had power but also because he felt Harris had cast aside his American citizenship to kowtow to Hawaiian royalty. Here's Twain's description of Harris:

> Harris is an American—a long-legged, vain, light-weight village lawyer from New Hampshire. If he had brains in proportion to his legs, he would make Solomon seem a failure; if his modesty equaled his ignorance, he would make a violet seem stuck-up; if his learning equaled his vanity, he would make [Prussian scientist] von Humboldt seem as unlettered as the backside of a tombstone; if his stature were proportioned to his conscience, he would be a gem for the microscope; if his ideas were as large as his words, it would take a man three months to walk around one of them; if an audience were to contract to listen as long as he would talk, that audience would die of old age; and if he were to talk until he said something, he would still be on his hind legs when the last trump sounded. And he would have cheek enough to wait till the disturbance was over, and go on again. [. . .] he was the King's most obedient humble servant and loving worshiper [. . .].[87]

Like many Americans, Twain seemed attracted to royalty, but his democratic principles caused him to hate the idea that power should be hereditary. As William Dean Howells put it, "he abhorred the dreadful fools who through some chance of birth or wealth hold themselves different from other men."[88] He highlighted this in *The Prince and the Pauper* (1881).

After the book was written, Twain began having second thoughts. While on the *Innocents Abroad* cruise, Twain became friends with another writer, Mary Fairbanks, and she became his informal proofreader and editor of his dispatches to the *Daily Alta California*. She continued assisting him in this capacity and supplying her opinions for many years, so Twain wrote to her "this book is not humorous but a serious book, and may damn me, tho' Livy says 'no.' I do wish you would come and read it in ms. [manuscript] and judge it, before it goes to the printers. Will you?"[89]

While the book was serious, it still had humor in it. And as with many of Twain's works, it looks like he satirized everybody in this novel—particularly the Hawaiians and the missionaries. And there are hints that he intended to overturn the racial and cultural assumptions of the American colonizers and tourists while highlighting the advantages of multiculturalism over monocultures.

The manuscript was due to the printers in March 1884, but apparently, Twain withdrew it. We don't know why. I suspect it was because the hidden theme of the book—the "little considered fact in human nature; that the religious folly you are born in you will die in"—was fatally flawed and bordered on racism. The question was whether religion is cultural or inborn (now we would say genetic, then they would have said it was their racial characteristic). Of course, many people change or abandon the religion they're born into. Twain himself is an example of this. It was around this time that he became an ardent agnostic.

> You will never, never know, never divine, guess, imagine, how loathsome a thing the Christian religion can be made until you come to know and study [George Washington] Cable daily and hourly. Mind you, I like him; he is pleasant company; I rage and swear at him sometimes, but we do not quarrel; we get along mighty happily together; but in him and his person I have learned to hate all religions. He has taught me to abhor and detest the Sabbath-day and hunt up new and troublesome ways to dishonor it.[90]

Cable was a southern author who was strongly antiracist and extremely religious. Twain wrote that letter in 1885 at the end of a 103-performance speaking tour with Cable called the "Twins of Genius." Twain remained a vocal agnostic the rest of his life, although he eased up on his criticism of Christianity later in his life.

I think it's also possible he abandoned his book because the idea that your family's background and your position in society is bred into you and cannot be changed goes against the democratic ideal that people are equal and can pull one's self up by their own bootstraps. It's interesting that a few years later, Twain wrote *Pudd'nhead Wilson* (1894), which takes the opposite view—that we are bound not by our genetics or "race" but by our culture. I should note that many people seem unaware that scientists disproved the theory that there are races more than half a century ago. The idea of races is a social myth with no basis in fact.[91] Unfortunately, this false belief still persists, causing untold harm to society.

I think he also may have had reservations about the novel because the general public held the missionaries in very high regard and wouldn't have responded well to his making fun of them and highlighting their flaws. He had already experienced some of this with his lectures. And then there were the racial issues the book would have raised. On top of that, it ends in tragedy with the hero dying a horrifying death from leprosy, while the American public practically demands a happy ending. Any or all of these things might be what he was referring to when he said the book "may damn me."

It was while Twain was working on the Hawai'i novel that Cable gave him a copy of Sir Thomas Malory's *Morte d'Arthur*, the classic book on the King Arthur legends. Some believe he rewrote the novel, moving the setting from Hawai'i to the sixth century and turning it into *A Connecticut Yankee in King Arthur's Court*.

More on that in a minute.

Hawaiian Legends and Myths

In 1884, Twain founded a subscription publishing company, which he called the Charles L. Webster & Company, named after his niece's husband, who became its director. It's first two publications were the American edition of Twain's *The Adventures of Huckleberry Finn* and former president Grant's *Personal Memoirs of Ulysses S. Grant*. It also published books by Leo Tolstoy and Walt Whitman.

One of its other authors was King Kalākaua, who cowrote *The Legends and Myths of Hawai'i: The Fables and Folk-Lore of a Strange People*, published in 1888. The other author was Rollin Daggett, who had previously been the US minister to Hawai'i. They were also assisted by Princess Liliuokalani, who would five years later become queen and Hawai'i's last monarch. Basically, it was a collection of ancient Hawaiian legends rewritten for a Western audience.

Twain explained in a letter to his partner Charles Webster,

> It was constructed by Daggett and the King of the Sandwich Islands, working together, and consists of the (historical) traditions and legends of the natives, reaching back connectedly 1,500 years, and of course is very curious—and *new*. It is fresh ground—untouched, unworn and full of romantic interest. I have read three of the legends and they impress me favorably. [...]
>
> It is the King who tells the ancient native legends (or sagas) to Daggett, and Daggett writes them down—and connects them, very plausibly into an historical chain, with names and dates and details.[92]

Twain first met Kalākaua in Honolulu when he was a prince at dinner the night before Twain visited the palace. Eight years, later the prince became king. Twain met the king again in 1874 on Christmas Eve in New York City.

The king's book is still in print.

Hawai'i's King Arthur

In 1958, Twain scholar Fred W. Lorch floated the idea that Twain rewrote his Hawai'i novel as *A Connecticut Yankee in King Arthur's Court* (1889).[93] He suggested Twain's King Arthur was inspired by King Kamehameha V (Lot), the feudal society took on the role of precontact Hawaiian society, the Catholic Church replaced the ancient Hawaiian religion, the Connecticut Yankee took the place of the missionaries, and, unlike the actual Arthurian tales, Twain's Merlin is a sorcerer who is more like the powerful priest in the Hawai'i novel than King Arthur's wise advisor. Also, the Church's use of the interdict in the novel may have been inspired by the kapu system.

The racial undertones are gone, and instead of converting the population to Christianity, the goal of the Yankee is to instill the American ideals of democracy, individuality, freedom, and equality. Where the missionaries worked for salvation first and then mechanical improvement, the Yankee sought freedom first and then mechanical improvement. While the missionaries were concerned with the adoption of their particular religious practices, the Yankee works to transform the feudal society with an industrial revolution and technology. He tries to replace religion with science and superstition with freedom, but his efforts are destroyed by an epidemic, perhaps inspired by the epidemics that wiped out so many Hawaiians and the leprosy that killed Bill Ragsdale. In both novels, a primitive society is suddenly introduced to the modern world with disastrous consequences.

While *The Connecticut Yankee in King Arthur's Court* went over well in America, it wasn't quite so popular in Britain since the Yankee tried to overthrow the monarchy. In the book, the Yankee says, "The blunting effects of slavery upon the slaveholder's moral perceptions are known and conceded the world over, and a privileged class, an aristocracy, is but a band of slaveholders under another name. [. . .] Men write many fine and plausible arguments in support of monarchy, but the fact remains that where every man in a state has a vote, brutal laws are impossible."

Whether Twain rewrote his Hawai'i novel as the *Connecticut Yankee* is unknown, but at the least it seems to have had some influence on it.

Note that Hawai'i may have also had an influence on *The Adventures of Tom Sawyer* and *The Adventures of Huckleberry Finn*. See David Zmijewski's book *Huck Finn and Hawaii: A Study of Hawaiian Influence on The Adventures of Huckleberry Finn*.

No Alien Land . . .

Twain was just finishing *Connecticut Yankee* when he was called on to make a dinner speech to celebrate the return of two all-star baseball teams from an around-the-world tour of exhibition matches designed to promote baseball in other countries. Part of this speech became known as Twain's prose poem and has been widely used to promote tourism to Hawai'i. It's one of his most popular quotations.

Hawai'i was their first stop on the tour, but they didn't play any exhibition games because their ship arrived too late and it was illegal in Hawai'i to hold nonreligious events on Sunday, so instead they got to meet the king and queen, were given a tour, and went to a luau.

The welcome home dinner in New York in 1889 was a major, highly publicized event, attended by future president Theodore Roosevelt, along with more than 250 other high-class guests, including many reporters. Twain's speech appeared in newspapers all across the country.

Twain was still so closely associated with Hawai'i that he was introduced as a native of the Sandwich Islands, probably as a joke.

> Though not a native, as intimated by the chairman, I have visited, a great many years ago, the Sandwich Islands—that peaceful land, that beautiful land, that far-off home of profound repose, and soft indolence, and dreamy solitude, where life is one long slumbrous sabbath, the climate one long delicious summer day, and the good that die experience no change, for they but fall asleep in one heaven and wake up in another. [. . .]
>
> Well, it is refreshment to the jaded, it is water to the thirsty, to look upon men who have so lately breathed the soft airs of those isles of the blest, and had before their eyes the inextinguishable vision of their beauty. No alien land in all the world has any deep, strong charm for me but that one. No other land could so longingly and so beseechingly haunt me, sleeping and waking, through half a lifetime, as that one has done. Other things leave me, but it abides; other things change, but it remains the same. For me its balmy airs are always blowing, its summer seas flashing in the sun, the pulsing of its surfbeat is in my ear; I can see its garlanded crags, its leaping cascades, its plumy palms drowsing by the shore, its remote summits floating like islands above the cloud-rack; I can feel the spirit of its woodland solitudes; I can hear the plash of its brooks, in my nostrils still lives the breath of flowers that perished twenty years ago.
>
> And these world-wanderers who sit before us here, have lately looked upon these things!—and with eyes of flesh, not the unsatisfying vision of the spirit. I envy them that![94]

Calling the descriptive part, "the prose poem" suggests that it should be a poem, so several people converted it into one. Will Sabin—the editor of *Paradise in the Pacific* magazine—did it for the magazine and his book *The Edge of the Crater, and Other Poems.*

No alien land in all the world
　　Has any deep, strong charm for me
But those fair mid-Pacific isles
　　That ever haunt me longingly;
Waking and sleeping, half a life,
　　They've called to me beseechingly.

With me those islands e'er abide.
　　Though other memories depart;
All else may change, still they shall be
　　The same forever in my heart
They hold me by some subtle spell,
　　Some all-compelling, magic art.

I know Hawai'i's balmy airs
　　Are ever blowing free for me;
Her spreading, sunlit summer seas
　　Are ever smiling flashingly;
The pulsing of her singing surf
　　Is in my ear incessantly.

I see her crags with garlands crowned,
　　Her leaping cascades; plumy palms
Still drowsing by the murmurous shore.
　　Indifferent to the world's alarms.
And whispering in their seeming sleep
　　The island spirit's soothing psalms.

Like islands o'er the sea of clouds,
    Enchanting, mystic and remote,
I see, in all their wondrous charm,
    Cathedral mountain summits float,
And spirits of the solitudes
    Speak to me in each woodland note.

I hear the plashing of her brooks,
    Now riotous, then soft and low,
And in my nostrils still there lives
    A perfume that I used to know—
The breath of fascinating flowers
    That perished twenty years ago.[95]

THE RETURN OF MARK TWAIN

TWAIN RETURNS TO HAWAI'I

The Trouble Begins

Twain was an excellent writer, but he was not a good businessman. By the beginning of the 1890s, he was in financial trouble. Much of it had been building for a while, and he wasn't aware of the extent, but he suddenly began finding out that his companies were deep in debt. There doesn't appear to have been any fraud or embezzlement. He had good men in control, but they seem to have been out of their depth. Also, Twain was too generous, paying people more than he should have, and his investments were losing money, so he had to invest more into them to keep them going. His publishing company began with two huge best sellers—Twain's and Grant's—but the subsequent books didn't do as well. After being liquidated, it still owed $80,000.

He had also invested much his funds and a good portion of his wife's inheritance in a machine that was supposed to revolutionize typesetting, but it failed. By 1891, he had invested $190,000—roughly $10 million in today's dollars—and although it worked, its retail cost would have been way too high, and by then, cheaper alternatives were on the scene. Much of that was his own money, but he ended up owing about $200,000. A large portion of that was to his wife.

To save money, he and his family closed up their mansion and moved to Europe for four years. This was shortly after both Twain's and Livy's mothers died a month apart. Then the Panic of 1893 hit. The United States spun into an economic depression that ran from 1893 to 1897. Even though he was the highest-paid author in America, in 1994, he had to declare bankruptcy. This wiped out his debts, but he vowed to pay back all of his ninety-six creditors, and eventually he did, but he had to go on an around-the-world lecture tour to do it.

In 1867, only Navy and merchant ships sailed around the world, but by 1895, tourism had become popular, and people who could afford it often toured the world, so Twain needed something to make his tour different if he was going to get a travel book published out of it. Since everyone already knew about his bankruptcy, he decided to emphasize that. He didn't want to lecture anymore, as the tour schedules were exhausting and he wasn't well, but he felt he had to pay back the creditors, probably to reestablish his dignity and get him out of his depression, but this also helped gain the public's sympathy and admiration.

Twain, Clara, and Livy as they were about to depart Vancouver for Hawai'i.
JAMES POND

An Around-the-World Tour

In 1895, at the age of fifty-nine, Twain began his tour in Paris and then traveled for forty days westward across America starting in New York and ending up in Oregon. He then sailed to Vancouver, Canada, and from there to Hawai'i—the island paradise he so desperately dreamed of returning to—before continuing on to Australia, New Zealand, Tasmania, India, Ceylon, and South Africa, then back to England. This became the around-the-world tour he had planned back in 1867 and was turned into the travel book *Following the Equator* (1896).

He probably expected his return to Hawai'i to be the high point of his trip, when he would give a lecture and see some of his old friends, even though the ship would be there for only a few hours. It was scheduled to drop off some passengers, load and unload cargo, drop off and pick up mail, and then leave right after Twain's lecture. That's what was planned, but it didn't work out that way by a long shot.

Their steamship CASS *Warramoo* ran aground in the fog and had to be repaired, putting them a week behind schedule. Twain, Livy, and daughter Clara finally sailed from Vancouver on August 23, 1895. Before they sailed, James Pond, Twain's manager for his US lectures, wrote in his diary that Twain "bought three thousand Manilla cheroots, thinking that with four pounds of Durham smoking tobacco he could make the three thousand cheroots last four weeks."[1] He did this even though he was very ill and was spending his days in bed. He had bronchitis, rheumatism, and a large carbuncle, which is an infected cluster of boils—similar to the saddle boils he had from his Big Island excursion.

Many people in Honolulu were anxiously awaiting Twain's arrival. Twain was supposed to be there on August 24, but when the ship didn't arrive, everyone became very concerned. The only method of communication with the Islands was by ship; there was no way for Honolulu to know Twain's ship had been delayed until another ship reported the *Warramoo* was in dry dock. They weren't sure when it would get there, but they began preparing for his lecture whenever Twain did arrive.

After a week at sea, they finally reached Honolulu at 9 or 10 p.m. on August 30. It was too late to enter the harbor, so the ship anchored a mile offshore. Because they were behind schedule, the captain planned to leave at 11 a.m., making it impossible for Twain to give his lecture, but what was more important was that Twain had finally returned to Hawai'i.

On the seventh day out we saw a dim vast bulk standing up out of the wastes of the Pacific and knew that that spectral promontory was Diamond Head, a piece of this world which I had not seen before for twenty-nine years. So we were nearing Honolulu, the capital city of the Sandwich Islands—those islands which to me were Paradise; a Paradise which I had been longing all those years to see again. Not any other thing in the world could have stirred me as the sight of that great rock did.

In the night we anchored a mile from shore. Through my port I could see the twinkling lights of Honolulu and the dark bulk of the mountain-range that stretched away right and left. I could not make out the beautiful Nuʻuanu Valley, but I knew where it lay, and remembered how it used to look in the old times. We used to ride up it on horseback in those days—we young people—and branch off and gather bones in a sandy region where one of the first Kamehameha's battles was fought. [. . .]

Seeing Honolulu Again

Many memories of my former visit to the Islands came up in my mind while we lay at anchor in front of Honolulu that night. And pictures pictures pictures an enchanting procession of them! I was impatient for the morning to come.

When it came it brought disappointment, of course. Cholera had broken out in the town, and we were not allowed to have any communication with the shore. Thus suddenly did my dream of twenty-nine years go to ruin.[2]

—◁

Most people today don't realize how terrible epidemics were in the nineteenth century. During the 1800s, diseases routinely swept across the United States, killing millions of people. It happened so often that it's pretty much been forgotten by everyone except those who work to protect us from it today. During that century, smallpox alone killed between 300 and 500 million. Improved health care, antibiotics, and vaccines became major tools in combatting and preventing outbreaks throughout the twentieth century.

The SS *Belgic* left China with more than 500 Chinese immigrants but stopped in Japan, which at that time was still struggling to get rid of the disease. Somehow, it was transferred to the ship, and three people died on the voyage to Honolulu. One sick man made it Honolulu's quarantine island, but he threw up in the small boat on the way. It's thought the disease was transferred into the ocean, where people became ill after swimming along the shore or by eating infected fish, shellfish, and crabs. The fact that raw sewage flowed down Nuʻuanu Stream right past the poor Hawaiian district of Iwilei probably helped spread the disease.

The first death beyond the quarantine island was on August 19, and the deaths continued through October 3. There were eighty-eight cases of cholera, with sixty-four deaths, most of them after Twain left. Eighty of those who caught the disease were Hawaiian, and fifty-nine of them died. Part of this was because the Hawaiians would hide their sick, thinking they would be taken away like those with leprosy. According to one official report, they also believed "the foreigners were trying to kill them off." That's not surprising considering the state of Hawaiian affairs, which I will get to shortly. Still, the quarantine successfully confined the disease to Honolulu, but it destroyed Twain's dream of ever visiting Hawai'i again.[3]

Talk of cholera had been circulating in Honolulu for more than a week, and the papers had thought it was contained, but the disease was spreading. At that point, fifteen people had already died. The Board of Health finally put the town under quarantine the morning after Twain arrived, closing the schools, preventing church services, and reducing the hours of the bars were open. They also shut down the harbor. People and cargo could be unloaded, but nothing—not even newspapers—could be brought aboard. This also meant no fresh fruit or vegetables.

Because there were paying passengers onshore who couldn't board and hoping that the Board of Health might end the quarantine, the captain said he'd keep the ship there until midnight on Sunday, September 1.

When a boat pulled alongside the ship, the crew refused to touch the rope, probably fearful it might be contagious. Twain's daughter Clara took it and secured it. Twain and other passengers secured the other ropes. At least two people were allowed to come aboard. One was one of the boats' captains, and another was customs officer Clarence Crabbe. Crabbe noticed Twain on a deck chair and asked, "Would you like to go ashore, Mr. Clemens?" In spite of his debts, Twain replied, "I would give a thousand dollars to go ashore and not have to return again."[4]

Twain was able to get a note delivered sending his aloha to Honolulu and saying he was wild to come ashore.

—⚓

Messages came from friends, but the friends themselves I was not to have any sight of. My lecture hall was ready, but I was not to see that, either.

On the deck of the CASS *Warramoo* in 1895.

Several of our passengers belonged in Honolulu, and these were sent ashore; but nobody could go ashore and return. There were people on shore who were booked to go with us to Australia, but we could not receive them; to do it would cost us a quarantine-term in Sydney. They could have escaped the day before, by ship to San Francisco; but the bars had been put up, now, and they might have to wait weeks before any ship could venture to give them a passage any whither. [...]

It is easy to make plans in this world; even a cat can do it; and when one is out in those remote oceans it is noticeable that a cat's plans and a man's are worth about the same. There is much the same shrinkage in both, in the matter of values.

There was nothing for us to do but sit about the decks in the shade of the awnings and look at the distant shore. We lay in luminous blue water; shoreward the water was green-green and brilliant; at the shore itself it broke in a long white ruffle, and with no crash, no sound that we could hear. The town was buried under a mat of foliage that looked like a cushion of moss. The silky mountains were clothed in soft, rich splendors of melting color, and some of the cliffs were veiled in slanting mists. I recognized it all. It was just as I had seen it long before, with nothing of its beauty lost, nothing of its charm wanting.

A change had come, but that was political, and not visible from the ship. The monarchy of my day was gone, and a republic was sitting in its seat. It was not a material change. The old imitation pomps, the fuss and feathers, have departed, and the royal trademark that is about all that one could miss, I suppose. That imitation monarchy, was grotesque enough, in my time; if it had held on another thirty years it would have been a monarchy without subjects of the king's race. [The decrease in the number of Hawaiians leveled off around this time and then began increasing.]

We had a sunset of a very fine sort. The vast plain of the sea was marked off in bands of sharply-contrasted colors: great stretches of dark blue, others of purple, others of polished bronze; the billowy mountains showed all sorts of dainty browns and greens, blues and purples and blacks, and the rounded velvety backs of certain of them made one want to stroke them, as one would the sleek back of a cat. The long, sloping promontory projecting into the sea at the west turned dim and leaden and spectral, then became suffused with pink dissolved itself in a pink dream, so to speak, it seemed so airy and unreal. Presently the cloud-rack was flooded with fiery splendors, and these were copied on the surface of the sea, and it made one drunk with delight to look upon it.

⁓

Hawai'i had changed considerably since 1866. Perhaps the most ground shaking was the 1893 coup d'etat led by a group of eighteen mostly American businessmen, headed by those in the sugar industry, who had been lobbying for annexing Hawai'i to the United States for decades. The US minister to Hawai'i was in on the plot and helped plan it. With the assistance of US troops, they overthrew the Hawaiian Kingdom and later placed Queen Lili'uokalani under house arrest in the 'Iolani Palace ironically for "treason." She was still there while Twain was sitting in the harbor.

President Grover Cleveland sent an official to investigate. Meanwhile, plotters spread rumors around Washington that if the queen was restored, she would behead them. This was clearly a lie to anyone who knew about Hawai'i since the queen was a Christian, but in those racist times, the idea of a brown woman cutting the heads off of white men caused a real stir. Congress refused to annex Hawai'i, and so the plotters formed their own republic, much like Texas and California had before being annexed.

It should be noted that according the 1890 census, there were around 90,000 people in Hawai'i, and only about 2,500 were American, some of whom wanted the monarchy restored. Since the supporters of the new Republic were greatly outnumbered, they continued the missionaries' tactic of preventing people from voting. Americans and Europeans, including noncitizens, could vote as long as they owned land. Asians couldn't vote at all. Very few Hawaiians were allowed to vote.

The plotters didn't really try to hide what they'd done. One of them, Theophilus Davies, the founder of one of the Big Five sugar firms, wrote four years later in the *Honolulu Daily Bulletin*, "the fact which can no longer be concealed is, that we rejected constitutionality, and we passed by simple treason, and we took our stand upon treachery, as our political basis."[5]

Eventually, President Cleveland told Sanford Dole, the Republic's president, to restore the monarchy, but he refused. Cleveland was soon voted out and replaced by President William McKinley, who believed in manifest destiny—that expanding the United States was God's will. Congress again voted down annexation, but it was attached to a popular bill, and the bill passed in 1898, taking effect in 1900. In 1898, Puerto Rico, the Philippines, and Guam also became US territories.

This was one of the few times where the United States has invaded a peaceful country and replaced the government. Another was the invasion of Panama in 1989, but in Hawai'i's case, the president and Congress were unaware of what was going on, and in Panama's case, a new Panamanian government was quickly set up. In both cases, the American people soon forgot about it.

In 1993, the US government officially said it was sorry, admitting the "illegal acts of the conspirators" and the subsequent US invasion were an "act of war" on "the government of a peaceful and friendly people." The US government hoped the apology would facilitate reconciliation with the native Hawaiians without doing anything further.

Twain didn't write about the overthrow. In 1895, Twain was relying on people coming to his lectures in order to pay off his debts, and he didn't want to do or say anything that might reduce his audiences. He was also trying to rehabilitate his image. In addition, he wasn't feeling well. But he had expressed his views against annexation in his 1873 *New York Tribune* articles. In his *Sacramento Union* articles, he was tasked with scouting business investment prospects in the Islands, so that's what he did, and he did seem to favor annexation in his early letters. In his lectures, it seemed like he was turning against it, although he clearly thought it likely. After traveling the world, he became an ardent anti-imperialist.

Imperialism was based on racism—the idea that the "civilized" people are superior to the "savage" natives. It wasn't just a portion of the population that believed this—it was the vast majority of Americans. They viewed Twain as a radical, but that didn't stop him.

Twain's views were complex. He valued the good things that came from colonialism and enjoyed being a tourist but hated the cultural destruction and the injustices committed against people in other lands. As American colonialism increased under President McKinley, Twain became much more vocal against it, even becoming a vice president of the Anti-Imperialist League of New York. He wrote in 1900 regarding America's war in the Philippines, "I am opposed to having the eagle put its talons on any other land."[6] When thinking of a flag for America's new Philippines province, he suggested, "we can have just our usual flag, with the white stripes painted black and the stars replaced by the skull and crossbones."[7]

Twain with John Lewis in 1903.

Concerning the Boxer Rebellion, where a group of Chinese peasants and laborers began attacking and killing foreigners, missionaries, and Chinese Christians, trying to drive them out of China, Twain said, "my sympathies are with the Chinese. They have been villainously dealt with by the sceptered thieves of Europe, and I hope they will drive all the foreigners out and keep them out for good. We have no more business in China than in any other country that is not ours."[8] Ironically, because of the Americans' behavior in China, the Boxers saw them as savages.

Twain also wrote, "I bring you the stately matron named Christendom, returning, bedraggled, besmirched, and dishonored, from pirate raids in Kiao-Chou, Manchuria, South Africa, and the Philippines, with her soul full of meanness, her pocket full of boodle, and her mouth full of pious hypocrisies. Give her soap and towel, but hide the looking-glass."[9]

You may recall that Twain was taking pokes at society back in his Virginia City days and even left the *San Francisco Daily Morning Call* because the editor didn't print his story about the attacks on the Chinese that were permitted by the police. His friends remembered him associating with people of all nationalities and cultures, which he did throughout his life. He paid the tuition for an African American student at Yale, saying, "he was doing it as his part of the reparation due from every white to every black man."[10] He also remained lifelong friends with John Lewis, the African American man who was the inspiration for Jim in *Huckleberry Finn*.

When it was first published, *Huckleberry Finn* was criticized for showing African Americans in a positive and sympathetic light. Now people ban it for being immoral, for uncritically portraying racists, and for using racist language—including the "n" word, which had different connotations in his time. First it was banned for being antiracist and now for being racist. Times sure have changed. *Tom Sawyer* was criticized for encouraging juvenile delinquency and insubordination.

Twain didn't mind when his books were banned. He wrote to a friend, "But the truth is, that when a library expels a book of mine and leaves an unexpurgated Bible lying around where unprotected youth and age can get hold of it, the deep unconscious irony of it delights me and doesn't anger me."[11]

One thing that hasn't changed from Twain's time is that both puritanism and racism continue to darken the world today.

But getting back to further changes in Hawai'i since Twain's initial visit, whaling was gone, and sugar was king. The Hawaiian population was still decreasing, but that was about to bottom out. The huge influx of foreign workers turned Hawai'i's society into a true melting pot of cultures. And most Hawaiians had been pushed further away from their subsistence lifestyle and into poverty or wage-paying work. But some things were still the same, such as Hawaiian generosity and their fun-loving nature.

—⟨⟩—

From talks with certain of our passengers whose home was Honolulu, and from a sketch by [journalist] Mrs. Mary H. Krout, I was able to perceive what the Honolulu of today is, as compared with the Honolulu of my time. In my time it was a beautiful little town, made up of snow-white wooden cottages deliciously smothered in tropical vines and flowers and trees and shrubs; and its coral roads and streets were hard and smooth, and as white as the houses. The outside aspects of the place suggested the presence of a modest and comfortable prosperity a general prosperity perhaps one might strengthen the term and say universal.

There were no fine houses, no fine furniture. There were no decorations. Tallow candles furnished the light for the bedrooms, a whale-oil lamp furnished it for the parlor. Native matting served as carpeting. [...]

There was nothing reminiscent of foreign parts, for nobody had been abroad. Trips were made to San Francisco, but that could not be called going abroad. Comprehensively speaking, nobody traveled.

But Honolulu has grown wealthy since then, and of course wealth has introduced changes; some of the old simplicities have disappeared. [...]

And the ladies riding astride. These are changes, indeed. In my time the native women rode astride, but the white ones lacked the courage to adopt their wise custom.

In my time ice was seldom seen in Honolulu. It sometimes came in sailing vessels from New England as ballast; and then, if there happened to be a man-of-war in port and balls and suppers raging by consequence, the ballast was worth six hundred dollars a ton, as is evidenced by reputable tradition. But the ice-machine has traveled all over the world, now, and brought ice within everybody's reach. [...]

The ladies of the Hawaiian capital learned too late the right way to occupy a horse too late to get much benefit from it. The riding-horse is retiring from business everywhere in the world. In Honolulu a few years from now he will be only a tradition.

We all know about Father Damien, the French priest who voluntarily forsook the world and went to the leper island of Molokai to labor among its population of sorrowful exiles who wait there, in slow-consuming misery, for death to come and release them from their troubles; and we know that the thing which he knew beforehand would happen, did happen: that he became a leper himself, and died of that horrible disease. There was still another case of self-sacrifice, it appears.

I asked after "Billy" Ragsdale, interpreter to the Parliament in my time, a half-white. He was a brilliant young fellow, and very popular. As an interpreter he would have been hard to match anywhere. He used to stand up

Top: Father Damien on the left in Kalawao ca. 1884 with his church next to the pandanus tree he slept under when he first arrived. This was before the colony was moved across the peninsula. Damien arrived in 1873 and died there in 1889 at the age of forty-nine. Bottom: The same spot from the air. Damien's church is the one on the left.

(TOP) DR. EDUARD ARNING; (BOTTOM) AUTHOR'S PHOTO

in the Parliament and turn the English speeches into Hawaiian and the Hawaiian speeches into English with a readiness and a volubility that were astonishing. I asked after him, and was told that his prosperous career was cut short in a sudden and unexpected way, just as he was about to marry a beautiful half-caste girl. He discovered, by some nearly invisible sign about his skin, that the poison of leprosy was in him. The secret was his own, and might be kept concealed for years; but he would not be treacherous to the girl that loved him; he would not marry her to a doom like his. And so he put his affairs in order, and went around to all his friends and bade them goodbye, and sailed in the leper ship to Molokai. There he died the loathsome and lingering death that all lepers die. [. . .]

And one great pity of it all is, that these poor sufferers are innocent. The leprosy does not come of sins which they committed, but of sins committed by their ancestors, who escaped the curse of leprosy!

Mr. Gowan has made record of a certain very striking circumstance. Would you expect to find in that awful leper settlement a custom worthy to be transplanted to your own country? They have one such, and it is inexpressibly touching and beautiful. When death sets open the prison door of life there, the band salutes the freed soul with a burst of glad music![12]

—⚓—

Throughout the Middle Ages, just about every large town in Britain and Europe had a leprosy hospital to separate the infected from the rest of the population. In fact, in Mark Twain's time, there were leprosy patients all around the world in quarantine, but nowhere else was there a colony like the one on Molokai. At its peak, more than 1,000 people lived there.

Twain's friend Charles Warren Stoddard wrote in his book *The Lepers of Molokai*, "The prospect of life banishment alarmed the natives, both the sick and the hale. They were not, and they still are not, afraid of the disease. They are a most affectionate people: they love their friends with a love passing the love of woman [. . .] At the approach of this health officer the lepers would be secreted by friends, who were willing to brave possible contagion rather than part with those so dear to them."[13]

The Hawaiians didn't believe the disease was caused by invisible bacteria, neither did they think it was contagious. What they couldn't stand was having

Kalaupapa peninsula. The town of Kalaupapa is along the shore, while Kalawao is on the far side of the peninsula.
AUTHOR'S PHOTO

their friends and loved ones taken away from them. They insisted it was a violation of their individual rights.

But options were limited, and the only thing that could prevent the spread of the disease was forcing people into quarantine. Because patients would escape or be taken from the hospital, the colony was established on the isolated peninsula of Kalapapua, a remote flatland at the base of 1,000- to 2,000-foot cliffs (300–600 m) and surrounded on three sides by ocean. There they were imprisoned for life without parole. They were even officially declared dead.

Unfortunately, the site was severely unprepared when the patients first began arriving in 1866—a couple of months before Twain's arrival—when it was little more than a barren landscape. Leprosy became an epidemic a few years later. News of Father Damien's work in the 1870s began publicizing the plight of the patients, prompting the government to improve their situation. Charles Warren

Stoddard was a Catholic and a friend of Father Damien. His book *The Lepers of Molokai*, published by a Catholic publisher, greatly contributed to Damien's fame. This was furthered by the writings of Robert Louis Stevenson and Jack London. By the 1890s, the patients were able to live relatively normal lives. At its peak, around 2 percent of Hawai'i's population were infected—about 1,000 people.

Twain's final visit to Hawai'i lasted just over two days in which he could see but not touch. At just past midnight, in the first few minutes of September 2, 1895, the steamer left Honolulu for Australia. All Twain wrote was:

> Sept. 2: Flocks of flying fish—slim, shapely, graceful, and intensely white. With the sun on them they look like a flight of silver fruit knives. They are able to fly a hundred yards.[14]

Flying fish are occasionally seen leaping out of Hawai'i's waters. I've seen them from the ferry in the channel between the islands of Maui and Lana'i. Some can glide for up to forty seconds covering about 1,300 feet (400 m)—a quarter of a mile. Hawai'i has nine species of flying fish that range in size up to around sixteen inches. You are more likely to see them in the summer months, and they travel in schools. Sometimes, they accidentally crash into canoers.

YOU CAN VISIT KALAUPAPA

Kalaupapa National Historical Park, PO Box 2222, Kalaupapa, HI 96742, (808) 567-6802, nps.gov/kala/index.htm. Two of the churches built by Saint Damien can be seen on the south side of Molokai. Saint Damien of Molokai Catholic Church & Parishes, 115 Ala Mālama St., Kaunakakai, HI 96748, (808) 553-5220, damienchurchmolokai.org/wp.

I have yet to see the Hawaiian flying squid (*Nototodarus hawaiiensis*). Flight data are scarce about our squid, but other species can sail about 100 feet in three seconds—faster than the fastest human sprinter. And they actually flap their fins and shoot jets of water to propel themselves while in flight. Squid have been seen flying in groups of more than twenty, and they seem to prefer flying at night.

Overall, you're more likely to see whales and dolphins leaping out of Hawai'i's waters. The humpback whales vacation here from November through April, while spinner dolphins are year-round residents.

When in New Zealand, Twain wrote this letter to Henry Whitney:

Frank Moeller's Masonic Hotel Napier, N.Z.,

Nov. 30, 1895.

Dear Mr. Whitney:

Your long-delayed letter has reached me today, and I was very glad to hear from you, and know that you are still hale and hearty—which I am not, it exasperates me to have to say.

I was perishing to get ashore at Honolulu, and talk to you all, and see your enchanted land again, and be welcomed and stirred up. But it was not to be, and I shall regret it a thousand years; for of course I shan't get another chance to see the Islands again. At least, I am afraid I shan't, life is so uncertain now-a-days.

I have had a very delightful time in Australia and New Zealand, notwithstanding my poor health.

Do please remember me most cordially to any of my old-time friends that still survive the thirty years interval since I was with them in Honolulu.

I thank you ever so much for your beautiful *Tourist Guide Through Hawai'i*, which arrived by recent mail.

Sincerely yours,
S. L. Clemens[15]

Continuing on his world tour, Twain gave a dinner speech in Fiji and then gave sixty three lectures all across Australia. After traveling eight hours by train, then changing clothes in a cab, he arrived to give his lecture in Sydney. This was what he called "At Home," which was more of a casual talk than a lecture.

> I know I'm late, but I couldn't help it. I have been travelling in a railway carriage, and the heat—whew! [. . .] The only heat that I've experienced like this was in the Sandwich Islands. But there they don't trouble themselves much with superfluous clothing. The women wore—well, I don't remember what they wore. There wasn't enough of it. And the men—well, just on ordinary occasions they didn't wear anything. But on State occasions they did. They wore smiles, and they even smiled too much. If you in Australia have this kind of weather in the middle of December, what must you have in July?[16]

He then went on to tell "some of his experiences in the Sandwich Islands." Unfortunately, we don't know what they were or whether they were new or old experiences. He then headed off for three months in India. While there, he summarized his career in an interview with the *Times of Bombay*.

—

How did I make my first start in journalism, you ask? Well, I first tumbled into it as a man falls over a precipice that he is not looking for. I wasn't as far as I could see, intended for a journalist, but out in Nevada in those early silver days it was a struggle—a scramble from pillar to post—and one had to get a living as best he could.

I was invited to take a place on the staff of a daily newspaper there—the *Territorial Enterprise*—and I took it. I should have taken command of a ship if it had been offered, for I wasn't particular in those days. I had had no training, but yet they offered me the post of first officer, not the chief editor, but a subordinate post, and I remained in the journalistic profession for four years in Nevada and San Francisco together. On the *Territorial Enterprise* I was what they called the city editor. It was a large title, but the pay was not correspondingly great—in fact, the name was merely for style. In reality the city editor should have been called the local reporter. The post was, so to speak, flung at me. I didn't ask for it.

There was a chief editor, a news editor, and a telegraphic editor, and in those days they gathered in from the San Francisco and Sacramento papers a good part of the reading matter of the journal. We were expected and supposed to furnish facts pure and simple for the columns of the *Enterprise*, but there were not facts enough to fill the required space, and so often the reading material was largely a matter of imagination—sometimes based on fact, but not always.

After about four years in these parts I went off to the Sandwich Islands to write a series of letters concerning the sugar industry there for the *Sacramento Union*. I was gone about five or six months, and when I came back I concluded to deliver a lecture or two on the Sandwich Islands, and I did so. It seemed an easier way of making a living than journalism. It paid better, and there was less work connected with it, so I dropped journalism and took to the lecturer's platform for two or three years. Then I went on an extended tour of Europe, which lasted for five or six months, and when I returned I was asked to write a book. I did so, and from that time on I have written books mainly.[17]

Here the importance of Hawai'i in the chain of events becomes clear. It's involved in two of the four links that led to his fame. Hawai'i was his primary stepping-stone from struggling reporter to international celebrity.

Later in *Following the Equator*, after describing the beauty and magnificence of Mauritius—an island to the east of Madagascar and Africa—Twain suggested a couple of minor improvements he would make to Hawai'i:

> The Sandwich Islands remain my ideal of the perfect thing in the matter of tropical islands. I would add another story [or level] to Maunaloa's 16,000 feet if I could, and make it particularly bold and steep and craggy and forbidding and snowy; and I would make the volcano spout its lava-floods out of its summit instead of its sides; but aside from these nonessentials I have no corrections to suggest. I hope these will be attended to; I do not wish to have to speak of it again.[18]

LIFE GOES ON

AFTER THE TOUR ENDED IN 1886, TWAIN, Livy, and Clara were in England when they received news that Suzy had died of spinal meningitis at their home in Hartford, Connecticut. She was twenty-four. Five months earlier, their daughter Jean was diagnosed with epilepsy.

In 1887, Twain's cousin became very ill while in London, and rumors circulated that Twain was at death's door or had died. When a reporter tried to confirm this, Twain wrote back, "The report of my death was an exaggeration."[19] His cousin also survived.

The Clemens family in 1884: Clara, Sam, Jean, Livy, and Suzy.

In 1904, Livy died, and this affected Twain deeply. His daughter Clara, who had been taking care of Jean, had an emotional breakdown. This left Jean's care to Twain and his staff. Epilepsy wasn't as treatable then as it is today. While she was perfectly normal most of the time, it was thought she would be better cared for in treatment centers and sanitariums, so she lived at those for much of the remainder of her life.

The Man in the White Suit

In 1906 when Mark Twain testified before a congressional committee about a new copyright law, he had a year earlier begun wearing his iconic white serge suits lined with white silk. The press took notice. These excerpts are from the *New York Times*:

An Advocate of Dress Reform

While waiting to appear before the committee Mr. Clemens talked to the reporters.

"Why don't you ask why I am wearing such apparently unseasonable clothes? I'll tell you. I have found that when a man reaches the advanced age of seventy-one years as I have, the continual sight of dark clothing is likely to have a depressing effect upon him. Light-colored clothing is more pleasing to the eye and enlivens the spirit. [. . .]

"After all, what is the purpose of clothing? Are not clothes intended primarily to preserve dignity and also to afford comfort to the wearer? Now I know of nothing more uncomfortable than the present day clothes of men. The finest clothing made is a person's own skin, but, of course, society demands something more than this.

"The best-dressed man I have ever seen, however, was a native of the Sandwich Islands, who attracted my attention thirty years ago [*sic*, forty years previous]. Now, when that man wanted to don especial dress to honor a public occasion or a holiday, why he occasionally put on a pair of spectacles. Otherwise the clothing with which God had provided him sufficed.

"Of course, I have ideas of dress reform. For one thing, why not adopt some of the women's styles? Goodness knows, they adopt enough of ours. Take the peek-a-boo waist, for instance. It has the obvious advantages of being cool and comfortable, and in addition it is almost always made up in pleasing colors, which cheer and do not depress.[20]

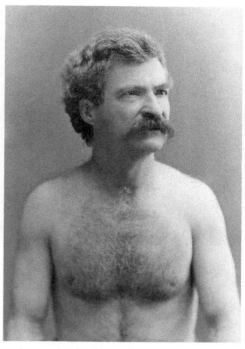

"The best-dressed man . . . ," Twain in about 1883.

Aloha from Hawai'i

In 1908, near the end of his life, Twain built an Italianate villa on 248 acres of forested rolling hills near Redding, Connecticut, that he named Stormfield. The mansion, which cost between $45,000 and $60,000 ($2.5 million to $3.5 million in today's dollars), was not yet completed when Twain moved in on June 18, 1908. He died just two years later on April 21, 1910, and his mansion burned down thirteen years after that.

The Hawaiian Promotion Committee decided to send Twain a mantel and a plaque for Stormfield to thank him for writing the prose poem, which they used to promote tourism and which had encouraged many people to discover Hawai'i. The Committee had adopted it as their first slogan, and according to the *Pacific Commercial Advertiser*, "It has been printed in almost every piece of literature concerning the Islands which the promotion committee has issued, and has been sent broadcast over the world. Every mail which leaves Hawai'i carries Mark Twain's wonderful message to the ends of the earth."[21]

Twain placed mantle on the fireplace in the billiard room. Across the center panel of the mantle was carved the word "Aloha." There was also a large carved wooden plaque of breadfruit and leaves to hang above the mantle.

Twain playing pool next to the mantel in 1908 or 1909. To the right are the mantel and the breadfruit plaque.
(LEFT) PAUL THOMPSON

His postcard thanking the Committee gave them another hugely popular promotional slogan.

Nov. 30, '08.

Dear Mr. Wood,

The beautiful mantel was put in its place an hour ago, and its friendly "Aloha" was the first uttered greeting my seventy-third birthday received. It is rich in color, rich in quality, and rich in decoration, therefore it exactly harmonizes with the taste for such things which was born in me and which I have seldom been able to indulge to my content. It will be a great pleasure to me, daily renewed, to have under my eye this lovely reminder of the loveliest fleet of islands that lies anchored in any ocean, and I beg to thank the Committee for providing me that pleasure.

Sincerely Yours,
S. L. Clemens.[22]

Nov. 30/08.

Dear Mr. Wood.

The beautiful mantel was put in its place an hour ago, + its friendly "Aloha" was the first uttered greeting my 73ʳᵈ birthday received. It is rich in color, rich in quality, + rich in decoration, therefore it exactly harmonises with the taste for such things which was born in me + which I have seldom been able to indulge to my content. It will be a great pleasure to me, daily renewed, to have under my eye this lovely reminder of the loveliest fleet of islands that lies anchored in any ocean, + I beg to thank the Committee for ~~xxxxxxx~~ providing me that pleasure.

Sincerely Yours
SL. Clemens

Mark Twain's postcard thanking the Hawaiian Promotion Committee for the mantel and plaque.

This color photograph of Twain was taken shortly before his death using the Autochrome process.
ALVIN LANGDON COBURN

"The loveliest fleet of islands that lies anchored in any ocean" has since been used to promote the Islands around the world.

In 1909, Clara married a Russian pianist, composer, and conductor named Ossip Gabrilowitsch, which sounds like it could be one of Twain's pseudonyms. That fall, they brought Jean back home, but a few months later on Christmas Eve, she died in her bathtub. It's thought that a seizure brought on a heart attack. She was twenty-nine.

Twain died the following year at the age of seventy-four. He was born in 1835, the year Halley's Comet was here, and died in 1910, when it came back. He never got to see it though. He was born after it had faded away and died before it became visible again. But his birth was two weeks after it was closest to the sun and his death the day after it was closest. An interesting coincidence.

He said, "I came in with Halley's Comet in 1835. It is coming again next year, and I expect to go out with it. It will be the greatest disappointment of my life if I don't go out with Halley's Comet. The Almighty has said, no doubt, 'Now here are these two unaccountable freaks; they came in together, they must go out together.' Oh! I am looking forward to that."[23]

Love for Hawai'i

When Twain arrived in Hawai'i, it had gone through a major social upheaval, discarding its ancient religion and laws, replacing them with new freedoms and restrictions. He was able to document the transition from being dominated by the conflicting whaling and missionary forces to the rise of the sugar industry and its not-so-peaceful exploitation of labor. This later led to the domination of the Big Five corporations that overthrew the Kingdom of Hawai'i, leading to its absorption by the United States. Ironically, it was the businesses that were primarily started and owned by the missionaries and their descendants that abolished the Christian government they had worked so hard to establish.

Also, in the 1860s, the seeds were being sown for the rise of tourism—the industry that came to dominate Hawai'i in the twentieth century and something Twain played a significant role in and helped to bring about.

But it's his love for Hawai'i that shines through. He wasn't here long, but the Islands remained with him for the rest of his life. His biographer, Albert Paine wrote, "The languorous life of the Islands exactly suited Mark Twain. All his life he remembered them—always planning to return someday, to stay there until he died."[24] Paine also added, "The Hawaiian episode in Mark Twain's life was one of those spots that seemed to him always filled with sunlight. From beginning to end it had been a long luminous dream [. . .]."[25]

Jack London, who followed Twain as one of America's greatest writers, wrote, "Somehow, the love of the Islands, like the love of a woman, just happens. One cannot determine in advance to love a particular woman, nor can one so determine to love Hawai'i. One sees, and one loves or does not love. With Hawai'i it seems always to be love at first sight. Those for whom the Islands were made, or who were made for the Islands, are swept off their feet in the first moments of meeting, embrace, and are embraced. [. . .] Truly, Hawai'i is a woman beautiful and vastly more persuasive and seductive than her sister sirens of the sea."[26]

John Steinbeck, in *Travels with Charley*, reflected, "Who has not known a journey to be over and dead before the traveler returns. The reverse is also true. Many a trip continues long after movement in time and space has ceased. I remember a man in Salinas who in his middle years travelled to Honolulu and back, and that journey continued for the rest of his life. We could watch him in his rocking chair on his front porch, his eyes squinted, half-closed, endlessly travelling to Honolulu."[27]

NOTES

Twain before Twain

1 Mark Twain, "Mark Twain's War Experiences," *New York Times*, October 7, 1877, p. 10.

2 Mark Twain's speech, Carnegie Hall, New York, February 11, 1901, in Albert Bigelow Paine, *Mark Twain: A Biography*, Volume 3, New York: Harper & Brothers, 1912, p. 1123.

3 Mark Twain, "Chapters from My Autobiography," Chapter XXIII, *North American Review*, October 1907, p. 116.

4 Albert Bigelow Paine, *Mark Twain: A Biography*, Volume 1, New York: Harper Brothers, 1912, pp. 221–22.

5 Mark Twain, *Mark Twain's Sketches, New and Old*, Hartford, CT: American Publishing Company, 1875 (1889), p. 239.

6 Mark Twain, "Petrified Man," *Territorial Enterprise*, October 4, 1862.

7 Mark Twain, *Mark Twain's Sketches, New and Old*, Hartford, CT: American Publishing Company, 1875 (1889), p. 242.

8 Mark Twain, "Mark Twain's Letters from Washington, Number IX," *Territorial Enterprise*, March 7, 1868.

9 Mark Twain, "Unpublished Chapters from the Autobiography of Mark Twain," Part 2, *Harper's Magazine*, March 1922, p. 456.

10 Rudyard Kipling, "Mark Twain Interviewed," *The Pioneer* (Allahabad, India), March 18, 1890. Reprinted as Rudyard Kipling, "Rudyard Kipling on Twain," *New York Herald*, August 17, 1890, p. 5, and in Rudyard Kipling, *From Sea to Sea*, Volume II, New York: Doubleday & McClure Co., 1899.

11 Mark Twain, "Unpublished Chapters from the Autobiography of Mark Twain," Part 2, *Harper's Magazine*, March 1922, p. 456.

12 "Mark Twain," *Chicago Tribune*, December 18, 1871, p. 4.

13 Mark Twain, "Chapters from My Autobiography," Chapter XX, *North American Review*, July 5, 1907, p. 72.

14 Hunter S. Thompson, "Richard Nixon Doll," *Pageant Magazine*, July 1968.

15 Hunter S. Thompson, "Fear and Loathing in Limbo: The Scum Also Rises," *Rolling Stone*, October 10, 1974.

16 Mark Twain (Frederick Anderson and others, eds.), *Mark Twain's Notebooks and Journals*, Volume 1, Berkeley: University of California Press, 1975, p. 92.

17 *Daily Alta California*, January 10, 1866, p. 1.

18 (Attributed to Edward House), "Mark Twain as a Lecturer," *New York Tribune*, May 11, 1867, p. 2.

19 Mark Twain, "Chapters from My Autobiography," Chapter II, *North American Review*, September 21, 1906, p. 450.

20 Mark Twain, "Take the Stand, Fitz Smythe," *Territorial Enterprise*, February 6–7, 1866.

21 Mark Twain, letter to Jane Lampton Clemens and Pamela A. Moffett, January 20, 1866. Reprinted in Mark Twain (Edgar Marquess Branch, Michael B. Frank, and Kenneth M. Sanderson, eds.), *Mark Twain's Letters*, Volume 1, Berkeley: University of California Press, 1987, pp. 329–30.

22 Mark Twain, letter to Pamela A. Moffett, March 18, 1864; in Mark Twain (Edgar Marquess Branch, Michael B. Frank, and Kenneth M. Sanderson, eds.), *Mark Twain's Letters*, Volume 1, Berkeley: University of California Press, 1987, p. 275.

23 "Important," *San Francisco Dramatic Chronicle*, February 19, 1866, p. 2.

24 Charles Henry Webb writing as "John Paul," "Letter from San Francisco," *Sacramento Daily Union* [California], November 3, 1865, p. 2.

25 Mark Twain, "My Début as a Literary Person," *The Century Magazine*, November 1899, pp. 76–77.

26 Ronald Hartwell, "To Kilauea," *Mark Twain Journal*, Spring 1983, p. 32.

27 Mark Twain (Albert Bigalow Paine, ed.), *Mark Twain's Letters*, Volume 1, New York: Harper & Brothers, 1917, p. 103; with a small addition from Mark Twain (Edgar Marquess Branch and others, eds.), *Mark Twain Letters*, Volume 1, Berkeley: University of California Press, 1987, p. 333.

28 *Montana Post* (Virginia City, Montana Territory—not to be confused with the Virginia City in the Nevada Territory), April 14, 1866, p. 1.

Journey to Paradise

1 Mark Twain, "San Francisco to Sandwich Islands—No. 1" (article 1), *Sacramento Daily Union*, April 16, 1866, p. 5.

2 Mark Twain, *Roughing It*, Hartford, CT: American Publishing Co., 1872.

3 Mark Twain, "San Francisco to Sandwich Islands—No. 1" (article 1), *Sacramento Daily Union*, April 16, 1866, p. 5.

4 Mark Twain, *Roughing It*, Hartford, CT: American Publishing Co., 1872.

O'ahu

1 Mark Twain, *Roughing It*, Hartford, CT: American Publishing Co., 1872.

2 For the use of "Molokai" instead of "Moloka'i," see Catherine Aki, "So Is It Molokai or Moloka'i?," *The Molokai Dispatch*, October 15, 2008, themolokaidispatch.com/so-it-molokai-or-moloka-i.

3 Mark Twain, "Scenes in Honolulu—No. 4" (article 4), *Sacramento Daily Union*, April 19, 1866, p. 2.

4 Mark Twain, *Roughing It*, Hartford, CT: American Publishing Co., 1872.

5 Richard Henry Dana, *Two Years before the Mast*, London: Hutchinson & Co., 1840, pp. 128, 127.

6 Ebenezer Townsend Jr., "The Diary of Mr. Ebenezer Townsend, Jr., the Supercargo of the Sealing Ship *Neptune . . .*," *Papers of the New Haven Colony Historical Society*, Volume 4, New Haven, CT: New Haven Colony Historical Society, 1888, p. 76. Also reprinted as Ebenezer Townsend Jr., "Extract from the Diary of Ebenezer Townsend, Jr., Supercargo of the Sealing Ship *Neptune on Her Voyage to the South Pacific and Canton*," Honolulu: Hawaiian Historical Society Reprints, Number 4, n.d. (1921?), p. 31.

7 Isabella L. Bird, *The Hawaiian Archipelago*, London: John Murray, 1875, p. 4.

8 Lawrence Downes, "Mark Twain's Hawaii," *New York Times*, May 14, 2006, p. TR10 of the New York edition, nytimes.com/2006/05/14/travel/14twain.html.

9 Mark Twain, "San Francisco to Sandwich Islands—No. 1" (article 1), *Sacramento Daily Union*, April 16, 1866, p. 5.

10 Mark Twain, "Scenes in Honolulu—No. 4" (article 4), *Sacramento Daily Union*, April 19, 1866, p. 2.

11 H. M. Whitney, "Better Fifty Years in Hawai'i Than a Cycle of Cathay," *The Pacific Commercial Advertiser* (Honolulu), January 1, 1900, p. 6.

12 *The Pacific Commercial Advertiser* (Honolulu), November 30, 1915, pp. 9, 12.

13 H. M. [Whitney], "Has No Equal as a Humorist," *The Pacific Commercial Advertiser* (Honolulu), August 21, 1895, p. 1.

14 A composite of Mark Twain, "Scenes in Honolulu—No. 4" (article 4), *Sacramento Daily Union*, April 19, 1866, p. 2, and Mark Twain, *Roughing It*, Hartford, CT: American Publishing Co., 1872.

15 Mark Twain, *Roughing It*, Hartford, CT: American Publishing Co., 1872.

16 Mark Twain, "Scenes in Honolulu—No. 4" (article 4), *Sacramento Daily Union*, April 19, 1866, p. 2.

17 Mark Twain, "San Francisco to Sandwich Islands—No. 2" (article 2), *Sacramento Daily Union*, April 17, 1866, p. 2.

18 Mark Twain, "Scenes in Honolulu—No. 5" (article 5), *Sacramento Daily Union*, April 20, 1866, p. 2.

19 Mark Twain (Frederick Anderson and others, eds.), *Mark Twain's Notebooks and Journals*, Volume 1, Berkeley: University of California Press, 1975, p. 200.

20 Mark Twain, "Scenes in Honolulu—No. 5" (article 5), *Sacramento Daily Union*, April 20, 1866, p. 2.

21 Mark Twain, *Roughing It*, Hartford, CT: American Publishing Co., 1872.

22 Mark Twain, "Scenes in Honolulu—No. 5" (article 5), *Sacramento Daily Union*, April 20, 1866, p. 2.

23 A composite of Mark Twain, "Scenes in Honolulu—No. 5" (article 5), *Sacramento Daily Union*, April 20, 1866, p. 2, and Mark Twain, *Roughing It*, Hartford, CT: American Publishing Co., 1872.

24 Mark Twain, "Scenes in Honolulu—No. 5" (article 5), *Sacramento Daily Union*, April 20, 1866, p. 2.

25 Mark Twain, "Scenes in Honolulu—No. 5" (article 5), *Sacramento Daily Union*, April 20, 1866, p. 2.

26 Mark Twain, "Scenes in Honolulu—No. 5" (article 5), *Sacramento Daily Union*, April 20, 1866, p. 2.

27 Mark Twain, *Mark Twain's Speeches*, New York: Harper & Brothers, 1910, p. 107.

28 W. D. Howells, "My Memories of Mark Twain," Part 2, *Harper's Monthly Magazine*, August 1910, p. 344, and W. D. Howells, *My Mark Twain*, New York: Harper & Brothers, 1910, pp. 45–46.

29 Major J. B. Pond, *Eccentricities of Genius*, New York: G. W. Dillingham Co., 1900, p. 223.

30 Mark Twain, "Scenes in Honolulu—No. 8" (article 8), *Sacramento Daily Union*, May 21, 1866, p. 3.

31 Henry M. Whitney, *The Hawaiian Guide Book for Travelers*, Honolulu: Henry M. Whitney, 1875, p. 21.

32 A composite of Mark Twain, "Scenes in Honolulu—No. 6" (article 6), *Sacramento Daily Union*, April 21, 1866, p. 3, and Mark Twain, *Roughing It*, Hartford, CT: American Publishing Co., 1872.

33 H. M. Whitney, "Better Fifty Years in Hawai'i Than a Cycle of Cathay," *The Pacific Commercial Advertiser* (Honolulu), January 1, 1900, p. 6.

34 A composite of Mark Twain, "Scenes in Honolulu—No. 6" (article 6), *Sacramento Daily Union*, April 21, 1866, p. 3, and Mark Twain, *Roughing It*, Hartford, CT: American Publishing Co., 1872.

35 "Report Committee on Horses," *The Transactions of the Royal Hawaiian Agricultural Society*, Volume 2, Number 1, 1854, pp. 105–6.

36 Mark Twain, "Scenes in Honolulu—No. 6" (article 6), *Sacramento Daily Union*, April 21, 1866, p. 3.

37 A composite of Mark Twain, "Scenes in Honolulu—No. 6" (article 6), *Sacramento Daily Union*, April 21, 1866, p. 3, and Mark Twain, *Roughing It*, Hartford, CT: American Publishing Co., 1872.

38 Mark Twain, "Scenes in Honolulu—No. 6" (article 6), *Sacramento Daily Union*, April 21, 1866, p. 3.

39 Mark Twain, "Scenes in Honolulu—No. 7" (article 7), *Sacramento Daily Union*, April 24, 1866, p. 4.

40 A composite of Mark Twain, "Scenes in Honolulu—No. 7" (article 7), *Sacramento Daily Union*, April 24, 1866, p. 4, and Mark Twain, *Roughing It*, Hartford, CT: American Publishing Co., 1872.

41 Henry M. Whitney, *The Hawaiian Guide Book for Travelers*, Honolulu: Henry M. Whitney, 1875.

42 A composite of Mark Twain, "Scenes in Honolulu—No. 7" (article 7), *Sacramento Daily Union*, April 24, 1866, p. 4, and Mark Twain, *Roughing It*, Hartford, CT: American Publishing Co., 1872.

43 Mark Twain, "Scenes in Honolulu—No. 7" (article 7), *Sacramento Daily Union*, April 24, 1866, p. 4.

44 Mark Twain, "Scenes in Honolulu—No. 7" (article 7), *Sacramento Daily Union*, April 24, 1866, p. 4.

45 Mark Twain, "Scenes in Honolulu—No. 7" (article 7), *Sacramento Daily Union*, April 24, 1866, p. 4.

46 Mark Twain, "Scenes in Honolulu—No. 7" (article 7), *Sacramento Daily Union*, April 24, 1866, p. 4.

47 Mark Twain, "Scenes in Honolulu—No. 7" (article 7), *Sacramento Daily Union*, April 24, 1866, p. 4.

48 Mrs. Thomas Bailey [Lillain Woodman] Aldrich, *Crowding Memories*, Boston: Houghton Mifflin Co., 1920, pp. 128–29.

49 Col. Thomas Marshall Spalding, "The Adoption of the Hawaiian Alphabet," in *Papers of the Hawaiian Historical Society*, no. 17, 1930, pp. 31–32.

50 Mark Twain, "Scenes in Honolulu—No. 11" (article 11), *Sacramento Daily Union*, May 24, 1866, p. 3.

51 Mark Twain, "Scenes in Honolulu—No. 8" (article 8), *Sacramento Daily Union*, May 21, 1866, p. 3.

52 A composite of Mark Twain, "Scenes in Honolulu—No. 8" (article 8), *Sacramento Daily Union*, May 21, 1866, p. 3, and Mark Twain, *Roughing It*, Hartford, CT: American Publishing Co., 1872.

53 A composite of Mark Twain, "Scenes in Honolulu—No. 8" (article 8), *Sacramento Daily Union*, May 21, 1866, p. 3, and Mark Twain, *Roughing It*, Hartford, CT: American Publishing Co., 1872.

54 Charles Warren Stoddard, *South-Sea Idyls, Boston: J. R. Osgood & Co.*, 1873, and as *Summer Cruising in the South Seas*, London: Chatto, 1873, pp. 135–36.

55 Charmian London, *Our Hawaii (Islands and Islanders)*, New York: The Macmillan Company, 1922, p. 186. This is the revised and expanded edition of her 1917 edition of *Our Hawaii*.

56 Mark Twain (Frederick Anderson and others, eds.), *Mark Twain's Notebooks and Journals,* Volume 1, Berkeley: University of California Press, 1975, p. 137.

57 Franklin H. Austin, "Mark Twain Incognito—A Reminiscence" (article 3), *The Friend,* Volume 96, Number 11, November 1926, p. 253.

58 A composite of Mark Twain, "Scenes in Honolulu—No. 8" (article 8), *Sacramento Daily Union,* May 21, 1866, p. 3, and Mark Twain, *Roughing It,* Hartford, CT: American Publishing Co., 1872.

59 A composite of Mark Twain, "Scenes in Honolulu—No. 8" (article 8), *Sacramento Daily Union,* May 21, 1866, p. 3, and Mark Twain, *Roughing It,* Hartford, CT: American Publishing Co., 1872.

60 Hiram Bingham, *A Residence of Twenty-One Years in the Sandwich Islands,* Hartford, CT: Hezekiah Huntington, 1947, pp. 124–25.

61 National Park Service, *Hawaiian Aboriginal Culture,* US Department of the Interior, 1962, pp. 51–52.

62 C. S. Stewart, *Journal of a Residence in the Sandwich Islands* (revised second edition), New York: John P. Haven, 1828, p. 111.

63 David Malo, *Hawaiian Antiquities (ca. 1835–1836), Honolulu*: Hawaiian Gazette Co., 1903, pp. 79–80.

64 *Picturesque Cuba, Porto Rico, Hawaii, and the Philippines,* Springfield, OH: Mast, Crowell & Kirkpatrick, 1898, p. 63.

65 A composite of Mark Twain, "Scenes in Honolulu—No. 6" (article 6), *Sacramento Daily Union,* April 21, 1866, p. 3, and Mark Twain, *Roughing It,* Hartford, CT: American Publishing Co., 1872.

66 Mark Twain, *Roughing It, Hartford, CT: American Publishing Co., 1872.*

67 Jack London, "My Hawaiian Aloha," Part 3, *Cosmopolitan Magazine,* November 1916, pp. 61–62.

68 Mark Twain (Frederick Anderson and others, eds.), *Mark Twain's Notebooks and Journals,* Volume 1, Berkeley: University of California Press, 1975, p. 114.

69 Mark Twain (Albert Bigelow Paine, ed.), *Mark Twain's Notebook,* New York: Harper & Brothers, 1935, p. 23.

70 Mark Twain, "Scenes in Honolulu—No. 14" (article 14), *Sacramento Daily Union,* July 16, 1866, p. 3.

71 Henry Wise, Los Gringos, New York: *Baker and Scribner, 1849, p. 339.*

72 Rev. Sereno Edwards Bishop, *Reminiscences of Old Hawaii*, Honolulu: Hawaiian Gazette Co., 1916, p. 41.

73 Otto von Kotzebue, *A New Voyage round the World*, Volume 2, London: Henry Colburn and Richard Bentley, 1830, pp. 256–57.

74 Commodore Charles Wilkes, *Narrative of the United States Exploring Expedition during the Years 1838, 1839, 1840, 1841, 1842*, Volume 4, Philadelphia: C. Sherman, 1844, pp. 58–59.

75 Walter Francis Frear, *Mark Twain and Hawaii*, Chicago: The Lakeside Press, 1947, pp. 49–50.

76 Mary Lawton, *A Lifetime with Mark Twain: The Memories of Katy Leary*, New York: Harcourt, Brace and Co., 1925.

77 Mark Twain (Albert Bigelow Paine, ed.), *Mark Twain's Notebook*, New York: Harper & Brothers, 1935, p. 345.

78 Mary Lawton, *A Lifetime with Mark Twain: The Memories of Katy Leary*, New York: Harcourt, Brace and Co., 1925.

79 Walter Francis Frear, *Mark Twain and Hawaii*, Chicago: The Lakeside Press, 1947, p. 53 footnote.

80 Henry M. Whitney, *The Hawaiian Guide Book for Travelers*, Honolulu: Henry M. Whitney, 1875, pp. 30–32.

81 A composite of Mark Twain, "Scenes in Honolulu—No. 4" (article 4), *Sacramento Daily Union*, April 19, 1866, p. 2; Mark Twain, "Honored as a Curiosity in Honolulu" in Mark Twain, *The Celebrated Jumping Frog of Calaveras County and Other Sketches*, New York: C. H. Webb, 1867; and Mark Twain, *Roughing It*, Hartford, CT: American Publishing Co., 1872.

82 Mark Twain, "Scenes in Honolulu—No. 9" (article 9), *Sacramento Daily Union*, May 22, 1866, p. 3.

83 Mark Twain (Albert Bigalow Paine, ed.), *Mark Twain's Letters*, Volume 1, New York: Harper & Brothers, 1917, p. 104. Also Mark Twain (Edgar Marquess Branch, Michael B. Frank, and Kenneth M. Sanderson, eds.), *Mark Twain's Letters*, Volume 1, Berkeley: University of California Press, 1987, pp. 334–35.

84 Mark Twain, "Scenes in Honolulu—No. 11" (article 11), *Sacramento Daily Union*, May 24, 1866, p. 3.

85 Walter Francis Frear, *Mark Twain and Hawaii*, Chicago: The Lakeside Press, 1947, p. 12. Also in Mark Twain (Frederick Anderson and

others, *eds.*), *Mark Twain's Notebooks and Journals,* Volume 1, Berkeley:University of California Press, 1975, p. 184.

86 Mark Twain (Frederick Anderson and others, eds.), *Mark Twain's Notebooks and Journals,* Volume 1, Berkeley: University of California Press, 1975, p. 232.

87 Charles Warren Stoddard, *The Lepers of Molokai, Notre* Dame, IN: Ave Maria Press, 1885.

88 Albert Bigelow Paine, *Mark Twain: A Biography,* Volume 1, New York: Harper & Brothers, 1912, p. 283.

Maui

1 E. S. Goodhue, "Mark Twain's Hawaiian Home," *The Mid-Pacific Magazine,* August 1916, pp. 179–80.

2 Mary C. Alexander, *William Patterson Alexander in Kentucky, the Marquesas, Hawaii, Honolulu, 1934, p. 448.*

3 E. S. Goodhue, "Mark Twain's Hawaiian Home," *The Mid-Pacific Magazine,* August 1916, p. 181.

4 Mark Twain, "About a Remarkable Stranger, Being a Sandwich Island Reminiscence," *The Galaxy,* April 1871. Twain also incorporated this article in *Roughing It.*

5 J. Arago, *Narrative of a Voyage Round the World,* London: Treuttel and Wurtz, Treuttel, Jun. and Richter, 1823, pp. 119–20.

6 Mark Twain, "About a Remarkable Stranger, Being a Sandwich Island Reminiscence," *The Galaxy,* April 1871.

7 Henry M. Whitney, *The Hawaiian Guide Book for Travelers,* Honolulu: Henry M. Whitney, 1875, pp. 34–36.

8 Mark Twain, "From the Sandwich Islands" (article 23), *Sacramento Daily Union,* September 26, 1866, p. 1.

9 Hiram Bingham, Levi Chamberlain, Lowell Smith, Henry Dimond, Amos S. Cooke, Horton O. Knapp, and Samuel N. Castle in a letter dated January 11, 1840, to Ladd & Co., submitted in evidence to the Hawai'i. Office of the Attorney General, *Report of the Proceedings and Evidence in the Arbitration between the King and Government of the Hawaiian Islands and Messrs. Ladd & Co.,* Honolulu: Government Press, 1846, Appendix, Item F, p. 44.

10 William H. Dorrance and Francis S. Morgan, *Sugar Islands*, Honolulu: Mutual Publishing, 2001, pp. 70–71.

11 Mark Twain, "The Sandwich Islands," *New York Tribune*, January 6, 1873, pp. 4–5. And reprinted in newspapers throughout the nation.

12 Mark Twain (Edgar Marquess Branch, Michael B. Frank, and Kenneth M. Sanderson, eds.), *Mark Twain's Letters*, Volume 1, Berkeley: University of California Press, 1987, pp. 336–37. Part in Mark Twain (Albert Bigalow Paine, ed.), *Mark Twain's Letters*, Volume 1, New York: Harper & Brothers, 1917, pp. 104–5.

13 Theodore Hornberger, *Mark Twain's Letters to Will Bowen*, Austin: University of Texas Press, 1941. Also, Mark Twain (Edgar Marquess Branch, Michael B. Frank, and Kenneth M. Sanderson, eds.), *Mark Twain's Letters*, Volume 1, Berkeley: University of California Press, 1987, pp. 338–40. And pbs.org/wgbh/roadshow/stories/articles/2015/2/9/hawaii-love-samuel-clemens-letter-william-bowen.

14 Henry M. Whitney, *The Hawaiian Guide Book for Travelers*, Honolulu: Henry M. Whitney, 1875, p. 38.

15 Charles Warren Stoddard, *Hawaiian Life*, Chicago: F. Tennyson Neely, 1894, p. 126.

16 Mark Twain, "The Sandwich Islands," *The Complete Works of Mark Twain, Volume 24: Mark Twain's Speeches*, New York: Harper & Brothers, 1923, p. 13.

17 Mark Twain, *Roughing It*, Hartford, CT: American Publishing Co., 1872.

18 Mark Twain (Albert Bigelow Paine, ed.), *Mark Twain's Notebook*, New York: Harper & Brothers, 1935, p. 22.

19 Mark Twain (Frederick Anderson and others, eds.), *Mark Twain's Notebooks and Journals*, Volume 1, Berkeley: University of California Press, 1975, p. 172.

20 Jack London, "House of the Sun," *Pacific Monthly*, January 1910, p. 1.

21 Mark Twain, *Roughing It*, Hartford, CT: American Publishing Co., 1872.

22 Mark Twain (Harriet Elinor Smith and Richard Bucci, eds.), *Mark Twain's Letters*, Volume 2, Berkeley: University of California Press, 1990, p. 21.

Back on Oʻahu

1 Mark Twain (Albert Bigalow Paine, ed.), *Mark Twain's Letters*, Volume 1, New York: Harper & Brothers, 1917, pp. 105–6. And Mark Twain (Edgar Marquess Branch, Michael B. Frank, and Kenneth M. Sanderson, eds.), *Mark Twain's Letters*, Volume 1, Berkeley: University of California Press, 1987, pp. 341–42.

2 Mark Twain, "Scenes in Honolulu—No. 12" (article 12), *Sacramento Daily Union*, June 20, 1866, p. 1.

3 A composite of Mark Twain, "Scenes in Honolulu—No. 12" (article 12), *Sacramento Daily Union*, June 20, 1866, p. 1, and Mark Twain, *Roughing It*, Hartford, CT: American Publishing Co., 1872.

4 Mark Twain, *Roughing It*, Hartford, CT: American Publishing Co., 1872.

5 David Lawrence Gregg (Pauline King, ed.), *The Diaries of David Lawrence Gregg: An American Diplomat in Hawaii, 1853–1858*, Honolulu: Hawaiian Historical Society, 1982.

6 Herman Melville, *Typee*, New York: Wiley & Putnam, 1846, p. 251. This is in the first edition and was removed by the publisher from later editions.

7 Noenoe K. Silva, "He Kanawai E Hoʻopau I Na Hula Kuolo Hawaiʻi: The Political Economy of Banning the Hula," *Hawaiian Journal of History*, Volume 34, 2000, p. 33; and others.

8 Mark Twain, *Roughing It*, Hartford, CT: American Publishing Co., 1872.

9 Mark Twain, "The Sandwich Islands," *New York Tribune*, January 9, 1873, pp. 4–5.

10 Mark Twain, *Roughing It*, Hartford, CT: American Publishing Co., 1872.

11 Mark Twain, "Scenes in Honolulu—No. 12" (article 12), *Sacramento Daily Union*, June 20, 1866, p. 1.

12 Mark Twain, "Scenes in Honolulu—No. 13" (article 13), *Sacramento Daily Union*, June 21, 1866, p. 3.

13 Mark Twain, "The Sandwich Islands," *New York Tribune*, January 9, 1873, pp. 4–5.

14 Mark Twain, "Scenes in Honolulu—No. 13" (article 13), *Sacramento Daily Union*, June 21, 1866, p. 3.

The Big Island

1   Mark Twain, *Life on the Mississippi*, Boston: James R. Osgood & Co., 1883, pp. 217–18.

2   Mildred Leo Clemens, "Mark Twain in Paradise" (Chapter 9), *Honolulu Star Bulletin*, December 17, 1935, p. 4.

3   Ebenezer Townsend Jr., "The Diary of Mr. Ebenezer Townsend, Jr., the Supercargo of the Sealing Ship *Neptune . . . ,*" *Papers of the New Haven Colony Historical Society*, Volume 4, New Haven, CT: New Haven Colony Historical Society, 1888, p. 62. Also reprinted as Ebenezer Townsend Jr., "Extract from the Diary of Ebenezer Townsend, Jr., Supercargo of the Sealing Ship Neptune on Her Voyage to the South Pacific and Canton," Honolulu: Hawaiian Historical Society Reprints, Number 4, n.d. (1921?), p. 26.

4   Archibald Campbell, *A Voyage round the World*, New York: Van Winkle, Wylie & Co., 1817, p. 134.

5   A composite of Mark Twain, "Letter from Honolulu" (article 18), *Sacramento Daily Union*, August 18, 1866, p. 1, and Mark Twain, *Roughing It*, Hartford, CT: American Publishing Co., 1872.

6   Mark Twain, "Letter from Honolulu" (article 18), *Sacramento Daily Union*, August 18, 1866, p. 1.

7   Mark Twain, "Letter from Honolulu." (article 18), *The Sacramento Daily Union*, August 18, 1866, p. 1.

8   Mark Twain, "The Sandwich Islands," *New York Tribune*, January 6, 1873, pp. 4–5.

9   Mark Twain, "Letter from Honolulu" (article 18), *Sacramento Daily Union*, August 18, 1866, p. 1.

10 John Ledyard, *Journal of Captain Cook's Last Voyage*, Hartford, CT: Nathaniel Patten, 1783, p. 128.

11 Mark Twain, "Letter from Honolulu" (article 18), *Sacramento Daily Union*, August 18, 1866, p. 1.

12 Mark Twain, "Letter from Honolulu" (article 18), *Sacramento Daily Union*, August 18, 1866, p. 1.

13 *The Pacific Commercial Advertiser* (Honolulu), January 26, 1867, p. 3.

14 Mark Twain, "Letter from Honolulu" (article 18), *Sacramento Daily Union*, August 18, 1866, p. 1.

15 Composite of Mark Twain, "Letter from Honolulu" (article 18), *Sacramento Daily Union*, August 18, 1866, p. 1, and Mark Twain, *Roughing It*, Hartford, CT: American Publishing Co., 1872.

16 Composite of Mark Twain, "Letter from Honolulu" (article 18), *Sacramento Daily Union*, August 18, 1866, p. 1, and Mark Twain, *Roughing It*, Hartford, CT: American Publishing Co., 1872.

17 A composite of Mark Twain, "From the Sandwich Islands" (article 19), *Sacramento Daily Union*, August 24, 1866, p. 3, and Mark Twain, *Roughing It*, Hartford, CT: American Publishing Co., 1872.

18 Mildred Leo Clemens, "Mark Twain in Paradise" (Chapter 9), *Honolulu Star Bulletin*, December 17, 1935, p. 4. Also in Mildred Leo Clemens, "Trailing Mark Twain through Hawai'i," *Sunset*, May 1917, p. 7.

19 Mark Twain, "From the Sandwich Islands" (article 19), *Sacramento Daily Union*, August 24, 1866, p. 3.

20 Lilikal K. Kame'eleihiwa, "The *Māhele* of 1848," in Sonia P. Juvik and James O. Juvik, eds., *Atlas of Hawai'i*, 3rd edition, Honolulu: University of Hawai'i Press, 1998, p. 173, ulukau.org/elib/cgi-bin/library?e=d-0atlas-000Sec--11en-50-20-frameset-book--1-010escapewin&a=d&p2=book.

21 Mark Twain, "From the Sandwich Islands" (article 19), *Sacramento Daily Union*, August 24, 1866, p. 3.

22 Mark Twain, "From the Sandwich Islands" (article 22), *Sacramento Daily Union*, September 22, 1866, p. 1.

23 A composite of Mark Twain, "From the Sandwich Islands" (article 22), *Sacramento Daily Union*, September 22, 1866, p. 1, and Mark Twain, *Roughing It*, Hartford, CT: American Publishing Co., 1872.

24 Mark Twain, "From the Sandwich Islands" (article 22), *Sacramento Daily Union*, September 22, 1866, p. 1.

25 Otto von Kotzebue, *A New Voyage round the World*, Volume 2, London: Henry Colburn and Richard Bentley, 1830, p. 229.

26 Otto von Kotzebue, *A New Voyage round the World*, Volume 2, London: Henry Colburn and Richard Bentley, 1830, p. 209.

27 Mildred Leo Clemens, "Trailing Mark Twain through Hawai'i," *Sunset*, May 1917, p. 7. Also in Mildred Leo Clemens, "Mark Twain in Paradise" (Chapter 9), *Honolulu Star Bulletin*, December 17, 1935, p. 4.

28 Composite of Mark Twain, "From the Sandwich Islands" (article 19), *Sacramento Daily Union*, August 24, 1866, p. 3, and Mark Twain, *Roughing It*, Hartford, CT: American Publishing Co., 1872.

29 Mark Twain, "From the Sandwich Islands" (article 19), *Sacramento Daily Union*, August 24, 1866, p. 3.

30 A composite of Mark Twain, "From the Sandwich Islands" (article 19), *Sacramento Daily Union*, August 24, 1866, p. 3, and Mark Twain, *Roughing It*, Hartford, CT: American Publishing Co., 1872.

31 Ebenezer Townsend Jr., "The Diary of Mr. Ebenezer Townsend, Jr., the Supercargo of the Sealing Ship *Neptune . . . ," Papers of the New Haven Colony Historical Society*, Volume 4, New Haven, CT: New Haven Colony Historical Society, 1888, p. 72. Also reprinted as Ebenezer Townsend Jr., "Extract from the Diary of Ebenezer Townsend, Jr., Supercargo of the Sealing Ship Neptune on Her Voyage to the South Pacific and Canton," Honolulu: Hawaiian Historical Society Reprints, Number 4, n.d. (1921?), p. 24.

32 Mark Twain, "From the Sandwich Islands" (article 20), *Sacramento Daily Union*, August 30, 1866, p. 3.

33 A composite of Mark Twain, "From the Sandwich Islands" (article 20), *Sacramento Daily Union*, August 30, 1866, p. 3, and Mark Twain, *Roughing It*, Hartford, CT: American Publishing Co., 1872.

34 Mark Twain, "From the Sandwich Islands" (article 20), *Sacramento Daily Union*, August 30, 1866, p. 3.

35 A composite of Mark Twain, "From the Sandwich Islands" (article 20), *Sacramento Daily Union*, August 30, 1866, p. 3, and Mark Twain, *Roughing It*, Hartford, CT: American Publishing Co., 1872.

36 Mark Twain, "From the Sandwich Islands" (article 20), *Sacramento Daily Union*, August 30, 1866, p. 3.

37 A composite of Mark Twain, "From the Sandwich Islands" (article 20), *Sacramento Daily Union*, August 30, 1866, p. 3, and Mark Twain, *Roughing It*, Hartford, CT: American Publishing Co., 1872.

38 Mark Twain, "From the Sandwich Islands" (article 21), *Sacramento Daily Union*, September 6, 1866, p. 3.

39 A composite of Mark Twain, "From the Sandwich Islands" (article 21), *Sacramento Daily Union*, September 6, 1866, p. 3, and Mark Twain, *Roughing It*, Hartford, CT: American Publishing Co., 1872.

40 Mark Twain, "From the Sandwich Islands" (article 21), *Sacramento Daily Union*, September 6, 1866, p. 3.

41 A composite of Mark Twain, "From the Sandwich Islands" (article 21), *Sacramento Daily Union*, September 6, 1866, p. 3, and Mark Twain, *Roughing It*, Hartford, CT: American Publishing Co., 1872.

42 Mark Twain, *Roughing It*, Hartford, CT: American Publishing Co., 1872.

43 Franklin H. Austin, "Mark Twain Incognito—A Reminiscence," *The Friend*, Volume 96, Number 9, September 1926, p. 202.

44 Mark Twain, "From the Sandwich Islands" (article 21), *Sacramento Daily Union*, September 6, 1866, p. 1.

45 Mark Twain, "From the Sandwich Islands" (article 21), *Sacramento Daily Union*, September 6, 1866, p. 1.

46 Mark Twain, *Roughing It*, Hartford, CT: American Publishing Co., 1872.

47 A composite of Mark Twain, "From the Sandwich Islands" (article 22), *Sacramento Daily Union*, September 22, 1866, p. 1, Mark Twain, *Roughing It*, Hartford, CT: American Publishing Co., 1872.

48 Mark Twain, "From the Sandwich Islands" (article 22), *Sacramento Daily Union*, September 22, 1866, p. 1.

49 Composite of Mark Twain, "From the Sandwich Islands" (article 22), *Sacramento Daily Union*, September 22, 1866, p. 1, and Mark Twain, *Roughing It*, Hartford, CT: American Publishing Co., 1872.

50 Mark Twain, "From the Sandwich Islands" (article 22), *Sacramento Daily Union*, September 22, 1866, p. 1.

51 Mark Twain, *Roughing It*, Hartford, CT: American Publishing Co., 1872.

52 A composite of Mark Twain, "From the Sandwich Islands" (article 22), *Sacramento Daily Union*, September 22, 1866, p. 1, and Mark Twain, *Roughing It*, Hartford, CT: American Publishing Co., 1872.

53 Lord George Anson Byron, *Voyage of H.M.S.* Blonde *to the Sandwich Islands in the Years 1824–1825*, London: John Murray, 1826, p. 200.

54 A composite of Mark Twain, "From the Sandwich Islands" (article 22), *Sacramento Daily Union*, September 22, 1866, p. 1, and Mark Twain, *Roughing It*, Hartford, CT: American Publishing Co., 1872.

55 William Ellis, *A Narrative of a Tour though Hawaii, or Owhyhee*, London: H. Fisher, Son, & P. Jackson, 1827 (revised second edition), p. 48.

56 John Ledyard, *Journal of Captain Cook's Last Voyage*, Hartford, CT, 1783, p. 131.

57 S. M. Kamakua, *Ka Nupepa Ku'oko'o (The Independent Newspaper*, Honolulu), September 26, 1868, translated in S. M. Kamakau, *Ruling Chiefs of Hawaii*, Honolulu: Kamehameha Schools Press, 1992 revised edition, p. 318.

58 S. M. Kamakua, *Ka Nupepa Ku'oko'o (The Independent Newspaper*, Honolulu), February 1, 1868, translated in S. M. Kamakau, *Ruling Chiefs of Hawaii*, Honolulu: Kamehameha Schools Press, 1992 revised edition, p. 252.

59 A composite of Mark Twain, "From the Sandwich Islands" (article 22), *Sacramento Daily Union*, September 22, 1866, p. 1, and Mark Twain, *Roughing It*, Hartford, CT: American Publishing Co., 1872.

60 A composite of Mark Twain, "From the Sandwich Islands" (article 22), *Sacramento Daily Union*, September 22, 1866, p. 1, and Mark Twain, *Roughing It*, Hartford, CT: American Publishing Co., 1872.

61 S. M. Kamakau, *Ruling Chiefs of Hawaii*, Honolulu: Kamehameha Schools Press, 1992 revised edition, p. 315.

62 A composite of Mark Twain, "From the Sandwich Islands" (article 22), *Sacramento Daily Union*, September 22, 1866, p. 1, and Mark Twain, *Roughing It*, Hartford, CT: American Publishing Co., 1872.

63 Mark Twain, "From the Sandwich Islands" (article 24), *Sacramento Daily Union*, October 25, 1866, p. 1.

64 E. S. Craighill Handy and Mary Kawena Pukui, "The Polynesian Family System in Ka'u, Hawaii, VII," *The Journal of the Polynesian Society*, Volume 62, Number 4, 1953, p. 326. Reprinted as E. S. Craighill Handy and Mary Kawena Pukui, *The Polynesian Family System in Ka'u*, Wellington, New Zealand: The Polynesian Society, 1958, p. 191.

65 Jack London, "My Hawaiian Aloha," Part 1, *Cosmopolitan Magazine*, September 1916, p. 170.

66 Mark Twain, "From the Sandwich Islands" (article 24), *Sacramento Daily Union*, October 25, 1866, p. 1.

67 A composite of Mark Twain, "From the Sandwich Islands" (article 24), *Sacramento Daily Union*, October 25, 1866, p. 1, and Mark Twain, *Roughing It*, Hartford, CT: American Publishing Co., 1872.

68 May H. Rothwell, "Unawares, a Laughing Angel!," *Paradise of the Pacific,* Volume 48, Number 3, March 1936, pp. 9–10.

69 Mark Twain, "From the Sandwich Islands" (article 24), *Sacramento Daily Union,* October 25, 1866, p. 1.

70 "Waiohinu, Mark Twain Tree to Have First Light Thursday," *Honolulu Star-Bulletin,* November 10, 1953, p. 5; "Mark Twain's Kau Monkeypod Is Blown Down," *Honolulu Advertiser,* December 3, 1956, p. 10; "Mark Twain Tree Somewhat Alive," *Honolulu Star-Bulletin,* August 10, 1957, p. 2; and Ron Bennett, "Mark Twain's Monkeypod," *The Honolulu Advertiser,* March 23, 1958, p. 78.

71 Mildred Leo Clemens, "Mark Twain in Paradise" (Chapter 8), *Honolulu Star Bulletin,* December 16, 1935, p. 3.

72 Mrs. Frederick Lyman quoted in Walter Francis Frear, *Mark Twain and Hawaii,* Chicago: The Lakeside Press, 1947, pp. 71–72.

73 Mark Twain, "From the Sandwich Islands" (article 24), *Sacramento Daily Union,* October 25, 1866, p. 1.

74 A composite of Mark Twain, "From the Sandwich Islands" (article 25), *Sacramento Daily Union,* November 16, 1866, p. 1, and Mark Twain, *Roughing It,* Hartford, CT: American Publishing Co., 1872.

75 Mark Twain, *The Innocents Abroad,* San Francisco: H. H. Bancroft & Co., 1869, p. 325.

76 Mark Twain, *Roughing It,* Hartford, CT: American Publishing Co., 1872.

77 A composite of Mark Twain, "From the Sandwich Islands" (article 25), *Sacramento Daily Union,* November 16, 1866, p. 1, and Mark Twain, *Roughing It,* Hartford, CT: American Publishing Co., 1872.

78 Mark Twain, *Roughing It,* Hartford, CT: American Publishing Co., 1872.

79 Mark Twain, "From the Sandwich Islands" (article 25), *Sacramento Daily Union,* November 16, 1866, p. 1.

80 Mark Twain, "A Strange Dream," *New York Saturday Press,* June 2, 1866, pp. 1–2. Reprinted in *The Californian,* July 7, 1866, p. 4; in Mark Twain, *The Celebrated Jumping Frog of Calaveras County and Other Sketches,* New York: C. H. Webb, 1867; and in a slightly different version hand-copied in the Volcano House register transcript.

81 "Map May Point to King's Burial Site," *Honolulu Advertiser,* June 11, 2005, the.honoluluadvertiser.com/article/2005/Jun/11/ln/ln01p.html.

82 Sally Apgar, "Maiʻohos Feel Drawn to Royal Burial Site," *Star Bulletin*, March 5, 2006, archives.starbulletin.com/2006/03/05/news/story04.html.

83 *Daily Hawaiian Herald*, December 5, 1866. Also in An American Girl [M.(innie) Leola Crawford], *Seven Weeks in Hawaii*, Chicago: Howard D. Berrett, 1913, pp. 49–50 (and San Francisco: John J. Newbegin, 1917, pp. 97–98); Walter Francis Frear, *Mark Twain and Hawaii*, Chicago: The Lakeside Press, 1947, pp. 125–27; *Honolulu Star Bulletin*, September 27, 1947; and the Volcano House Register transcript, which was copied from Crawford's book after the two original pages were stolen around 1915.

84 Franklin H. Austin, "Mark Twain Incognito—A Reminiscence" (article 3), *The Friend*, Volume 96, Number 11, November 1926, p. 250.

85 Mark Twain in a letter to Albert Francis Judd, December 20, 1870.

86 Franklin H. Austin, "Mark Twain Incognito—A Reminiscence" (article 3), *The Friend*, Volume 96, Number 11, November 1926, p. 253.

87 Franklin H. Austin, "Mark Twain Incognito—A Reminiscence" (article 3), *The Friend*, Volume 96, Number 11, November 1926, pp. 250–52.

88 Twain's seventieth birthday speech at Delmonico's on December 5, 1905, in Mark Twain, *Mark Twain's Speeches*, New York: Harper & Brothers, 1910, p. 429.

89 Franklin H. Austin, "Mark Twain Incognito—A Reminiscence" (article 3), *The Friend*, Volume 96, Number 11, November 1926, pp. 252–54.

Returning to Oʻahu

1 Mark Twain, "Scenes in Honolulu—No. 14" (article 14), *Sacramento Daily Union*, July 16, 1866, p. 3.

2 Mark Twain, "Chapters from My Autobiography," *North American Review*, July 5, 1907, pp. 466–67. Also in Mark Twain (Albert Bigelow Paine, ed.), *Mark Twain's Autobiography*, Volume 1, New York: Harper & Brothers, 1924, pp. 239–40; *Mark Twain (Charles Neider, ed.), The Autobiography of Mark Twain*, London: Chatto & Windus, 1959, p. 150; and Mark Twain (Harriet Elinor Smith and others, eds.), *Autobiography of Mark Twain*, Volume 1, Berkeley: University of California Press, 2010.

3 Mark Twain, "Scenes in Honolulu—No. 14" (article 14), *Sacramento Daily Union*, July 16, 1866, p. 3.

4   Mark Twain letter to Mrs. Jane Clemens and Mrs. Moffett, June 21, 1866, in Mark Twain (Albert Bigalow Paine, ed.), *Mark Twain's Letters,* Volume 1, New York: Harper & Brothers, 1917, pp. 106–8. And Mark Twain (Edgar Marquess Branch, Michael B. Frank, and Kenneth M. Sanderson, eds.), *Mark Twain's Letters,* Volume 1, Berkeley: University of California Press, 1987, pp. 343–44.

5   *The Pacific Commercial Advertiser* (Honolulu), May 24, 1903, p. 2.

6   Mark Twain (Albert Bigelow Paine, ed.), *Mark Twain's Autobiography,* Volume 1, New York: Harper & Brothers, 1924, pp. 124–25. And Mark Twain (Harriet Elinor Smith and others, eds.), *Autobiography of Mark Twain,* Volume 1, Berkeley: University of California Press, 2010, p. 369.

7   Mark Twain, "An Autobiography," *The Aldine,* April 1, 1871, p. 58.

8   Mark Twain, "My Début as a Literary Person," *The Century Magazine,* November 1899, pp. 76–77, 87. This article is very different from the original *Harper's New Monthly Magazine* article (1866), but I didn't use anything from *Harper's.* I compared the *Century Magazine* version to the versions listed below, but I don't think I used anything from any of these:

Mark Swain (Mark Twain), "Forty-Three Days in an Open Boat," *Harper's New Monthly Magazine,* December 1866, pp. 104–13.

Mark Twain, "My Début as a Literary Person," in Mark Twain, *The Man That Corrupted Hadleyburg and Other Stories and Essays,* New York: Harper & Brothers, 1900, pp. 84–127.

Mark Twain, "My Début as a Literary Person," in Mark Twain, *My Début as a Literary Person with Other Stories and Essays.* Hartford, CT: The American Publishing Co., 1903, pp. 11–47.

Mark Twain (Harriet Elinor Smith and others, eds.), *Autobiography of Mark Twain,* Volume 1, Berkeley: University of California Press, 2010, pp. 127–44.

9   Bailey Millard, "Mark Twain in San Francisco," *The Bookman,* June 1910, pp. 370–71.

10 Mark Twain (Albert Bigalow Paine, ed.), *Mark Twain's Letters,* Volume 1, New York: Harper & Brothers, 1917, pp. 108–9. Also in Mark Twain (Edgar Marquess Branch, Michael B. Frank, and Kenneth M. Sanderson, eds.), *Mark Twain's Letters,* Volume 1, Berkeley: University of California Press, 1987, pp. 347–48.

11 Mark Twain (Frederick Anderson and others, eds.), *Mark Twain's Notebooks and Journals,* Volume 1, Berkeley: University of California Press, 1975, p. 118.

12 Max Planck Institute for the Science of Human History, "A European Origin for Leprosy? The Largest Study to Date on Ancient Leprosy DNA Reveals Previously Unknown Diversity of Strains in Medieval Europe," *ScienceDaily,* May 10, 2018, sciencedaily.com/releases/2018/05/180510150208.htm.

13 "Mark Twain's Lecture," *Providence Evening Press* (Providence, RI), November 10, 1869, p. 2.

14 Letter to Olivia Langdon, October 18, 1868, Hartford, CT, in Mark Twain (Harriet Elinor Smith and Richard Bucci, eds.), *Mark Twain's Letters,* Volume 2, Berkeley: University of California Press, 1990, p. 268.

15 A composite of Mark Twain, "Scenes in Honolulu—No. 15" (article 17), *Sacramento Daily Union,* August 1, 1866, p. 1, and Mark Twain, *Roughing It,* Hartford, CT: American Publishing Co., 1872.

16 A composite of Mark Twain, "Scenes in Honolulu—No. 15" (article 17), *Sacramento Daily Union,* August 1, 1866, p. 1, and Mark Twain, *Roughing It,* Hartford, CT: American Publishing Co., 1872.

17 Mark Twain letter to Jane Lampton Clemens and Pamela A. Moffett, June 27, 1866 in Mark Twain (Edgar Marquess Branch, Michael B. Frank, and Kenneth M. Sanderson, eds.), *Mark Twain's Letters,* Volume 1, Berkeley: University of California Press, 1987, p. 347.

18 Mark Twain in a letter to William Bowen, August 25, 1866 in Mark Twain (Edgar Marquess Branch, Michael B. Frank, and Kenneth M. Sanderson, eds.), *Mark Twain's Letters,* Volume 1, Berkeley: University of California Press, 1987, p. 359.

19 Mary Anthony, part of a 1925 letter to Mrs. Bishop quoted in Mark Twain (Edgar Marquess Branch, Michael B. Frank, and Kenneth M. Sanderson, eds.), *Mark Twain's Letters,* Volume 1, Berkeley: University of California Press, 1987, p. 333.

20 Mildred Leo Clemens, "Trailing Mark Twain through Hawaii," *Sunset,* May 1917, p. 96.

21 Mark Twain (Albert Bigelow Paine, ed.), *Mark Twain's Notebook,* New York: Harper & Brothers, 1935, pp. 22–23.

Leaving Hawai‘i

1 Mark Twain, *Roughing It*, Hartford, CT: American Publishing Co., 1872.

2 Mark Twain (Frederick Anderson and others, eds.), *Mark Twain's Notebooks and Journals*, Volume 1, Berkeley: University of California Press, 1975, p. 158.

3 Mark Twain in a letter to Jane Lampton Clemens and Pamela A. Moffett, July 30, August 6, 7, 8, 10, and 20, 1866, in Mark Twain (Albert Bigalow Paine, ed.), *Mark Twain's Letters*, Volume 1, New York: Harper & Brothers, 1917, pp. 115–19. Also Mark Twain (Edgar Marquess Branch, Michael B. Frank, and Kenneth M. Sanderson, eds.), *Mark Twain's Letters*, Volume 1, Berkeley: University of California Press, 1987, pp. 350–53.

4 Mark Twain (Albert Bigelow Paine, ed.), *Mark Twain's Notebook*, New York: Harper & Brothers, 1935, p. 29. And Mark Twain (Edgar Marquess Branch, Michael B. Frank, and Kenneth M. Sanderson, eds.), *Mark Twain's Letters*, Volume 1, Berkeley: University of California Press, 1987, p. 355.

5 Mark Twain in a letter to Jane Lampton Clemens and Pamela A. Moffett, July 30, August 6, 7, 8, 10, and 20, 1866, in Mark Twain (Edgar Marquess Branch, Michael B. Frank, and Kenneth M. Sanderson, eds.), *Mark Twain's Letters*, Volume 1, Berkeley: University of California Press, 1987, p. 353.

6 Mark Twain, "My Début as a Literary Person," *The Century Magazine*, November 1899, p. 77.

7 Mark Twain (Frederick Anderson and others, eds.), *Mark Twain's Notebooks and Journals*, Volume 1, Berkeley: University of California Press, 1975, p. 153.

8 "Mark Twain," *Pacific Commercial Advertiser* (Honolulu), May 19, 1866, p. 1.

9 Mark Twain, "An Epistle from Mark Twain," *Daily Hawaiian Herald*, October 17, 1866.

10 "'Mark Twain' on Photographs," *Daily Hawaiian Herald*, September 5, 1866.

11 Mark Twain, *Roughing It*, Hartford, CT: American Publishing Co., 1872.

12 George E. Barnes, "Mark Twain as He Was Known during His Stay on the Pacific Slope," *San Francisco Morning Call,* April 17, 1887, p. 1. Reprinted in *The Inter Ocean* (Chicago), April 30, 1887, p. 4, and Mark Twain (Gary Schamhorst, ed.), *Twain in His Own Time,* Iowa City: University of Iowa Press, 2010, p. 54.

13 Twain's advertisement, *Sacramento Daily Union,* October 11, 1866, p. 3.

14 A circular advertising Twain's lecture in Angels Camp. Quoted in "Twain's First Lecture Tour: Based on the Original Newspaper Accounts," *Mark Twain Quarterly,* Volume 3, Number 3, Summer–Fall, 1939, p. 24.

15 *Daily Alta California,* June 29, 1868, p. 2.

16 "Mark Twain," *Daily Missouri Republican* (St. Louis), March 24, 1867, p. 1.

17 *Brooklyn Union,* May 10, 1867. Quoted in Fred W. Lorch, *The Trouble Begins at Eight,* Ames: Iowa State University Press, 1968, p. 66.

18 Mark Twain, *Roughing It,* Hartford, CT: American Publishing Co., 1872.

19 "Mark Twain's Lecture," *San Francisco Dramatic Chronicle,* November 17, 1866, p. 3.

20 "Letter from New York," *Sacramento Daily Union,* June 4, 1867, p. 1.

21 *San Francisco Examiner,* quoted in *Sacramento Daily Union,* October 5, 1866, p. 2.

22 William A. Croffut, in "Mark Twain Smoked Out," *Daily Patriot* (Harrisburg, PA), June 4, 1889, p. 3.

23 "A Boston Critique on Mark Twain," *Boston Advertiser,* November 11, 1869, p. 1. Reprinted in the *Daily Alta California,* November 20, 1869, and *The Leavenworth Times* (Leavenworth, KS), November 16, 1869.

24 Albert Bigelow Paine, *Mark Twain: A Biography,* Volume 1, New York: Harper & Brothers, 1912, p. 295.

25 *The Golden Era* (San Francisco), October 7, 1866.

26 *Chicago Evening Post,* December 19, 1871. Reprinted in the *Lowell Weekly Journal* (Lowell, MI), January 10, 1872, p. 4, and an excerpt as "Mark Twain as a Lecturer," *Riverine Herald* (Echuca, Australia), August 14, 1872, p. 3.

27 "Mark Twain," *Chicago Tribune,* December 20, 1871, p. 4.

28 *Evening Telegraph* (Philadelphia), November 20, 1869, p. 6.

29 *The Observer* (UK), quoted in "Mark Twain," *Daily Graphic* (New York), November 5, 1873, p. 5.

30 Pele, "San Francisco Correspondence," *The Pacific Commercial Advertiser* (Honolulu), January 12, 1867, p. 1.

31 Lecture transcript sources:

1) *San Francisco Evening-Bulletin,* November 17, 1866, p. 5.

2) Pele, "San Francisco Correspondence," *The Pacific Commercial Advertiser* (Honolulu), January 12, 1867, p. 1.

3) "Mark Twain at the Mercantile Library Hall Tuesday Night," *Daily Missouri Democrat* (St. Louis), March 28, 1867, p. 5. Portions reprinted in "The Sandwich Islands," *Marshall County Republican* (Plymouth, IN), April 12, 1867; "A Humorous Description of the Sandwich Islanders," *The National Republican* (Washington, DC), April 16, 1867, p. 1; "A Humorous Description of the Sandwich Island [sic]," *Hillsdale Standard* (Hillsdale, MI), April 30, 1867, p. 1; "Mark Twain's Lecture," *The Pacific Commercial Advertiser,* August 24, 1867; and Fred W. Lorch, "Mark Twain's Sandwich Islands Lecture at St. Louis," *American Literature,* Volume 18, Number 4, January 1947, pp. 299–307 (where it's mistakenly cited as being from the *Missouri Republican).*

4) *Washington Chronicle* (Washington, DC), February 24, 1868. Reprinted in "The Sandwich Islands," *Chicago Republican* (Chicago), February 28, 1868, p. 11.

5) "Mark Twain's Lecture," *Providence Evening Press* (Providence, RI), November 10, 1869, p. 2.

6) *Boston Times,* reprinted in "The Sandwich Islands," *Chicago Tribune,* November 21, 1869, p. 6.

7) "A Boston Critique on Mark Twain," *The Boston Advertiser,* November 11, 1869. Reprinted in the *Leavenworth Times* (Leavenworth, KS), November 16, 1869, *Daily Alta California,* November 20, 1869, *Cairo Evening Bulletin* (Cairo, IL), November 24, 1869, *Evening Telegraph* (Philadelphia), November 20, 1869, and *Owyhee Tidal Wave* (Silver City, Idaho Territory), December 16, 1869.

8) "Franklin Lyceum Lectures," *Manufacturers' and Farmers' Journal* (Providence, RI), November 11, 1869, p. 1.

9) "Mark Twain's Lecture," *Hartford Currant* (Hartford, CT), November 24, 1869, p. 2.

10) *Cairo Evening Bulletin* (Cairo, IL), November 24, 1869.

11) "Mark Twain's Lecture," *The Cohoes Cataract*, January 15, 1870.

12) "Mark Twain," *Troy Daily Times* (Troy, NY), January 12, 1870.

13) *Chicago Evening Post*, December 19, 1871. Reprinted in the *Lowell Weekly Journal* (Lowell, MI), January 10, 1872, p. 6; and as "Mark Twain as a Lecturer," *Riverine Herald* (Echuca, Australia), August 14, 1872, p. 3.

14) *Brooklyn Eagle*, February 8, 1873, combining elements from the versions reprinted in Walter Francis Frear, *Mark Twain and Hawaii*, Chicago: The Lakeside Press, 1947, pp. 431–36, and Thomas B. Reed, ed., *Modern Eloquence*, Volume 4, Chicago: Geo. L. Schulman & Co., 1900, pp. 253–59.

15) "Cracking Jokes," *Once a Week* (London), November 8, 1873, pp. 402–5.

16) Albert Bigelow Paine, *Mark Twain: A Biography*, Volume 4, New York: Harper & Brothers, 1910, appendix D.

17) Mark Twain, "The Sandwich Islands," *The Complete Works of Mark Twain, Volume 24: Mark Twain's Speeches*, New York: Harper & Brothers, 1923, pp. 7–20.

18) Fred W. Lorch, *The Trouble Begins at Eight*, Ames: Iowa State University Press, 1968, pp. 274–84.

19) Mark Twain (Paul Fatout, ed.), *Mark Twain Speaking*, Iowa City: University of Iowa Press, 1976 (2006 edition), pp. 4–14.

32 "Cracking Jokes," *Once a Week* (London), November 8, 1873, p. 403.

33 "Local Matters," *Evening Bulletin*, October 3, 1866, p. 5.

34 "Academy of Music," *San Francisco Dramatic Chronicle*, October 3, 1866, p. 3.

35 Prentice Mulford, "Mark Twain," *The Golden Era* (San Francisco), October 7, 1866.

36 Alf Doten, *Daily Territorial Enterprise* (Virginia City, NV), November 1, 1866.

37 "Cracking Jokes," *Once a Week* (London), November 8, 1873, p. 403.

38 *San Jose Mercury*, November 26, 1866.

39 *New Haven Daily Palladium*, December 28, 1869.

40 *San Francisco Evening-Bulletin*, November 28, 1866.

41 *Daily Hawaiian Herald* (Honolulu), October 23, 1866.

42 *Philadelphia Press*, December 8, 1869.

43 "Cracking Jokes," *Once a Week* (London), November 8, 1873, p. 402.

44 "'Mark Twain's' Consolation," *San Francisco Dramatic Chronicle*, October 3, 1866, p. 4.

45 R. T. Macoun, "A Glimpse at the Sandwich Islands," *The Knickerbocker*, November 1851, p. 483.

46 James Jackson Jarves, *History of the Hawaiian or Sandwich Islands*, Boston: James Munro & Co., 1843, p. 50.

47 "Mark Twain's Lecture on the Sandwich Islands," *New York Times*, February 6, 1873.

48 *Boston Advertiser. Reprinted in Cairo Evening Bulletin* (Cairo, IL), November 24, 1869, and *Owyhee Tidal Wave* (Silver City, Idaho Territory), December 16, 1869.

49 Mark Twain in a letter to Henry G. Blasdel and others, November 1, 1866, published in the *Territorial Enterprise* (Virginia City, NV), November 4, 1866. And Mark Twain (Edgar Marquess Branch, Michael B. Frank, and Kenneth M. Sanderson, eds.), *Mark Twain's Letters*, Volume 1, Berkeley: University of California Press, 1987, p. 364.

50 Twain quoting his youngest daughter Jean Clemens in Twain's letter to his daughter Clara, May 20, 1905. Mark Twain Papers, Bancroft Library, University of California, Berkeley.

51 A composite of a George Barnes article, *San Francisco Call*, probably December 1878, reprinted in "Mark Twain," *Iola Register* (Iola, KS), January 3, 1879; and George E. Barnes, "Mark Twain as He Was Known during His Stay on the Pacific Slope," *San Francisco Morning Call*, April 17, 1887, p. 1.

52 Mark Twain, *Roughing It*, Hartford, CT: American Publishing Co., 1872.

53 *San Francisco Evening-Bulletin*, November 17, 1866, p. 5. Also in Walter Francis Frear, *Mark Twain and Hawaii*, Chicago: The Lakeside Press, 1947, appendix D3.

54 Mark Twain (Benjamin Griffin and Harriet Elenor Smith, eds.), *Autobiography of Mark Twain*, Volume 3, Berkeley: University of California Press, 2015, p. 245.

55 Mark Twain in a letter to his mother, Jane Clemens, and family, December 4, 1866, in Mark Twain (Albert Bigalow Paine, ed.), *Mark Twain's Letters,* Volume 1, New York: Harper & Brothers, 1917, p. 122.

56 Howard G. Baetzhold, "Mark Twain's 'Lost Sweetheart,'" *American Literature,* November 1972, pp. 414–29.

57 National Park Service, *Hawaiian Aboriginal Culture,* US Department of the Interior, 1962, p. 56.

58 Mark Twain, "'Mark Twain' in New York," Letter Number 11, *Daily Alta California,* April 9, 1867, p. 1.

59 Albert Bigelow Paine, *Mark Twain: A Biography,* Volume 1, New York: Harper & Brothers, 1912, p. 311.

60 Mark Twain, *New York Herald,* November 19, 1867.

61 Mark Twain in a letter to his mother, Jane Clemens, and family, June 7, 1867, in Mark Twain (Albert Bigalow Paine, ed.), *Mark Twain's Letters,* Volume 1, New York: Harper & Brothers, 1917, p. 127.

62 Frank Fuller, "Utah's War Governor Talks of Many Famous Men," *New York Times,* October 1, 1911, p. 46.

63 Mark Twain (Albert Bigelow Paine, ed.), *Mark Twain's Autobiography,* Volume 2, New York: Harper & Brothers, 1924, pp. 352, 355–56. Also in Mark Twain (Benjamin Griffin and Harriet E. Smith, eds.), *Autobiography of Mark Twain,* Volume 2, Berkeley: University of California Press, 2013.

64 Frank Fuller, "Utah's War Governor Talks of Many Famous Men," *New York Times,* October 1, 1911, p. 46.

65 Mark Twain, "Letter from Mark Twain, No. 18," *Daily Alta California,* June 23, 1867, p. 1.

66 Mark Twain, *The Innocents Abroad,* Hartford, CT: American Publishing Company, 1869.

67 Mark Twain (Albert Bigalow Paine, ed.), *Mark Twain's Letters,* Volume 2, New York: Harper & Brothers, 1917, pp. 168–69.

68 *Philadelphia Bulletin.* Reprinted as "Mark Twain in Philadelphia," *The Idaho World* (Idaho City, Idaho Territory), January 27, 1870, and as "Mark Twain in Philadelphia," *Boise News* (Boise, Idaho Territory), January 27, 1870, p. 2.

69 Mark Twain, "Dining with a Cannibal" (Around the World—Letter Number 8), *Buffalo Express* (Buffalo, NY), January 29, 1870, p. 2; and all across the country.

70 Mark Twain in a letter to Albert Francis Judd, December 20, 1870.

71 Mark Twain, "Memoranda," *The Galaxy,* Volume 10, Number 6, December 1870, pp. 878, 884.

72 "Mark Twain," *The Pacific Commercial Advertiser* (Honolulu), September 10, 1870, p. 3.

73 Mark Twain, "The Sandwich Islands," *New York Tribune*, January 6, 1873, pp. 4–5.

74 Mark Twain, "The Sandwich Islands," *New York Tribune*, January 9, 1873, p. 5.

75 Mark Twain in a letter to Whitelaw Reid, January 3, 1873, in James E. Caron, "The Blessings of Civilization," *The Mark Twain Annual, Number 6,* University Park: Penn State University Press, 2008, p. 60.

76 *Sacramento Daily Union,* February 13, 1873, p. 3.

77 Mark Twain, "Letter from Mark Twain, No. 18," *Daily Alta California,* June 23, 1867, p. 1.

78 Mark Twain letter to the editor of the *London Evening Standard,* October 9, 1873. Reprinted in Mark Twain (Albert Bigalow Paine, ed.), *Mark Twain's Letters,* Volume 2, New York: Harper & Brothers, 1917, p. 490, and Mark Twain (Lin Salamo and Harriet Elinor Smith, eds.), *Mark Twain's Letters,* Volume 5, Berkeley: University of California Press, 1997, pp. 448–49.

79 *Sacramento Daily Union,* November 10, 1873; *Daily Alta California,* November 10, 1873; *Hawaiian Gazette,* December 24, 1873.

80 *Danbury News* (Danbury, CT). Reprinted in the *Daily Missouri Democrat* (St. Louis), March 27, 1875, p. 2; and many others.

81 *Paxton Weekly Record* (Paxton, IL), January 21, 1875, p. 1.

82 *St. Louis Post-Dispatch* (St. Louis), January 7, 1875, p. 2; *Pittsburgh Daily Commercial* (Pittsburgh, PA), January 8, 1875, p. 2; *Baltimore Sun* (Baltimore, MD), January 21, 1875, p. 1; many others.

83 Mark Twain in a letter to Charles Warren Stoddard and another to William Dean Howells, both October 26, 1881, in Mark Twain (Albert Bigalow Paine, ed.), *Mark Twain's Letters,* Volume 1, New York: Harper & Brothers, 1917, pp. 404–6.

84 Walter Francis Frear, *Mark Twain and Hawaii*, Chicago: The Lakeside Press, 1947, pp. 89–90.

85 Mark Twain (Albert Bigalow Paine, ed.), *Mark Twain's Letters*, Volume 2, New York: Harper & Brothers, 1917, pp. 439–40.

86 "Poor Bill Ragsdale," *Daily Alta California*, July 13, 1873, p. 1.

87 Mark Twain, "The Sandwich Islands," *New York Tribune*, January 9, 1873, p. 5.

88 W. D. Howells, "My Memories of Mark Twain," Part 3, *Harper's Monthly Magazine*, September 1910, p. 516. And as W. D. Howells, *My Mark Twain*, New York: Harper & Brothers, 1910, p. 68.

89 Mark Twain in a letter to Mary Fairbanks, January 24, 1884, quoted in Mark Twain (Dixon Wecter, ed.), *Mark Twain to Mrs. Fairbanks*, San Marino, CA: Huntington Library, 1949, p. 255.

90 Mark Twain in a letter to William Dean Howells, February 27, 1885, quoted in Mark Twain (Albert Bigalow Paine, ed.), *Mark Twain's Letters*, Volume 1, New York: Harper & Brothers, 1917, p. 450.

91 There are a huge amount of sources for this, but here are a couple to begin with: Emma Bryce, "What's the Difference between Race and Ethnicity?," *Live Science*, February 7, 2020, livescience.com/difference-between-race-ethnicity.html, and R. C. Lewontin, "Confusions about Human Races," *Social Science Research Council*, June 7, 2006, raceandgenomics.ssrc.org/Lewontin.

92 Mark Twain to his partner Charles Webster, November 11, 1885, in David W. Forbes, *Hawaiian National Bibliography, 1780–1900: Volume 4, 1881–1900*, Honolulu: University of Hawai'i Press, 1998, pp. 295–96.

93 Fred W. Lorch, "Hawaiian Feudalism and Mark Twain's A Connecticut Yankee in King Arthur's Court," *American Literature*, March 1958, pp. 50–66.

94 A composite of the *Boston Daily Globe*, April 9, 1889, p. 1; "New York Greets the Boys," *The Sun* (New York), April 9, 1889, p. 1; *Mark Twain, Mark Twain's Speeches* (1923 edition), New York: Harper & Brothers, 1923, pp. 145–49; Albert Bigelow Paine, *Mark Twain: A Biography*, Volume 3, New York: Harper & Brothers, 1912, pp. 878–79.

95 Will Sabin, *The Edge of the Crater, and Other Poems*, Honolulu: Paradise of the Pacific Press, 1915, pp. 67–68.

The Return of Mark Twain

1 Major J. B. Pond, *Eccentricities of Genius*, New York: G. W. Dillingham Co., 1900, p. 224.

2 Mark Twain, *Following the Equator*, Hartford, CT: American Publishing Company, 1897, pp. 48–58.

3 Board of Health, *Special Report by the Board of Health on the Cholera Epidemic in Honolulu, Hawaiian Islands in August and September, 1895*, Honolulu: Hawaiian Gazette Co., 1895.

4 Mildred Leo Clemens. "Mark Twain in Paradise" (Chapter 19), *Honolulu Star Bulletin*, December 30, 1935. Quoted in David Zmijewski, "Hawaii Awaits a Legend," *Mark Twain Journal*, Fall 1988, p. 26.

5 Theo. H. Davies, "Letter from Mr. Davies," *Daily Bulletin* (Honolulu), January 31, 1894, p. 2.

6 *New York Herald*, October 15, 1900.

7 Mark Twain, "To a Person Sitting in Darkness," *North American Review*, February 1901, p. 176.

8 Mark Twain in a letter to Rev. J. H. Twitchell, August 12, 1900. Reprinted in Mark Twain (Albert Bigalow Paine, ed.), *Mark Twain's Letters*, Volume 2, New York: Harper & Brothers, 1917, p. 699.

9 Mark Twain, "Salutation Speech from the Nineteenth Century to the Twentieth, Taken Down in Shorthand by Mark Twain," *Minneapolis Journal*, December 29, 1900.

10 W. D. Howells, "My Memories of Mark Twain," Part 2, *Harper's Monthly Magazine*, August 1910, p. 340. And as W. D. Howells, *My Mark Twain*, New York: Harper & Brothers, 1910, p. 35.

11 Mark Twain, in a letter to Hariett E. Whitmore, February 7, 1907, in Mark Twain (Albert Bigalow Paine, ed.), *Mark Twain's Letters*, Volume 2, New York: Harper & Brothers, 1917, p. 805.

12 Mark Twain, *Following the Equator*, Hartford, CT: American Publishing Company, 1897, pp. 60–64.

13 Charles Warren Stoddard, *The Lepers of Molokai*, Notre Dame, IN: Ave Maria Press, 1885.

14 Mark Twain, *Following the Equator*, Hartford, CT: American Publishing Company, 1897, p. 65.

15 Mark Twain, "Letter from Mark Twain," *The Pacific Commercial Advertiser* (Honolulu), January 6, 1896, p. 1. Also in Mark Twain, "Letter from
   Mark Twain," *Hawaiian Gazette* (Honolulu), January 7, 1896, p. 6.

16 "Experience of Australian Heat," *Daily Telegraph* (Sydney, New South
   Wales, Australia), December 21, 1895, p. 10.

17 "Interview with Mark Twain," *Times of India* (Bombay), January 23,
   1896, p. 5. Reprinted in Mark Twain (Gary Scharnhorst, ed.), *Mark
   Twain: The Complete Interviews,* Tuscaloosa: University of Alabama
   Press, 2006, pp. 274–75.

18 Mark Twain, *Following the Equator,* Hartford, CT: American Publishing Company, 1897, p. 629.

19 Frank Marshall White, "Mark Twain Amused," *New York Journal,* June
   2, 1897, p. 1. Reprinted in Mark Twain (Gary Scharnhorst, ed.), *Mark
   Twain: The Complete Interviews, Tuscaloosa:* University of Alabama
   Press, 2006, pp. 137–38.

20 "Mark Twain in White Amuses Congressmen," *New York
   Times,* December 8, 1906, p. 5.

21 Rolyat, "If Missouri Really Has to Be Shown," *The Pacific Commercial
   Advertiser* (Honolulu), January 22, 1911, section 3, p. 1.

22 *The Pacific Commercial Advertiser* (Honolulu), December 20, 1908, p. 1.
   And in the Hawaiian Gazette (Honolulu), December 22, 1908, p. 3.

23 Albert Bigelow Paine, *Mark Twain: A Biography,* Volume 4, New York:
   Harper & Brothers, 1910, p. 1511.

24 Mark Twain (Albert Bigalow Paine, ed.), *Mark Twain's Letters,* Volume
   1, New York: Harper & Brothers, 1917, p. 103.

25 Mark Twain (Albert Bigalow Paine, ed.), *Mark Twain's Letters,* Volume
   1, New York: Harper & Brothers, 1917, p. 115.

26 Jack London, "My Hawaiian Aloha," reprinted in Charmain London, *Our Hawaii,* New York: Macmillan, 1922 revised edition, p. 13.
   The original October 1916 *Cosmopolitan* magazine article left out the
   second part of the quotation, which Jack London wrote after quoting
   Mark Twain's Hawaiʻi prose poem, also not included in *Cosmopolitan.*

27 John Steinbeck, *Travels with Charley,* New York: Viking 1962.

ABOUT THE AUTHOR

John Richard Stephens began writing books in 1987. Prior to becoming an author, he held a wide variety of occupations ranging from work as a psychiatric counselor in two hospitals to being an intelligence officer and squadron commander in the US Air Force. John has had twenty-three books published so far, including *Wildest Lives of the Frontier: America through the Words of Jesse James, George Armstrong Custer, and Other Famous Westerners, Gold: First-Hand Accounts from the Rush That Shaped the West* (both by TwoDot), *Commanding the Storm* (Lyons Press), *Weird History 101*, and *Wyatt Earp Speaks*. He lives in the Hawaiian Islands.